MIDDLE TENNESSEE STATE UNIVERSITY
A CENTENNIAL LEGACY

MIDDLE TENNESSEE STATE UNIVERSITY
A CENTENNIAL LEGACY

Janice M. Leone, Editor

TWIN
OAKS
PRESS

ISBN-13: 978-0-9844354-6-3

First Edition

Printed in The United States of America

Twin Oaks Press
twinoakspress@gmail.com
www.twinoakspress.com

Cover and Interior design
By Art Growden
artgrowden.com

TABLE OF CONTENTS

ACKNOWLEDGEMENTS

This collection came about through the efforts of the late Dr. Anne Sloan, Assistant to the Provost for International Education, professor of political science, and a graduate of MTSU. As early as 2006, Anne had the foresight to begin preparing for MTSU's centennial, still a few years in the future. When a group of history faculty suggested that this would be a propitious time for a new history of the university, Anne wholeheartedly agreed. Sadly, Anne passed away in the spring of 2009 and never saw the fruition of this idea, but we hope she would be happy with the result.

In addition to Anne's inspiration, we benefitted tremendously from the unflagging encouragement of June McCash and Ron Messier of Twin Oaks Press. From the beginning of this project they read endless drafts, guided us through the publication process, and always shared with us their confidence in our efforts. A special thanks goes to Nora Hibbard and Art Growden who worked tirelessly and patiently to bring this book to completion. Their careful attention to detail in every aspect of the book's creation has made us all look good, and they have our sincere appreciation and respect for sharing their talents with us. John Vile, Dean of the Honors College, read early drafts of each essay, lent his considerable editing expertise, and always believed in what we were doing. He has our unending gratitude. We also greatly appreciate the support of Rebecca Conard and Kathy Slager who made invaluable contributions to the success of this collection. And thanks to Dean Mark Byrnes and our colleagues in the College of Liberal Arts who generously supported this project with their opinions, suggestions, and good-humored patience with "the book" that never seemed to end.

Support comes in many forms. A project of this scope could not have been possible without funding. Joe Bales and the MTSU Centennial Committee provided much of the initial support as we first ventured into uncovering and updating MTSU's hundred-year history. In addition, the generosity of the MTSU Public History Program came at a crucial moment and allowed us to move forward with our research and writing. Some of the book's contributors also benefitted from research grants awarded by the university. As editor of this collection, I would especially like to thank all of the writers who gave of their time voluntarily to craft essays that are a credit to their professionalism and to the history discipline as a whole.

The contributors based their essays on careful research, and we found valuable sources in several places. Archivists at the Albert Gore Research Center, James Walker Library, particularly Special Collections and the Digital Memory Project, Rutherford County Archives, and Tennessee State Library and Archives all provided material that answered many of the questions we encountered in our efforts to re-tell the MTSU story. In addition, MTSU Creative and Visual Services generously gave us access to campus photos. Throughout this search into MTSU's past, we also benefitted greatly from the expertise and knowledge of our fine students. Natalie Goodwin, Meaghan Peterson, Kelsey Fields, John George, Dallas Hanberry, Matthew Hibdon, and Richard Wilhite all contributed in their own ways toward recreating MTSU's history. And finally, we are indebted to our many colleagues, friends, and family members who helped in so many ways to make the sometimes lonely business of writing a little less solitary and a lot more enjoyable.

A Remarkable Legacy

DAVID L. ROWE

Soon after I arrived in 1981 to teach in the History Department of Middle Tennessee State University in Murfreesboro, I heard of a cosmic event that people in town were anticipating. Expectations were high in some quarters of a mystical, spiritual "great convergence" scheduled for a particular day at a particular place— the southwest intersection of Tennessee Boulevard and East Main Street. While news of the convergence circulated broadly through the town, no one could explain clearly what was supposed to happen or what effect it might have. But one thing was clear: the appointed spot was as unlikely a location for a cosmic spiritual upheaval as one could imagine. Davis's Market was a family-run business conveniently located adjacent to the university campus. It enjoyed a colorful reputation in town for many things, not least of which was its remarkable variety of beers. If anything actually happened that day no one could say but, since my research interest was "creative" religious movements, the story made my upstate New York heart beat warmly. Perhaps this southern university town was more like home than I thought.

Thirty years later, as I approach retirement age, another convergence looms, this one more tangible. October 2011 marks the bicentennial anniversary of the state legislation that called for a new town and courthouse seat for Rutherford County, initially to be called Cannonsburgh, soon changed to "Murfreesborough" to honor a local Revolutionary War veteran. One month earlier, in September 2011, Middle Tennessee State University celebrates the centennial of its official inauguration and opening. Town and gown share oddly similar creation stories. In each case, the state's legislature mandated the institution and the name, but left open each one's precise location. The result was a stiff competition and maneuvering in which eager developers and local boosters found ways to sway the commissions that made these respective decisions. In 1812, Captain William Lytle, proponent of the site near his property for the county seat, hosted the commissioners to an outdoor feast with "a good supply of liquors on hand."[1] After considerable fellowship and boisterous discussion of the matter, Lytle offered to give 60 acres of land gratis for the county seat should the commissioners vote for his site. Almost needless-to-say, his proposal beat out his competitors' offers.

Likewise, the General Education Act of 1909 established three normal schools, one in each of Tennessee's grand divisions. Selecting Johnson City as the home for East Tennessee's campus and Memphis for the campus in West Tennessee was not controversial. But, once again, several communities in Middle Tennessee competed, this time to host its school. The committee that would decide the matter visited each prospective city, where elected officials and boosters lured them with offers of free city services and glowing descriptions of their town's advantages. But prominent Murfreesboro lawyer and civic leader Andrew L. Todd chaired the committee and made sure that, when members visited his hometown, the city put its best foot forward. Particularly appealing was the offer of two local realtors to provide 80 acres without charge for the site. It was a selfless offer, no doubt, but they also stood to profit handsomely from developing housing around the campus. This offer, as with Lytle's gift, was too good to pass up.[2] So Middle Tennessee Normal School became a Murfreesboro landmark. The rest, as they say, is history.

But what kind of history, and what will we make of it? Anniversaries invite hagiography: lists of accomplishments, heroes and heroines, contributions to the greater community, triumph over tragedies, victories of all sorts. So, in 2006, several members of the MTSU History Department and related disciplines set out to explore what has happened at MTSU. In large part, because of the passage of a hundred years, topics for inclusion in this history of the school were influenced heavily by availability of sources as much as by specializations and interests of those writing them. Not so much a history of MTSU, this is a collection of essays in celebration of that history. Each writer has taken a vertical slice in time, focused on a specific theme, and, in some chapters, revealed how the threads of time have woven the fabric of change.

THE FOUNDING AND DEVELOPMENT OF MTSU

Despite what seems like the writers' variegated interests, their essays comprise snapshots of four essential qualities of university life. The first four chapters depict the development of the institution. With a view of situating the gown within the town, in the first essay, John Lodl, Rutherford County Archivist and alumnus of the History Department's graduate program in Public History, and Dr. Janice Leone, specialist in the history of education and general editor of this volume, detail the intricacies of creating and locating the normal school, while also exploring the central role education played in the history of Murfreesboro in the nineteenth century. Both progressivism in education and town boosterism ensured that politics and the lure of profits would play central roles in the battle to locate Middle Tennessee's normal school in Murfreesboro. Having already hosted several colleges, academies, and female institutes, Murfreesboro enjoyed a reputation as an education center, a fact that alone made it a logical location for the normal school.

Dr. Lorne McWatters, public historian and environmentalist, explores the changing landscape of MTSU as it evolved from normal school to state teachers college, to state college, and finally, in 1965, to university; from the classical architecture of Kirksey Old Main to the postmodern versions of brick and glass of the new College of Education and the soon-to-be-completed student center. Here, too, the developmental context, considering a growing and changing student population and continuously evolving educational ideas and practices, is critical in understanding the campus's distinctive footprint.

Dr. Rebecca McIntyre and Dr. Nancy Rupprecht, MTSU historians, examine the campus culture for women students and teachers from 1911, when both groups were subject to prescribed community norms that guided their behavior and career patterns, to the post-1965 university days of increased advocacy for women, as evidenced especially in the growth and development of the Women's Studies program. "Learn to Stand Alone," motto of an early woman's club on campus, describes well the continuous goal of women at MTSU.

Murfreesboro is not only a southern town, but it encompasses one major Civil War battlefield and is close to others. Dr. Derek Frisby, who earned his undergraduate degree at MTSU and teaches in the Department of History, rounds out the first section of the book by examining the developing identity of MTSU, focusing particularly on the tension over its attachment to a Confederate past. Not only did that tension provoke an institutional crisis, but it also created strained relationships with a community of alumni and supporters who did not always understand the university's extraordinary growth and changing needs.

CAMPUS LIFE

The quality of student life has attracted three contributions to this collection. Professor Emeritus Reuben Kyle of the College of Business, who has done extensive research on the Nobel Prize winner James Buchanan and his family's relationship to the institution, reconstructs the lives of students at State Teachers College in the 1930s, when they used only six buildings, all arranged around the Kirksey Old Main classroom building. Living conditions and expectations of young people were different then, but their concerns will sound very familiar to today's students.

Professor Emeritus Fred Colvin, another MTSU historian who is well known for his engaging lectures in sports history among other subjects, tackles the fascinating story of athletics. It is a story that begins with little more than sandlot football and baseball teams and continues through MTSU's evolution to today's NCAA Division I status. Dr. Colvin introduces us not only to colorful students but also to committed coaches and athletic directors whose influence on the lives of their student athletes is memorialized in the names of many of MTSU's buildings and streets. Dr. Colvin does in prose what MTSU's new Hall of Fame accomplishes in brick and steel.

Jordan Kirkman, an undergraduate history major when he completed this research as an assignment in the Historian's Craft course, tells the story of the dramatic year 1968 and its impact on MTSU students. The war in Vietnam, student protests, continuing struggles for civil rights, and space travel all precipitated local responses including student debates, protests, and taking the first steps in growing beyond our segregationist past. Due in part to the leadership of the faculty and of President Mel Scarlett, students chose to work to effect change on campus and in the community without rioting in the streets.

FACULTY AND ADMINISTRATION DEVELOPMENT

Faculty and administration development is an essential quality of MTSU's story that reflects community involvement. Dr. James Williams, MTSU historian and director of the Albert Gore Research Center, begins this section of the book by recounting the firing of English professor Philip Mankin and its aftermath. President Q. M. Smith's action had political, religious, and moral implications, and it provoked a public controversy when town supporters of Mankin appealed the decision to the State Board of Education. Notwithstanding, Mankin lost his job, and his firing led the American Association of University Professors to censure the administration.

Dr. David L. Rowe, long-time AAUP member and chapter leader, picks up the story and examines the rapid growth of the MTSU chapter following Mankin's firing, during which time it became the largest chapter in the Tennessee Board of Regents system. He sees these developments as signs of the faculty's transformation from teachers to professors, a process of professionalization that, ironically, President Q. M. Smith initiated and encouraged in his quest to modernize the institution. That process continued long after President Smith's administration. Modernization required desegregation, and while MTSU, like all state schools, was admitting African American students by the mid-1960s, progress was slow.

Dr. Ken Scherzer explores the university's response to the US District Court's famous "*Geier* decision" in 1968, requiring the state to desegregate Tennessee State University (the former all-black college) and to ensure greater racial diversity among the students, faculty, and administrators at all Tennessee Board of Regents institutions. Even though the decree is no longer in effect, MTSU continues to feel its consequences.

CREATION AND GROWTH OF SELECT ACADEMIC PROGRAMS

Two writers have focused on the creation and growth of significant academic programs. Dr. Ellen Garrison, professor and public historian, recounts the impact of World War II on academic life when President Q. M. Smith successfully negotiated for the development of military training facilities on campus, particularly a pilot training program. At a time when male students were leaving to serve in the war and funding was otherwise scarce, these programs increased the number of students and brought the school badly needed financing, allowing it to survive difficult times. The pilot training program, especially, transformed the campus by adding new facilities and revolutionizing student life for both men and women. Today the Aerospace Major, like Recording Industry Management, remains a signature program at MTSU that continues to attract students from across the nation and beyond.

Dr. Phil Mathis, professor emeritus and former dean of the University Honors College, recounts the story of honors education at MTSU. Founded in 1973, the program reflected the post-Sputnik urge to improve education, particularly in math and the sciences, around the country. Established as an academic program, in 1998 it became the first honors college at a public university in Tennessee and now boasts its own building, financed in part by the first of its many impressive graduates. It was here that in fall 2009 the college hosted a lecture series on MTSU history that served as the progenitor for this book.

The essays in this book are labors of respect and love, both for the institution and for the disciplines and values the stories convey. While readers may find a certain synergy in reading the chapters together, they are organized so that readers can pick and choose the topics they find most interesting. As with all histories, each consumer takes away something different. The stories may perhaps produce understanding, memories, renewed appreciation, or more questions. As a body, though, the contributors are happy here to present their work as just another opportunity to celebrate MTSU's centennial legacy in the way that comes naturally, by serving both the public and the institution that has been for us more than a work place but a collegium, a community of learning and teaching.

David L. Rowe
History Department
2011

NOTES

1   John C. Spence, *The Annals of Rutherford County*, vol. 1 (Murfreesboro, TN: Rutherford County Historical Society, 1991), 68–69, 86–87.

2   John Pittard, *The First Fifty Years: Middle Tennessee State College, 1911–1961* (Murfreesboro: Middle Tennessee State College, 1961), 9–13.

CHAPTER ONE

Middle Tennessee State Normal School Comes to Murfreesboro, 1909–1911

JANICE M. LEONE
JOHN LODL

On September 11, 1911, almost a thousand people gathered in the auditorium of the Main Building in Murfreesboro, Tennessee, to celebrate the dedication of the Middle Tennessee State Normal School. They listened to presentation speeches by Murfreesboro Mayor G. B. Giltner and Andrew L. Todd, representing Rutherford County. State Superintendent of Education J. W. Brister delivered the acceptance address. Other notables who participated in the speech making of the day included the presidents of the yet-to-open West and East Tennessee Normal schools, S. A. Mynders and S. G. Gilbreath, respectively, Dr. Brown Ayers, president of the State University (now known as University of Tennessee–Knoxville), as well as US Commissioner of Education P. P. Claxton. The Murfreesboro Band, along with Tennessee college students, provided the music.

The speeches presented that day clearly looked to the future as they described Middle Tennessee State Normal as an institution designed for a very specific purpose. According to State Superintendent Brister, that purpose was "to create a professional atmosphere in which teachers are to grow, to offer a favoring environment for their development." The school would provide "training for as important and noble a vocation as ever engaged the activities of man."[1] He ended his speech with what would sound familiar to current listeners. He answered his own question of whether Tennessee would benefit from schools focused on teacher preparation with a plea for state financial support. As Brister noted, ". . . we can hope for no permanent gain unless from some source comes more money for the schools."[2]

While the crowds who gathered for the dedication of Middle Tennessee State Normal had been justly apprised of both the future promises and pitfalls of this new institution, most were unaware of the past efforts it had taken to bring the school to Murfreesboro. Had they known, perhaps their enthusiasm for the school would have been even greater. The dedication of Middle Tennessee State Normal in 1911 was the culmination of a long struggle to improve education in Tennessee. One of the earliest calls in the state legislature to create a teacher training school in the state occurred in October 1855, when a Wilson County politician introduced a bill in the House to establish a state normal school in Lebanon, Tennessee. The measure passed in the House but failed in the Senate.[3] Again, in 1874, a normal school bill made it through the state Senate but got "lost" in the House just before adjournment.[4]

While the legislature had little success in the years after the Civil War, support for normal schools came from the private sector as well as from educators' professional organizations. For example, trustees of the George Peabody Fund for a few years contributed money for the support of normal students at various schools in the state, but eventually focused support on Peabody Normal College once it was established in Nashville in 1875.[5] Additional support for normal schools had come from the State Teachers Association in 1865 in the form of a resolution that stated:

> Resolved, by this Association, that we recommend to the legislature to establish, for the present, one normal school, with a view of establishing two more, at some future time, one in each geographical division of the State. [6]

But the battle continued. Twenty-two years later, in 1887, the Public School Officers Association, under the auspices of the state school superintendent, put on their meeting agenda a discussion of the creation of state normal colleges.[7] Clearly, the schools had yet to be created. A more indirect method of support for educational reform came through the Summer School of the South, held in 1902, along with other teacher institutes. Teachers who attended were provided with academic improvement as well as necessary information and materials to carry on educational campaigns to improve education in the state.

While these various legislative and associational efforts failed to result in the actual building of state supported normal schools by the turn of the century, they did keep the issue alive and laid the groundwork for the successful education campaign of the early twentieth century. For example, in 1903 a group of state school administrators met in Nashville to begin a statewide educational campaign. They created a set of objectives that guided their efforts for the next three years. Among their goals they included the "higher training of teachers and the encouragement of those who wish to make teaching a life profession,"[8] an early reference to teacher training. By 1906, these same administrators petitioned the State General Assembly to provide an "annual appropriation of $75,000 for the establishment and maintenance of three normal schools."[9] Although it took another three years of lobbying, the calls for the creation and support of normal schools were eventually folded into the General Education Bill, passed in 1909. The final bill provided an appropriation of 25 percent of the gross revenue of the state to create a general education fund to support a number of projects, including building and maintaining "three normal schools for white teachers—one in each grand division of the state, and one normal school for colored teachers."[10] In the first years after the bill's passage, 13 percent of this general education fund was set aside for the support of the three normal schools, as well as for "an Agricultural and Industrial Normal School for negroes in Nashville."[11]

Of the many school officials who worked for the passage of the General Education Bill of 1909, Robert Lee Jones, who served as state superintendent of education from 1907 to 1911, was given much credit for the bill. According to one historian of these early education campaigns, the bill was "largely a monument to his tact, diplomacy, and ability to direct a legislature."[12] Jones resigned as state superintendent in 1911 to become the first president of Middle Tennessee State Normal School. Andrew L. Todd, who served as Rutherford County superintendent of schools from 1900 to 1907, also earned recognition for his active involvement in the education improvement efforts. And Todd continued his activities as he worked to bring Middle Tennessee State Normal to Murfreesboro and to nurture the school in its early years.[13]

With passage of the General Education Bill, the stage was set, so to speak, for the next phase of normal school education—determining in which three Tennessee towns the schools would be built. The Tennessee legislature had also authorized municipalities and counties who intended to vie for one of the schools to issue $100,000 of 5 percent or less interest-bearing bonds "for the purpose of purchasing sites, erecting and equipping buildings for State Normal Schools."[14] Murfreesboro and Rutherford County officials wasted no time in putting the finances in place that would allow them to compete for one of these institutions. The Murfreesboro City Council met in late June 1909 to authorize the mayor to offer $25,000 in bonds to the State Board of Education "for the location of one of the State Normal Schools in Rutherford County." Council members passed this ordinance after its third reading on July 1, 1909, just a few months after the legislature had approved the education bill.[15]

Likewise, members of the Rutherford County Quarterly Court (now the County Commission) presented a resolution in early July 1909 to issue $100,000 in bonds at 5 percent interest to be paid semi-annually. Thirty-seven magistrates (now commissioners) voted in favor of the resolution, while 14 opposed it. All of this, of course, was contingent on the normal school being located someplace in Rutherford County, and in July 1909 that was yet to be determined.[16] But city officials had reason to be optimistic about their chances of winning over other competitors. Not only would a prominent Murfreesboro resident, Andrew L. Todd, sit on the selection committee, but the town had already established itself as a center for educational endeavors that went back to the days of its founding. Murfreesboro had enjoyed the fruits of higher education for many years.[17]

Rutherford County, Tennessee, was created in October 1803, and officially began operating as a new center of local government in January 1804. Shortly thereafter, in 1806, the state legislature passed an act to establish academies in all counties. Bradley Academy was created to serve the needs of this new county but as a private institution. An 1809 advertisement, announcing the school's opening, stated that "Bradley Academy . . . will be open for the reception of students" and that the students would be "taught the English language grammatically, the Latin and Greek languages, writing and Arithmetic, the most useful branches of Mathematics, Geography, natural and moral philosophy, and astronomy, and such other useful and ornamental branches of literature as are usually taught in similar institutions."[18] By the time that future president, James K. Polk, attended Bradley Academy in 1815, the school had moved from the frontiers of the county into the county's new seat, Murfreesboro. In the 1830s, Bradley Academy moved into a new, two-story brick structure in Murfreesboro and remained in this new location until the academy dissolved around 1840. The building itself survived the ravages of the Civil War, and thereafter became synonymous with black education in Rutherford County from 1884, when the school was authorized for the exclusive education of African Americans, until the 1950s, when the city schools began to integrate.

After Bradley's founding, Murfreesboro residents continued their interest in education when, in 1842, the Baptists of Middle Tennessee passed a charter to create a new college. This new institution would be called Union University, and they elected to construct the college in Murfreesboro. From its inception in 1842, until funds could be raised to build a new structure, the Tennessee State Legislature placed the former Bradley Academy building under the same stewardship as Union University so the Baptist leaders were able to use this location for their operations. In 1848, after several years of raising funds, Baptists laid the cornerstone for a new campus on East Main Street, although the new university was not completed until 1853. Union University was highly successful before the Civil War, but sustained extensive physical and financial damage during the war. The college re-opened for a brief time in Murfreesboro, from 1868 until 1873, before ultimately closing again because of financial constraints and a cholera epidemic. The Baptists finally moved Union University to Jackson, Tennessee, in 1874, where it is still in operation today.[19]

Women were not ignored in this educational growth. In 1853, Baptists also opened the Tennessee Baptist Female Institute, also known as Eaton College, which Union University's Board of Trustees managed. The building for this new college for women was located just north of Union University in Murfreesboro and accommodated one hundred students. The school closed during the Civil War and, like many of the larger buildings in town, its building served as a hospital. After the war, Baptists abandoned their mission to educate young ladies at Eaton College. The school was re-chartered in 1866, however, as the Murfreesboro Female Institute and remained in operation until 1899 as a private institution for young ladies.

Not to be outdone, the Murfreesboro Methodist Church established Soule Female Academy in 1851, on Maple Street, just north of the town square. While the young ladies utilized an older school building for the first two years, monies were raised to construct a new structure across the street, which opened in November 1853. The school was forced to close for a short time during the Civil War but reopened in January 1866. This quick recovery of the school was short lived, however, as the Soule Female Academy was forced to close again in 1868 due to a financial crisis. From this point until its final closing in 1917, the school was operated as a private, secular school, not associated with any main denomination. Famous alumni from the school included Tennessee writer Will Allen Dromgoole and Jean Faircloth, who later married General Douglas MacArthur. From its inception through its demise, Soule Female Academy was the "most long lived and prestigious of all . . . private schools for girls" in Rutherford County.[20]

The Tennessee College for Women was the last major institution to open in Murfreesboro prior to the grand opening of Middle Tennessee State Normal School. In 1905, the Baptist State Convention of Tennessee created an educational committee "to locate and establish a college for women." They settled on Murfreesboro once again, and acquired the former Union University campus consisting of 14 acres on East Main Street. The new building was completed and ready for operations by September 1907. Andrew L. Todd, who later became a key player in the establishment of Middle Tennessee Normal School in Murfreesboro, served on the board of directors for the new college for women. The Tennessee College for Women survived for almost 40 years before being closed in 1945 by the executive board of the Southern Baptist Convention. The school was then merged with Cumberland University in Lebanon, Tennessee.[21] Today a historical marker on East Main Street in Murfreesboro, dedicated to the legacy of the school, states: "On this site was Tennessee's only senior college for women for thirty-eight years, training students from throughout the United States to be educators, missionaries, and homemakers. The ideal of its Baptist founders was to offer the very best educational advantages under positive Christian influence." So Murfreesboro had a long tradition of supporting education. Town residents may have felt that this legacy not only prepared them to become home to one of the new state normal schools, but also that their experience may have simply made them more deserving than others.

And, indeed, the plans for the location decision were already moving forward. In June 1909 members of the State Board of Education met in Nashville to determine how to proceed in locating the proposed normal schools. At this meeting the board constituted a subcommittee of three of its members: P. L. Harned from Montgomery County, Robert Lee Jones, the state superintendent originally from White County and then Nashville, and Andrew L. Todd from Murfreesboro. This committee of three was to prepare guidelines for the "method of procedure on the part of the Board and also to formulate a uniform plan of action for all bidders." All bids for a normal school would be due to the board no later than September 1, 1909.[22]

Although there is no surviving record of the specific rules and regulations developed by the subcommittee, counties and municipalities submitted 22 bids to the board by the September 1 deadline. By that date the board had constituted itself as the search committee and, between September 8 and October 14, visited 20 proposed sites, two of the original bidders having withdrawn their proposals. These visits, of course, took board members all over the state. Towns vying for the school in East Tennessee included Athens, Cleveland, Dayton, Johnson City, and Sweetwater. The West Tennessee towns that wanted a normal school were Covington, Humboldt, Huntington, Jackson, McKenzie, and Memphis. Middle Tennessee had the largest number of towns competing for the school, including Columbia, Cookeville, Clarksville, Fayetteville, Monterey, Murfreesboro, Shelbyville, Tullahoma, and Winchester. According to the newspaper, the total offered in money, bonds, land, and property by all 20 bidders amounted to $3,250,000.[23] Indications are that board members were surprised by the positive response from these communities. As they wrote in the board minutes for November 1909: "The interest manifested over the State in establishing these schools far exceeded our expectations and the arguments offered for each place applying were strongly presented each had its particular merits considered and the responsibility of deciding between rival claimants has been very great, as every competing place possessed some merit and all were intensely interested in obtaining the school."[24] Stories carried in local papers about each site visit also described enthusiastic citizens of municipalities and counties who turned out in large numbers to promote the advantages of their respective towns as the ideal location for the school. Not only was this civic boosterism at its best, but as an editorial noted, "The amount of money and lands and buildings offered in some of the towns is remarkable. Such offers show the value placed upon educational institutions of merit."[25] Governor Malcolm Patterson was quoted in another article as stating that "[a] great deal of enthusiasm has been observed; certainly this means well for the great cause of education in Tennessee. I think it is a most hopeful sign for the State and for its people."[26] Clearly, state officials were pleased with the support that Tennessee residents exhibited in the search process for improved education.

Citizens of Murfreesboro were no exception when it came to enthusiasm. In an effort to ensure an anticipated crowd of five thousand city and county residents at the October 4 visit of the board of education, the *Nashville American* reported that all toll roads leading to Murfreesboro had "been thrown open to all."[27] According to the newspaper account of the visit, the five board members who arrived from Nashville on October 3 "were met at the station by committees in automobiles, and a large crowd of citizens in carriages and buggies."[28] Board members represented all portions of the state. (These board members included J. L. Brooks from Johnson City, J. M. Barker from Bristol, W. N. Billingsly from Spencer, J. L. Bynum from Jackson, and T. B. Loggins from Dickson.) But what must have encouraged Murfreesboro boosters was that board member, Andrew L. Todd, Rutherford County native and well-known lawyer and businessman in Murfreesboro, also served on the site visitation committee. Board members toured the city, were entertained in private homes, and attended a song service at the Methodist church after dinner on the first day of their visit. When Governor Patterson and State Superintendent R. L. Jones arrived in the town the next day, the official visit began. After an informal reception at the Elks Club and another tour of the city, board members assembled on the town square as Governor Patterson briefly addressed "an assemblage of 2,500 or 3,000 public school children and citizens from the courthouse steps."[29] The next venue was the Opera Hall, which, according to press accounts, "was packed to its full capacity." Here, "concrete arguments" as to why Murfreesboro was the ideal location in Middle Tennessee for the normal school were presented by local officials including Mayor J. H. Crichlow. Yet, if the timeline for site activities is correct as recounted in the newspaper then the arguments made in Murfreesboro's favor on this day were brief. The gathering at the Opera Hall began approximately at noon, after which board members and other officials moved to the nearby Jordan Hotel for lunch, and then returned to Nashville "in automobiles, accompanied by citizens of Murfreesboro."[30] All of this suggests that the site visit was more of an opportunity to showcase the physical attributes of the town itself as well as the enthusiasm and support of local residents for situating the school in their community. And when board members later announced the three chosen locations, it is obvious from their explanations of their choices that they had access to additional information about each site in the form of written documents. It is also likely, but undocumented, that Murfreesboro officials took advantage of meetings in "private homes" and even the ride back to Nashville to highlight the town's advantages. Unfortunately, this is all speculation as to how the process worked since conversations, of course, were not recorded and written documentation supporting Murfreesboro's bid for the school is yet to be found.

The board completed its last site visit on October 14 in Clarksville, also a strong contender for the Middle Tennessee normal school. The board met the following day and, after accepting travel claims from board members for their site visit expenses, voted to "defer action for a few days as to the location of the schools."[31] The few days turned into several weeks, however, and the board did not meet officially again until November 29 to discuss the issue. This delay did not stop the general public, as well as local newspaper editors, from speculating as to which of the 20 towns visited would win the three normal schools. Although a story in the *Nashville American* for November 7 described the towns as "serenely waiting for the decision of the Board," there were indications that interested parties continued to lobby the board to choose their respective towns. The paper's editor also felt confident in predicting that Johnson City would be selected in the Eastern Division; Memphis would get the nod in the Western Division; and either Columbia or Clarksville would win the Middle Tennessee location.[32] By the time the board gathered on November 29 to begin serious deliberations, the *Nashville American* editor had narrowed his predictions enough to eliminate Columbia as a contender and identify Clarksville as the site of the future Middle Tennessee Normal School.[33]

The board took its time with deliberations, meeting in five official sessions over the course of two and a half days, from November 29 to December 1. During this time, delegations from several of the contending towns set up headquarters in Nashville, intending to improve the chance that their hometowns would be selected, even though the board had earlier ruled that no further hearings would be granted.[34] As the *Nashville Tennessean* reported after the second day of meetings:

> Many of the delegations which came to Nashville on the first day of the meeting to push the claims of their respective cities and towns continue to crowd the corridors of the capitol, and whenever one of the members of the board dares show his head outside the governor's office, where the sessions are being held, he is immediately buttonholed, while the advantages and merits of this or that town are whispered into his ear. These "boosters" realize what is at stake, and will, no doubt, remain in Nashville until the board announces its final decision and the locations of the three normals are made known.[35]

Although reporters covered the deliberation closely, they seemed to have had trouble getting information out of board members. As the *Nashville Banner* reported after the first day of meetings, "None of the members of the State Board will give out anything regarding the probable location of the three normal schools. They are everyone reticent on the subject."[36] Yet this did not stop reporters from continuing to make predictions. Memphis and Johnson City remained favorites in their respective divisions. In the day before the final decision was announced, Murfreesboro appeared for the first time, along with Clarksville, as a favorite for Middle Tennessee.[37] Apparently the choice of the location for the normal school in Middle Tennessee proved to be a sticking point for the board and may have held up the announcement of the final decision.

Clarksville and Murfreesboro had submitted equally attractive proposals. When the board announced its decision on December 1, awarding the schools to Memphis, Johnson City, and Murfreesboro, members issued clear reasons for the choices. In describing the selection of Murfreesboro, board members noted that the town and county had offered the proceeds of $180,000 of bonds as well as a free site to be selected by the board. Of almost equal importance was the guarantee from city officials "that a sewer system would be inaugurated in the city of Murfreesboro before the school is located and ready to begin work." The board went on to note that "[t]his bid by Murfreesboro and Rutherford County is about equal to that of Clarksville and Montgomery County and is greater than that of any other County or municipality bidding for the Normal in Middle Tennessee, hence a majority of the Board has considered this to be the proper place for the establishment of the Middle Tennessee State Normal." The board made it clear, however, that should Murfreesboro officials fail to uphold any part of its proposal, the board was free to select a different site, a stipulation presented to each winning town.[38] Given the hard-fought competition for the schools, there was actually little chance that city officials would not work to ensure that they delivered on all promises in the proposals.

The response to the selection was varied, but local press seemed unable to resist the temptation to engage in a discussion, at least for a brief time, of the "real" reasons for the choices, especially in the case of Murfreesboro and Middle Tennessee. The

Nashville Banner informed readers of a rumor that five members of the board had originally supported a combination of Jackson, Murfreesboro, and Johnson City, but had abandoned this effort in the face of opposition from Governor Patterson. When questioned about this, board members denied any such agreement. According to the *Banner* reporter, "These members said that while those on the board had talked among themselves in twos and threes, nothing like a caucus had been held by any of the members."[39]

Careful readers of the *Banner* would, however, have noticed in the same article, mention of board members, "with two or three other guests," being "delightfully entertained at dinner at the home of State Supt. R. L. Jones." Up until that time, the board had accomplished nothing, according to the *Banner*. But by the following day, the day after the dinner, the contest "had narrowed down considerably." The board was in session for only one hour before making the announcement of the chosen sites.[40] (While there is no record of the dinner conversations, of course, it does raise the question of whether more than dinner was served that night at the home of the state superintendent, who went on to become the first president of Middle Tennessee State Normal School.)

Other responses indicate that the choice was a simple matter of geography. The *Nashville American* editor used location to explain Murfreesboro's selection over Clarksville, even though the latter town had offered $185,000, a free site, and free water, compared to Murfreesboro's bid of $180,000 and a free site. As the editor noted, with regard to the map of Tennessee, "If a rule is placed on the drawing with one end on Memphis and the other on Johnson City, it will fall directly over Murfreesboro. Besides this feature the Board took into consideration the accessibility of all the towns and concluded that the three chosen could be the easiest reached from all points and sections."[41]

Response to the selection decision appears to have been, at last publicly, very civil. Along with their regrets to the disappointed officials in the towns not chosen, board members extended congratulations to them for "the educational spirit" they had experienced in all the towns they had visited.[42] Newspaper accounts reveal a generally positive consensus about the choices. The *Chattanooga Times* encouraged readers "to acquiesce cheerfully and cordially." Although the paper's preference was for Dayton and Winchester, rather than Johnson City and Murfreesboro, they praised both winners. The school in Murfreesboro would surely succeed since "its people are among the best in the State and such an institution can not fail to flourish there by sheer force of the high quality of its environment."[43] The *Nashville Banner* writers praised the wisdom of the selection, and, in reference to the choice of Murfreesboro over Clarksville, stated matter-of-factly that the board chose Murfreesboro because it was the most centrally located and easily accessible.[44] The *Nashville American* described Murfreesboro as "a fine town, one of the very best in the state." Being in "the center of a splendid territory, with excellent railway facilities and inhabited by a most hospitable, high minded people," the selection of Murfreesboro was certainly supported by the Nashville press.[45]

Columbia's response, however, was not so positive. An editorial in the town's newspaper, the *Daily Herald*, described the decision as political and noted, "Not a site selected is altogether a fortunate one. Murfreesboro has not a single advantage that is not possessed by Columbia. . . . Murfreesboro is a delightful little city. It is a splendid place to live, but it will hardly be seriously claimed that it is as admirably situated for the location of the Normal as is Columbia." The choice of Memphis also merited criticism in the same editorial. Questioning the city's "moral and religious tone," the paper argued, "It will not be a fortunate thing for the future of Tennessee to have its teachers trained in an atmosphere reeking with vice and lawlessness." Columbia residents were to be consoled in knowing that the town's bid for the school was not defeated "on merit" but rather resulted from the "fine Italian hands of several of the chief advisors of the Patterson administration," a reference to the area's political stance on the governor who had served on the selection committee. Yet the paper encouraged residents to be satisfied with the campaign the city officials had conducted, a campaign that "never degenerated into a secret lobby."[46]

The other major contender for the school in Middle Tennessee was Clarksville, and here, too, was the contention that politics was involved. Just after the decision was announced, the *Leaf Chronicle* of Clarksville printed an editorial that listed all the well-known advantages of the town that had led many to just assume that Clarksville would win the school. The editor went on to argue that what interested people did not know was "that the game of politics would be played and that before the final vote would be taken there could be a trade made that would prevent the schools being located at points where under the statutes they should have been. . . . it wasn't down in the cards that Clarksville, fortified as she was by such splendid advantages in this unequal contest, should meet with such a Waterloo. How it came about we leave to wiser and better informed heads than ours as to the devious ways of politics."[47]

Regardless of the less-than-subtle suggestions that the choice had not been fair, the decision stood, and the state board moved on to selecting the specific sites within each chosen town. As many as seven potential sites were offered in Murfreesboro for the school. After considering them all, the board decided in February 1910 to accept the offer made by T. H. Harrison and Joe Black, local real estate developers. The offer included 80 acres of land given free of charge with another 20 acres sold for $5000. This, of course, is the current site of MTSU; and in 1910 this one hundred-acre plat was bordered on the west by Broad Street (now Middle Tennessee Boulevard), on the south by Main Street and Woodbury Pike, on the north by Lascassas and Hall's Hill Pike (now Greenland Avenue), and on the east by a road to be constructed as part of the offer. The *Nashville Tennessean* reported very favorably on the selection of this site mainly because of its location. East Main Street was considered the "most beautiful residence street in the city," the site itself was "located high and dry with excellent sewerage advantages," and was not far from the Murfreesboro School for Boys and the Tennessee College for Women.[48] While the choice of this site may have been considered beneficial to the future school and, by connection, the town, the fine print of the deed indicates that Harrison and Black succeeded in furthering their own development goals. Not only had the state board agreed to construct paved roads around the entire property, but board members would also be responsible for extending Bell and Lytle Streets to the western boundary of the school's campus, thus connecting the town with the school.[49] Since Harrison and Black owned property surrounding the school site, it seems safe to speculate that, with paved roads and close proximity to the public square, they envisioned further real estate development in the near future.

With the site selected, the state board moved rapidly to construct the normal schools and prepare them to open in 1911. In the next 18 months, after first rejecting architectural plans because they were over the approved appropriation, the board awarded the architectural contract to C. K. Colley and the construction contract to George W. Moore and Son of Nashville. At a cost of $137,855, Moore and Son would erect the main building, a women's dormitory, kitchen and dining hall, and the powerhouse. Separate contracts for heating, plumbing, and lighting were awarded to other contractors at an additional cost of approximately $28,000. The bid for the president's house came in at $10,000. The board noted clearly that they had accepted only the lowest bids.[50]

In the fall of 1910, R. L. Jones was named as the first president of the school, at a salary of $3600 and a house, for a term of five years. The board went on to appoint a local committee, made up of the representatives from each grand division as well as the state superintendent for each of the schools, to handle their continuing development. As a member of the Middle Tennessee local committee, Andrew L. Todd played an active role in the many details required in setting up the school. By the time of the September 11 dedication, the first buildings were completed, most of the faculty was in place, and approximately 125 students had paid tuition of $2/ month. MTSU was off to a promising beginning.

NOTES

1   "Middle Tennessee Normal School is Dedicated," *Nashville Tennessean,* 12 September 1911, 4; Proceedings of the Tennessee State Board of Education, Record Group 91, vol. 62, 11 September 1911, 47, Tennessee State Library and Archives, Nashville, TN.

2   Ibid.

3   Robert Hiram White, *Development of the Tennessee State Educational Organization, 1796–1929* (Kingsport, TN: Southern Publishers, 1929), 72–73.

4   Ibid., 126.

5   Creation of Peabody Normal College was approved by the Tennessee State Legislature in the Law of 1875. See Andrew David Holt, *The Struggle for a State System of Public Schools in Tennessee, 1903–1936* (New York: Teachers College, Columbia University, 1938), 55.

6   Ibid., 50.

7   Ibid., 61.

8   Ibid., 94.

9   Ibid., 95.

10 Ibid., 96.

11 Ibid., 248. Text of the Act can be found in J. W. Brister, *Public School Laws of Tennessee* (Nashville, TN: Department of Public Instruction, 1911), 76–87.

12 Holt, *Struggle for a State System,* 126.

13 Unpublished biography of Andrew Lee Todd in Leone's possession.

14 TN, Senate Bill No. 699, Chapter 580 in *House Journal of the Fifty-Sixth Assembly of State of Tennessee,* 4 January 1909, 2030.

15 City Council of Murfreesboro Minute Book, June 1909, Walker Library, Middle Tennessee State University, Murfreesboro, TN.

16   Minutes of Rutherford County Quarterly Court, July 1909, Rutherford County Archives, Murfreesboro, TN.

17   Minutes of Rutherford County Quarterly Court, Book 4, 179-80, Rutherford County Archives, Murfreesboro, TN.

18   *Nashville Clarion,* 2 June 1809, Tennessee State Library and Archives.

19   *Tennessee Encyclopedia of History and Culture*, Version 2.0, s.v. "Union University," http://tennesseeencyclopedia.net/entry.php?rec=1417.

20   Eugene H. Sloan, "Soule College," *Rutherford County Historical Society Publication* 11(Summer 1978): 58.

21   *Tennessee Encyclopedia of History and Culture*, Version 2.0, s.v. "Tennessee College for Women," http://tennesseeencyclopedia.net/entry.php?rec=1319.

22   Proceedings, TN State Board, 3 June 1909, 27.

23   "State Board Meets Monday," *Nashville American*, 24 November 1909, 3.

24   Proceedings, TN State Board, 30 November 1909, 36.

25   "The Normal Schools," *Nashville American*, 6 October 1909.

26   "Hopeful Sign for the State," *Nashville American*, 4 October 1909.

27   Ibid.

28   "Murfreesboro to the Fore," *Nashville American*, 5 October 1909.

29   Ibid.

30   Ibid.

31   Proceedings, TN State Board, 15 October 1909, 33–34. Six board members turned in requests for reimbursement of expenses incurred in visiting prospective normal school sites. The total requested for Pullman rail travel, laundry, telephone calls, hotel accommodations, cab fare, and clerical work amounted to $689.85.

32   "Where Normals May Be Located," *Nashville American*, 7 November 1909.

33   "Twenty Towns Taking Notice," *Nashville American*, 29 November 1909.

34 Ibid.

35 "Normal Site for Middle Division Ties Up Board," *Nashville Tennessean,* 1 December 1909.

36 "Site for Three Normal Schools," *Nashville Banner,* 29 November 1909.

37 "Normal Site," *Nashville Tennessean.*

38 Proceedings, TN State Board, 30 November 1909, 38.

39 "State Normal Sites Selected," *Nashville Banner,* 1 December 1909.

40 Ibid.

41 "Normal Sites Are Selected," *Nashville American,* 2 December 1909.

42 Proceedings, TN State Board, 30 November 1909, 39.

43 "Duty to Acquiesce," *Chattanooga Times,* reprinted in *Nashville American,* 4 December 1909.

44 "The State Normals," *Nashville Banner,* 2 December 1909.

45 "The Normals Located," *Nashville American,* 2 December 1909.

46 "Normal School Sites," *Daily Herald,* 2 December 1909, 2.

47 "The Normal School," *Leaf-Chronicle,* 3 December 1909, 4.

48 "Selects Site for Normal School," *Nashville Tennessean,* 11 February 1910.

49 Joe Black and Tom Harrison, owners of this property, referred to the present Middle Tennessee State University Blvd. as Broad St. See Proceedings, TN State Board, 10 February 1910, 48–52.

50 Proceedings, TN State Board, 6 September 1910, 64.

CHAPTER TWO

A History of Place

D. LORNE McWATTERS

It was February 10, 1910, and Murfreesboro attorney Andrew L. Todd was on a mission. In 1909, Todd had deployed his considerable political skills on the Tennessee State Board of Education to engineer the selection of Murfreesboro as the site of one of four new "normals" (teaching schools) in Tennessee. On this Thursday in 1910 he was taking the selection committee on a tour of several possible sites, but Todd himself had already made up his mind. Homer Pittard, author of a history of Middle Tennessee State University (MTSU), explains: "Loading the Board into his Lincoln, [Todd] pulled out from his law office, circled the public square and began the precarious descent down [South] Maple Street into the 'Bottoms.'"[1] Todd was deliberately taking the board through a poor African American neighborhood, steering his motor car on a route designed to create a "bad impression"[2] of the sites closer to the downtown area,[3] the better to also steer the board toward his choice, a one hundred-acre plot of open fields and farmland east of town.

It is no surprise that the board seconded Todd's pick as the place where Middle Tennessee State Normal School (MTSN) would begin when its first four buildings were erected in 1911 (Figure 1).[4] This piece of land actually defines the western, southern, and northern boundaries of today's university.[5] From this small start, MTSN expanded physically eastward, eventually to encompass 515 acres. It also grew organizationally, to become Middle Tennessee State Teachers College (MTSTC) in 1925, Middle Tennessee State College (MTSC) in 1943, and Middle Tennessee State University (MTSU) in 1965.

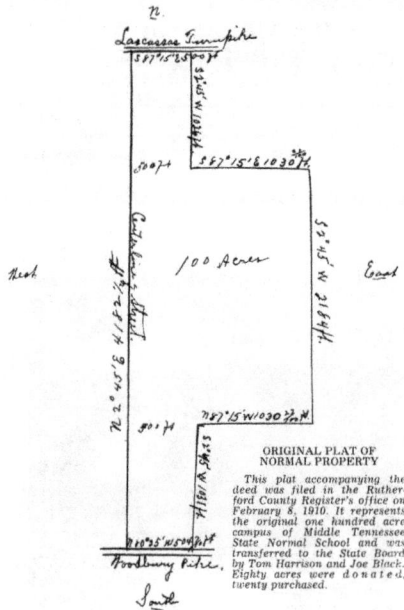

Figure 1: Tom Harrison/Joe Black property, 1910. Pittard, n.p.

This essay explores the physical growth of MTSU, over its one hundred-year history, as revealed in its ever-changing "footprint." MTSU was born as MTSN in 1911, a normal school where teachers and farmers were trained, and it developed over the decades into the Comprehensive Doctoral academic "city" of MTSU, offering PhDs in several disciplines and producing citizens of the world able to take classes in Kurdish and Chinese. Who, standing amidst the first four buildings of MTSN, would have thought that this small school in the geographic center of Tennessee, with 125 inaugural students and 19 faculty would boast, a mere one hundred years later, a student body of 26,430 (Fall 2010) on a campus of 515 acres with 137 permanent buildings and over nine hundred faculty, and a 2009 ranking in *Forbes* as one of the top 100 (#57) public universities in the nation?

Knitting together photographs and text, this essay focuses on the physical/ architectural layout of the major campus buildings[6] and traces the evolution of MTSU by dividing its one hundred-year history into five roughly 20-year periods reflecting phases of building construction and expansion on campus:

Early Years, 1911–1931
Depression and World War II, 1932–1949
Postwar Boom, 1950–1971
Quiet Years, 1972–1989
Postmodern Boom, 1990–2011

This approach calls for an exploration of the history of MTSU as a complex place, or "cultural landscape,"[7] in this case a built environment with the spatial and cultural characteristics of an institution of higher education. Perry Chapman notes that a college campus "stands apart from most organized places because it blends the qualities of the natural world with the evocative order of the designed environment such as to foster human interaction." The American campus, he continues, is a "cultural landscape imbued with deep social purpose."[8] Close examination of the construction (and occasional destruction) of MTSU buildings yields illuminating examples of the creation and expansion of its cultural landscape by referencing the historical forces shaping the design and layout of the buildings. MTSU is one of many American campuses that can be described as "Vernacular American," where structures and landscaping are added over time as needed, creating a readable "layered history."[9]

It is, of course, through the construction of its buildings that a university becomes or grows into itself. An example of this process is provided by the 1968 construction of Peck Hall in the midst of the oldest part of campus, or the recent placement of the Veterans Memorial in front of Jackson Hall (1911; Figure 2). The accretion of layers formed by interweaving buildings can yield the beauty of a pearl, or it can result in graceless, and possibly needless, visual incursion. In either case, such on-the-ground changes are the "making" of a university that almost everyone comes to love, with time.

Figure 2: Jackson (1911))/ Veteran's Memorial Project (2010) and KOM (1911)/ Peck Hall (1968). Photos by author, 2011, 2008.

THE EARLY YEARS: 1911–1931

The Tennessee General Education Act of 1909 authorized four normal schools in the state, three for whites and one for African Americans. Middle Tennessee and East Tennessee opened their schools in Murfreesboro and Johnson City, respectively, in 1911. West Tennessee State Normal opened in Memphis in 1912, as did the African American normal, referred to as "Tennessee State Agricultural and Industrial School," in Nashville. Creation of the normal schools was the result of an educational reform movement that began after the Civil War and jelled into a massive campaign launched in the early twentieth century. Led by Philander P. Claxton, a professor at the University of Tennessee–Knoxville, and supported by northern philanthropists as well as educators throughout Tennessee, the reformers were able to convince the general assembly between 1907 and 1917 to pass legislation that replaced district school directors with county school boards, increased educational funding, enacted compulsory education, required teacher certification, and mandated that each county establish a high school.[10]

Local backing for the normal school was perhaps as important as Andrew Todd's influence, and reflects a regional tradition of support for educational institutions. On September 11, 1907, for example, the Tennessee College for Women (1907–1945) opened on the site of the former Union University (1842–1873) on East Main. Murfreesboro was also the location for Soule Female Academy (1851–1899), and Bradley Academy which became a school for African Americans in 1884, although it originated as an all-white school in 1809 and was the alma mater of James K. Polk in 1814.[11] Asserting that this educational tradition was a factor in local support for the "Normal," Pittard notes that residents "turned out in circus style" when the State Board Selection Committee first came to town in 1909. Business was suspended, the buildings around the square hung with bunting, and the Opera House, where city and county officials promised $180,000 for the school, "jam packed."[12]

Nashville architect C. K. Colley was chosen to design the new Middle Tennessee State Normal School (MTSN). Placement of three of the original buildings, the Administration Building (now Kirksey Old Main, KOM), the cafeteria (now Jackson) and the girls' dormitory (now Rutledge) began a pattern of large, widely separated buildings arranged around an open quadrangle (Figure 3). Architectural historian Paul V. Turner identifies this pattern as an "American Tradition," reflecting not only the availability of land in the United States as compared to Europe, but also a desire to move away from the cloistered, closely attached college buildings typical of Europe.[13]

Colley's original buildings were all neoclassical (classical revival) in style, displaying such typical features as imposing, columned porticos, parapets, balustrades, dentils, and numerous multipane windows on all sides (Figure 4). This classical look, also influenced by the "City Beautiful" movement in American architecture, intended to impress viewers with a sense of history, permanence, and power, to launch MTSN

STATE TEACHERS COLLEGE • ESTABLISHED 1911 • MURFREESBORO, TENN.

Figure 3: Aerial of Middle Tennessee State College, c.1934. Midlander, 1934.

as a place to be taken seriously.[14]

MTSN opened for business on September 11, 1911 (Figure 5). A distinctly utilitarian power plant had been built, its smokestack easily visible just north of the Administration Building, and a "hitch-barn" was constructed near the plant to house the horses that pulled buggies to MTSN before the age of automobiles and many, many parking lots.[15] Housing for students, particularly women (who, it was believed at the time, required careful supervision), was a problem from the start. The three-story girls' dormitory (Rutledge) had 56 rooms, not enough for the female students, and until 1921 all male students lodged off campus.[16]

In its first decade, the most important building at MTSN was the large Administration Building, a multipurpose structure common to many American colleges, where it was usually referred to as "Old Main."[17] MTSU's Old Main contained not only classrooms, but also administrative and business offices, a library, laboratories, rooms for clubs, the training school for students and teachers, an auditorium, and a combination study hall-gymnasium. While buildings constructed in the 1920s relieved some space pressures, the Administration Building continued as the main administrative and classroom structure on campus until the 1960s.

By the end of its first decade, MTSN had become a fully functioning normal school, although still offering only two years of college-level instruction. From 125

Figure 4: President's House, Rutledge, Administration Building (KOM), and Cafeteria (Jackson). Midlander, 1929; Midlander, 1945; AGRC, c. 1926; and AGRC, 1911.

students in Fall 1911, enrollment had grown to 625 by 1916, falling to 393 in 1920 but rising again to 594 in 1921. Since the school's focus was on training elementary school teachers, the student body was dominated by women, typically over 60 percent of the total (66 percent in 1921). In the 1920s, several new buildings were added, part of a state-directed process by which the normals moved from offering two-year to three-year diplomas, becoming four-year state colleges by 1925. MTSN dropped "Normal" from its name and became Middle Tennessee State Teachers College (MTSTC) in 1925, offering a four-year bachelor of science degree. Achieving these educational ambitions required new or upgraded facilities for accreditation from the

Figure 5: First students and faculty at Middle Tennessee Normal, 1911. AGRC, 1911.

American Association of Teachers Colleges (AATC).[18]

These historical forces resulted in a substantial building program from 1921 to 1931.[19] Funding was authorized in 1917, when state officials discussed plans to turn all the normal schools into teachers colleges, but was interrupted by World War I. Monies became available in 1921, allowing the college to construct a 25-room boys' dormitory, a gymnasium inside the Administration Building, a laundry, and a barn. The Moffitt House (now Ellington Annex) on Normal Boulevard was purchased as both a dormitory for 60 women and a lab for "domestic science." The 25-room boys' dormitory, the first new building since 1911, was completed in 1921 (Figure 6) and named Jones Hall after the school's first president, Robert Lee Jones (1911–1919 and 1921–22). While somewhat smaller and less ornate than Rutledge, Jones was designed in the same neoclassical style and placed on the east side of the

Figure 6: Jones Hall (1921) and Campus Barn (1922),
later "Art Barn." Midlander, 1945; AGRC, n.d.

Administration Building facing the quadrangle, reinforcing the basic layout of the campus. The new dairy barn, large enough for 50 cows, was added to already existing agricultural facilities north and west of Jones Hall (north of the current Nursing Building), intended for use as both a dairy and a teaching lab. The college supplied most of the fruits and vegetables and all of the milk consumed in the cafeteria, the latter achievement continuing today as an MTSU tradition. The new barn would later achieve iconic status at MTSU, first because of its size and distinctive pair of silos and later as the art department's "Art Barn" facility (Figure 6).[20]

The surge in construction in the 1920s included building a new library (1926; Figure 7). It might be argued that placing the library inside the quadrangle is inconsistent with the rectangular arrangement; that may be so, but its location just a hundred yards from KOM appears to be a quirk resulting from a visit to the campus by Governor Austin Peay with a committee discussing construction plans, at which time, standing on the steps of KOM, he pointed to the quadrangle and suggested, "why not right there."[21] The library's neoclassical design, however, was consistent with the other buildings. Also classical, and placed south of Rutledge on the west side of the quadrangle, was Lyon Hall (1927; Figure 7), a second large girls' dormitory (120 students) named after the university's second president, Alfred P. Lyon (1922–1938).

One of the most important new buildings, the Training or Demonstration School, was constructed on 15 acres donated by the city several hundred yards west of Normal Boulevard (west of today's Bell Road parking lot). Strikingly similar in design to the Administration Building, but smaller (1929; Figure 8), the new facility replaced the Administration Building's six-room "Model School" where budding teachers practiced their skills on young elementary and high school students (Figure 8). The location of the Training School intensified an already existing drainage problem along Sinking Creek, which ran between the President's house and campus.

Figure 7: Library (1926) and Lyon Hall (1927).
AGRC, before 1968; Midlander, 1945.

Figure 8: "Lake Unnecessary," c. 1929, Training School students on steps of school, 1929, Demonstration (Training) School (1929), and Training School students at KOM, 1920s. Midlander, 1929; Midlander, 1929; AGRC, 1929; AGRC, 1920s.

Since students had to walk across this wet weather channel, which frequently flooded, on their way to the Training School, "Lake Unnecessary" became even more unnecessary (Figure 8).[22]

In the early years of the school, it appears that the grounds were landscaped informally by students and faculty, with the remaining acreage utilized for crops.[23] In 1930 J. H. Bayer, "custodian of property" at MTSC, brought a paper bag of walnuts from George Washington's Mount Vernon estate to plant south and west of the library. The resulting trees became Walnut Grove, an attractive wooded area of the quadrangle often used for football tailgating and other gatherings.[24] More revealing of land-use patterns at MTSTC is a drawing from the 1931 *Midlander*, which shows not only the seven major buildings, power plant, tennis courts, athletic field (today Horace Jones Field), and road system, but also all of the crops being grown on campus and all of the agricultural buildings. The President's House appears to be enveloped in a field of alfalfa (Figure 9).

By 1931, the college was a well-established Tennessee teachers college with neoclassical architecture on a traditional American open quadrangle. Enrollment in 1930 was 629 students, 66 percent female. But the building program of the 1920s had one last act: $225,000 for a new Science Building, a "magnificent . . . splendidly equipped" three-story facility (Wiser-Patten, 1931; Figure 10).[25] One of the most aesthetically pleasing buildings at MTSU, the new Science Building was the icing

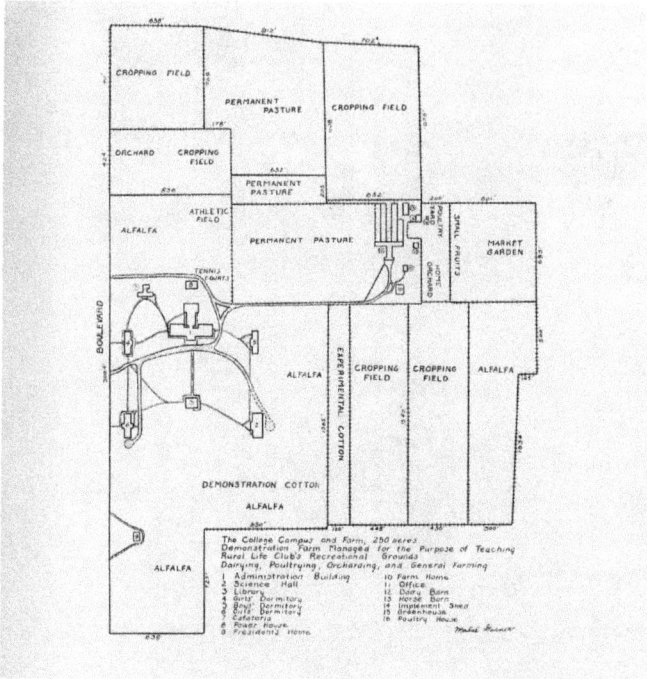

Figure 9: Drawing of MTSTC buildings and grounds, 1931. Midlander, 1931.

on the construction cake of MTSC's first 20 years. The next period, 1932 to 1949, saw almost no new construction, but students, faculty, and staff had to deal with the Great Depression and World War II before witnessing a major transformation after the War.

DEPRESSION AND WORLD WAR II: 1932–1949

The Depression and World War II were emergencies for MTSU during which construction came to a screeching halt. The 1930s were difficult, not only because of reduced funding, but also because of talk about closing all state teachers colleges permanently.[26] Some New Deal resources were made available to MTSTC, such as National Youth Administration (NYA) projects that improved the athletic field (Horace Jones Field), the cafeteria, and the campus landscape as students gained work experience. The Works Progress Administration (WPA) provided funding for various projects, including landscaping, and a Civilian Pilot Training program introduced in 1940 constructed an an airstrip on campus, making MTSTC/MTSC for a time one of only four US colleges with its own airport. Funding for the college was also forthcoming when the federal government selected MTSC to educate cadets

Figure 10: Science Building (1931). Midlander 1941.

for the 11th College Training Detachment of the American Air Force Flying Training Command.[27]

The arrival of the Army Air Force Cadets in 1943 turned the campus into a hive of activity (Figure 11). There was also a great deal of military activity around Middle Tennessee, as over one million soldiers came to a 20-county area between 1942 and 1944 to train in the "Tennessee Maneuvers" for the looming invasion of Europe. Military service caused student enrollment to drop to its lowest numbers ever; only 20 males and 180 females registered in 1944. In the years 1942 through 1945, in fact, the average number of male students on campus was 55, compared to 207 from 1911 to 1941.[28]

The airport (1940) survived until 1954, when it moved to leased facilities at Murfreesboro's Municipal Airport. Many frame structures appeared in the airport area of campus during and after the war, including long, single-story buildings used

Figure 11: Tennessee Maneuvers, c. 1943 and
War Training, 1943. AGRC, c. 1943; Midlander, 1943.

by Tennessee fire fighters and by MTSC building and garden maintenance staff. The hangar became the armory for Forrest Hall in 1954, and the frame buildings were torn down in the 1960s.[29]

Another group of frame buildings that reflected the impact of World War II was used as housing for returning soldiers, many now married. The college imported 57 frame buildings (for apartments) and 50 trailers, creating new areas east of Jones Hall and the Science Building known as "Vet Village" and "Trailer Town" (Figure 12).[30] Vet Village, which survived until the 1960s, was part of a transformation of the student population of the school. By 1950 there was an enrollment spike to 1,211 students, well beyond prewar levels. The postwar expansion also affected gender balance, as the GI Bill, in combination with the school's shift from a focused "teachers" college to a broader "state" college, led to a 56-percent male student body in 1950 (679 men, 532 women), neatly reversing previous figures. This was the beginning of a trend that would accelerate in the booming years of the 1950s and 1960s.[31]

Figure 12: Trailer Town, 1947, MTSC Aerial of Vet Village and Trailer Town, 1953, and Trailer Town Kids, 1947. Midlander, 1947; AGRC, 1953; Midlander, 1947.

The trailers of Trailer Town would disappear in a few years, replaced by a new men's dormitory (Smith Hall) in 1951. Vet Village was a special place at MTSU for over twenty years, surviving after the war until it was torn down for a new science building (Davis Science, 1967). The only permanent building constructed during the 1932–1949 period, other than the airport hangar, was the Industrial Arts Building (Voorhies Industrial Technology Building, 1942; Figure 13),[32] the first major building constructed away from the quadrangle (and not designed in a neoclassical style).

Figure 13: Industrial Arts Building (Voorhies, 1942). Midlander, 1952.

THE POSTWAR BOOM: 1950–1971

The 20-year period from 1950 to 1971 witnessed a massive building boom, first when the GI Bill expanded access to higher education for millions of veterans, later when federal and state governments expanded funding (such as the National Defense Education Act of 1958, in response to the 1957 launching of Sputnik by the Soviet Union) to increase citizens' access to college education, and finally when the postwar baby boomers produced by GI families reached college age. Enrollment at MTSC more than doubled from 1,211 in 1950 to 2,850 in 1960, then almost tripled to 8,093 by 1970.[33] The college added an MA-level graduate program in 1950, racially integrated in 1962 and introduced its first computer that same year, became a university (MTSU) in 1965, and began a doctor of arts degree program in 1970.

The physical appearance of the campus changed dramatically during this period, expanding north, south, and especially east, also adding buildings to the historic west side of campus. As new buildings were constructed and old ones torn down, "modernist" structures with spare lines and heavy use of glass, steel, and concrete replaced the earlier neoclassical styles. This style of architecture was less expensive and more utilitarian than earlier traditional styles, its simplified buildings like a "machine for learning" in Richard Dober's words.[34]

The enrollment of a more diverse student body also broadened the responsibilities of American universities. "Institutions," writes Perry Chapman, "added a prodigious set of functions," becoming "research arms for national defense and science policy, economic and cultural resources for their localities, purveyors of ever more student educational and social services, and partners in wide-ranging enterprises."[35] Before World War II, Chapman continues, "a typical American campus had a spatial clarity reflecting its classical heritage"; after the war colleges became larger and more complex, "laced with roads and vast parking areas." Changes in the scale, order, and character during such rapid growth, he concludes, "often eclipse[d] the gentler settings and the nature of the campus experience that had prevailed for 300 years."[36]

Figure 14: Natatorium (1953) and Memorial Auditorium (1950).
Midlander, 1952; AGRC, 1950.

The boom of 1950–1971 was launched by the new Memorial Auditorium (1950; Figure 14), built on a rise at the west entrance to campus on Faulkinberry Drive. Meant to honor World War II veterans, its main feature was a large gymnasium. The building's imposing facade, with hints of art deco, represented a transition in style toward modern architecture. An aesthetically pleasing structure, it also provided offices and training facilities in the basement used by the newly arrived Reserve Officer Training Corps (ROTC) program until Forrest Hall (1954) was built. A separate, similarly styled indoor swimming pool, the "Natatorium" (1953; Figure 14), was placed next to Memorial.

The longstanding issue of student housing was addressed in 1951 with the construction of a men's dormitory, Smith Hall (Figure 15), on the east side of the quadrangle south of the Science Building, followed by a women's dormitory, Monohan Hall (1954; Figure 15), on the exact opposite west side. In the late 1950s, the campus experienced an enormous expansion of dormitories to accommodate the student explosion. Most of these facilities spread eastward from Smith Hall along the southern edge of the campus. Huge additions to Monohan and Lyon Halls on the west side of campus made up a second grouping, while the two seven-story "hi-rises," Corlew and Cummings Halls, now contributions to the center of campus, made up a third (Figure 15). Both Smith and Monohan, erected on the quadrangle, were constructed in a neoclassical style; the other dormitories, placed away from the quadrangle, were modern in style.

Growth in enrollment was also reflected in the construction of another neoclassical building, MTSU's first Student Union (James Union Building, JUB, 1942; Figure 16). Resting atop a steep stairway in a manner somewhat reminiscent of the Administration Building, JUB became the center of campus life in the 1950s with a cafeteria, bookstore, pool hall, and auditorium (Tennessee Room) that was used for registration, special events, and regular dances.[37]

The year 1954 marked the appearance of Forrest Hall (Figure 17), a building whose name would become controversial in the 1960s because it was named after Nathan Bedford Forrest, the Confederate colonel (later general) who occupied

Figure 15: Monohan (1954), Smith (1951),
Corlew (1967) with Cummings construction, and Corlew cake, 1967.
Photo by author, 2009; AGRC, c. 1950s; AGRC, 1967; AGRC, 1967.

Murfreesboro briefly in 1862 but who was also a slaveholder, commander of Fort Pillow at the time of the slaughter of African American soldiers in 1864, and founder of the Ku Klux Klan. The new facility, including the nearby hangar and annexes, allowed the ROTC to move from Memorial. It retains its name today, despite protests that have erupted from time to time over the past 40 years.[38]

The university's new library (Andrew L. Todd Hall, 1958; Figure 18) was significant as the first modernist-style building on the quadrangle. Located between Jones Hall and the Science Building, with its original entrance facing the quadrangle, it was clearly a departure from the neoclassical style of the other buildings, and yet somewhat understated and not architecturally obtrusive. As the first intrusion into the neoclassical consistency of the historical core of the campus, however, it pointed in the direction of things to come.

Reflecting a longstanding interest in art, music, and theatre at the college, a new fine arts building (Saunders; Figure 19), also modernist but with a nod toward the neoclassical in its use of a large portico with columns, appeared in 1959. It was placed away from the quadrangle, just north of Jones Hall. In that same year, officials also made a dramatic alteration to the rear of KOM by adding glass-enclosed hallways with contemporary colored panels on the outside of both the east and west elevations (Midgett, 1959; Figure 19). The Midgett renovation displays a trend on campus in

Figure 16: James Union Building (1952). Midlander, 1952.

this period of altering the size and shape of windows in various ways, such as bricking them in, a process which undermines the architectural integrity of historic buildings.

The first major building of the 1960s was the impressive Dramatic Arts Building (Boutwell, 1964; Figure 19). With its large auditorium, this was also the first building to be dedicated exclusively to theatrical productions. For a brief time it sat alone on the east side of campus, where its design and ornamentation, including colored panels and glass, reflected Midgett and made a definite modernist statement.

The following year, 1965, modern architecture struck the historic quadrangle

Figure 17: Forrest Hall (1954). Photo by Author, 2008.

Figure 18: Todd Library (1958). AGRC, c. 1958.

with a vengeance when the now "Middle Tennessee State University" erected a new administration building on the south side of the quad (Cope Administration Building, 1965; Figure 20). With a tall columned portico, Cope was oriented toward a new southern entrance to campus, facing a new road that ran north from East Main Street and circled around Cope and the quadrangle in a "loop" (Figure 20). More so than any other building to that date, Cope screamed "modern" with its large foyer encased in concrete, glass, and steel. The 1965 *Midlander* exulted, "progress never stops," praising Cope for bringing "the beauty of modern art" to campus. The "forcefulness of the New Administration building," it concluded, "is a superb introduction to the physical MTSC."[39]

Boutwell and Cope were the beginning of a rapid acceleration of building construction at MTSU, reflecting the arrival of the first baby boomers on campus and, perhaps, the change of status from state college to state university. In 1967 the university added a new student union, a large modernist structure with features similar to Cope, just east of Todd Library. Now called Keathley University Center (KUC; Figure 21), it assumed the role of JUB, whose life as a student union expired after only 14 years. The same year, 1967, also saw construction of a new science building, Davis Science, modern in style, larger than the original 1931 Science Building, and displaying a distinctive mosaic on its east side (Figure 21). The frame buildings of Vet Village were removed to make way for Davis, thereby ending a distinctive era in MTSU's physical and cultural history.

Architecturally, perhaps the most dramatic change on the MTSU campus occurred in 1968 with the construction of Peck Hall inside the quadrangle (Figure 22). An enormous modern classroom and office facility, with a style sometimes referred to as architectural "brutalism," Peck required destruction of the 1926 library (Figure 22) in a process that not only eliminated an original neoclassical building in the historical core, but also replaced it with a structure completely out of scale with

*Figure 19: Saunders Fine Arts (1959), Midgett (1959)
and road construction, and Boutwell Dramatic Arts (1964).
Photo by Author, 2009; AGRC, c.1960; AGRC, 1964.*

Figure 20: Aerial of MTSC, 1960, Cope Administration (1965) aerial, and Cope entrance, 2009. AGRC, 1960; AGRC, 1965; Photo by Author, 2009.

the other historic buildings around it.

In 1969 the university doubled the size of Todd Library with a huge addition on the east side, also adding a dramatic new entrance on the south that reoriented the building toward the east side of campus (Figure 23). This was consistent with the shift away from the historic core inaugurated by KUC and Davis Science in 1967 and sealed in 1975 by the McWherter Learning Resources Center.

The last major building to be erected in this period is one of the largest, Murphy Center, north of Memorial and west of the athletic field (1971; Figure 24). With its large gymnasium and track, Murphy Center became an important building on campus, hosting not only basketball and other sporting events, but also serving as a venue for all kinds of civic and business activities, for concerts, and for MTSU's graduation ceremonies. A modern, glass-encased building with an overhanging roof,

Figure 21: Keathley University Center (KUC, 1967) and Davis Science (1967). AGRC, 1973; Photo by Author, 2009.

*Figure 22: Peck Hall (1968), Library (1926) teardown for Peck in 1967,
and Peck Hall construction with graduates in 1967.
Photo by Author, 2008; AGRC, 1967; AGRC, 1967.*

Murphy's appearance and scale introduced a dramatic quality to the northwest part
of campus, later augmented by the expansion of Floyd Stadium.

When 1950 began, the MTSC main campus had seven major buildings, plus
the airport hangar, power plant, agricultural facilities, tennis courts, athletic field, and

*Figure 23: Todd Library addition (1969) and Todd addition completed.
AGRC, 1969; AGRC, 1969.*

Figure 24: Murphy Center (1971) construction and Murphy completed.
AGRC, 1970; AGRC, 1971.

Vet Village. Between 1950 and 1971 the university constructed 18 major buildings, including four new large dormitories.[40] It also built 23 smaller dormitories, although additions to Monohan (Schardt and Reynolds, 1960) and Lyon (Miss Mary and McHenry, 1962) were very substantial. MTSU also added the Agriculture (Stark, 1968) and Health Services (McFarland, 1969) Buildings.[41] When compared to the 38 years before 1950, this reckoning reveals the rapid growth of MTSC into MTSU in just two decades. Enrollment grew almost 700 percent during this era, from 1,211 in 1950 to 8,093 in 1970. Surprisingly, the university was about to enter a quiet period, as reflected by an almost complete absence of new construction for the nearly 20 years between 1972 and 1989.

QUIET YEARS: 1972–1989

Although physical growth slowed during these decades, student enrollment continued to rise, from 8,093 in 1970 to 11,275 in 1980 and 14,865 in 1990, resulting in serious space problems that plague MTSU even today. Trailers placed for a time south of KUC became home to numerous feral cats, and were sarcastically referred to as the "Sunquist Homes," after then-Governor Don Sunquist. Only two major buildings were added during this period: the innovative McWherter Learning Resources Center (LRC, 1975) and the Wright Music Building (1980; Figure 25). The LRC, strikingly modern with its large glass, concrete, and steel entrance, was also architecturally unusual due to its special and very round "Environmental Simulation Library" jutting out from the southeast corner of the building. This room could alter temperature, humidity, air flow, lighting, and odors to simulate different environments, with the hopeful result of opening up "not only the four classroom walls but [also] the students' awareness of lifestyles in different geographical areas."[42] It did not meet expectations, however, becoming for a time an inappropriate location for the Albert Gore Research Center, which did not mix well with round walls and high humidity.

The second major building of these years, Wright Music (1980), was constructed

*Figure 25: McWherter Learning Resources Center (LRC, 1975),
LRC entrance, and Wright Music (1980). All photos by author, 2009.*

behind, and connected to, Saunders Fine Arts. A brutally plain brick building,
Wright is home to a state-of-the-art performing auditorium with specially designed
acoustics. Although other facilities, such as the Tennessee Livestock Center (1972),
the Abernathy and Ezell dormitories (1973), the Strobel Biology annex (1974), and
the Telescope Building (1986) were built during the "Quiet Years," the serious lag in
construction would not be addressed until the next 20-year period.

POSTMODERN BOOM: 1990–2011

The Quiet Years of the 1970s and 1980s ended noisily in the 1990s when a new
architectural style spread across campus so quickly, and on such a scale, that what
was previously the east side of campus in the 1980s became the middle of campus.
In addition to the new buildings, a number of other changes emerged: an elaborately
redesigned entrance to campus from Rutherford Boulevard; a roundabout near the

Figure 26: Mass Communications (MassComm, 1990), MassComm with columns, Nursing (1994, 2006), Recreation Center with 2007 entrance, Walker Library (1998), and Business and Aerospace (1997). All photos by author, 2008–2010.

Recreation Center to ease vehicular congestion on the east side; large fringe parking lots designed to shift students away from the west and central campus; a small parking lot for Womack housing plunked down on land liberated by the destruction of four homes in the historic Ragland Court neighborhood; the "Naked Eye" Observatory placed almost as infill on the southeast corner of the original historic quadrangle; a new Sports Hall of Fame (Emmett & Rose Kennon) building; a third addition to the Todd Building, making it a structure with three entrances; a Fraternity Row on Rutherford Boulevard;[43] a new housing complex (Scarlett) in the northeastern part of campus; an attractive new Cogeneration Plant; and a monument to MTSU's fallen soldiers, surprisingly placed in front of the 1911 Cafeteria (Jackson), in the heart of the original campus, rather than by Memorial Auditorium, MTSU's other site of memory. During this period, significant changes were also made to the athletic facilities, including the massive new addition to Floyd Stadium, a new baseball park, and a new track and field structure.

The foregoing array of changes occurred over a period of two decades, as part of an era launched by construction of the exciting new Mass Communications Building (MassComm, 1990; Figure 26). MassComm became the most architecturally innovative modern building on campus, with its huge, two-story open interior[44] and curving brick western facade, a curvature that was repeated in a row of pillars on the north side of the structure. The Cason-Kennedy Nursing building (1994, expanded 2006; Figure 26) also displayed the popular new style of postmodern "architecture," with arcing porticos graced by simple columns at its main entrances.[45] Such arrangements of building elements seem to be looking back to 1911 and forward to 2011 at the same time, and these arcing and round shapes have been repeated on most of the new buildings since 1990. For example, the next new building in the 1990s, the Recreation Center, utilized this style on its entrance in 1995 and reinforced it on the 2007 addition (Figure 26). The utilitarian Telecom Building (1996) had no need for such artifice, but the enormous Business and Aerospace Building (BAS; Figure 26) includes elaborate, columned porticos on both its north and south entrances. The same kind of statement is made by the Walker Library (1998; Figure 26), with its massive columned entrance and curving shapes. Also promoting a classical feel is the placement of Walker, MassComm, and BAS around an elaborately landscaped

Figure 27: Salvaged columns on MTSU roundabout. Photo by Author, 2010.

*Figure 28: Honors Building (2003) and College of Education (Back)/
Student Union (Front) Buildings under construction.*

quadrangle much smaller than it historic cousin on the west side of campus.

This architectural style seems to assert both postmodern dynamism and classical reliability. The attitude is also demonstrated in the roundabout, where 160-year old sections of large limestone columns (salvaged from Nashville's capitol; Figure 27) have been artfully placed, as if to unite disparate elements on campus. This symbolic and sculptural use of the column, as an icon of permanence, strength, and stability, surely intends to convey MTSU's strong sense of purpose.

The next major structure, the Paul W. Martin Sr. Honors Building (2003; Figure 28), is an architectural compromise between the classical and modern, with the prominence of its impressive, and very traditional, bell tower and a row of non-functional decorative columns.[46] The Honors Building sat somewhat forlornly alone until recently, as if guarding the space between MassComm and the Recreation Center, but it suddenly seems almost crowded by the new neighboring, and much larger, College of Education and Student Union buildings due to open in 2011 and 2012, respectively (Figure 28).

As construction at MTSU increased in recent decades, a pathway with a strong east-west axis was developed between the historic western buildings and the new eastern structures, carefully marked with banners and light posts. Running all the way from Middle Tennessee Boulevard on the west to Rutherford Boulevard on the east, it is an aesthetically delightful and highly functional feature that unifies the campus both physically and metaphorically, as if to display a one hundred-year cross section

Figure 29: Pathway looking east and Pathway looking west. Photos by author, 2010.

Figure 30: Natatorium dwarfed by Floyd Stadium, 2009. Photo by author, 2009.

of this "place" (Figure 29).[47]

Perhaps expedience or even pragmatism has occasionally caused MTSU to disrespect its architectural heritage. In addition to the intrusion of Peck Hall and other structures into the historic core, historic buildings have sometimes been neglected or altered carelessly.[48] The enormous structure on the west side of Floyd Stadium dwarfs the Natatorium and reduces the impact of the first modern building at MTSU, Memorial Auditorium (Figure 30). The destruction of the Art Barn in 2005 (Figure 31), a reminder of how this place looked close to its birth, seems an unfortunate price to pay for "progress." Of course, the historic western core has survived, with KOM

Figure 31: Art Barn (1922), Art Barn tear down in 2005.
Art Barn photos courtesy of Brenda Johnson, MTSU Art Department, 2005.

and Rutledge receiving badly needed facelifts and the other buildings around the quadrangle being carefully maintained, and football fans continue to flock to Floyd Stadium, first stopping to tailgate in Walnut Grove.

Yet, the newer parts of campus reflect changing trends in higher education and American life, and their presence raises the question: what might the future hold, not only for MTSU, but for all universities? This is surely difficult to answer, particularly in the midst of the Great Recession and the ongoing digital revolution. As funds dry up, criticisms mount. Should the university provide a classical liberal arts education or job-training? Can it do both? Will students be taught by tenure-track and tenured faculty, or by full-time temps or adjuncts who save the state a great deal of money? Or will they learn online, also a less "expensive" form of education? In fact, will the bricks-and-mortar campus soon give way to a more virtual world of higher education where pajama-clad students toil at home "wired" to their computers? Will the Walker Library be overtaken by its fabulous new "Digital Media Studio," with its books digitally scanned into searchable computer "clouds" and the physical books themselves either destroyed, recycled, or housed for possible retrieval in underground silos? Most important of all, will college parking lots be abandoned, reclaimed for community gardening, or turned into parks or walking trails?

Whatever the fate of MTSU, its campus continues to grow, as seen in the currently rising College of Education and Student Union buildings and in the plans for a new science building, authorized but not yet funded. At least in the near future, MTSU will be treasured as a beautiful place dedicated to the endless adventures of teaching and learning. Its footprint will change as history unfolds but surely it will never disappear, for who would we be without our "place"?[49]

NOTES

1   Homer Pittard, *The First Fifty Years: Middle Tennessee State College, 1911–1961* (Murfreesboro: Middle Tennessee State College, 1961), 17. Pittard's story has not been verified by other sources, but it seems probable.

2   Ibid. Pittard fails to explain that the "Bottoms" was an African American section of town or that Murfreesboro's 1910 population of 4,679 included 2,080 blacks, almost 40 percent of the total. The Normal was being built in Jim Crow Tennessee and would be a "whites only" segregated school for its first 50 years, until 1962.

3   Locals also referred to this area, or at least part of it, as "Mink Slide." For details on this part of town, see Greg Tucker, "Mink Slide Mammals were only Human," *Daily News Journal*, 21 February 2010. See also Charles B. Arnette, *From Mink Slide to Main Street* (Nashville: Williams Printing, 1991); and Deborah Wagnon and Christian Hidalgo, *Images of Murfreesboro* (Charleston: Arcadia Publishing, 2007), which includes an excellent photo of the area on page 13.

4   This plat is included among Pittard's photos, *First Fifty Years*, n.p. The sources for the figures in this essay will be captioned and cited as follows: Albert Gore Research Center, Middle Tennessee State University (cited as AGRC, year); *Midlander*, the MTSU yearbook (cited as *Midlander*, year); Pittard, *First Fifty Years* (Pittard, page number); or Photo by Author (Photo by Author, year).

5   Middle Tennessee Boulevard, originally "Normal Boulevard," runs along the west side. "Lascassas Turnpike" on the north became Greenland Drive and "Woodbury Pike" on the south became East Main. MTSU's current eastern boundary, Rutherford Boulevard, was defined as the campus expanded eastward. The university extends slightly past these boundaries in some places.

6   Space limitations prevent consideration of all 137 permanent structures built or maintained by MTSU both on and off the main campus. However, some facilities such as agricultural buildings, dormitories, and athletic facilities will be discussed briefly.

7   The National Park Service defines college campuses as "historic designed landscapes," a form of "cultural landscape." See http://www.nps.gov/history/hps/tps/briefs/brief36.htm.

8   M. Perry Chapman, *American Places: In Search of the Twenty-first Century Campus* (Westport, CT: Prager Publishers, 2006), xxxiv.

9   Richard P. Dober, *Campus Landscape: Functions, Forms, Features* (New York: John Wiley & Sons, 2000), 46.

10 Andrew David Holt, *The Struggle for a State System of Public Schools in Tennessee, 1903–1936* (PhD dissertation, Teacher's College, Columbia University, 1938); Paul H. Bergeron, Stephen V. Ash, and Jeannette Keith, *Tennesseans and Their History* (Knoxville: University of Tennessee Press, 1999), 223–24; and *Tennessee Encyclopedia of History and Culture*, Version 2.0, s.v. "Higher Education," http://tennesseeencyclopedia.net/.

11 *Tennessee Encyclopedia of History and Culture*, Version 2.0, s.v. "Tennessee College for Women." See also the Rutherford County Tennessee Historical Society, Heritage Partnership for Rutherford County, and Bradley Academy websites online for further information.

12 Pittard, *First Fifty Years*, 12.

13 Paul Venable Turner, *Campus: An American Planning Tradition* (Cambridge: MIT Press, 1984), passim. See also Chapman, *American Places*, Introduction and 3–56.

14 Turner, *Campus*, 163–214.

15 Pittard, *First Fifty Years*, 50.

16 Ibid., 24, 92–93. "Craddock" and "Forrest" Halls, two rooming houses for men, can be seen on the 1914 Sanborn Fire Insurance map, and men also occupied the "Kittrell House" on East Main. Women also lived off campus, some at two identical houses which still stand directly across "Normal Boulevard" (Middle Tennessee) from Rutledge.

17 Richard P. Dober, *Campus Heritage: An Appreciation of the History & Traditions of College and University Architecture* (Ann Arbor, MI: Society for College and University Planning, 2005), 31–32, notes that universities typically develop a "sentimental attachment" to their "Old Mains," often built on "stark sites and bleak landscapes." He reports 31 Old Mains listed in the National Register of Historic Places as of 2003.

18 Pittard, *First Fifty Years*, 130, 136. MTSC was accredited by the Southern Association of Colleges and Schools (SACS) in 1929 and by AATC in 1931.

19 Ibid., 136–39, explains this process in detail. See also Frank B. Williams Jr., *East Tennessee State University: A University's Story, 1911–1980* (Johnson City: East Tennessee State University Press, 1991), 41–59.

20 Pittard, *First Fifty Years*, 114–17; Allison Norman Horton, "An Abstract of Origin and Development of the State College Movement in Tennessee," (EdD thesis, George Peabody College for Teachers, Nashville, August 1953), 91–92.

21 Pittard, *First Fifty Years*, 22.

22 Ibid., 18, describes the problems of "Lake Unnecessary."

23 Ibid., 47, explains that agricultural instructor Verd Peterson implemented a "landscaping scheme set up by Dr. Charles Heffer from the University of Tennessee," and that Peterson and his students "scoured the wooded areas" around the school for trees and flowering shrubs.

24 Plaque dedicated to Walnut Grove, MTSU National Alumni Association, 2004.

25 Pittard, *First Fifty Years*, 138–39.

26 Williams, *East Tennessee State*, 101–18, and Pittard, *First Fifty Years*, 140–65. At some points, faculty and staff were not paid their normal salaries. Williams notes that the normals saw funding of $175,000 in 1930–31 reduced to $56,000 from 1933 to 1937.

27 Pittard, *First Fifty Years*, 177. On the NYA projects, see MTSC student newspaper, *Sidelines*, 19 and 27 September 1939, 8 November 1939, and 10 January 1940. See also Joe Nunley, *The Raider Forties* (New York: Vantage Press, 1977), 38–39; and *Tennessee Encyclopedia of History and Culture*, Version 2.0, s.v. "Murfreesboro."

28 Pittard, *First Fifty Years*, "Data," 261. See also *Tennessee Encyclopedia of History and Culture*, Version 2.0, s.v. "Second Army (Tennessee) Maneuvers."

29 Pittard, *First Fifty Years*, 193, 222, notes that the fireman facilities buildings appeared in 1944 and that a fire-training tower was built in 1956. These buildings are readily visible in aerial photos.

30 Horton, "An Abstract of Origin," 91–92; Pittard, *First Fifty Years*, "Data," 261.

31 Pittard, *First Fifty Years*, "Data," 261. Between 1911 and 1941, women averaged 62 percent of enrollment, and average total enrollment was 539.

32 Horton, "An Abstract of Origin," 92.

33 Pittard, *First Fifty Years*, "Data," 261. Arthur M. Cohen, *The Shaping of American Higher Education* (San Francisco: Jossey-Bass Publishers, 1998), 196, notes that enrollment in American universities rose by 500 percent from 1945 to 1975, from 2 to 11 million students. Universities were 70 percent male in 1950.

34 Richard P. Dober, *Campus Architecture: Building in the Groves of Academe* (New York: McGraw Hill, 1996), 1–48, quotation on page 8. See also, Turner, *Campus*, 251–60.

35 Chapman, *American Places*, 2.

36 Ibid.

37 *Midlander*, 1953–1966.

38 The name "Forrest Hall" was not contested in its earlier years, but became so after integration in the 1960s, when issues such as the Nathan Bedford Forrest university mascot adopted in the 1930s and the playing of "Dixie" at football games became intertwined.

39 MTSC, not MTSU, is the precise term used by the *Midlander*, 1965. Pittard, *First Fifty Years*, 205–6, describes this "new thoroughfare" as providing a road "to view the broad vistas of the campus described by many as the most beautiful in the state."

40 Because of their size, this list of 18 major buildings includes the Smith (1951), Monohan (1954), Corlew (1967), and Cummings (1969) dormitories.

41 Most of the new relatively smaller dormitories were built along the south side of campus. The Lyon and Monohan additions greatly enlarged the original buildings.

42 *Midlander*, 1975.

43 The Tennessee General Assembly passed a law in 2003 clearing up the "myth" that sorority houses were not allowed because more than eight women living in the same house made it a brothel. Katie Broderick, "Sigma Kappa Opens UTC's First Residential Sorority House," UT Echo Online 1/25/07, http://media.www.utecho.com/media/storage/paper483/news/2007/01/25.

44   Dober, *Campus Landscape*, refers to these features as "interior landscapes," xxv.

45   The term "arc-itecture" is the author's. Chapman, *American Places*, notes on page 2 that the late twentieth century witnessed a "renewed appreciation for the attributes of human scale, collegial vitality, and quality of the campus experience," a process that altered attitudes toward campus architecture and led designers away from modern designs. It should also be noted that these postmodern buildings display a corporate aesthetic.

46   The inclusion of the bell tower and other architectural details was influenced by Dr. John Paul Montgomery, the third director of the Honors Program established in 1973.

47   The use of banners and light posts to decorate, indeed to "brand" MTSU, is occurring throughout the campus, and includes newly elaborate entrances and other changes to the road system, such as signage that refers to historic buildings and names. This is a form of "place marking," the development of a unique campus feel, an adjunct to the usual place making, the structuring of an overall campus plan. See Richard P. Dober, *Campus Design* (Ann Arbor, MI: The Society for College and University Planning, 2003 (1992 originally)), 1–14.

48   The huge additions to Lyon, Monohan, and Jones were not careless, but they distort the original feel of the much smaller buildings on the quadrangle.

49   The photo on page 1 is from the 1950s. AGRC, c. 1950s.

CHAPTER THREE

Learn to Stand Alone

Women on Campus

REBECCA CAWOOD MCINTYRE
NANCY ELLEN RUPPRECHT

On April 26, 1964, faculty, staff, and students of Middle Tennessee State College (MTSC) gathered at the new Woodmore Dining Hall to hear Tennessee Governor Frank Clement dedicate eight new buildings on campus. These structures were only some of the new buildings commissioned by MTSC President Quill Cope as part of a massive growth campaign. To name the buildings, Cope had asked the faculty and staff to list colleagues they believed were the most deserving of such an honor. When the names came in, five women topped the list. The honorees were longtime secretary Bonnie McHenry and faculty members, "Miss Tommie" Reynolds, Elizabeth Schardt, "Miss Mary" Hall, and E. May Saunders.[1] These five joined two other women, Katherine Monohan and Elma Rutledge, with campus buildings named in their honor. Dotting the MTSU landscape, these sturdy brick and mortar structures are appropriate memorials to each woman's dedication and commitment to the school. Reynolds Hall, Schardt Hall, McHenry Hall, Monohan Hall, Rutledge Hall, Miss Mary Hall, and the Saunders Fine Arts Building are also indicative of the importance of women at the institution. Though history often marginalizes women's contribution to higher education, campus women need to be examined critically, especially at MTSU. Whether faculty, staff, or students, these women's experiences reveal the difficulties of being an educated woman in the South. For decades, campus women have negotiated between the cultural ideals of women's supposed submissiveness and women's own needs "to learn to stand alone." This motto from the Dromgoole Literary Society, an early campus club for women, was hard to achieve in the patriarchal southern culture of the early and mid-twentieth century, more of an aspiration than a reality.[2] By going to and often working at a college, generations of MTSU women challenged their preordained roles in the private sphere of the home; yet instead of rebelling, most women worked within cultural boundaries to quietly, but effectively, create a place in the public sphere of higher education. By the 1960s, the culture had changed and women across the nation openly proclaimed their equality. At MTSU, change came, though slowly. In the late 1960s, campus women were protesting inequities and limited opportunities, but it took another 20 years for women to have the same rights as campus men and for women to be part of the academic curriculum. Such progress would have been inconceivable to the women who came to the Middle Tennessee Normal School in 1911.[3]

THE TEACHING YEARS: 1911–1943

The first generation of faculty women at Middle Tennessee Normal School (MTN) did stand alone, but only within certain parameters. In 1911, Miss Tommie Reynolds, Katherine Monohan, and E. May Saunders were three of the eight women hired for the original 20 member faculty. At 40 percent of the faculty, this high number of women professors was inconceivable at a coeducational college, but normal schools, with their focus on teaching, welcomed female faculty.[4] American society regarded teaching as a respectable, albeit underpaid, profession for women. By 1890, most states realized the need for qualified teachers and were willing to use public monies to create and operate normal schools. The term "normal" derived from the French *école normale*, a school that instructed students on pedagogy and used their own model school for student teaching. American normal schools followed this model, offering two or three years of classroom instruction with hands-on experience at a campus school. Upon completion, graduates received a diploma that was a permanent teaching certificate.[5]

Tennessee lagged behind other states when it came to public education. The situation was dire, as the state's mainly rural schools overflowed with students without the basics of an elementary education, and teachers often lacked a high school diploma.[6] In 1909, the government finally acted. That year, the state legislature passed the General Education Bill, which, besides increasing funding for public schools, also created three normal schools for whites and one for African Americans, making Tennessee the 45th and last state to have a publicly funded normal school system. Being last did have some consolations. By the time MTN opened its doors in 1911, the State Board of Education and the school's administrators had plenty of examples of both successful and unsuccessful policies for teacher education.[7]

Women educators played a large role in the new normal school. With a majority of female students, administrators realized that experienced women in front of the classroom would be excellent teachers and effective role models. For three decades at MTN, and its successor Middle Tennessee State Teachers College (STC), women comprised roughly half of the faculty.[8] The female hires had more similarities than just education. For one, they were all white women. MTN was segregated like every southern school, despite the fact that, in 1911, African Americans comprised almost 25 percent of Rutherford County citizens, and 40 percent of Murfreesboro.[9] In addition to race, all of the women faculty were local and the majority were from farms, with a good number from tiny Murfreesboro, slightly larger Chattanooga, and moderately sized Nashville. Like their male counterparts, female faculty had earned at least a bachelor's degree from the George Peabody College for Teachers in Nashville and a good number had master's degrees from either Peabody College or Columbia University. With little deviation, and unlike their male counterparts, these women professionals remained single their entire lives.[10] And, without exception, administrators paid male faculty considerably more than women, regardless of educational level or teaching experience. Publicly though, they neither complained nor challenged the system. Instead, like women across the country, they tacitly accepted this inequity, preferring to work within cultural constraints to effect change.[11]

Tommie Reynolds, the most unconventional woman faculty member, still adhered to the cultural script assigned to southern women. Described as the perfect Athenian, Reynolds was tall and imposing. She dressed plainly and styled her hair in a tight helmet of curls that framed a stern expression. She possessed an air of absolute confidence and authority, not giving off even a whiff of frivolity. Yet, students often remembered Miss Tommie as kind and generous.[12] A native of Rutherford County, Reynolds began her career at Rockvale School teaching rural students from first grade to high school. She earned her bachelor's degree from Peabody College in 1911, specializing in mathematics and physical education. Immediately hired at MTN, she taught in the math department and coached women's sports. In 1923, she switched to teaching physical education full time, alongside Frank Faulkinberry, and became his assistant coach for the new intercollegiate women's basketball, soccer, and tennis teams.[13]

Reynolds, at least in combination with Faulkinberry, appears to have been a good coach. Though records are sketchy for her years as a head coach, during her time as assistant coach the women's basketball team went undefeated for two years and won both the state and then southern championship in 1926.[14] Besides coaching, Reynolds created the women's intramural program and formed the Women's Athletic Council (WAC) that provided leadership and logistical support for women's teams. Through the WAC, female students earned points and when they reached certain levels, they received certificates, medals, and finally a letter to sew unto their school cardigan. Reynolds's role in athletics was unusual, even for a normal school, according to a colleague who commended her accomplishments "in an era of deep suspicions that competitive athletics should still remain in a man's world." In 1936, Reynolds returned to the math department and stayed until she retired 21 years later. Miss Tommie certainly broke boundaries and even though she seems the most likely candidate to break free of the constraints of southern womanhood, no evidence exists that she ever did.[15]

Though she always remained supportive of women's intramurals, Reynolds, in her later years, expended more time advancing the cause of women's education. Particularly important was her role in establishing the Tennessee branch of Delta Kappa Gamma, an honor society for women's education. After 46 years, Reynolds retired in 1957. Seven years later, she was present at the dedication ceremony at Woodmore Cafeteria. The picture shows an older woman wearing a gray suit, a flowered hat, a dour expression, and her gloved hands primly crossed on her lap. Even though she had just had Reynolds Hall, the new neoclassical women's dormitory, christened in her name, Miss Tommie remained a perfect Athenian.[16]

Reynolds Hall was connected to another women's dormitory, erected a decade earlier in 1954. Also neoclassical in design, Monohan Hall was named for history professor Katherine Monohan. Born in Tennessee in the early 1870s, Kate Monohan was the daughter of Irish immigrants and a devout Catholic. Little is known of her childhood, but by 1893 she had earned a master's degree from Peabody College and the next year began teaching at Knoxville High School.[17] In 1911, President Robert Lee Jones hired Monohan, along with A. Max Souby, to teach history to the "Normalites," as students were nicknamed. The two teachers could not have been more different. Souby was from Fort Worth, Texas. With little money but lots of ambition, he went to Nashville where he eventually graduated from Vanderbilt University. The 30-year-old Souby was considered a dashing bachelor when he arrived at MTN, and students commented on his easygoing style and sense of humor.[18] When "Miss Monohan" arrived, she was older than other female faculty members. A confirmed spinster, she was never easygoing and her Victorian sensibility about morality was strict even for the time. She abhorred any public display of affection and was fanatical about her own person, becoming hysterical if a man even grazed her arm. Students occasionally laughed at her supersensitive nature but, like Souby, she was a popular teacher. Even 30 years later, her students fondly remembered her moving lectures on Andrew Jackson. In 1930, she was honored with a dedication in the yearbook as a southern lady "whose charming manners, loyal devotion, high ideals, and sterling character" were an inspiration to others. Like her female peers, Monohan devoted herself to her students, while working hard to maintain the aristocratic bearing of an elite southern woman.[19]

Elizabeth Schardt, however, was more adept at testing the boundaries of southern womanhood. Like Monohan, Schardt was Catholic and grew up in Nashville, where she attended St. Cecilia's Academy.[20] After high school, she went to Knoxville, earned a bachelor's degree the University of Tennessee, and then returned to Nashville to earn a master's degree from Peabody College in French and Spanish. In addition, Schardt spent summers earning language certificates at the University of Ghent and the University of Mexico. Well traveled, well educated, and well dressed, Schardt appeared very worldly and sophisticated for rural Rutherford County in the 1920s. But students, particularly women, adored her. Margie Mitchell claimed she was the dearest of all her teachers. In 1964, she clearly remembered her first French class with

Schardt 40 years earlier, when "Miss Elizabeth" seemingly skipped into the room as the final bell rang, "exuberant and lovable, and just a few years out of university."[21] Another student and later close friend, Lois Kennedy, regarded Schardt as "a fine womanly woman" who gave her students a "peek at the world beyond the campus."[22] Besides spending most summers traveling or studying, Schardt devoted herself to advancing women's education. She was a cofounder of the Tau Omicron women's honor society in 1931, was active in the Delta Kappa Gamma, and the American Association of University Women (AAUW), the latter a group of faculty women that provided each other with support and intellectual companionship. These were just a few of her many organizational affiliations. At the dedication of her dormitory, congratulatory letters spoke of her great mind, congenial personality, and tremendous legacy as the one person who, more than anyone else, shaped how French and Spanish were taught in Tennessee's public schools for decades. Senator Albert Gore Sr. even found time to send her a note in admiration of his former teacher, friend, and mentor.[23]

As popular as Schardt and just as dedicated to women's education was "Miss Mary" Hall. Born in 1895 in Kittrell, Tennessee, Hall was the youngest daughter of a Rutherford county doctor. As a young girl, everyone realized that Mary was smart and ambitious. Devoted to her father, young Mary helped him with his practice, riding along for house calls and later keeping his paperwork. As a teenager, she asked her father to let her enroll at Vanderbilt to study medicine. Though the money was available, Dr. Hall told her that the medical profession was too hard a life for a woman and that she would be going to college to be a teacher.[24] A dutiful daughter and a woman who retained the norms of her rural southern upbringing, Mary never questioned her father's wishes and went to the University of Tennessee for a teaching degree. The only hint of her disgruntlement was when she admitted years later that she had no interest in teaching children when she enrolled in college.[25] She stayed at the University of Tennessee for two years, but when her father became ill she transferred to Peabody College to be closer to him. Peabody, though, proved a blessing. Hall found her true passion, training teachers for elementary school.[26]

In 1929, Hall was hired to teach in the Department of Education, where she stayed until her retirement in 1960. Students remember her as upbeat and practical, occasionally stern, but always compassionate.[27] Ambitious and clearly a leader for women's education, Hall was, nonetheless, traditional and conservative. She never married, claiming that she never found the right man; others said that her father never thought any boys were worthy of his daughter or maybe that Miss Mary could not find a man as worthy as her father. She did advise married women students to put their husbands first and their careers last. Like Monohan, Hall also wanted to guard the morals of her single students and made sure that the women never made "inappropriate advances" in public. After she retired, she bemoaned what she saw as the waywardness of students in the 1970s, blaming it on the "general deterioration of morals of society."[28]

Though a vigilant guardian of public morality and a woman accepting of the often patriarchal strictures on female professionals, Mary Hall should also be remembered as a pioneer. When she was hired, she was the only woman professor in the Department of Education, and when she retired, she was still the lone female.[29] In photographs, she looks dainty, with matching dress and short jacket ensembles and the ever-present flower hat atop her short gray hair. Although demure looking, Hall's spirit allowed her to excel in what was clearly a man's domain. During her years at the school, she also worked as the state supervisor of elementary education, a powerful job for anyone, but especially for a woman. As a supervisor and more so as a teacher, Hall influenced how children were educated in public schools for generations. Seemingly tireless, Hall was involved in her church, her community, and her profession. She was a leader in Delta Kappa Gamma and AAUW. She was also a strong force in the Dames Club, an MTSU social club that brought together female staff, faculty, and spouses. Yet even though Hall was a path breaker, she surely appreciated that the dormitory dedicated in her name is not the Hall building but rather "Miss Mary" Hall.[30]

In this group, only one woman had a classroom building named for her. E. May Saunders came to Murfreesboro in 1913 to teach music, and stayed until her retirement almost 50 years later. From Kentucky, E. May studied at Forest Park University in St. Louis, Missouri, before coming to MTN as the first director of music.[31] In the classroom, she demanded high standards and many of her nonmusical students feared her class. All future teachers where required to take her vocal music class, a terrifying ordeal according to many students. To pass the class, each student stood up in front of the class and performed a solo with music picked by Saunders, pieces that were sure to be obscure and difficult. Outside of this tribulation, students who were musically inclined adored Miss Saunders because of her commitment to her craft and her students. She built an appreciation and awareness of music and nurtured talent through concerts, orchestras, bands, and glee clubs. Saunders's colleagues applauded her drive and skill at mentoring students and faculty.[32] Margaret Wright, who came to teach music in 1947, regarded Saunders as a mother and the glue that held the department together. Wright also respected Saunders's work in music education in the state and throughout the region, particularly as chairman of the music section of Middle Tennessee Educational Association and the vice president of the Southern Conference for Music Education.[33] Like Tommie Reynolds and Mary Hall, she was a founding member of the school's branch of Delta Kappa Gamma, and like her female peers, Saunders never married. Even after her retirement, Saunders remained active in the musical community, and when the Saunders Fine Arts Building was dedicated in 1964, the style reflected her personality. A jumble of styles, the Saunders Building combines a modernist approach with neoclassical columns and a echo of the art deco style, a fitting legacy for E. May Saunders who combined a traditional approach with a touch of whimsy.[34]

Another appropriate legacy is Rutledge Hall. As one of the original four campus buildings from 1911, it was simply dubbed the women's dormitory. It was later named for Elma Rutledge, the dormitory's "matron" for over a decade. Born in Huntland,

Tennessee, Rutledge married and relocated to Fort Worth, Texas, where her husband owned several stores. Rutledge returned to Tennessee in 1904, a widow with two young children. In 1917, with her children married, Rutledge took the job as MTN's third matron of the women's dormitory. She was deemed by the administration as a "lady of highest culture." Dormitory life was meant to conform to life at "a well-ordered home" and Rutledge's mission was to protect and inspire young women and enforce a culture of *in loco parentis* where the school took on parental responsibilities. The rules and regulations seem punitive now but were standard in women's dormitories across the country. Rutledge meant to prevent any behavior considered untoward, and she routinely shooed boys from lingering on the dormitory steps or parted any couple who stood a bit too close. There were curfews, quiet hours, and mandatory dorm inspections. If women habitually broke these rules, they could be dismissed. Yet students retained fond memories of Rutledge. They might have come in a few minutes after curfew or snuck food in their rooms, but these students did not rebel. Rather, Rutledge's discipline was accepted as necessary and as a maternal comfort for women who were often away from home for the first time.[35]

There were women, though, who never lived in the dormitory. In 1920, Cornelia Clark lived on a farm at the edge of the city and hitched her horse to a buggy to get to school. She regarded herself as a country girl who "didn't fix up much" but wanted, just like the other students, a good practical education.[36] Practicality was the hallmark of MTN women, whether they boarded or lived at home. They came to be teachers, and in the first year 250 women were enrolled in the program.[37] The women students, known as "coeds," dominated the campus until the late 1940s. As the student majority, women studied the typical curriculum provided by normal schools with pedagogy, English, history, and mathematics being required and an assortment of courses offered as electives. Because this was rural Tennessee, future teachers, regardless of sex, took courses in manual and industrial arts, home economics, and agriculture in order to pass these necessary skills on to their students. To elevate its standing from "just a normal school," MTN also offered courses like science, languages, classical history, and modern literature, typically the province of four-year colleges.[38]

The coeds varied widely in age in the normal school years. Some were as young as 16, though many were nontraditional students, mature women with teaching experience who returned to the school to earn their normal certificates. Courses were offered during the traditional school year through the quarter system, and in the summer the school had an accelerated teacher certification program class aimed at students who were already teaching in the public schools. The women who boarded during the school year were single, though many of the returning teachers were married. Quite a few came with their husbands who also wanted the skills and official certification to be better and higher paid teachers. These married women integrated easily into the student body. Like Mrs. Grace Stephens Zumbro of Woodbury, Tennessee, "a noble type of good, heroic, womanhood," they stood as examples for the young coeds.[39] Whether married or single, these women, like their teachers, tended to come from rural backgrounds. They could afford room and board but were not so wealthy as to turn away the free tuition offered at MTN. This opportunity for a free education was a boon for Middle Tennesseans, many who could not afford an elite school like Vanderbilt.[40]

When women entered MTN in the 1910s and 1920s, the administration expected them to join campus clubs. Most of these were divided by sex, though often with a brother-sister partnership for similar clubs, such as the pairing of the YMCA with the YWCA.[41] The most important clubs in the early years were the literary societies. MTN had four: Dromgoole and Murfree for women, and Claxton and Grady for men. These societies thrived in most normal schools. Though somewhat social, the clubs' true mission centered on intellectual pursuits that offered a way to attain "a higher degree of culture." This cultural uplift was considered especially important in normal schools like MTN, whose students often had little exposure outside their small towns or remote farms. Beyond uplift, though, female societies also helped assuage a certain loneliness many women felt at leaving home for the first time. As one club member claimed, "work is the greatest panacea for homesickness."[42]

Dromgoole was the most popular group for MTN women. Founded in 1912, the society was named in honor of Murfreesboro native, Miss Will Allen Dromgoole. Though forgotten today, Dromgoole wrote "local color" pieces, with stories featuring poor whites and even poorer blacks, crude stereotypes, seemingly amusing in 1900. Dromgoole had retired to Murfreesboro in 1912 and was pleased the society wanted to use her name. She often had the girls over to her home and even supplied the club's motto, "Learn to Stand Alone."[43] The other slightly less popular society was named after the more well-known Murfreesboro author, Mary Noailles Murfree. Writing under the pseudonym Charles Egbert Craddock, Murfree also wrote local color pieces about Tennessee, but her stories were less racially charged than Dromgoole's works. Also retired in her hometown, Murfree happily lent her name to the Murfree Society and attended a yearly meeting as an honored guest though not an active member.[44]

For the clubs' first year, the 33 members of Murfree Society studied Greek myths, and the 40 Dromgoolians focused on modern writers. Each society met weekly and once a month paired with its respective brother society.[45] Members designed meetings to be educational and uplifting. Officers created a themed program and assigned members to perform various activities such as singing, acting in small plays, playing piano solos, and offering topical lectures. The clubs presented holiday programs, such as a 1920 Halloween program put on by Murfree Society in which members offered a short history of the holiday, a reading, a ghost story, and some spooky music. Debates were also popular, uplifting entertainment for the women at MTN as at other normal schools. The tone of the debates varied wildly. Most were serious affairs, such as the debate between Dromgoole members in October 1914, assessing whether Germany was the cause of the Great War, or the 1921 debate between members of the Murfree Society, arguing for or against the United States' entry into the League of Nations. But topics also ran to the trivial, such as the 1921 Murfree Society debate on whether

"Blondes are fickle and deceitful."[46] The highlights of the year happened at the school graduation ceremony when the school president awarded best essay prizes to one Dromgoole and one Murfree member. The end-of-the-year ceremonies also featured performances by each female literary society paired with its brother group. Dramatic plays were popular, but so were musicals where women could show off their dancing skills—as in the chorus line performed by Murfree members in the 1920s. [47]

Civic duties played a large part in these societies and other campus clubs. Dromgoole members planted trees on Arbor Day, and Murfree women worked with the Red Cross in the twenties. Other civic-minded ventures were planned by the YWCA and, until 1920, the Women's Suffrage Club. An assortment of specialized clubs rose in the 1920s as enrollment increased. Not surprisingly, the Home Economics Club was popular with women with its goal of setting "high standards for girls" while improving school and home life with greater knowledge.[48] The Science and Agricultural Clubs were well attended by women, the latter having a popular hayride every spring. Other coeducational groups focused on music and drama. Other clubs open to men and women were the county clubs, such as the Franklin, the Grundy, and the Rutherford Clubs, that automatically included all students from those respective counties.[49]

A variety of athletic teams, some intramural and some intercollegiate, offered other extracurricular activities for women. Beginning in 1914, Miss Tommie coached the women's basketball team and her Normalites played against rivals such as Peabody College and Western Kentucky until well into the 1920s. The WAC also offered an array of intramural sports for participating students. Of course, not every woman could afford such an active campus life. Many students were like Cornelia Clark who, at three o'clock each day, hitched a horse to her buggy and hurried home to cook, clean, and do chores on the family farm.[50]

The more prosperous 1920s led to major changes for women students. Enrollment grew dramatically with female students outnumbering men two to one.[51] With the large enrollment, and a nationwide trend toward abolishing the normal school concept, the Tennessee Board of Education elevated the school's standing to a four-year teachers college. In 1925, Middle Tennessee State Teachers College (STC) offered new curriculum, tightened entrance requirements, raised course standards, and hired new faculty, ten more in only two years. Many of these new hires were women. Among them were Rebecca Buchanan, in public speaking, Ollie Green in geography, and Agnes Little, chair of the Home Economics Department, who like campus mainstays Reynolds, Monohan, and Saunders were from Tennessee, active in the campus and the community, and never married. Exceptions to the rule were Flora Gillentine, Sarah Beasley, and Annie Frazier, women married to male faculty members. By 1927, women made up 54 percent of the faculty, 100 percent of the secretaries, and none of the administration. Again, they were paid less then men but never publicly complained.[52]

In the 1920s, coeds appeared to have adopted the new flapper persona.[53] Replacing the long skirt, middy blouses, and swept-up hair of the Normalite, the new coeds bobbed their hair and shortened their dresses. They called themselves flappers and wrote about themselves as flappers like the anonymous author in the *Normalite*, the school's newspaper. "The flapper," she wrote, "was on campus and alive and well." These women "study and think how to come up against the world and its many problems" but were also "pleasure seekers," looking for excitement. "The modern maid," she claimed, "is unafraid."[54] Evidence suggests a more nuanced reality. While the *Midlander* yearbook occasionally lauded a woman as "a live wire," more often coeds were praised as "quiet, unassuming girls," "a treasure for some good man," and overall "dainty and charming."[55] As reflected in the strict campus codes, the "new woman" of the 1920s did little to challenge the institution's status quo of *in loco parentis*. These were, after all, rural girls of modest means from the South. They may have cherished fun but foremost, they wanted an education. Mary Francis Snell was typical. During the 1920s, she lived on campus even though she was from Murfreesboro. Since her family farm was four miles away and she had no vehicle, it was more pragmatic to board. She never had much money, as her father was a farmer/mule trader and her mother stayed home. The highlights of her school years were club meetings and weekly chapel.[56]

Louise Mott also wanted an education but represented the more socially active coed of the 1920s. From Smyrna, Mott was comfortably off and devoutly Christian. She spent several years living in Rutledge Hall and had enough money to spend on a few luxuries. A striking blond, Mott did have trouble balancing extracurricular activities with school work. Besides going to church daily, she attended YWCA meetings and headed the Murfree Society. Classes were a challenge for her, and she confided in her diary the miseries of organic chemistry, her "fateful subject." She also lamented that she had to take five exams in one day, though she ended up with three B's and a C in English. As for chemistry, Mott only recorded that she passed the class. On top of all this, Louise was also dating Kenneth Miles, a STC basketball player and stellar student. Kenneth took her to see movies at the Princess Theater on the town square, escorted her to dances, went on nightly walks, and helped her with homework. For her part, she cheered him on at home games, wrote him long letters, and supported his choice to be the football coach at Central High School in Nashville. And when she graduated, she married her beloved Kenneth and taught home economics at Central High.[57]

Louise Mott may have preferred to watch her future husband play basketball, but there were may coeds who wanted to play competitively like the men. As noted earlier, Frank Faulkinberry and Tommie Reynolds coached the winning women's basketball team. Intramurals expanded dramatically and included horseback riding, hiking, and stunts. Dromgoole and Murfree Societies were still important in the 1920s, but they were soon superseded in popularity by new art clubs, drama societies, orchestral groups, singing clubs, and a band. Women also found positions on the *Midlander*, the new yearbook, and *Sidelines*, the new weekly newsletter. Never the editor in chief, women, nonetheless, had managerial and writing opportunities on these campus publications.[58]

The stock market crash of 1929 and the subsequent depression hurt STC as it hurt the nation. Opportunities stagnated, particularly in the mid-1930s, as agricultural prices plummeted and banks closed. For school administrators the goal was to stay afloat. The school's bursar, Thomas B. Woodmore, found innovative ways to pay his faculty and staff, giving out vouchers for local stores instead of the dreaded "payless payday" found at other state institutions.[59] There was no money for new faculty, but they were unnecessary anyway as enrollment dropped in the worsening economy. Women who boarded at Rutledge Hall or the new Lyon Hall often stayed on campus during the weekend because, as Mabel Baxter Pittard from Lawrenceburg explained, it was either bus fare home or a meal ticket for the week. She picked food.[60]

In this depression, the students who self-identified as children of farmers, 40 percent, were hard hit. And even though STC charged no tuition, prospective students still had to pay room and board and buy books. Before the depression, students at MTN and STC did not work while enrolled.[61] If they needed money they would drop out for a year, get a job and save up, so they could come back to school full time. The New Deal changed that mentality. The National Youth Administration (NYA) was part of the Works Progress Administration (WPA), the largest program of the New Deal. A key mission of the NYA was creating campus jobs so that students could work and go to school, an early version of work-study programs of today. A powerful group at STC, the NYA operated from 1935 to 1948. While male students worked outdoors constructing buildings and improving existing structures, women stayed inside. The jobs were competitive. Katherine Butler remembered being ecstatic at landing an NYA job at the school library. Another librarian work-study student was Mabel Baxter Pittard, who was finally able to complete the degree that she had delayed twice in four years when she dropped out to make money so she could enroll for another year. With the library job, she finished her degree in two years.[62]

Jobs or not, women were strictly accounted for by dorm mothers. As highlighted in Reuben Kyle's essay in chapter five on the campus culture of the 1930s, women could not sit in cars with men, had to be in the dorm by dark, and were required to get permission before going to town. And if a student broke the rules, she would be "campused" and lose her privilege to leave the grounds. There were even monitors to make sure lights were out and rooms were clean. The situation bears similarities to modern boarding schools for teenagers. Although some women rebelled against this overbearing atmosphere, the rebellions were minor. As Kyle demonstrates, the most common misdemeanor was sneaking food into the dormitories and, even with strict rules, romances still began on the steps of Old Main and blossomed outside Rutledge Hall until the matron shooed the couple away.[63]

Though money was tight, female students still formed strong bonds at STC in the 1930s. Typical of the period, women were openly expressive in their affections for other women. Louise Rankin, the most popular girl of 1934 and 1935, had dozens of female friends who wrote in her yearbook how much they loved and admired her. She was the "perfect model" and the "perfect girl" for men and women. But affection did not equal equity. For students and faculty in the 1930s, learning to stand on one's own was difficult, but change was around the corner.[64]

MIDDLE TENNESSEE STATE COLLEGE: 1943–1965

In 1943, the school experienced yet another identity change, from a teaching college to the Middle Tennessee State College (MTSC).[65] With a new name came a broader mission. But the mission had to wait because of circumstances beyond the school's control. When America went to war in Europe and the Pacific, the young men of Middle Tennessee went too. By 1943, the government had enlisted or drafted most male students and some male faculty. Naturally, enrollment plummeted, but not just for men. In 1944, there were only 20 male and 180 female students, down from a high in 1923 of 431 men and 662 women. By necessity, classes were small and new faculty rare.[66] The professors were mainly women who had been at the school for years. Yet, the bonds between student and teacher remained strong. Blanche McClure felt her teachers were like her extended parents, mentors from whom she could learn. Kathryn Kerby was excited to be elected to the Tau Omicron Honor Society but was also thrilled to be working with the talented E. May Saunders.[67]

President Q. M. Smith looked for innovative ways to keep the school afloat and money coming in. The most successful venture was a Civilian Pilot Training program. Started in 1941, Smith and Professor Horace Jones created a three-month course with a ground and flying school taught by the American Aeronautical Association. Though the program began at the Murfreesboro airport, operations were transferred in 1943 to the new airstrip on the MTSC campus. That same year, the Army Air Force used the airport and school to train pilots at the newly designated 11th College Training Detachment.[68]

As explored in Ellen Garrison's chapter about the campus during World War II, the 11th Training Detachment did bring men on campus, though not in the classroom. Instead, women took on the leadership roles traditionally reserved for men. For students that meant a woman was head of the student body and editor of the *Midlander* and of *Sidelines*. Organized sports for women, which had petered out after the death of Coach Frank Faulkinberry in 1932, returned as the new Lady Raiderettes basketball team took the court in 1944 with Baxter Hobgood as coach and Miss Tommie as his assistant.[69]

Besides new sporting opportunities, women of the war years built even stronger bonds as students. The type of woman who came in the 1940s resembled earlier coeds. MTSC was segregated, and women were local, largely rural, and certainly middle class. They were often daughters of graduates or had some relative or close family member who had attended the school. Overall, these were still practical women who wanted an education in order to find a job rather than land a husband, a common accusation women students at other colleges and universities faced. Blanche Cook, 1946 graduate, went to MTSC for an education degree because teaching, nursing, and secretarial jobs were still the best options for women, particularly in the

South. Her friend, Jane Kittrell, never questioned going to college, since her father, a Smith County farmer, demanded that his daughter get educated.[70]

Kittrell and McClure, with a group of about 25 coeds, banded together as "The Forties Bunch."[71] These women arrived on campus in 1942 and 1943 and were housed in Lyon Hall dormitory. When the 11th Training Detachment arrived, the men got the rooms and the young women were told to pack up and move to the other dorm, Rutledge Hall. Miffed, the Lyon women still complied and walked with their baggage to the older and slightly dilapidated dormitory built in 1911. The Lyon women did not only double up; instead, they shared a room with at least five and sometimes six students. In an act of solidarity, the Lyon girls banded together. They did not rebel against coed rules but did engage in little acts of defiance. Circumventing the rules involved a trip off campus. Cook and other students remember hitchhiking up to the town square to eat at Mrs. Shipp's Restaurant, see a movie at the Princess Theater, or dance at The Little Brown Jug.[72]

Still, dancing at The Little Brown Jug could not change the sadness women felt for men fighting overseas. Blanche Cook wrote letters to the servicemen she had met at the USO Center in Hartsville, Tennessee. Kathryn Kerby spent a lot of time running to mailboxes to see if a boy from overseas had written. Jane Kittrell would wake up with other students at 4 a.m. so they could see every boy off to war. The sense of patriotism ran high in the campus newspaper and in the *Midlander*, which dedicated the yearbooks to "the boys who had left." When a vet came home, the whole MTSC community celebrated.[73]

The celebration was glorious at war's end. The community welcomed returning soldiers with opened arms, parades, and parties. After the jubilation came the reality. The school lost at least 38 students overseas and many more who did not want to come back to college.[74] But there were also many blessings. The passage of the GI Bill dramatically increased enrollment with the government footing the bill. Male veterans flocked to MTSC to earn their bachelor's and sometimes graduate degrees.[75] They typically brought with them wives and often small children. To house the families, President Q. M. Smith used federal monies to erect Vet Village, at first just trailers and then semipermanent buildings for the families. The veterans kept coming and, as early as 1946, men outnumbered women on campus and, by 1949, men made up the majority of graduating seniors for the first time in the school's history. It was a case of more men entering but also fewer women enrolling.[76]

Male students may have dominated, but MTSC women in the late 1940s and through the 1950s were still enrolled and active. In many ways, they mirrored earlier generations. Still overwhelmingly from Middle Tennessee, students typically were second-generation college students like Rebecca Lovell who graduated in 1954, following in the footsteps of her mother, who graduated from STC in 1929. When Ella Jolly enrolled in classes in the early 1950s, she was the last of eight siblings to go to the school. Jolly lived in the dorms but many women commuted from home.[77] Elizabeth Bradley stayed at home because it was her only option. As she recalled, her father had lost everything in the 1930s depression. She had her own work-study plan, milking 15 cows before walking to morning classes. Even though she was part of the respected Buchanan family, Elizabeth had no money for frivolities—certainly a hardship, but one that she credits for lessening her need for material goods.[78]

Campus codes remained strict for women and nonexistent for men. In the 1950s, though, evidence shows that the rules were often broken and definitely bent by a new generation of coeds. Frances Carter Gill, who graduated in 1954, remembered that "ladies" did not wear blue jeans to school and codes required women to cover up their gym shorts with a raincoat if outside. Yet, Gill remembers a campus panty raid, and a candid snapshot in the *Midlander* from the 1950s featured a woman sunbathing in a two-piece bathing suit, modest by current standards but scandalous as "campus clothing."[79] Overall, 1950s women dressed as most coeds across the country, in poodle skirts and sweater sets, with bobby socks and saddle shoes. Students still spoke fondly of their housemothers as akin to mothers and grandmothers who were strict but loving. This does not mean they did not try to pull one over on the housemother. Jean Moser, a 1956 graduate, remembers her days at MTSC fondly. Although she lived at home she had plenty of campus friends, who wanted to spend weekends at her house because her mother did not have a 10 p.m. curfew. Her mother, dubbed Aunt Rene by the adoring girls, never knew how many she would have in the house Sunday morning. Jean credited these sleepovers for an active social life and "lots of company."[80]

Even when they were not trying to get around curfew, many women went home on weekends. Martha Turner left Rutledge Hall most Fridays to return home to Woodbury. She still had an active social life and many campus friends who in later years had frequent get-togethers, much like "The Forties Bunch." The school offered dances on Tuesday nights in the Tennessee Room of the James Union Building (JUB), well-attended affairs occasionally featuring a live band.[81]

Women also enjoyed clubs and other extracurricular events. Unfortunately, the gains in women's athletics during the war years disappeared quickly. In 1947, the Raiderettes basketball team reached the semifinals in the southeastern tournament and the coed tennis team had an 8 and 5 record. The next year intercollegiate teams for women were gone. Intramurals were as strong as ever, with new activities like tumbling and modern dance, but the only intercollegiate team to compete was the Raiderette Rifle Team, formed in 1952 as a counterpart to the men's team.[82] Though athletics waned, most clubs proliferated in the 1950s as enrollment rose. Religious denominations sponsored students, and the campus had Baptist, Methodist, Episcopal, Catholic, Presbyterian, and Church of Christ clubs by 1960.[83] There were still the traditional drama clubs, speech clubs, home economic clubs, and new groups like the Sacred Harp Choir, founded in 1947, and the Aquatic Club that started in 1952 and offered spots for men and women. Women, though, in order to be a "mermaid" on the team, had to demonstrate ability and gracefulness.[84]

Being a mermaid fit with the campus culture of the 1950s. More than ever before, MTSC judged women by their beauty. Though established in 1925, Homecoming took on new importance by adding several courtiers to the Homecoming Queen's court. The number of titles a girl could win simply tripled by midcentury. Starting in 1926, the school voted on the most popular girl and the most beautiful coed. By the 1950s, there was Miss MTSC, Miss *Midlander* and six ladies in waiting, and the coveted ROTC Queen. The yearbooks even featured pages of girls simply deemed "lovely to look at." Such emphasis on beauty conformed to the middle-class, white culture of the time.[85] That does not mean that beauty beat brains. Women were the majority of the students picked for inclusion in the *Who's Who Among American University and College Students*, and women gained entrance into honor societies like Pi Gamma Mu, Pi Omega Phi, and Pi Kappa Delta and filled the membership of women's societies like Tau Omicron. The school never barred women from any academic major. Home Economics offered popular job opportunities, and women still sought teaching degrees, although many went into business and science.[86]

Even as job opportunities rose for graduates, women were rarely hired as faculty members. As David Rowe notes in chapter nine, President Q. M. Smith worked to strengthen the faculty, typically at the expense of qualified women. In the 1950s, some of the old guard like Hall, Saunders, Schardt, and Reynolds were still teaching, but when they retired their spots were most often offered to men. By the early 1960s, only home economics had a majority of women professors. In departments like science, math, social science, and business, one or two women and at least half a dozen men taught. The departments of agriculture, aviation, art, and industrial arts had no women on the faculty.[87]

Administration was also a man's domain. Sometimes women squirmed when comments by males reached levels unacceptable today. In 1960, Dean Beasley, by all accounts a good administrator, hesitated in hiring Sandra Stott as his secretary. She wanted the job but, because she had just married, Beasley told her, "I know you won't be here very long, but I am going to hire you." Stott retired 45 years later as the James Union Building facilities coordinator.[88] Dean Beasley, though, had different advice for Jane Warner; he advised her to finish her degree in education as "you are going to marry somebody and your husband may move and there won't be any other jobs except teaching, and you will need to get that certificate."[89]

MIDDLE TENNESSEE STATE UNIVERSITY: 1965–2011

When MTSC became MTSU in 1965, women's place on campus had changed only minimally. There were, however, moves toward desegregating the campus. Even though in 1954 the US Supreme Court decreed that schools must be desegregated, the judges did not include a specific timeline for compliance. With their mandate to integrate "with all deliberate speed," southern colleges took no immediate action. By the early 1960s, African Americans began the process of enrolling in public colleges where they often met fierce resistance. At what was still MTSC, Olivia Woods, the first African American student on campus, faced little resistance and certainly no violence when she began classes in 1962. [90]

Nationally, demands for women's rights also emerged on college campuses, though MTSU women seemed divided on this second wave of feminism. The accent on beauty actually grew stronger in the sixties when students voted for a Circle K Sweetheart, a Vet's Beauty, 8 class favorites, and 21 ROTC sweethearts in addition to the earlier Homecoming Queen and Miss *Midlander* with their respective courts.[91] The college rules for women were still strict. The ten-page "Co-ed Codes" pamphlet listed dozens of do's and don'ts for campus women. Rules required women to sign in and out of dorms, follow strict curfews, and obtain permission from parents to spend the night away from dorm rooms. House mothers could enter coeds' rooms at any time and checked weekly for "order and cleanliness." Sportswear was not permitted on campus, and students wearing gym clothes needed to cover up with a coat when walking outside or use the circuitous back route outlined in the code book. Men were only allowed in the women's dormitory parlor during certain hours and were not even allowed to carry luggage to a girl's room without written permission. On or off campus, visiting a man's room was grounds for severe disciplinary action. Punishments ranged from expulsion to being "campused." When campused, a woman was confined to her dorm after 7 p.m. and to her room at 10 p.m. No visitors were allowed. The time spent in confinement varied. For students who were ten minutes late for curfew, the punishment lasted a weekend. For other infractions, however, it could be much longer, such as a coed put on "social probation" for three weeks.[92]

By 1968, women openly challenged such punitive measures and demanded the end of restrictions. Even the fairly conservative president Quill Cope realized that change was necessary, telling an interviewer that "the role of the college acting *in loco parentis* has gone the way of the passenger pigeon" and students were old enough and responsible enough to be independent. The next year, Cope's successor, Dr. M. B. Scarlett, moved into action. First, he implemented another Cope decree, finally allowing Greek fraternities and sororities on campus. Next, he formed a Rules Committee, a group of administrators, faculty, and selected students, whose job was to recommend codes to delete. One of the faculty chosen was Judy Smith, a sociology professor who knew the time had come for change.[93]

Smith grew up in Murfreesboro and started MTSC in the 1950s. Smith was an anomaly in many ways. When she began classes, she was married with one child. She was an education major, minoring in English, but when it was time to student teach, she was pregnant with her second child. Pregnant students were not allowed to student teach and so Smith went to professor Richard Peck for advice. The head of the English Department, Peck advised her to change her minor into her major, as she needed only a few English classes, and then go back and get her teaching credentials later. Smith never did get her teaching certificate. Instead, five years after graduating from MTSC in 1960, she earned a master's degree in social work from the University of Tennessee. A year later in 1966, she was hired by MTSU as a sociology instructor. By then, Smith had four young children, and she became one of the few working mothers on the faculty roster. The administration had been hiring more women by the 1960s; however, few had children. Many female faculty were either single, like

Dr. Thelma Jones in the History Department, or were married to another faculty member, like English professor Dr. Virginia Peck, wife and colleague of Richard Peck. But all these faculty women did have two things in common. They were well educated and underpaid. Without exception, women were paid less than any of the male department members, regardless of degree or rank.[94]

This inequity was not confined to MTSU and was typically *de rigueur* in most workplaces. When Smith began teaching sociology, though, a new activism and a new law made the country aware of women's legitimate discontent. Betty Friedan's book, *The Feminine Mystique*, published in 1963, became a bestseller. Friedan, a college graduate and mother, recorded the discontent among a generation of married women for whom being a housewife was the only acceptable identity. In 1966, Friedan and a group of women formed the National Organization for Women (NOW) whose mission was to secure for women the same legal rights as men. An important way to gain those rights, NOW contended, was through enforcement of the Civil Rights Act of 1964. Signed into law by President Lyndon Johnson, the act was the cornerstone for protecting the civil and legal rights of all citizens by enforcing desegregation laws and bringing to trial anyone accused of taking away a person's rights as an American citizen. Though created as a response to the civil rights movement of the 1950s and early 1960s, the act did not protect just African Americans but anyone facing discrimination. For women activists, Title VII of the act had special significance. This section prohibited discrimination in employment based on race, color, religion, national origin, or sex and listed the actual areas it covered, such as hiring, firing, promotions, and pay. The Equal Employment Opportunity Commission (EEOC) was created to investigate charges of employment discrimination and the US Attorney General was authorized to bring civil suits against any group including, but not limited to, colleges and universities.[95]

NOW had little direct effect on campus culture at MTSU, but Smith and her participation in the demise of the coed codes did change the way female students were treated. The curfew changed slowly, extended an hour or two each year, until the mid-1970s when curfews and all such rules for women were abolished. And when President Scarlett offered Smith the job of dean of women in 1971, replacing Martha Hampton, Smith hesitated; she had four children. Clayton James, a former dean of students and sociology professor, advised his friend and colleague not to take the job because with children "your time will not be your own." But Scarlett kept insisting and Smith agreed to stay for a year and ended up holding the office for another three years.[96]

As dean of women and then associate dean, Smith found that her female students differed somewhat from previous generations. Most students were local, first-generation college students, unsure of what they would face as their family's first coed. Smith spent much of her time counseling these young women who were conflicted about being treated both as children and then as adults in a culture, particularly by the mid-1970s, where changes for women were enormous and sometimes just a bit frightening.[97]

When Smith started teaching at MTSU in 1966, another faculty member took women's rights in a completely new direction. June Anderson was a pathbreaker in women's education.[98] Born in West Tennessee in 1926, Anderson was smart and ambitious. After high school, she earned a BS in chemistry and biology in 1947 and, the next year, a master's degree in chemistry and English from Peabody College. With her degrees in hand, she was hired by a public school and taught for over a decade, winning several prestigious awards including the Tennessee Distinguished Science Teacher Award. In 1958, Quill Cope hired Anderson to teach chemistry at MTSC. She accepted and then took a brief hiatus to earn her PhD from Florida State University in 1964 before returning to the school and teaching until her death in 1984. Anderson never married and was never shy. Tenacious and talented, she rose quickly as the sole female faculty member in the Chemistry Department and eventually was one of the few women to be promoted to full professor. In 1975 Anderson founded an advocacy organization for women, the Concerned Faculty and Administrative Women (CFAW) at the university. The group, later renamed the Association for Faculty and Administrative Women (AFAW), had lofty goals and a determined president in June Anderson.[99] As her colleague, Margaret Ordoubadian, remembered, she was "energetic and assertive . . . totally interested in the welfare of women on campus."[100]

June Anderson and CFAW fought for academic parity regardless of gender. For MTSU women employees, pay equity and status were still in a sorry state in the 1970s. A study conducted by the American Association of University Professors (AAUP) found that in 1972, in the 28 departments on campus, there were 336 male and only 102 female faculty members. The study revealed that these 102 faculty women were rarely in the higher ranks, with a paltry 8 women as full professors compared to the 72 men at that top rank. Regardless of rank, women earned at least five hundred dollars a year less than their male counterparts—typically the inequity was much wider. Women were denied paid maternity leave and had no job protections if they took unpaid maternity leave.[101] By 1976, the numbers had not improved. A CFAW study found that of the 432 full-time faculty members, only 92 were women and these women were concentrated in five of twenty-six departments, including Home Economics, Nursing, and Health and Human Performance. Six departments—Aerospace, Criminal Justice, Geography, Industrial Arts, Mass Communications and Philosophy—had no women teaching at all.[102] This situation gained the attention of the EEOC and the US Justice Department. Anderson went to Washington to testify before the National Council for the Education of Women about discrimination against women at MTSU. The EEOC eventually awarded 35 faculty women compensatory back pay and adjusted their salaries accordingly.[103]

But numbers can be deceptive. While it is true that MTSU did not provide equitable pay or advancement, and women were woefully underrepresented in 1976, campus women were, nonetheless, making their mark in academia and administration. Joining Judy Smith in higher administration was Dr. Mary Tom Berry, the first woman assistant vice-president for academic affairs. Besides establishing Tennessee's first kindergarten program, Berry was instrumental in developing the Department of Elementary and Special Education in the College of Education, a department that she headed in the 1980s. The first director of the University Honors Program was June Hall McCash. With a doctorate in comparative literature from Emory University, McCash came to MTSU in 1967 as an assistant professor in the Department of Foreign Languages where she taught French and humanities. In 1973, President Mel Scarlett appointed McCash as the first director of the MTSU Honors Program. As detailed by Phil Mathis in chapter 12, her contributions to the program were immense, particularly the creation of the core structure of what became the Honors College and the institution of a distinguished lecture series. McCash remained director until 1980 when she became the first woman to chair the Department of Foreign Languages.[104]

When McCash took office in 1980, four other women chaired MTSU's academic departments.[105] Home economics and nursing were two departments dominated by female faculty. Dr. Hattie Arthur of home economics and Betty McComas of nursing were both long-time faculty members and full professors. Dr. Marlyne Kilbey was the chairperson of the Psychology Department, and Dr. Barbara Haskew led the Department of Economics and Finance. Haskew was a woman who garnered many "firsts." Raised on a farm outside Franklin, Tennessee, Haskew was an outstanding student. She went to the University of Tennessee where, in 1969, she became the first woman in the school's history to earn a PhD in economics. In 1970, she arrived at MTSU as a new assistant professor in the Department of Economics and Finance, a traditionally male-dominated field.[106] Five years later, Haskew became the first woman to chair the department. She held the position until 1981 when she went to work for the Tennessee Valley Authority. In 1988 Haskew returned to MTSU as the first female dean of the College of Business; eight years later, she was named provost of the university.[107]

Just as women like McCash and Haskew made strides in administration and acted as mentors and role models, June Anderson worked to help other women come to MTSU and make the transition to higher education. There were few avenues of support or mentorship for college women in the 1970s, particularly married women with children. To help solve this situation, Anderson founded the Women Information Service for Education (WISE) in 1977. A women's advocacy center, WISE began in a room in Jones Hall. Staffed by volunteers from CFAW, the center offered support and encouragement for women, along with workshops, counseling, referrals, legal clinics, scholarships, and a daycare. Renamed the June Anderson Women's Center (JAWC) in 1984, the program grew exponentially in function and size, expanding in 2010 to include all nontraditional students, regardless of gender. The center worked with other women's advocacy programs to improve safety on campus and initiate sexual assault awareness programs such as the popular "Take Back the Night" event. A yearly event, it featured speakers promoting sexual assault awareness on campus and then a candlelight vigil. The JAWC has also sponsored an impressive lecture series featuring such luminaries as Maya Angelou (1991), US

Surgeon General Joycelyn Elders (1998), feminist icon, Gloria Steinem (2010), and civil rights activist, Angela Davis (2011).[108]

JAWC also organized and assisted in several educational programs for women, including National Women's History Month. The notion of setting aside time to recognize women's part in history began in a school district in Santa Rosa, California, in 1978. In response, other school districts created their own special women's history days, and the movement mushroomed with a congressional resolution in 1981 that mandated a weeklong celebration, and a 1987 resolution dedicated the month of March to women in history. MTSU began a formal women's history week in 1983 and English professor and CFAW president Dr. Ayne Cantrell put together an impressive slate of scholars for a women's history conference. The program expanded along with national initiatives, and by 1985 the MTSU Women's History Month Committee raised funds and awareness for a month of events that March. The program continues to attract impressive speakers and large audiences.[109]

A month of women's history was one step to arouse awareness but women's experiences also needed to be in the curriculum. Nationwide, women's studies programs began in the 1960s with San Diego State University offering the first bachelors degree in 1969. Broadly conceived, women's studies is an interdisciplinary field that examines traditional academic disciplines from a feminist perspective. By 1980, there were 300 women's studies programs in American colleges and universities.[110] MTSU was not on the cutting edge of the movement, but in 1978 a group of women faculty and students asked for and got permission for a course focused on women. At first, Women's Studies was just a single class, "Introduction to Women's Studies." Taught on a volunteer basis, the course consisted of a series of lectures given by members of the campus community. Appropriately, June Anderson organized, coordinated, and graded the course. With the positive response from students and faculty, Anderson and other faculty members created a Women's Studies minor in 1980 which included the introductory course, a directed readings course, and a combination of ten woman-centered courses in a variety of academic programs. June Anderson was appointed the first coordinator of the program, originally housed in the Honors Program but governed by an independent faculty board.[111]

Over the course of the 1980s, the program grew slowly. Sadly, June Anderson passed away in 1984 and subsequent coordinators encountered difficulty in obtaining funding and faculty release time. The program lacked an office and a budget, and the coordinators worked without additional compensation. By the late 1980s, though, Women's Studies rebounded. Faculty like Cantrell, Dr. Jeanette Heritage (psychology), Dr. Charisse Gendron (English), Dr. Linda Badley (English), Dr. Nancy Rupprecht (history), and JAWC director, Rebecca Rice, lobbied effectively for the facilities, budget, and faculty to make Women's Studies a true force on campus.[112] The Women's Studies minor expanded so quickly that by 1993 it was designated as an independent program, with Nancy Rupprecht as director. Its mission was "to inform and enlighten students about the lives, history, socialization, and culture of women." Besides academic courses, Women's Studies also sponsored a biennial conference that began in 1995 and continues to the present. Renamed the Women's and Gender Studies Program in 2010 and offering a graduate certificate, the program's mission is secure. Under the direction of Dr. Tina Johnson, Women and Gender Studies seeks to "enlighten, inform, and inspire students of all genders about the lives and history of diverse women."[113]

Female students have also made major strides. Since the 1980s, women have been represented in all majors and minors. They have been leaders on campus and the community. They are welcome as members in every club, save the fraternities. A strong sorority system offers sisterhood for women wanting the support and friendship Greek life can offer. While queens still reign at Homecoming, women also excel academically and compete on equal footing in all student competitions. This is partly due to the adoption of Title IX in 1972 that changed the landscape for many collegiate women. A federal law, Title IX made it illegal to deny equal opportunity to males and females in all collegiate areas. One of the most visible results is the rise of women's sports on campus. Intercollegiate sports for women had died out in 1947 but, with Title IX, women's teams came back full force. The first woman athletic director, Sue Stanley, took over in 1975, and by 1976 the Lady Raiders were represented in basketball, tennis, and volleyball. In 2001, track, softball, soccer, and golf rounded out women's sports.[114]

In administration and academics, women have also moved beyond traditional barriers. Dr. Mary E. Martin became the first woman dean of the Graduate School in the early 1980s. A native of St. Louis, Martin came to MTSU in 1968 and spent the next 13 years as a professor in the Department of Education before going to the Graduate School.[115] Three MTSU alumnae from the 1970s came back to their alma mater to serve as administrative deans. Dr. Rosemary Owens became dean of Continuing Studies and Public Service a little more than a decade after earning her bachelors of education and then masters of education from MTSU, and Dr. Gloria Bonner joined the Department of Education in 1985, just 11 years after earning her bachelors and then masters of education. In 1988, she earned an EdD from Tennessee State University. In 1999, she then became the first female dean of the College of Education and Behavioral Science. Following in her footsteps in 2009 was Dr. Lana Seivers. Raised in East Tennessee, Seivers was a 1972 graduate of MTSU. After a distinguished career in state education, she was chosen as the new dean of the reorganized College of Education in 2009.[116]

These are but a few of the outstanding campus women of the last 25 years of MTSU history, and such advances are to be celebrated. At this centennial year, several thousand women will come to the school and begin the process of becoming college women, educated and independent, poised to succeed. They will have little knowledge of the struggles for women's education in the early history of the school. One wonders too what the previous generation would think of MTSU at its centennial. No doubt, Miss Tommie Reynolds would be impressed with women's athletics, especially the Lady Raider's basketball team. Miss Schardt would be pleased with the international flavor of the school and its newest addition, the Confucius Center. Miss Mary Hall would be proud of the beautiful new education building, and Miss Monohan likely would be pleased that women faculty are a good portion of the history department. Some of these women might be a bit shocked with the lack of a dress code and the couples holding hands while strolling to class on a sunny spring afternoon. But, one hopes that even the straight-laced Miss Monohan could overlook these differences and join in celebrating women at MTSU, a school that at one hundred years old offers all the tools necessary to learn to stand alone.

NOTES

1   "MTSC Lauded By Governor," D*aily News Journal,* 27 April 1964, 1, 7; Quill E. Cope to Elizabeth Schardt, 17 August, 1963, box 1, folder 1, Elizabeth Schardt Papers, Albert Gore Research Center (AGRC), Middle Tennessee State University, TN (hereinafter cited as Schardt Papers, AGRC).

2   Anne Firor Scott, *The Southern Lady: From Pedestal to Politics, 1830–1930* (Chicago: University of Chicago Press, 1970).

3   This essay is only a small sampling of women's history at MTSU and a more comprehensive study remains in the future. Holly Barnett, Nancy Morgan, and Lisa Pruitt, *Middle Tennessee State University* (Charleston, SC: Arcadia Publishing, 2001), 91; Homer Pittard, *The First Fifty Years, Middle Tennessee State College, 1911–1961* (Murfreesboro: Middle Tennessee State College, 1961), 203–24.

4   For the best treatment of normal schools, see Christine A. Ogren, *The American State Normal School: "An Instrument of Great Good"* (New York: Palgrave Macmillan, 2005). For faculty at MTN, see *Bulletin* (Murfreesboro: Middle Tennessee State Normal School), vols 1–12, 1911–1923, Special Collections, James Walker Library, Middle Tennessee State University, TN (hereinafter cited as *Bulletin*, MTN).

5   Ogren, *American State Normal School,* 1–10.

6   In the years prior to the 1909 Education Bill, Tennesseans complained vociferously about the lack of teacher education, particularly for female teachers. See, for example, Tennessee Department of Public Instruction, *Statistical Report, 1908* (Nashville: State Department of Public Instruction, 1908), 28–29.

7   *Public School Laws of Tennessee* (Nashville, TN: State Printer, 1911), 77. The George Peabody School in Nashville was a private normal school. Delaware, Nevada, and Wyoming never had public normal schools and educated teachers at their state universities. Ogren, *American State Normal School,* 213–35.

8   *Bulletin,* MTN, 1911–1923; *Bulletin of Middle Tennessee State Teachers College,* 1924–1929, and *Bulletin of State Teachers College, Murfreesboro,* 1930–1943, Special Collections, Walker Library (hereinafter cited as *Bulletin,* STC).

9   Mary Hoffschwelle, *Rebuilding the Rural Southern Community: Reformers, Schools, and Homes in Tennessee, 1900–1930* (Knoxville: University of Tennessee Press), 174n23.

10   Ogren, *American State Normal School*, 125. Only a few married women taught at MTN. They were all spouses of a faculty member or administrator. *Bulletin, MTN*. For another example of opposition to married women at normal schools, see Penina Migdal Glazer and Miriam Slater, *Unequal Colleagues: The Entrance of Women into the Professions, 1890-1940* (New Brunswick: Rutgers University Press, 1987), 50–67; and Barbara Speas Havira, "Coeducation and Gender Differentiation in Teacher Training: Western State Normal School, 1904–1929," *Michigan Historical Review* 21, no. 1 (Spring, 1995): 56.

11   For the first ten years, all MTN employees had to sign a ledger to be paid. These ledgers listed each faculty member's salary in the space before their signature. There would have been no way that faculty did not know of the inequity. See Middle Tennessee State Normal School Payroll Ledgers, 1911–1918, AGRC. For insights into pay discrepancies for women in education, see Lynn D. Gordon, *Gender and Higher Education in the Progressive Era* (New Haven: Yale University Press, 1990), 90; and Havira, "Coeducation and Gender Differentiation in Teacher Training": 52–53.

12   Tommie Reynolds was born in Rutherford County on 3 September 1887 and passed away in Murfreesboro on 25 August 1966. *Daily News Journal*, 27 April 1964, 1, 7; Susan G. Daniel, *Cemeteries and Graveyards of Rutherford County, Tennessee* (Murfreesboro: Rutherford County Historical Society, 2005), 264.

13   Pittard, *First Fifty Years*, 47; Bobbie Sue Shelton-Lomas, "Old Rockvale School," http://eaglevilletimes.com/Backintime/OldRockvaleSchool.pdf.

14   *Midlander*, 1927, 92. *Midlander* yearbooks are located in the AGRC; online at http://library.mtsu.edu/digitalprojects/mtsumemory.php; and Special Collections, Walker Library.

15   Though records are sometimes incomplete, there is nothing to suggest that Reynolds was forced out of her position in athletics. One source notes that she left coaching because the women's basketball team was disbanded. "MTSC Lauded By Governor," *Daily News Journal*, 27 April 1964, 1, 7; Pittard, *First Fifty Years*, 47; "Miss Reynolds Dies; Joined Faculty in 1911," *Daily News Journal*, 26 August 1966, 1, 3.

16   The WAC was later renamed the Woman's Athletic Association (WAA). Audrey Mae Doak and Martha Marshall, *XI State History* 2 (1994), 15, 16, 31–32, http://www.xistate.org/history/history.html; *Daily News Journal*, 27 April 1964, 7.

17   Monohan's birth is either 1870 or 1874. She was born in Tennessee though sources vary as to which city. Far from the aristocratic southern heritage she often

claimed, Monohan was the daughter of Irish immigrants. Her sister and brother worked at a dry goods store in Nashville. How Monohan got the money to go to college is unknown. US Department of Commerce, Bureau of the Census, *12th Census of the Population, 1900* (Washington DC: Government Printing Office); US Department of Commerce, Bureau of the Census, *13th Census of the Population, 1910* (Washington DC: Government Printing Office).

18   Max Souby taught at MTN until he enlisted in World War I. Pittard, *First Fifty Years*, 47–48; Phi Beta Kappa, *The Phi Beta Kappa Key: The Official Publication of the United Chapters of Phi Beta Kappa* 5 (1922): 132; J. Duncan Spaeth, "Obituary," *The Trend: A Bulletin of Current History and Letters* (1922): 91.

19   Pittard, *First Fifty Years*, 44–45; Joe Nunley, *The Raider Forties* (New York: Vantage Press, 1977), 24–25.

20   *Sidelines,* 1 July 1971. The 1910 census lists an Elizabeth Schardt as living with her uncle in Nashville. Her parents were second-generation Irish and she was a practicing Catholic, though not as overt as Monohan.

21   Margie Mitchell to Elizabeth Schardt, 22 March 1964, Schardt Papers, AGRC.

22   Lois Kennedy to Elizabeth Schardt, 28 March 1964, Schardt Papers, AGRC.

23   Dorothy MacClean to Elizabeth Schardt, 8 April 1964, Schardt Papers, AGRC; Quill E. Cope to Elizabeth Schardt, 19 March 1964, Schardt Papers, AGRC; Albert Gore Sr. to Elizabeth Schardt, 27 March 1964, Schardt Papers, AGRC.

24   Rita Schaerer King, "Mary Hall: A 20th-Century Pioneer for Educational Progress in Tennessee" (EdD dissertation, Peabody College for Teachers of Vanderbilt University, 1993), 15–17.

25   Ibid., 19–20.

26   Ibid., 24–25.

27   Pittard, *First Fifty Years*, 211.

28   King, "Mary Hall," 15–17, 74–75.

29   This does not include the Training School, also called the Campus School, which included women teachers. *Bulletin*, STC.

30   Doak and Marshall, *XI State History*, 32–33.

31   As a young teacher, Saunders referred to herself as E. Mai but soon changed the spelling to E. May. E. May is used for consistency. Saunders later earned a graduate degree from Columbia in 1929. *Bulletin*, STC.

32   Pittard, *First Fifty Years*, 38–39, 66, 81; Nunley, *The Raider Forties*, 45.

33   Margaret Wright, interview by Regina Forsythe, 12 July 1995, transcript QMS.1995.25, Q. M. Smith Oral History Collection, AGRC (hereinafter cited as Smith Collection, AGRC; all interviews in the collection were conducted by Regina Forsythe).

34   Doak and Marshall, *XI State History*, 33–34.

35   Pittard, *The First Fifty Years*, 135; *Bulletin,* MTN, 1916, 70; *Bulletin,* MTN, 1917.

36   Cornelia Clark Davidson, 1 September 1995, transcript QMS.1995.84, Smith Collection, AGRC; Clark graduated in 1920 and spent two years teaching Domestic Arts at a Chattanooga school before marrying William Hall Davidson in 1922 and resettling in Murfreesboro. *Normalite*, November 1922, 29, http://library.mtsu.edu/digitalprojects/mtsumemory.php.

37   Ninty-seven men enrolled the first year. It was quite typical for normal schools to have a majority of women students. Ogren, *American State Normal School*; *Bulletin*, MTN, 1916.

38   *Bulletin*, MTN.

39   *Midlander,* 1928.

40   *Midlander*, 1928, 44. See *Bulletins*, MTN. Instead of charging tuition, the school made students promise that they would teach for six years in the Tennessee schools, a standard pledge for normal schools.

41   "Be a Jiner," *Normalite*, 30 October 1923, 3.

42   Ogren, *American State Normal School*, 108–18; *Normalite*, October 1922.

43   *Dromgoole Literary Society: Minutes and Records*, October 1914, Special Collections, Walker Library.

44   Dromgoole was a prolific writer whose style and content have dated her work. Murfree was also prolific though her writing, then and now, attracted a larger audience than Dromgoole's work. Both were unmarried and retired in Murfreesboro. *Tennessee Encyclopedia of History and Culture*, Version 2.0, s.v. "Will Allen Dromgoole," http://tennesseeencyclopedia.net/; C. Brenden Martin, *Tourism in the Southern Mountains* (Knoxville: University of Tennessee Press, 2007), 84–85; Henry Shapiro, *Appalachia on Our Mind* (Chapel Hill: University of North Carolina Press), 25–26; *Murfree Literary Society: Minutes and Records, 1920–22*, Special Collections, Walker Library; *Dromgoole Literary Society*, October 1914.

45   Dromgoole paired with Claxton and Murfree with Grady. The bonds between brother and sister clubs were strong, though the brother club dominated decision-making between the paired societies.

46   *Murfree Literary Society, 1920–22*, October, 1920 and November 22, 1921; *Dromgoole Literary Society*, October 1914.

47   *Murfree Literary Society, 1920–22*.

48   Agnes Nelson, *Home Economics Club* (Murfreesboro: Middle Tennessee State College, 1958) Special Collections, Walker Library.

49   For club information, see *Signal* and *Normalite*, 1923; Mabel Jesse Baxter Pittard, 25 September 1995, transcript QMS.1995.106, Smith Collection, AGRC.

50   Davidson interview.

51   For faculty numbers, see Pittard, *First Fifty Years*, appendices. *Midlander* yearbooks and school bulletins corroborate the numbers from the period.

52   *Bulletin*, STC 1927.

53   There are several books on the myths and realities of the flapper on college campuses. Good examples include Paula Fass, *The Damned and the Beautiful: American Youth in the 1920s* (New York: Oxford University Press, 1977); Helen Leftkowitz Horowitz, *Campus Life* (New York: Alfred P. Knopf, 1987); and Lynn Dumenil, *The Modern Temper: American Culture and Society in the 1920s* (New York: Hill and Wang, 1995).

54   *Normalite*, November 1922.

55   *Midlander*, 1927, 39, 42, 47; *Midlander*, 1929, 47.

56   Mary Francis Snell McNeill, 12 August 1995, transcript QMS.1995.56, Smith Collection, AGRC.

57   They were married 43 years until Kenneth's death in 1972. Louise Mott Miles lived for another 40 years, until she passed away at the age of 101 in 2009. Louise Miles diary, AGRC; Louise Mott Miles, interview by Jim Williams, 15 April 2008, transcript MT0380, Middle Tennessee Oral History Project, AGRC, (hereinafter cited as MT Oral History Project, AGRC).

58   *Midlander*, 1926, 1927, 1929. See Fred Colvin's essay on sports at MTSU, chapter 6 in this volume.

59   Thomas Brinton Woodmore, *Up the Winding Staircase* (self published, Murfreesboro, TN, 1984), copy at Special Collections, Walker Library; Pittard, *First Fifty Years*, 135–64.

60   Pittard interview.

61   *Sidelines*, 16 November 1935; Pittard inteview.

62   Carroll Van West, *Tennessee's New Deal Landscape: A Guidebook* (Knoxville: University of Tennessee Press, 2001), 9; Pittard, *First Fifty Years*, 177; Katherine Butler Holden, 25 September 1995, transcript QMS.1995.110, Smith Collection, AGRC. For a critique of the NYA, see Herbert M. Kliebard, *Schooled to Work: Vocationalism and the American Curriculum, 1876–1946* (New York: Teachers College Press, 1999), 192–204.

63   See, for example, Pittard interview.

64   *Midlander*, 1935, 67–76.

65   Pittard, *First Fifty Years*, 166–77.

66   Ibid., 261. One suspects that many women took jobs left behind by the men and pushed education into the future. The *Midlander* yearbooks from the war years provide a good picture of the demography of the student body.

67   Women who attended the school in the mid-1940s were interviewed as part of the MT Oral History Project housed at the AGRC. See, for example, interviews of Jane Kittrell Ogles, Blanche Cook McClure, Norma Rousseau Burgdorf, and Fay Brandon.

68   Though women were not part of the training detachment they were in the Aviation Club and then the Aviation Teachers Training Program, a forerunner of today's highly successful Department of Aviation. Anna Marie Lanier, "The Flight of the Aerospace Program: A Detailed Look at the History of Middle Tennessee State University's Department of Aerospace," unpublished manuscript, 3 May 2010, 4–8; Pittard, *First Fifty Years*, 177.

69   Faulkinberry committed suicide in 1933 for reasons that remain murky. "Popular S.T.C. Faculty Member Dies Instantly," *Daily News Journal*, 13 May 1933, 1, 4.

70   Blanche Cook McClure, interview by Betty Rowland, 23 February 2006, transcript MT0281, MT Oral History Project, AGRC; Jane Kittrell Ogles, interview by Betty Rowland, 24 July 2006, transcript MT0263, MT Oral History Project, AGRC.

71   Suma Clark, "1940s reunite in 2005," *The Alumni Record* 3, no. 2 (1 December 2005), 3.

72   See Kathryn Tolle, interview by Bety Rowland, 28 April 2006, transcript MT0285, MT Oral History Project, AGRC; McClure interview; Ogles interview; *Daily News Journal*, 9 August 1985.

73   *Daily News Journal*, 9 August 1985.

74   Nunley, *The Raider Forties;* Pittard, *First Fifty Years*, 182–83.

75   Even though women, who had served the military were eligible for the GI Bill, fewer than 3 percent of the 350,000 female veterans nationwide used their benefits and barely any did at MTSC.

76   For the stories of returning vets and the loss of so many of their schoolmates, see Nunley, *The Raider Forties*. It is hard to say why enrollment plummeted for women, though a strong economy might play a role. *Vet Village: the Little MTSC City* (Murfreesboro: Middle Tennessee State College, 1955).

77   Ella Jolly, 22 September 1995, transcript QMS.1995.102, Smith Collection, AGRC.

78   Elizabeth Whorley Bradley, 4 November 1995, transcript QMS.1995.138, Smith Collection, AGRC.

79   Frances Carter Gill, 20 July 1995, transcript QMS.1995.41, Smith Collection, AGRC.

80   Jean Hudgens Moser, 21 September 1995, transcript QMS.1995.101, Smith Collection, AGRC. See *Midlanders* from the 1950s.

81   Martha Turner Roach, interview by Eric Preston, transcript MT0335, MT Oral History Project, AGRC.

82   Barnett, Morgan, and Pruitt, *Middle Tennessee State University*, 82.

83   See *Midlander,* 1950–1960.

84   Barnett, Morgan, and Pruitt, *Middle Tennessee State University*, 86; *Midlander* 1957, 66.

85   On the culture of beauty, see Horowitz, *Campus Life*; Lois Banner, *American Beauty* (New York: Alfred Knopf, 1983). For the different beauty titles see *Midlander*, 1955–1960. Barnett, Morgan, and Pruitt, *Middle Tennessee State University*, 92, 103.

86   Anna Marie Smith, 4 August 1995, transcript QMS.1995.51, Smith Collection, AGRC.

87   See the *Bulletins*.

88   Jennifer Holder, "Stott retiring after 45 years of service,"*Daily News Journal,* 27 April 2005; Sandra Stott, 14 September 1995, transcript QMS.1995.97, Smith Collection, AGRC.

89   Jane Warner, 3 October 1995, transcript QMS.1995.114, Smith Collection, AGRC.

90   MTSU remained relatively quiet during the 1960s. See Jordan Kirkman's essay for the campus culture of 1968, chapter 7 in this volume. Stenia Olivia Woods, interview by Betty Rowland, 19 June 2001, transcript MT0046, MT Oral History Project, AGRC.

91   Barnett, Morgan, and Pruitt, *Middle Tennessee State University*, 92, 103. See also *Midlander*, 1965–1970.

92   Co-Ed Codes, 1967–1968, 1–10, http://library.mtsu.edu/digitalprojects/mtsumemory.php.

93   Judy Smith, interview by Betty Rowland, 12 September 2000, transcript MT0022, MT Oral History Project, AGRC.

94   Ibid. For salaries, see MTSU Budget Books, 1966, 1967, 1968, AGRC.

95   Good surveys of the women's rights movements are Ruth Rosen, *The World Split Open: How the Modern Women's Movement Changed America* (New York: Penguin Press, 2000); Sara M. Evans, *Tidal Wave: How Women Changed America at Century's End* (New York: Free Press, 2003).

96   Smith interview.

97   Ibid.

98   Mopsy Gascon and Bill Fisher, "All that she left behind," *MTSU Magazine*, Fall/Winter 2002, 6.

99   Clara Rasmussen, "June Anderson: Women's Rights Pioneer," *Sidelines*, 21 October 2009.

100 Gascon and Fisher, "All that she left behind," 4.

101 "The Status of Women at MTSU, 1972–1973," prepared by MTSU chapter of American Association of University Professors. In AAUP Papers, AGRC.

102 John Pitts, "Washington probes MTSU job bias," *Sidelines*, 22 June 1976, 1.

103 Gascon and Fisher, "All that she left behind," 5; Rasmussen, "June Anderson," 5. The EEOC returned a second time but it was a third salary study in 1990 that led to major salary adjustments. The salary studies have been an ongoing, though sometimes erratic process. A lawsuit was initiated by Dr. Lani Ford that sued the TN Board of Regents for sexual discrimination when she was not rehired in 1972, after having been an assistant professor for a year in the Department of Education. In her place the department hired several men, one with fewer qualifications and less experience than Dr. Ford. She won her lawsuit but the case dragged on for more than a decade as the Board of Regents filed numerous appeals. See *Dr. Lani Ford, et al. v. Chancellor Roy S. Nicks, et al.*, US District Court of Appeals, Sixth Circuit, Case number 88-5260.

104 McCash has had a long and distinguished career at MTSU. She wrote several books, authored dozens of articles, book reviews, and papers, and still found the time to serve on a huge number of university, community, and professional committees. She has been Professor Emerita since 2004. Among numerous honors, she was awarded a career achievement award from MTSU, an outstanding alumni award from her alma mater, Agnes Scott College, and in 2011 the Georgia Author of the Year award for her first novel, *Almost to Eden.*

105 There were 29 departments on campus and four "schools" that would later become the basis for the present colleges. No women held the position of dean of these schools, though Jessie Warren was associate dean of the Department of Continuing Education and Public Service until 1984 when she became the Franklin County school superintendent. In 1988, she came back to MTSU as the first female vice president. "Dr. Jessie H. Warren, former MTSU VP, dies," *MTSU Record,* 3 June 2006, 3. In 1980, there were several administrative heads including Dot Harrison as director of public relations, Joy Callahan as affirmative action officer, and Judy Smith as associate dean of students. "MTSU Directory of Faculty and Staff, Fall 1980," http://library.mtsu.edu/digitalprojects/mtsumemory.php.

106 Sarah Fryer, "Barbara Haskew Leaves MTSU," *Murfreesboro Post,* 4 July 2010, 1.

107 Like McCash, Haskew's accomplishments are enormous. She was the university provost until 2002, when she returned to the classroom. In 2010, she retired from the university after President Barack Obama appointed her as a director on the TVA Board of Directors, a position confirmed by the US Senate in 2011. "A History of the Economics and Finance Department at Middle Tennessee State University," 5–6, 10, frank.mtsu.edu/~econfin/documents/history.pdf.

108 Gascon and Fisher, "All that she left behind," 5. See also "Working Papers," file at June Anderson Women's Center, MTSU.

109 The Education Task Force of the Sonoma County Commission on the Status of Women began a Women's History Week in early March 1978 and chose the week of March 8 to coincide with International Women's Day.

110 For the evolution of Women's Studies, see Evans, *Tidal Wave,* 94–96.

111 Women's Studies committee, "University Self Study Report," in possession of Nancy Rupprecht; *MTSU Undergraduate Catalog, 1980–1981,* 180.

112 Nancy Rupprecht, "Women's Studies Report," memo to VPAA James Hindmann, October 9, 1991, unpublished, in possession of Nancy Rupprecht.

113 *MTSU Undergraduate Catalog, 1995–1997*, 59; http://www.mtsu.edu/
womenstu.

114 See Fred Colvin's essay on sports in chapter 6 of this volume. On Title IX, see
Deborah L. Brake, *Getting in the Game: Title IX and the Women's Sports Revolution*
(New York University Press; 2010).

115 "Mary Martin," *The MTSU Record* (25 January 2010): 8.

116 As the campus grew in the 1990s and 2000s, the number of women employed
at MTSU also reached new heights. While this is good news, such numbers make it
impossible to include all their stories in such a short essay. One hopes that they will
record their experiences for future generations who don't realize the barriers women
faced. "Lana Seivers," *The Alumni Record* (March 2010): 1–2; *The MTSU Record*
(21 April 2008): 1, 5.

CHAPTER FOUR

The Blue Raiders and the Gray Wizard

A Struggle with Memory and Identity

DEREK FRISBY

The opening of Middle Tennessee State Normal School in 1911 promised to reinvigorate Murfreesboro's economy and rekindle its rich educational heritage that the Civil War had nearly extinguished. The town's selection to host one of the state's normal schools also offered the community a chance to reshape the town's identity from one of lost causes to new-found opportunities. Yet, lingering controversies over the use of Confederate iconography as part of the school's persona, most notably the infamous Confederate cavalryman Nathan Bedford Forrest, challenged the school's community allegiances and complicated the institution's transition from a rural teachers' academy to a nationally recognized research university.

Tennessee's present tranquility belies its violent past. The complex relationships between warfare and culture are embedded in nearly every community within its borders, a product of Tennessee's warrior-statesman tradition and the prodigious response of its citizens to any call to arms. Few places demonstrate the influence of these relationships more than Murfreesboro. Founded by veterans on Revolutionary War land grants, Murfreesboro stands in the heart of the Volunteer State and served for several years as the state's capital. By 1860, Murfreesboro was a burgeoning political, commercial, and educational center hosting a number of state politicians, a few thriving industries, and several renowned academies and colleges. But war irrevocably scarred Murfreesboro's physical and psychological landscape. Caught in the vortex of the Civil War, this strategically located town was the target of several Confederate raids and arguably the site of the conflict's bloodiest and most crucial battles.[1]

The Civil War dominated Murfreesboro's public memory and impeded its postwar recovery. Despite its strong antebellum record of educational development, Murfreesboro largely forgot the studies of a young James K. Polk and John Bell at the distinguished Bradley Academy and, after languishing throughout Reconstruction, the three colleges that had sprung up in the town's environs before the war teetered on the verge of dissolution. Murfreesboro's wartime tribulations also weighed heavily upon its residents' psyche. Many locals still harbored pro-Confederate proclivities 50 years after Appomattox, as they vividly recalled Federal "mutilations" upon them (or their relatives) and their town. Evidence of the war was still visible in 1909, when officials inspected potential sites around the town for a new normal school. Decades-old battle damage on buildings, the deteriorating earthworks of Fortress Rosecrans, as well as the public square's prominent Confederate monument served as constant reminders of the war's tragic effects upon Murfreesboro. With these specters of war hovering over them, citizens had made the conflict a centerpiece of the town's public memory and identity, even as a wave of reconciliation swept over the country in the 1890s.[2]

THE NAMING OF THE FIRST TWO DORMITORIES

Murfreesboro aggressively sought, and ultimately received, the opportunity to host one of the state's regional normal schools at the turn of the twentieth century. With an inaugural class comprised largely of aspiring local educators and little infrastructure to build upon, Middle Tennessee State Normal School (MTN) relied upon community support, and officials quickly began integrating the institution into the community. Normal's lone female dormitory was at capacity at its opening, and the male students were without campus housing. As a solution, administrators rented two houses near campus in 1912, and converted them into dormitories to accommodate the relatively small number of men attending the predominately female school.[3] MTN named these residence halls for notable Murfreesboro Civil War-era-related figures. Their choices appeared to be a way to link the town and the school, an important development given Normal's absence of traditions, the preponderance of local residents attending the school, and the concurrent Civil War golden anniversary celebrations.

One dorm was christened Craddock Hall in honor of local author Mary Noailles Murfree, whose pen name was Charles Egbert Craddock. Born in 1850, she was a descendent of the namesake of Murfreesboro and had gained celebrity as a "local color" author writing several fictional works, typically set in Tennessee. Among her first literary laurels was *Where the Battle Was Fought*, a Reconstruction-era novel that highlighted the Civil War's integral role in Murfreesboro's postwar identity and described Grantland, the Murfree's family home northwest of town that had been destroyed in the conflict. At the time, Murfree had recently returned to Murfreesboro where she lived until her death in 1922.[4]

The other dormitory was named Forrest Hall, in homage to Confederate cavalry commander and local legend, Nathan Bedford Forrest. Forrest had earned his laurels as a wily and fearsome combat commander during his daring raid on Murfreesboro 50 years earlier. Curiously, Forrest's lack of formal education was among his most noted attributes. This "untutored genius" had emerged as one of the South's most prominent antebellum businessmen and slavetraders, and during the war this "wizard of the saddle" often defeated better-educated and West Point-trained opponents. His mercurial personality and popularity among the southern populace also earned him the enmity of the West Point clique within the Confederate Army, who often ostracized Forrest, and left him to conduct independent commands and raids. Forrest's role in the racial atrocities at the 1864 Fort Pillow Massacre severely tainted his postwar reputation, and a number of bad Reconstruction-era investments left him practically destitute. Until his death in 1877, he remained largely an unrepentant Confederate whose reported affiliation as the first Grand Wizard of the emerging Ku Klux Klan (KKK) saw him hauled before Congress to testify about the increasingly disturbing levels of southern racial violence. In hindsight, naming a college building after someone with little or no academic credentials and a controversial past may appear unusual and inappropriate, even if it was simply a dormitory. But the circumstances and timing of events surrounding MTN's establishment and the cultural imperatives of a lost cause ideology overrode any concerns about its potential legacy. It unknowingly set in motion a series of events that later clouded the school's identity and tested its bonds with community.[5]

MIDDLE TENNESSEE'S "BLUE RAIDERS"

Middle Tennessee State Normal changed significantly over the course of the next 20 years. The campus and community prospered in the 1920s and, as a result of this growth and the success of its graduates, MTN expanded, constructing numerous buildings and hiring more faculty to accommodate increasing enrollments. As the normal school concept gradually fell out of favor and a more comprehensive four-year curriculum for teacher training became the vogue in education, Middle Tennessee State Normal became Middle Tennessee State Teachers College (STC) in 1925. The new STC clung tenaciously to the lost cause identity prominent in the period. The 1930 *Midlander* yearbook paid homage to the Old South and the Civil War. The editor wrote that the "Old South is gone but today its ideals, culture, traditions, manners and chivalry remain . . . [and have] served as an inspiration to the student body since the birth of this college." Graduates of southern colleges, he continued, have an almost sacred mission "to live and work for a greater South and greater America." The foreword recalled that into "balmy Dixie came the deep-throated growlings and ravages of that monster called War" and afterwards "came new people to build a new and greater South." The endpapers featured slaves picking cotton on a plantation, and the borders of the pages included steamboats, cotton bales, and the flags of the Confederacy and United States. The yearbook also featured, interspersed with quotes from Henry W. Grady's 1886 speech lauding the "New South," images from the Stones River National Battlefield and paintings of Southerners standing amidst the ruins of war. One image even depicted white-hooded klansmen riding through a desolate, war-scarred forest at night. The staff dedicated the yearbook to Miss Katherine Monohan, the *Midlander* faculty advisor and history instructor, who was, they declared, the epitome of the southern lady.[6]

The connection between the traditions of the Old South and the school may have served as a palliative for a campus suffering under severe economic distress. The Great Depression led to declining enrollments and financial retrenchment for STC, and students and staff looked for distractions to Depression-era hardships. Athletics served as one of those pleasant distractions in communities across the country, particularly at colleges. STC had the sports teams but lacked an official nickname to distinguish itself from its competition or to inspire the fan base. Other Tennessee schools had chosen nicknames, and the University of Tennessee "Vols" and Vanderbilt "Commodores" were already in use at the turn of the century. West Tennessee Normal had adopted the "Tigers" in 1914, and Tennessee Polytechnic had been the "Golden Eagles" since 1925.[7] Typically, reporters dubbed Middle Tennessee in the box scores simply as MTN or STC, and unofficial team names among the students such as "the Pedagogues," "the Teachers," or "the Normalites" failed to rally the faithful fans. Thus, late in the 1934 season Murfreesboro's newspaper, the *Daily News Journal*, sponsored a contest for a nickname more appropriate to a school of its stature. The paper narrowed approximately 240 entries down to about 25 and allowed the football team to choose the winner. Charles Sarver, a guard on the team, had submitted an entry based upon the successful Colgate University "Red Raiders" and simply substituted "Blue," one school color for STC, for Colgate's "Red" on the entry form. Since Sarver was one of their own, the team's choice was perhaps predestined. The "Blue Raiders" became the school's official nickname—though they lost the only game that season while using their new moniker. At least Sarver received some consolation by collecting $5 for his winning entry.[8]

The college's struggles sadly continued both on and off the field during the Great Depression. The 1936 *Midlander* commented that due to its mediocre record and poor attendance, STC athletics "lay at the bottom of the heap...the flowers had already wilted in the vase . . . the murky depths beckoned."[9] By 1938, STC had witnessed a precipitous decline in enrollments, while internal squabbling among the legislature, the faculty, and STC President P. A. Lyon over the institution's future compounded the anxiety around campus. After a contentious debate, President Lyon resigned, and a search began for someone who could rescue the foundering college.[10]

THE SMITH YEARS

Middle Tennessee Normal graduate and former Tennessee Polytechnic Institute President Q. M. Smith became STC's president in 1938. Smith had been Middle Tennessee Normal's second student applicant in 1911 and, during his academic career in Murfreesboro, he had served as class president, as the first campus newspaper editor, as a member of the first football team, and later as the first president of the alumni association. In 1912, he was the only student representative on a committee which chose the official university colors of blue and white. Smith later attended the University of Tennessee and Peabody College. Almost everyone recognized Smith's "unrelenting spirit" and administrative ability, honed from over three decades of educational leadership, supplemented by service as a Navy officer in World War I and as an Army Reserve officer until 1942. However, his gruff, no-nonsense, uncompromising approach to campus governance was controversial and ruffled more than a few feathers, both on campus and in the community, during his tenure. Undaunted by his critics, President Smith set about revitalizing his alma mater even as the world stood at the brink of another world war.[11]

As the war clouds gathered, Smith launched a campaign to redefine the institution's mission and image as a move toward greater "respectability." He carefully managed a groundswell of support by the students, the public, and the legislature to redesignate STC as a state college with enhanced curriculum options. When the legislature approved this transition in 1943, discussions abounded about changing the institution's name in order to distinguish it from the variety of similar regional institutions. Suggested names for the new college included "Stones River State College" and "Murfreesboro State," but Coach E. W. Midgett, perhaps influenced by the America's entrance into World War II, vociferously suggested "Forrest State College," to reflect its community roots and connect the Raider nickname with that local legend, Nathan Bedford Forrest. President Smith and the state legislature eschewed this advice and eventually chose the less creative "Middle Tennessee State College" as the new title.[12]

World War II consumed the public's attention and, with the draft and romantic allure of wartime service, Middle Tennessee State College (MTSC) male enrollments significantly declined. President Smith recruited a number of campus-based wartime occupational training programs, particularly in aviation, to offset the loss of tuition revenue. When the war ended, many of these programs remained, positioning MTSC as an attractive option for the influx of new students under the auspices of the GI Bill program.[13]

Intensely anti-communist and heavily influenced by the Southern Agrarian movement based at nearby Vanderbilt, Smith also made the decision to strengthen MTSC's link with Nathan Bedford Forrest. He directed MTSC Public Relations Director Gene Sloan to offer suggestions for a mascot name. Sloan forwarded the names of Confederate "raiders" John Hunt Morgan and Nathan Bedford Forrest to the president. Smith unhesitatingly selected Forrest. He intended Forrest's allegedly oft-quoted maxim, "the First with the Most," to represent a spirit and a philosophy that would inspire students, particularly those in Middle Tennessee, by emphasizing the Southern Agrarian virtues of physical courage, loyalty to family and region, independence, initiative, and citizenship. The Southern Agrarians' manifesto, *I'll Take My Stand*, contained a series of essays denouncing the increasing role of nationalization, industrialization, and urbanization in American culture. The contributors' works advocated a return to the local, agrarian, and rural virtues of the antebellum South to cure the ills of American modernity. This philosophy also contained tenets of the "Lost Cause" that mythologized the Confederacy. Lost Cause proponents explained that the Confederacy's defeat was from overwhelming force rather than innate skill and attempted to divorce the Confederacy from the preservation of slavery, while promoting the perceived chivalry and nobility of the antebellum South.[14]

Agrarians and Lost Cause supporters quickly latched onto Forrest as a symbol for their arguments, and they perpetuated these "myths" throughout the early twentieth century. The general became a resonant and daring symbol of southern society. According to two professors who have chronicled the Forrest myth, "the fact that an uneducated rube, an American plebeian, could so adroitly, so intuitively, master the art of warfare, indeed make it into an art form, was a reminder to the professional soldier and the aristocrat that much could be learned from a common man." Forrest's words were often preserved in southern dialect with misspelled words to stress his uneducated background, as a literary device that utilizes local speech patterns to "maintain one's individual dignity in a homogenizing world."[15]

Newspaper editorials and advertisements highlighted the virtues of American citizen-soldier myth and superior capitalist values by employing Forrest's "First with the Most" philosophy during World War II and the Cold War era. During this period, Forrest's tactics and military maxims became synonymous with the popular perception of the "American Way of War" and American business acumen. One advertisement for *Business Week* magazine, just two weeks prior to the Japanese attack on Pearl Harbor, displayed a Memphis statue of Forrest and the famous proverb, "Git thar furstest with mostest," proclaiming "Long, long ago this burly general had the secret of American success down pat." A 1960 Delta Airlines full-page ad in the *Chicago Tribune,* complete with an actor dressed as Forrest in an airliner, declared, "'Fustest with the Mostest' . . . Spare of Word and square of jaw, [Forrest] cut complicated strategy down to a simple formula…and one uniquely appropriate to Delta today." The corporate promotion of Forrest in modern American business practices was an irony the Southern Agrarians surely appreciated. Forrest by the mid-1940s was no longer a regional curiosity, the villain of the Fort Pillow Massacre, or the perceived leader of the KKK; instead, his image had been magically transformed into that of an American military and business icon. Given this cultural and intellectual atmosphere, it is not surprising that Memphians erected a statue to Forrest over his grave and turned the surrounding area into a local park, that the Tennessee General Assembly declared Forrest's birthday a state holiday in the 1920s and 1930s, and that Q. M. Smith mandated that the "untutored genius" Forrest be enlisted to represent MTSC's new status as a state college.[16]

The connection between Smith's Agrarian values and those of the community surrounding MTSC's campus were heightened by Murfreesboro native and leading Southern Agrarian Andrew Nelson Lytle, who wrote one of the most influential works celebrating the Forrest myth. *Nathan Bedford Forrest and His Critter Company* was an example of a culture seeking a usable past, and it emphasized the agrarian values of the protean folk hero Forrest as "an antidote to industrial modernism and its inevitable spiritual corrosion." In one telling passage, Lytle romanticized Forrest's age as one "closer to Henry II's than it is to ours. They are centuries apart yet those centuries knew the orderly return of the seasons, saw the supernatural in the natural, moved about by foot, by horse, and at sea by the wind. We have put our faith in the machine." In 1944, another Forrest biographer, Robert Selph Henry, also used Forrest as "nature's soldier" to elaborate further on his character traits that Agrarians admired. Twenty years later, the 1964 *Midlander* used Henry's description of the intrepid Forrest to epitomize the Raider spirit saying, "[Forrest] is a man of great self-confidence, self-reliance, and reticence; man of quick resolves and prompt execution, of inexhaustible resource, and of ready and clever expedients . . . panic and fear flew and hid at his approach, and the sound of his cheer gave courage to the weakest heart." Smith and others in Murfreesboro almost assuredly knew both works. Lytle's and Henry's Forrest must have appeared as a natural choice for a college in a community steeped in the Forrest myth and so closely linked in geographical and intellectual proximity to the Southern Agrarians. Thus Smith, and MTSC Public Relations Director Gene Sloan, apparently began incorporating Forrest's myth into college official communications sometime in the late 1940s, though the first extant university-sanctioned image of Forrest remains the 1951 *Midlander*.[17]

By the 1950s, Confederate iconography became increasingly visible in campus traditions across the South, and MTSC embraced the latest Confederate kitsch and "flag fads." Confederate flags proudly waved at MTSC football games, and MTSC's band adopted "Dixie" as the school's fight song. These developments were the local manifestations of MTSC's integration of the Southern Agrarian / Forrest myth into campus traditions and the growing national incorporation of Confederate symbols into American culture. In 1948, Strom Thurmond and his Dixiecrats broke away from the national Democratic Party to protest the Democrats' support of civil rights. The Dixiecrats, emboldened by the Southern Agrarian philosophy, railed against the oppressive nature of the federal government as antithetical to the southern way of life. Thurmond's Dixiecrats quickly raised the old Confederate battle flag as a symbol of their party and ignored the desperate pleas of the United Daughters of Confederacy (UDC) and Sons of Confederate Veterans (SCV) to cease using Confederate symbols in what these Lost Cause organizations considered an ahistorical context. Although the Dixiecrat movement was short-lived and received only token support in Tennessee, its use of the Confederate battle flag ushered in an age of flag fads across the country. These flag fads transitioned Confederate iconography from embodying solely a political message to one with a myriad of meanings. The approach of the Civil War centennial accelerated the process of stripping these symbols of their historical context and turned them into a ubiquitous presence in American culture, emblazoned on every trivial and tacky souvenir imaginable. Strangely, the increased use of Forrest and other Confederate symbols during this critical period of growth allowed MTSC to sustain community involvement by emphasizing its local heritage, while simultaneously striving to become more relevant at the state and national levels without appearing too provincial.[18]

By the 1950s, the Forrest myth and the use of Confederate iconography had become "a microcosm of the larger national mythology." It seemingly embraced "individualism and rebellion, the conquest of frontiers, whether geographic or political, constantly recommitting itself to the idealized notions of democracy, and taking full advantage of practical politics and economics." Forrest, in particular, was the personification of "the paradox of the mythical American man, symbolizing both the common and uncommon," and therefore, he seemed a not-so-unusual choice to represent an institution of higher education that often attracted first-generation, low-income students. The fact that so many in the campus population were veterans accentuated Forrest's appeal among the student body and staff. MTSC warmly received Forrest back on campus, and his new college compatriots proudly wore Confederate hats and carried Confederate battle flags to athletic events as the band blared "Dixie." A bust of Forrest stood in the new student center.[19]

MTSC was one of several other regional schools that had also adopted Confederate-themed mascots or traditions. At least one similar school, Mississippi Southern College (later the University of Southern Mississippi), also used Forrest as a mascot for their team. Most interestingly, the MTSC athletic department resisted the adoption of Confederate iconography for its official use, although Forrest's seemingly omnipresent appearance at athletic events, the Stars and Bars waving in the stands, and the "Dixie" fight song tacitly sanctioned their use to inspire local support. Images or themes of Forrest and the Confederacy never replaced the standard "MT" on football helmets or other athletic gear, and the figure of Forrest rarely appeared prominently in official publications. The only extant athletic department use of any significant Confederate iconography was printed on the 1964 football media guide cover and, rather than Forrest, it depicted a simple cavalry trooper riding roughshod over its opponents. Interestingly, the man who originated the Blue Raiders, Charles Sarver, later remarked that the only unpleasant memory about his decision was when Smith and Sloan decided they "needed a reason for the name" and chose Forrest to represent the Blue Raiders.[20]

Beyond the athletic fields, the arrival of a Reserve Officers' Training Corps (ROTC) unit on campus in 1950 further embedded Forrest into MTSC's identity. The MTSC ROTC unit specifically trained in armored maneuver tactics and guerilla warfare, both similar to the widely heralded and much-mythologized aspects of Forrest's military career. Many officers believed studying this "Wizard of the Saddle" would be essential to US strategy for countering Soviet mass armored formations as well as Communist insurgents. Few were shocked then, in 1954, when the MTSC administration named their new ROTC building, Nathan Bedford Forrest Hall. Fort Lee, Fort Bragg, Fort Hood, Fort A. P. Hill, Fort Rucker, and Fort Gordon are just a few of the prominent United States military installations that had already been named to honor former Confederates and, given this trend, there was an immediate consensus about the appropriate name for the building to train future military leaders at MTSC. "There was no search made for a name for the ROTC building," said Dean of Students Belt Keathley in his 1958 Forrest Hall dedication speech; "the name was simply present and at hand. The spirit of the man for whom the building is named resides on our campus." Later, the cadets formed several related student and professional organizations with local Confederate namesakes, such as the Sam Davis Rifles drill team and the Forrest Raiders, an elite cadet professional organization. Students also composed the Dixie All-Star Majorettes and the Track and Sabre Club.[21]

General Forrest had made his first formal appearance as MTSC's mascot on the cover of the 1951 *Midlander*. During the 1950s he appeared on the cover five times, but the 1956 *Midlander* stands out among all others, marking a significant change in the level of Confederate iconography associated with the campus. The 1956 *Midlander* staff commissioned *Nashville Banner* illustrator Jack Knox to create a unique Forrest image to symbolize the spirit of MTSC. Knox's illustration depicted a very aggressive, masculine Forrest astride his steed, King Phillip, with pistol in hand. That image became the standard visual logo of MTSC for over a decade. The 1956 *Midlander* also featured a cartoonish Confederate member of Forrest's cavalry wearing a MTSC belt buckle on his uniform. This stereotypical Johnny Reb guided readers around the campus making frequent references to being "fustest with the mostest." The commentary omitted the more controversial elements of Forrest's character and reputation, except for one rather disturbing image on the Campus Organizations page, which shows the Confederate character removing a KKK hood from a "C.S.A." haversack.[22]

The 1956 *Midlander*'s publication and Forrest Hall's dedication appeared in the tenuous period surrounding the 1954 *Brown* Supreme Court decision overturning racial segregation in education. Other than the aforementioned depiction of the KKK hood, there is little evidence suggesting that the student body or the administration at MTSC consciously chose to identify with Forrest as part of the massive resistance initiated by Southerners to thwart federal integration efforts. Instead, the increasing association of Forrest and Confederate iconography appears as part of the trendy Confederate kitsch of the Civil War centennial: "merely one of those fads which the American people eagerly like to grab up and promote and then drop just as quickly" when the commercial value fades. It remained to be seen just how quickly such a trend would fade in Murfreesboro, where the Civil War centennial ran alongside MTSC's 50th anniversary. The boundaries between campus and community had all but disappeared since 1945, as many local veterans returned to MTSC to embark upon new educational and professional opportunities. With the campus and community's public memory and identity tied inexorably with their martial heritage, Forrest rode boldly into Murfreesboro again.[23]

To celebrate its golden anniversary, MTSC unveiled a new flag, a new alma mater, and a new Forrest mascot. The new incarnation of Forrest emerged as a student astride King Phillip, the general's trusted steed, and dressed in full Confederate uniform with the instantly recognizable goatee to resemble Forrest's visage. The first student to portray Forrest was actually Connecticut native Dick Schoonman. This "Connecticut Yankee in King Phillip's Court" proudly paraded down Main Street during Homecoming and patrolled the sidelines at sporting events, against a backdrop of Confederate flags, for the next two years. The tradition continued throughout the 1960s as other students who resembled Forrest in physical stature volunteered to replace Schoonman. According to the campus newspaper, *Sidelines*, the Forrest mascot was indicative of the "honor, loyalty, courage, integrity, and 'stick-to-it-tive-ness'" of MTSC students and served as a "unifying symbol and as a builder of high goals." By 1968, Forrest and the college's identity were so intertwined that officials placed an eight-foot, 600-pound bronze medallion featuring Jack Knox's rendition of Forrest outside the new Keathley University Student Center (KUC).[24]

THE BATTLE FOR A NEW IDENTITY

The KUC medallion marked Forrest's zenith as the school's representative. Although the medallion evidenced the administration's desire to continue the school's affiliation with Forrest, it was increasingly apparent that students sought a reconsideration of the institution's image. MTSU's enrollments between 1959 and 1969 had ballooned from 2,363 to nearly 7,500, expanding at an average rate of 10 percent per year as a result of the "baby boom" generation. The baby boomers challenged traditional culture and sought a new identity of their own. Some began to question the utility of the past as a part of MTSU's image. They chafed at MTSU's antiquated campus coed codes that dictated attire and behavior. As for the institution's past and traditions, these baby boomers noted that MTSU had "been enshrouded in the gloomy mist of underestimation," but remained optimistic that "our image is still in the formative state and we have the opportunity to make MTSU what we think it should be. As we continue to grow, much of our former personality will change."[25] Fewer campus publications made direct references to Forrest after the college's notably calm integration in 1962 and its transition to university status in 1965. The 1966 *Midlander* noted that the change to university status was "a birth of new era, with a new spirit but remaining with old traditions and holding to her heritage," yet the students made significant changes to the university's identity to diminish the use of Confederate imagery and references in campus publications. Though the core image of a Confederate, goateed cavalryman remained, it was increasingly referred to simply as "The Raider," and representations of the Raider also became less dignified and more caricatured as reverence for Forrest waned. Compounding the image problem, a string of disappointing football seasons and a plethora of new opportunities in the area for the growing numbers of car-mobile students caused officials to estimate that fewer than 30 percent of students had ever been to a Raider contest of any type.[26]

 The success of the Nashville sit-ins and the Civil Rights Movement, and shaken confidence in authority stimulated by the escalating Vietnam War, as well as the assassinations of Civil Rights figures John Kennedy, Martin Luther King, Malcolm X, and Robert Kennedy, created a discernable inner restlessness and aura of change on campus in the 1960s. Furthermore, the proposed establishment of a University of Tennessee campus in Nashville, in 1968, had sparked a group led by Rita Geier to file a lawsuit claiming the new UT–Nashville campus would perpetuate a racially segregated "dual system of higher education" in violation of the 14th Amendment and the *Brown* decision. In this period of heightened racial and generational tensions, MTSU students in late 1960s were developing "a growing concern for their university . . . a concern with its place in the South and as an American institution."[27]

On October 21, 1968, *Sidelines* published "*Dixie*: What Does It Mean?" an editorial by Associated Student Body senator Sylvester Brooks. Brooks, an African American student, condemned the school's Confederate-themed traditions by reminding readers that slavery was the Confederacy's cornerstone and of Forrest's culpability in the Fort Pillow Massacre, as well as his involvement in the Ku Klux Klan. He argued that, instead of unifying the student body, these symbols were divisive on an increasingly multicultural, progressive campus. "As long as these remnants of slavery and Black inferiority are allowed to persist on this campus," Brooks proclaimed, "I will never choose to be a full part of this school." He also expanded his attack to include the Murfreesboro community, charging that by clinging "passionately to the relics" of "America's worst yesterday" southern society would never move forward.[28]

Brooks's criticism for MTSU's use of "Dixie," Confederate flags, and the Forrest mascot unleashed a torrent of responses that filled the editorial pages for months. Supporters of these traditions rode to Forrest's defense by recounting his military prowess and revered character traits that reflected southern values. Others steadfastly defended the use of "Dixie" and the Confederate flag as symbols of school spirit rather than symbols of white supremacy.[29] Former *Sidelines* editor, Tony Pendergrass, commented that the symbols represented "a fighting spirit which is appropriate for athletic squads and are symbols—not bigotry."[30] Joseph Smith, director of MTSU's Band of Blue, angrily defended MTSU's use of these symbols and vowed to keep playing "Dixie" until the administration declared an official ban.[31]

Brooks's editorial garnered support, too. Jim Leonard appreciated Brooks's "moral firmness" in challenging the relevancy of these symbols to "a progressive institution in the New South." Several editorials called for greater communication to close the chasm between the black and white students. "If MTSU is to become a progressive university then [the] corroding tradition of a decadent South must be abandoned," student Karen Thomas said, and "If tradition impedes progress, then tradition must succumb." Thomas continued, "Until the students at MTSU emerge from the smallness of their environment and realize the boundaries of the world are not the boundaries of Tennessee and until they realize that white people are not the only people, there can be no solution."[32] A long-time Murfreesboro resident, with professed generational ties to Confederate veterans and an MTSU parent, recalled her first view of the Forrest mascot and Confederate accoutrements as shocking and offensive in a university setting. She begged, "Please let us keep their flag and hatred buried. Let us honor them by keeping their mistakes at rest along with their bones."[33]

The ASB debated the issue throughout the Fall 1968 semester. In December, they voted to reject any change in the school's symbols. Although many students had argued that their support of Forrest, "Dixie," and the Confederate flag as MTSU symbols was based upon the lack of "racial overtones or undertones" in their original selection, it quickly became obvious that some racial connotations did indeed exist. *Sidelines* editor in chief David Mathis wrote shortly after the ASB vote, "the student voice was heard to keep things as they are, thus the issue did not receive any of the changes that a 'minority' sector of our population desired."[34] But the administration overruled the ASB. Subsequent MTSU presidents, M. G. Scarlett and Sam Ingram, prohibited Confederate flags and the playing of "Dixie" on campus.[35] The university discharged Forrest from further service as the university mascot and formed a special committee to choose a less controversial, "more generic" mascot, "more palatable to minorities on campus and in the community." Their choice, apparently a compromise between the traditionalists and those that favored change, was a St. Bernard dog named "Beauregard" attended by a Blue Raider that resembled a hybrid Yosemite Sam–Zorro-inspired infantryman. This new mascot, even with its reference to another Confederate general, failed to inspire, and it too was quickly retired. Animosities over Scarlett's summary actions in this issue lingered and, in 1970, an unknown group burned a cross on campus, apparently in protest of the university's growing diversity.[36]

MTSU's subsequent attempts over the next two decades to find a distinctive identity fell flat. Homer Pittard, a revered faculty member and local historian, chaired a committee to find yet another image to represent the university "that would maintain an area of identification and a student relationship." Beginning with the 1976 football home opener, a Tennessee walking horse, ridden by a blue-and-white uniformed caped horseman, became the new MTSU mascot. The mascot came fully equipped with its own specially decorated horse trailer. Its choice was intended to showcase Middle Tennessee's famous equestrian tradition, and "the whole habilitation ties in with the tradition of heroic figures on horseback," supposedly to satisfy those still pining for Forrest's return. Of course, the horse's unique gait took its toll on the field and surrounding track and was impractical for indoor sports such as basketball. After just four years, officials replaced this mascot with another, a character nicknamed "Old Blue" outfitted in blue-dyed dog costume. MTSU administrators had struggled to find "a more popular figure that the crowds would respond to," so they chose Old Blue, a figure invented by an unofficial booster club, the Raider Roadies. The new mascot received a rather unenthusiastic review in the 1980 *Midlander*, and Old Blue, with its close resemblance to Ol' Smokey, MTSU's Knoxville-based rival's Blue Tick hound mascot, gradually disappeared from the scene.[37]

By 1989, MTSU had dramatically improved its organization and garnered new resources to accommodate another period of extraordinary growth. The university had established six colleges and had begun offering doctoral-level degree programs. Its black population had increased to about 10 percent of the now more than 10,000 enrolled students, and students elected their first African American Homecoming Queen, Barbara Gibson, in 1978. MTSU and Rutherford County had swelled as a result of the new Nissan auto plant, and this growth began to break the Civil War's hold on the campus and the community. Despite this success, the university still had no distinctive identity. An innocuous new logo was adopted in 1978, simply featuring the letters, "MTSU," in a futuristic font, with no mascot. Only two campus vestiges of Forrest remained: the KUC medallion and Forrest Hall.[38]

Students returned in January 1990 to find a large circular void where the Forrest medallion had once been. MTSU officials had removed the plaque while students were away on Christmas break. Again, controversy erupted, though it is hard to tell how much of the controversy came from the removal of Forrest's image or from the manner in which it was done. A few citizens and students protested the university's covert action as an attempt to erase their heritage. Those who specifically mentioned their objections to the removal did so using the standard defense: Forrest's veneration as mascot had more to do with his purported character virtues and endearment to the community than to commemorate slavery. Some even hoped to mollify the connection to slavery by claiming the figure was not Forrest at all, but a generic representation of a Civil War–era cavalryman. Others claimed the removal damaged the historical integrity of the building since the medallion was an original architectural embellishment.[39] But most shared the sentiments of Norman Dasinger Jr. who wrote to Interim MTSU President Wallace Prescott to defend his Confederate relative's honor, charging, "In removing this plaque you have denied Southerners and their history rightful remberance [sic] at your institution."[40] Three years later, local physician Dr. Richard Soper inquired through his state senator about the circumstances of the plaque removal, presumably to protest its removal as a violation of state policy or law. MTSU's first African American president, James Walker, disputed such charges. He responded to allegations that MTSU was abandoning its community ties by removing the image, or that his race had anything to do with this decision, by saying pointedly, "Though there appears to be concern of the removal of the plaque, I do want to inform you that we have a building on our campus named for Nathan Bedford Forrest. Forrest Hall houses our Military Science Department and is centrally located on our campus."[41]

The Forrest Hall debate was indicative of a broader national movement challenging the use of controversial symbols and buildings depicting Native American or Confederate themes, as many southern universities, like MTSU, shed their regional distinctiveness for increasingly national recruitment and recognition. Indeed, Confederate-related names or images were retired at a number of southern higher education institutions in the late twentieth century. In the early 1970s, the University of Southern Mississippi changed its image from a Forrest-themed mascot, General Nat. Their athletic teams were known as the "Confederates," and later as the "Southerners." In a runoff referendum on a new mascot, students and alumni chose to replace their Southerners nickname with the "Golden Eagles." The University of Mississippi, often criticized for its use of Confederate flags and the plantation owner Colonel mascot, has endured decades of turmoil over its identity. Although Ol' Miss retains the "Rebels" as their nickname, they have banned the Confederate flag from athletic events and, in 2010, students chose to supplant Colonel Reb with a black bear figure. Officially, Colonel Reb, dating from 1936, was banished in 2003; however, the university redesignated their former logo of an antebellum plantation owner as a "historical trademark" to satisfy some of the Colonel Reb loyalists. Yet the controversy continues, and some Ol' Miss alumni have created a Colonel Reb Foundation that continues to promote the use of the traditional logos.[42]

A 2002 decision to rename Confederate Hall embroiled the home of Southern Agrarianism, Vanderbilt University, in a bitter debate on the value of public memory and the Confederacy's legacy. The United Daughters of the Confederacy, who had donated a substantial portion of the funds to construct the building in 1933, sued the university. Rhetoric around this decision turned vitriolic, and Vanderbilt officials later accepted a legally nuanced compromise requiring them to keep the Confederate Hall inscription on the building's facade and memorial plaque in the lobby, but officially changed the name to "Memorial Hall," and established a lecture series to discuss "issues of race, history, memory, and the Civil War."[43]

MTSU also determined to change its identity to reflect its evolution from a regional to national institution while attempting to retain its established community connections. In the early 1990s, the university began its rebranding campaign by redesigning its official academic logo to incorporate the ubiquitous "swoosh" visual element, perhaps intended to convey a sense of motion or progress for the fastest-growing university in Tennessee. In 1998, MTSU prepared to enter Division I-A athletics (now the Football Bowl Subdivision, or FBS), and choose a new visual identity to represent its teams. Chosen by a committee of students, alumni, and community leaders, the new image featured the long-established "MT" alongside a mythical winged horse, nicknamed "Lightning" for the belief that this creature carried lightning bolts for Greek gods. Possessing "superior cunning and speed," the new Lightning mascot would represent the school's character, talent, and strength. This latest incarnation of MTSU's institutional identity according to the official description, recognizes "the soaring school spirit" and traditions of excellence in a number of academic and extracurricular endeavors, "including historic preservation, teacher training, aerospace, political science, horse science and the recording industry."[44]

In a strange twist of fate, the Lightning reference even has a connection to Civil War Murfreesboro to enhance its suitability to represent the university and community. Shortly after the battle of Stones River, Union commander Colonel John A. Wilder formed the Lightning Brigade in Murfreesboro, using the fresh supply of local horses and the newly acquired Spencer repeating rifles. Federal forces deployed the powerful new unit that married firepower and speed as the army's offensive punch during the Tullahoma campaign and in a key defensive role at the Battle of Chickamauga. The importance of the Lightning Brigade is often underappreciated by the general public, particularly those in Murfreesboro still harboring Confederate sentimentalities, though among professional military leaders and historians this unit of Blue Raiders served as a model for reintroducing maneuver warfare to the US military doctrine following the Civil War.[45]

Despite the popularity and commercial success of the Lightning mascot, the specter of Forrest and the Confederacy still looms over the institution's public memory and identity. Some still insist that Forrest remain a part of campus traditions and perpetrate myths, half-truths, and outright lies concerning Forrest and his connections with the Blue Raiders even when the elements of these tales contradict the historical record to support their case. Among the most popular are the myths that Forrest commonly confiscated the blue uniforms of his Federal enemies to outfit his command—hence the "Blue Raiders"—and that Forrest's cavalry often donned blue uniforms to trick Union forces into holding fire until it was too late, or that the school named their ROTC Building "Forrest Hall" in memory of Forrest's great-grandson, Memphis native and US Army Air Force General Nathan Bedford Forrest III, who was killed in action during a B-17 bombing raid over Germany in 1943.[47] These types of stories probably stem from earlier attempts to divorce the Forrest name from the more negative aspects of the Civil War's and slavery's legacy. In the fierce, albeit misguided, defense of those seeking to keep Forrest and similar Confederate iconography as part of the Blue Raiders image, the deeply enmeshed nature of the community's and college's identities is clearly evident in the public's memory. Even into the twenty-first century, the MTSU community still debates the contested legacy of Forrest and the Confederacy. In 2006, calls to rename Forrest Hall generated passionate comments from both sides on the issue, compelling the university to convene a special forum discussing the relationship between the community, campus, and the Confederacy. The 2012 Sons of Confederate Veterans national convention scheduled to be held in Murfreesboro will certainly renew similar discussions about the complex relationships of heritage, history, memory, and identity throughout Middle Tennessee.[47]

MTSU drew from the community for its strength and identity during its tumultuous early decades. By the late 1930s, college officials cemented this connection by identifying the institution with a local legend, Confederate cavalryman Nathan Bedford Forrest. This identity with the community became more ensconced as national cultural trends and Civil War centennial commemorations popularized and secularized Confederate iconography, largely stripping Forrest and other Confederate symbols of their historical context. The campus and the community that sponsored it struggled to retain their strong regional identities with the past as both developed a national and global presence. As William Faulkner once wrote, in the South, "the past isn't dead. It isn't even past." On the eve of Murfreesboro's bicentennial and MTSU's centennial, the ghosts of those old Civil War soldiers, like Forrest, are finally fading away from prominence, but will forever remain a part of public memory and identity.

NOTES

1   For a survey of Tennessee history, see Paul Bergeron, Steven Ash, and Jeannette Keith, *Tennesseans and Their History* (Knoxville: University of Tennessee Press, 1999).

2   Homer Pittard, *The First Fifty Years: Middle Tennessee State College, 1911–1961*, (Murfreesboro: Middle Tennessee State College, 1961), 15–16.

3   For the selection of Murfreesboro as site for a state normal school see chapter one by Janice Leone and John Lodl, in this volume. Pittard, *First Fifty Years*, 85; *Signal*, 1912, Albert Gore Research Center (AGRC), Middle Tennessee State University, Murfreesboro, TN, 35.

4   Alice Fay Taylor, "Mary Noailles Murfree: Southern Woman Writer" (PhD thesis, Emory University Graduate Institute of the Liberal Arts, 1988); Richard Carey, *Mary N. Murfree* (New York: Twayne Publishing, 1967), 115.

5   *Bulletin* 20 (Middle Tennessee State Normal School, 1912), Special Collections, James Walker Library, Middle Tennessee State University, TN. The *Bulletin* served as the catalog containing information about the institution and its course offerings. Of the many Forrest biographies, two recent works stand out above the rest: Brian S. Wills's *The Confederacy's Greatest Cavalryman: Nathan Bedford Forrest* (Lawrence: University of Kansas Press, 1998) [Originally published under the title, *A Battle from the Start*, in 1992], and Jack Hurst's *Nathan Bedford Forrest: A Biography* (New York: Vintage Press, 1994).

6   *Midlander* 5, 1930, in the Internet Archive database, http://www.archive.org/details/middletennesseestateuniversity. The *Midlander* yearbooks (1926–2004) are available through the Internet Archives as digital images or in hardcopy in Special Collections, Walker Library, or the AGRC. The *Midlander* ceased publication in 2004.

7   References to the University of Tennessee's football team as the "Volunteers" began in 1902, and Vanderbilt's mascot has been portrayed as a naval officer since the 1880s due to the connection with its namesake, Cornelius Vanderbilt, and the shipping industry. The University of Memphis used the motto, "We fight like tigers!" after a football game in 1914, and Tennessee Tech's student body voted for the nickname, "Golden Eagles," in 1925. See James R. Montgomery, Stanley Folmsbee, and Lee S. Greene, *To Foster Knowledge: A History of the University of Tennessee, 1794–1970* (Knoxville: University of Tennessee Press, 1984), 350–51; Austin Wheeler Smith, *The Story of Tennessee Tech* (Nashville: McQuiddy Printing, 1957), 194–96; University of Memphis Athletic Department—Traditions, http://www.gotigersgo.com/trads/mem-mascot.html; Vanderbilt University, http://www.vanderbilt.edu/spirit/mascot.html.

8   Pittard, *First Fifty Years*, 150–51; Matt Bolch, "Name Chosen In Contest: Raider Name Evolved, But Not Without Controversy," *Daily News Journal*, undated, Forrest Mascot Controversy file, AGRC; "Economy Dictated Colors; Sarver Suggested 'Raider,'" *Mid-Stater Alumni Bulletin* 1, no. 2 (Spring 1960): 1–3; Bobby Newby, *They Bled Raider Blue* (self published, 1996), 25–26; "Everything But Confederate Money: Old Bed's in Trouble," *Mid-Stater* (Winter 1968), 8.

9   *Midlander*, 1936, 67.

10   Pittard, *First Fifty Years*, 152–59.

11   Ibid., 160--66. In 1995 Regina Forsythe interviewed 138 people about Quintin Miller Smith during his association with Middle Tennessee State University both as a student (1911–1913) and as president (1938–1958). These interviews of students, staff, friends, and classmates are in the Q. M. Smith Collection housed at the AGRC. "Quintin Miller Smith: A Brief Biography," Smith Collection, AGRC.

12   Pittard, *First Fifty Years*, 170–74.

13   Ibid., 177–84; Joe Nunley, *The Raider Forties* (New York: Vantage Press, 1977), 43.

14   Pittard, *First Fifty Years*, 151; Bloch, "Name Chosen in Contest"; Paul Ashdown and Edward Caudill, *The Myth of Nathan Bedford Forrest* (Lanham, MD: Roman & Littlefield Press, 2005), 5. According to Gene Sloan, MTSC's public relations director, he submitted the names of Forrest and John Hunt Morgan to Smith for final approval. Despite Morgan's Murfreesboro connections and that he was considered "more of a Raider than [Forrest]," Forrest's "first with the most" philosophy had a greater appeal to Smith. Sarver later said he opposed Smith's and Sloan's decision. "Economy Dictated Colors," *Mid-Stater* 1, no. 2 (Spring, 1960): 1, 3.

15   Ashdown and Caudill, *Myth of Nathan Bedford Forrest*, xvii–xviii; Eva M. Burkett, *American English Dialects in Literature* (London: Scarecrow Press, 1978), vii.

16   *Chicago Tribune*, 26 November 1941; *Chicago Tribune*, 1 March 1960; Court Carney, "The Contested Image of Nathan Bedford Forrest," *Journal of Southern History* 67 (2001): 601–30; "Everything But Confederate Money," 8.

17　Ashdown and Caudill, *Myth of Nathan Bedford Forrest*, 109; Andrew Nelson Lytle, *Bedford Forrest and his Critter Company* (New York: McDowell, Oblensky, 1960), xv; Robert Selph Henry, *First with the Most: General Nathan Bedford Forrest* (Indianapolis: Bobbs-Merrill, 1944), xx; or Field Marshal Viscount Garnet Joseph Wolseley, *The American Civil War: An English View*, ed. James A. Rawley (Mechanicsburg, PA: Stackpole Books, 2002), xxxiii; or "General Forrest," *United Service Magazine* 228 (1892), 1–14, 113–24. Henry quote cited used in *Midlander*, 1964, 2; Pittard, *First Fifty Years*, 149–50.

18　John Coski, *The Confederate Battle Flag: America's Most Embattled Emblem* (New York: Belknap Press, 2005), 112.

19　Paul Ashdown and Edward Caudill, *The Mosby Myth: A Confederate Hero in Life and Legend* (Wilmington, DE: Scholarly Resources, 2002), xxv, 141.

20　Bloch, "Name Chosen in Contest"; Gayle McCain, "Biggers, Smith, and Gracy Direct New Student Center," *Sidelines*, 4 March 1968. The University of Southern Mississippi's evolution, as well as their struggle with identity and memory, parallels that of MTSU's in many ways. See Chester M. Morgan, *Treasured Past, Golden Future: The Centennial History of the University of Southern Mississippi* (Jackson: The University Press of Mississippi, 2010).

21　Dedication of the Murphy, Forrest, and Todd Buildings, 25 March 1958, Dedication of the Nathan Bedford Forrest R.O.T.C. Building by Belt Keathley, http://content.mtsu.edu/cdm4/audiofiles/fifthieth/Dedication%20Forrest.mp3.

22　*Midlander*, 1956, 50.

23　Ruth Danehower Wilson, "Confederate Flag-Wavers," *Crisis* 59 (April 1952): 242, as quoted in Coski, *The Confederate Battle Flag*, 112. Constructed in 1953–54, the Forrest Hall dedication was delayed until 1958, as was customary, until all buildings in that particular funding outlay, including the library in 1958, had been completed. Thus, there is no evidence that the *Brown* decision affected the timetable for the dedication in order to make a political statement or avoid controversy. Although, curiously, the only image of the the Raider that appears in the 1964 *Midlander*, appears on the same page as Olivia Woods, MTSC's first African American graduate who enrolled in 1963. *Midlander*, 1964, 226.

24　"Yankee, Dick Shoonman, Plays Role of Southern General, 'Blue Raider,'" *Sidelines*, 7 November 1962; *Midlander*, 1962, 221.

25　"Does MTSU have an Inferiority Complex?," *Sidelines*, 19 April 1966.

26 *Midlander,* 1966, 3–9; and "School Spirit A Must," *Sidelines,* 21 March 1968. For examples of the dramatic change to a caricature-like appearance of the Raider, see the *Midlander,* 1966, 6 and 23, or "Raider's Raider on Display in Library," *Sidelines,* 16 May 1968.

27 *Midlander,* 1969, 83.

28 Sylvester Patrick Brooks, "*Dixie*: What Does It Mean?" *Sidelines,* 21 October 1968.

29 David C. Hooven, "Author Proud Of Heritage," *Sidelines,* 28 October 1968.

30 Tony B. Pendergrass, "Former Editor Looks For Hidden Question," *Sidelines,* 28 October 1968, 3.

31 Ron Thompson, "Smith Comments On 'Dixie,'" *Sidelines,* 24 October 1968.

32 Karen Thomas, "Rebel Flag Called Treasonous," *Sidelines,* 7 November 1968; Jim Leonard, "Praise for Brooks' Column," *Sidelines,* 24 October 1968.

33 Margaret Lowe Hibbett, letter to the editor, "Local Citizen Scorns Use Of Confederate Flag," *Sidelines,* 23 October 1968, 5.

34 David Mathis, "As I See It A Joke Ended 'Dixie,'" *Sidelines,* 19 December 1968, 4.

35 "Forrest to Stay: Pres. Scarlett Sent Decision," *Sidelines,* 19 December 1968, 1; Matt Bloch, "Many Mascots Have Cheered Fans," *Middle Tennessee State University Diamond Anniversary,* 7 September 1986, Special Collections, Walker Library, 10–11; Fact Sheet on MTSU Nathan Bedford Forrest/"Dixie" Controversy, 1990, Forrest Mascot Controversy File, AGRC.

36 "Cross Burning Initiates Protest by Blacks at President's Home," *Sidelines,* 11 December 1970, 1, 3.

37 "New Mascot and Symbol Debut on September 25," *Mid-Stater* (Fall 1976), 17.

38 *Midlander,* 1978.

39   Albert H. Baxendale, "Stand up for the cause: Removal of a plaque is another example of how our Southern Heritage is belittled," *Tennessean*, 17 May 1992; Sue S. Kolbe to Ed Murray, 22 February 1990; Ed Murray to John Bragg, 12 March 1990; "Fact Sheet on MTSU Nathan Bedford Forrest/'Dixie' Controversy," 1990, Forrest Mascot Controversy File, AGRC.

40   Norman R. Dasinger Jr. to Wallace Prescott, 25 February 1990, box 2, Nathan Bedford Forrest folder, John Bragg Collection, AGRC.

41   James Walker to Richard G. Soper, 25 February 1993, box 2, Nathan Bedford Forrest folder, John Bragg Collection, AGRC.

42   David Sansing, *The University of Mississippi: A Sesquicentennial History* (Hattiesburg: University Press of Mississippi, 1999), 275–76; "Ol' Miss Mascot Selection Committee," http://mascot.olemiss.edu; Rick Cleveland, "Colonel Not Exactly a Longtime Tradition," *Clarion Ledger*, 19 June 2003.

43   *Vanderbilt Ledger*, 2 September 2002, 5 May 2005, and 25 July 2005. Critics have also decried the use of Native American mascots and nicknames in collegiate and professional sports since the 1960s. In 2005 the National Collegiate Athletic Association (NCAA) directed member institutions to reassess their use of Native American symbols and names, resulting in numerous schools rebranding themselves, although there were a few high-profile holdouts, including Florida State University and the University of Utah.

44   "The Legend of Lightning," MTSU Athletic Department, 18 August 2003, http://www.goblueraiders.com/content.cfm/id/2171.

45   For a history of the Lightning Brigade, see Richard A. Baumgartner, *Blue Lightning: Wilder's Mounted Infantry Brigade in the Battle of Chickamauga* (Huntington, WV: Blue Acorn Press, 1997), and Robert S. Brandt, "Lightning and Rain in Middle Tennessee: The Campaign of June–July 1863," *Tennessee Historical Quarterly* 52 (Fall 1993): 158–69.

46   Biography of Brigadier General Nathan Bedford Forrest, III at http://www. arlingtoncemetery.net/forrest.htm.

47   Byron Hensley, "'An Educated Debate' on Forrest," *Daily News Journal*, 30 November 2006; Scott Broden, "MTSU Will Hold Forums to Discuss the Life of Forrest," *Daily News Journal*, 5 December 2006; Andy Harper and Josh Daugherty, "Forrest Battle Persists: City Sponsors Lecture, Hall Vandalized Over Weekend," *Sidelines*, 11 April 2007.

CHAPTER FIVE

Student Life in the 1930s

REUBEN KYLE

In the fall semester of 2011, the centennial year for Middle Tennessee State University (MTSU), about 3,000 incoming freshman students joined the more than 20,000 sophomores, juniors, seniors, and graduate students on campus. These students come from across the state of Tennessee, from across the country, and from around the world, yet only about 3,000, or 12 percent of the enrollment, actually make their home on campus. Many of the rest live in private apartments and houses within walking distance of campus, and thousands of others drive their cars and complain about the lack of parking. Tennessee residents now pay about $3,000 per semester to enroll in classes, with out-of-state students paying three times that amount. To gain admission, all prospective students have to demonstrate that they have a sufficiently high aptitude by means of standardized entrance exams and high school transcripts.

Contrast those images with the situation facing a student enrolling at State Teachers College (STC), Murfreesboro, as MTSU was known in the 1930s. In the fall quarter of 1935 about 150 freshmen entered Teachers College, as the students called it.[1] Total enrollment in the fall term numbered about 500 students with perhaps 350, or 70 percent, of those living on campus in three dormitories. (In the spring and summer quarters the total enrollment would increase with the arrival of teachers returning to complete requirements for a college degree.) The remainder lived at home somewhere in the area or in private boarding houses in Murfreesboro. In 1935 there was no tuition for Tennessee residents while the very few out-of-state students paid $30 per quarter. All students also paid a quarterly registration fee of $15 and an activity fee of $3, and some paid minor lab fees.[2] Admission requirements for Tennessee residents were that students have completed "the full four-year course of an approved high school."[3] In a day when completing high school was not common, this latter requirement was no mean accomplishment.

The 1935 campus covered 250 acres with five principal buildings arranged around the building we now know as Kirksey Old Main. Students lived in three dormitories, two for the women and one for the men, and attended class in Old Main or the new science building. Today the campus covers 500 acres and comprises nearly 140 buildings. Parking has become a major inconvenience for students as well as for faculty, staff, and visitors. In 1935 only a few faculty members and very few students drove to campus. Commuting students either walked or rode their bicycles or, if they lived outside of town on nearby farms, shared rides to campus.

Today's students would have a difficult time finding much familiar on the 1930s campus. Rules imposed on students, particularly upon the women, would seem very strange. Women wore skirts or dresses to class; shorts were definitely not allowed outside of physical education classes. Women residents were required to sign out whenever they left the Rutledge or Lyon Hall dormitories. Supervision of the men was less strict but an assistant football coach served as "Dormitory Daddy." With the relatively small student body, the faculty—and even the President—often knew many students personally. For most, living away from home was a privilege and a novelty so the majority of students were serious. "We thought it was wonderful to go to breakfast and wonderful to be at an 8 o'clock class." It would be the unusual student of today who expressed those sentiments. With fewer opportunities and distractions, the small campus community was closer knit than is the case today. On Wednesday nights following dinner there was dancing in the cafeteria. Some students even stayed on the weekends to attend ball games on Saturday. Simply put, the 1930s decade was a different time at a different institution.

Without question, dormitory life can be a memorable part of the college experience. Frances Sweeney Brandon, who attended Teachers College between 1934 and 1939, lived in Lyon Hall. She described the dorm rooms as having no bathrooms, only a lavatory, with each floor sharing a communal bath with shower stalls. As Frances noted, "[W]e thought we were very modern." Frances and her roommate, a friend from her Nashville elementary school, shared a double bed. Because the room was large enough, another single bed was added in their sophomore year to accommodate a student who needed to be on the first floor. The rooms were "neat, not glamorous," painted gray or blue and white. Most students brought their own lamps because the lighting was not adequate for studying. Frances's room was on a corner with a view of the campus grounds. There was one telephone for all four floors of the dormitory. In the lobby of Lyon there was an old grand piano that anyone was allowed to play.[4] Life in Rutledge Hall was similar. Anne Davis Lokey described her room as having twin beds and a dresser. Her room was on the ground floor and had two big windows. In those times, before air conditioning, the windows certainly were appreciated.[5]

In the dorms, the women often shared snacks brought from home on the weekends. Anne reported a time when she and her dorm mates planned to celebrate her birthday. They were warming some sausages on a hot plate—no microwaves then—and enjoying soft drinks when one girl developed a severe pain that turned out to be an attack of appendicitis. The dorm mother had to be called in and she contacted a doctor. She also, naturally, smelled the sausages, and the party came to an end. Leona O'Neil Murphy reported a similar experience when someone tried to fix popcorn in her room. The aroma gave the party away.[6]

The rules for women students living in the dormitories were very strict. A bell signaled lights out at 10 p.m. After supper at the cafeteria a couple could walk back to the dorm, but they had to be there by 6:30 p.m. According to Charles Murphy, "[T]hat was your date that night." In the spring, as the days grew longer, the time was extended to 7 p.m.[7] Residents could receive special permission to study in the reception room of Lyon Hall, but they had to at least have paper or a notebook to show that they were working. Men were not allowed in the dormitory. If a man—a maintenance man or parent—did appear in the dorm, a call would be sounded, "Man in the hall."

The campus night watchman, C.W. Daniels, kept an eye on couples returning to the dorms at curfew. Leona Murphy recalled that Daniels "had a little flashlight that he carried around . . . he would come around there with that flashlight and flash on you and say 'all right, move on.'" Her husband, Charles, added, "A boy would try to get his girl in the doorway to hug on her a little bit and [Daniels] would flash that light and make you move on." So the men students decided to "get even with him." "[W]e all got referee whistles and got on different parts of the campus and blow the whistle . . . he would dash over there, someone on the other side would blow the whistle and he would dash over to the other side . . . ." The students then named him Dashing Dan.

Life in the men's dorm, Jones Hall, was also interesting. Even though he did not live in the dorm, William Patterson spent many nights in Jones Hall. The men's rooms had concrete floors and plaster walls with beds on either side and an open closet at the head of each bed.[8] According to Patterson, "They might have had a couple of desks in there but that was it."[9] There was some disagreement over the extent of the rules in the men's dorm. As Patterson commented, "Forget the house rules. Everybody broke them." On the other hand, Charles Murphy remembered that Coach Nooby Freeman was in charge of Jones Hall during his years at Teachers College. Freeman, in Murphy's words, was strict about the men keeping their rooms neat. He would check twice a week and if a room did not meet his standards "he would give you a little extra work to do . . . ." Lights had to be out at 11 p.m. —except for athletes during their sport's season; players had to be in their rooms by 9 p.m. Murphy remembered that Freeman "was real strict . . . you had to dress properly . . . he was like a second father to you . . . ." So, though not to the extent of the women students, men at STC also had strict rules to follow.

Hazing was common among both men and women students. They held a kangaroo court that might call freshmen students out of their beds at night to be "tried" by upperclassmen. A student would be brought to a room lit only by candlelight and quizzed on her behavior and knowledge of the rules. She was asked questions such as, "Are you minding the rules of the dormitory? Do you sign the book when you go out? Are you smoking in your room?" Frances Brandon recalled, "[W]hen you went into kangaroo court they make some ugly, weird noises, like ghosts or something, and when you went back to bed that night, you didn't sleep anymore." The punishment of the court would be an assignment to serve an upperclass woman student, such as making her bed or sweeping her room.[10] Leona Murphy remembered that "it went off all right as long as you were a good sport." Frances Brandon reported that she became head of the kangaroo court in her second year. But she decided that it was "inhumane" and dispensed assignments only halfheartedly. On reflection, she said later that it taught the "girls to be neat . . . " and so it "was a pretty good plan." For the boys, hazing was much more severe but it happened in the open in front of Old Main. The men students would run a belt line in addition to being forced to clean rooms, put out the garbage, and take sheets to the campus laundry.

The men also played tricks on each other in the dorm. One trick involved removing the furniture from a person's room without his knowing about it. Called "stacking" a room, the tricksters would move the furniture to the porch of Jones Hall. In one case, according to William Patterson, a student was intercepted on his way to his room and enlisted in stacking a room only to discover when finished that it was his own room. Both Patterson and Charles Murphy were the targets of some of these pranks. As Patterson recalled, "Back when I was on the football squad, I'd come back from home, and [his Model A Ford with a rumble seat] would be hanging up a tree, or they'd jack up the back wheels a little bit—right off the ground where it wouldn't run." In another instance, Murphy and another student bought a Model T Ford for $14 or $15. They painted it blue and white and called it "Little Audry." One day Charles found that the car was missing, only to discover that some others had moved it to the porch of Old Main. The President thought that Charles himself had done it and "raised Cain with us . . . . We had a hard time getting that thing down."

The women "stacked" rooms, too. Isa Lee Sherrod Freeman worked as a librarian at Teachers College from 1935 to 1940 and lived in Lyon Hall. Once, while Isa Lee was attending a concert in Nashville, the students stacked her room and "draped toilet paper all over." Fortunately for Isa Lee, Margaret Mitchell, the hostess of the dorm and dean of women discovered the trick and made the students clean the room before Isa Lee returned.[11] Clearly, women students were not to be outdone by the men.

MTSU students have, since the early 1970s, enjoyed a variety of options for meals. Today, on campus, several cafeterias and the Grill offer many choices, from complete meals to burgers and sushi. Off campus there are even more choices, ranging from the familiar fast-food places to sit-down restaurants. In the 1930s, however, eating establishments near campus were limited. A Mr. Bach operated a tearoom across the street now known as Middle Tennessee Boulevard. A plate lunch cost 25 cents. On campus, there was a single cafeteria and students typically purchased meal tickets for five or ten cents each or $6 for a book that was good for a month or six weeks. A lost meal ticket book was a disaster. According to Frances Brandon "[e]veryone was hungry." The country was suffering in the Great Depression and money was scarce.

The cafeteria was located in what later became Alumni Hall and is now known as the Tom H. Jackson Building, which now houses the News and Public Affairs office. In the 30s the cafeteria was, Charles Murphy remembered, where "everyone ate at the same place. . . and where you got to know people . . . ." Obviously, the cafeteria was an important site for students and the sense of community there was strong. A story about one student, who was struggling to stay in school, demonstrates just how strong. Students brought their coupon books to the cafeteria and a coupon would be torn out when they selected their food. This particular student, who was short on money, would go to the cafeteria with tickets that had already been used. He did this, evidently, with the connivance of another student working in the cafeteria. As William Patterson stated, "That's the way that boy existed. Everybody in the school knew he was doing it, and nobody said anything about it. But that was the kind of school it was then."

Another place students gathered was Old Main, both on the front steps and in the lobby. Leona Murphy recalled, "They didn't have those rails up . . . Everybody just sat around outside on the steps. That was just the place to come and kind of congregate, talk, and get acquainted." William Patterson also remembered the steps as "a great place to sit around and loaf . . . and dodge the teachers. They'd be coming up the sidewalk and you'd hide behind the columns and cut class. It was a great day." Maybe the students of the 1930s were not so different from those of today.

One regular campus activity was chapel, which all students were required to attend two or three times per week; although, apparently not every student abided by this rule. Charles Murphy remembered that the football coach expected his players to attend. Anne and James Lokey recalled going to chapel, too. James remembered that Miss E. May Saunders, for whom the Saunders Fine Arts Building is named, always called for the singing of the same hymn whenever there was a guest attending chapel. "[I]t was the funniest thing to watch the people start to get the songbooks out and turning to 'Onward Christian Soldiers' to have it ready before she announced the song . . . ."

Students also worked together to support the campus entrepreneur, Randy Wood from Morrison, Tennessee, who operated a store from his dorm room in Jones Hall. John Bragg, a student in the class of 1940, said that Wood kept an icebox—not a refrigerator but a box that used ice to cool things—from which he sold soft drinks. In addition, he sold Moon Pies, razor blades, and other things. One weekend Wood left campus forgetting to empty the ice. When the ice melted, the water ran into Coach Nooby Freeman's room. President Q. M. Smith almost kicked shopkeeper Wood out of school.[12] Years later, after graduating from Teachers College and following World War II, Randy Wood became an important entrepreneur in the music business. He was the owner of Randy's Record Shop in Gallatin, Tennessee, founder of Dot Records, and producer of many hit popular records from 1950 through the 1970s. He also became a great benefactor of MTSU in later years.

Women students also participated in entrepreneurial ventures. They had a laundry located behind Old Main. To have a sheet laundered cost 25 cents. Men, on the other hand, did not have a laundry. One student would pick up laundry and dry cleaning in the dorm and take it to town. As mentioned, part of the hazing of both women and men students involved collecting the laundry for upperclass women and men. Clearly, STC students during the 1930s were inventive outside the classroom.

Attention to academic work was expected and skipping classes was frowned upon. Many of those interviewed for the Q. M. Smith Oral History Collection remembered that they did not have much to do as students except to go to class and study. Still, students were students. In a handout to new freshmen students in the fall quarter of 1937, the following observation was offered: "This is your first time to register in college. You will have in college more freedom than you have had in high school." Lurlene Dill Rushing was surprised on her arrival to find that very freedom. "What impressed me was that no one cared whether you did your homework or studied. It was a very free situation." When asked what his major was, William Patterson replied: "Well, let's see, everything that came after 9 a.m. and then in the afternoon." On beginning his junior year, as required by the college bulletin, he was asked the same question by the dean. "'Bill, you're supposed to be a junior now, what are you majoring in?' I said 'what's that?'...That's how some of us were doing in school. We were taking the things that we liked." Nonetheless, Bill was happy with his experience at Teachers College. "We had the best professors, without a doubt, the best anywhere."

Another memory related by Patterson concerned his experience in economics class. Taken during Patterson's freshman year, the economics course was taught by William Benton Judd, and the class included James Buchanan, another freshman. Patterson sat next to Buchanan, "and I learned as much from him [as from the professor]. He helped me get through, so I always said that 'that boy is going somewhere.'" Today, Buchanan ranks among the most distinguished of Teachers College graduates as a world-renowned scholar and winner of the 1986 Nobel Prize in Economic Science.

Sports have been popular at the institution from its founding. When he first entered Teachers College in the mid-1930s, John Bragg stated that there was no football stadium but games were played in a field behind the science building. During his student years the football stadium and the Alumni Memorial Gym were built. Bragg reported that many students stayed on campus during the weekend to attend football games on Saturday night. An athlete himself, John Bragg was a star baseball player and played basketball and golf as well during his Teachers College years. Later in life John Bragg served in the Tennessee legislature and was a highly respected member of that body for many years. The Bragg Mass Communications building is named for him.

Charles "Bubber" Murphy is remembered as, perhaps, the greatest all-round athlete ever to play for Middle Tennessee State. He played football, basketball, baseball, and tennis between 1935 and 1938, but baseball was his favorite sport. The baseball diamond was in front of the science building in 1937–38 and the library, where Peck Hall is now located, was in center field. Murphy recalled, "Sometimes the baseball would be hit over in the Faculty Library." After graduating, he signed a contract to play professional baseball for a signing bonus of $100. He played professional ball for two or three years after leaving Teachers College. Following his service in World War II, Murphy returned to become head football coach and athletic director. Murphy Center is named for him.

Unlike today's students, a very high percentage of whom work as they attend school, the students of the 1930s did not typically have jobs off campus, although some did work on campus. Leona O'Neil Murphy, for example, along with her twin sister Leota, got a National Youth Administration (NYA) job on campus.[13] Leona and Leota shared $15 a month to assist teachers in the Training School.[14] Leona said that she helped "with the children and remedial work and things like that." Lida Loughry Lasseter worked as a grader for a history teacher. Her pay was $5 per month. In addition, she assisted with some student testing for which she was paid about two or three dollars for each group tested for grade placement. She recalled: "I suppose it was to see how the rural schools ranked with the city schools . . . ."[15] Others worked in the cafeteria, and Isa Lee Freeman remembered that some football players worked in the library. "They hated it but they had to have some kind of work for their scholarship."

Madison Dill, a member of the class of 1940, held a job managing instruments and sheet music for the Music Department. Later he became the student director of music, a job for which he did receive "a small sum."[16] John Bragg became editor of *Sidelines*, the student newspaper, and in compensation received a dormitory room; previously he had lived at home. Bragg also became a stringer—a reporter paid by the column rather on salary—for the *Tennessean* newspaper writing sports stories. He was paid 10 cents for each story the paper ran.

A more unusual case of student employment was that of Whitney Stegall, an STC student in the middle 1930s. When he entered Teachers College he remembered having only two and a half dollars in his pocket but, "much to the disgust of some of the professors," he was assisted in enrolling. When asked what students did for fun, he replied: "I worked." In return for his room, breakfast, and supper, he was a janitor at Aunt Bette's boarding house on the corner of Highland and Lytle streets. For lunch he was on his own. When asked what he did on weekends, he replied, "Well, the second year, I worked for Woodfin–Moore Funeral Home. I drove the ambulance and assisted with funerals." He had a furnished room over the funeral home and lived there until he graduated.[17]

In the 1930s, just as today, many students did not live on campus. Most of those living off campus lived at home, and that meant in or near Murfreesboro. John Bragg and Madison Dill, both from local families, always lived at home, except for the short time that Bragg was given the dormitory room. Another member of the class of 1940, James Buchanan, recalled that he only came to campus to attend class; otherwise he was needed on the family farm outside of town.[18]

The day students used assigned lockers under the gymnasium for storage, and the spot became a meeting place. They referred to themselves as the "locker room boys." Buchanan recalled that they spent a lot of time shooting craps, playing pickup basketball, and horseshoes. Among this group, in addition to Buchanan, were Cranor Elrod, Ralph McGee, Ed Loughry, Marshall Duggan, and Grover Maxwell. Ed Loughry became a banker and a prominent member of the Murfreesboro community. Maxwell became a distinguished professor and scholar of the philosophy of science at the University of Minnesota.[19]

James Buchanan grew up on a farm south of Murfreesboro in the community of Gum. During his years at Teachers College he lived at home and rode to campus with a minister who lived in the area while working on a degree at the college. Buchanan recalled life on the farm in his memoir:

> there was work: plowing, manuring, harrowing, planting, cultivating, hoeing, haying, threshing, picking, milking, herding, feeding—work for long hours on days during growing seasons and in weather foul and fair throughout the year.[20]

The 1940 yearbook, next to James Buchanan's senior class picture, lists as his only activities membership in the Science Club and the Sigma Club, the latter being an honor society of "serious-minded men interested in intellectual and cultural development and actuated by worthy aims."[21] While he noted that he might have been more challenged at another institution, he also admitted that he could have taken greater advantage of the intellectual opportunities available to him at Teachers College. Still, he managed multiple majors in English, mathematics, and social science. Among the people who influenced his intellectual life were Ann Ordway and Eva Mai Burkett in English, and William Mebane in physics, and especially Dr. C. C. Sims who inspired him eventually to attend the University of Chicago where he earned his doctorate in economics in 1947. Other students also remembered Dr. Sims as an exceptional teacher.

There were women students, as well, who came to campus only for class and study. Like Buchanan, Lida Loughry Lasseter came from a farm family; her family lived in Lascassas on the north side of Murfreesboro. They had no electricity and raised much of their own food. Besides growing corn and wheat, "[w]e had beef, lamb, pork all from the farm." As for school, "[i]t was all just going to school as far as I can remember."

Katherine Butler Holden lived in Murfreesboro and was among the very few students who drove a car to campus. She recalled that she parked in front of Old Main and that there was "[n]o parking problem whatsoever . . . ." Katherine attended Teachers College for two years beginning in 1935 before transferring to Randolph Macon College in Virginia. Prior to entering Teachers College she attended the Demonstration School when it was located in Old Main.[22]

Mary Lurlene Dill Rushing lived about two and a half miles from campus. She was able to ride to campus with her sister but walked home after classes.[23] Another town student was Geraldine Eaton Garner who lived at home and walked to campus. She says that, like many others, she could not afford to attend any other school. Like James Buchanan, she also had three majors: biology, English, and social studies. As a serious student, Geraldine finished her bachelor's degree in three years at the age of 19. Sadly, she was a victim of the inadequate opportunities for women college graduates during that era. After she graduated she returned to campus for a business course so that she could work as a secretary for a building contractor. Later she married a pharmacist and helped him manage a pharmacy in Murfreesboro. That business is still in existence as Beckman's Pharmacy.[24]

Another student who maintained ties with Murfreesboro was Thelma Jennings, who attended Teachers College in the late 1930s. She lived in Wilson County, about 17 miles from Murfreesboro, and commuted to campus with a young man from Statesville. A number of Jennings's cousins had attended Teachers College, and she preferred to go there rather than to Cumberland College in Lebanon, Tennessee. As a commuter she was not involved in campus activities during the two years she was in the Permanent Professional Elementary Certificate program. She came to class and studied in the library so that she could begin her teaching career as soon as possible. She returned to Middle Tennessee State College later, however, and earned her BS degree in 1953. Still later, in 1962, she returned to earn an MA degree. Jennings eventually received a PhD from the University of Tennessee and joined the faculty of the Middle Tennessee State University History Department in 1966.[25]

In the early 1930s Albert Gore, later US Senator Gore and father of Vice President Al Gore, did his student teaching during his years at Teachers College. Katherine Holden remembered, "He was such a cutup. . . the story was that he was the only person that ever flunked practice teaching. It made a good tale anyway." Isa Lee Freeman also remembered Albert Gore attending sporting events after he graduated. "He would stand at the door and shake hands with every person and call them by name when they came in or out. . . . He was always interested in politics."[26]

Students of State Teachers College, Murfreesboro, of the 1930s did find plenty of activities. Remember that John Bragg was an athlete playing basketball, baseball, and golf. He was editor of *Sidelines* and advertising manager of the *Midlander*, the college yearbook. He began his political career at Teachers College as president of the freshman class of 1936 and was president of the Associated Student Body in 1940. His friend, Madison Dill, was active in the Music Department and was president of the senior class of 1940.

James Lokey, who attended Teachers College from 1931 to 1935, organized the first school marching band, ultimately named the Band of Blue, in October 1931. James had begun learning to play the trumpet as a freshman in high school. He took the initiative to gather 20 musicians to form the band and march at halftime during football games. The band of 20 marched the length of the field while playing "Our Director March" and returned to the center of the field to form a T where they played the Alma Mater. On Thanksgiving Day 1931, the new band took their first road trip to Tennessee Preparatory Institute, in Nashville, with James as the band leader. In 1934 he asked the president, then P. A. Lyon, to assist the band in accompanying the football team scheduled to play the University of Chattanooga. As the college was in difficult financial straits, the president could not help, so James approached the

Nashville, Chattanooga, and St. Louis Railway. He offered to recruit 200 students to take the train to Chattanooga if the company would give them a low fare. The company agreed to provide two cars on the train and to allow the band to ride free if James could get the students. He recalled that they paid less than two dollars and that the 200 students made the trip along with the band. Although the Teachers College football team lost the game, the students and the band had a great trip.[27]

James Lokey also helped to organize the first dance on campus in 1935. President Lyon was able to get permission for the occasion, and he asked Lokey to locate an orchestra. Because of concern for the women students, Lokey arranged for the matron of the women's dormitories to chaperone the dance and the women. In later years dances were held every Wednesday night in the school cafeteria.

From the perspective of the twenty-first century, student life at State Teachers College, Murfreesboro, seems limited and hard to imagine. Nevertheless, the students from the 1930s looked back on those days as a happy time in their lives. Despite the generational differences and the changes brought about by new technologies, there is continuity in college life. The goal of colleges in the 1930s, and in the twenty-first century, is to introduce young men and women to the world of ideas and to let them begin to experience life as adults. In recounting student life in the 1930s, it is clear that STC, later to become MTSU, succeeded in advancing this mission.

NOTES

1   [Editor's Note:] Although the official name of the school was Middle
Tennessee State Teachers College, it was widely known as State Teachers College,
Murfreesboro. Students of the period referred to the school simply as "Teachers
College."

2   *Bulletin of the State Teachers College, Murfreesboro* (May 1935), Special
Collections, James Walker Library, Middle Tennessee State University,
Murfreesboro, TN, 26.

3   *Bulletin of the State Teachers College, Murfreesboro* (July 1934), Special
Collections, Walker Library, 18.

4   Howell Frances Sweeney Brandon, interview by Regina Forsythe, transcripts
QMS.1995.95–96, Q. M. Smith Oral History Collection, Albert Gore Research
Center (AGRC), Middle Tennessee State University, Murfreesboro, TN (hereinafter
cited as Smith Collection; all interviews in the collection were conducted by Regina
Forsythe).

5   Anne Davis Lokey, transcript QMS.1995.113, Smith Collection, AGRC.

6   Leona O'Neil Murphy, transcripts QMS.1995.42–44, Smith Collection,
AGRC.

7   Charles Murphy, transcripts QMS.1995.42–44, Smith Collection, AGRC.

8   This writer's first office on campus in 1972 was in one of those old dorm rooms
and, aside from the beds, they remained as Patterson describes.

9   William Lytle Patterson, transcript QMS.1995.7, Smith Collection, AGRC.

10 Brandon interview.

11 Isa Lee Sherrod Freeman, transcript QMS.1995.17, Smith Collection, AGRC.

12 John Thomas Bragg, transcripts QMS.1995.82–83, Smith Collection, AGRC.

13 National Youth Administration, http://www.archives.gov/research/guide-fed-
records/groups/119.html.

14 From its founding in 1911 the institution included an elementary school that also served as a teacher training facility. Over the years the name has been variously the Training School, the Demonstration School, the Campus School, and now the Homer Pittard Campus School.

15 Lida Loughry Lasseter, transcript QMS.1995.2, Smith Collection, AGRC.

16 Jesse Madison Dill, transcript QMS.1995.69, Smith Collection, AGRC.

17 Whitney Stegall, transcript QMS.1995.22, Smith Collection, AGRC.

18 James M. Buchanan, *Economics from the Outside In: "Better Than Plowing" and Beyond* (College Station: Texas A&M University Press, 2007).

19 Personal correspondence from James M. Buchanan, 1 March 2010. Professor Maxwell left Middle Tennessee Teachers College and transferred to the University of Tennessee where he graduated in 1941. http://special.lib.umn.edu/findaid/xml/uarc00480.xml.

20 Buchanan, *Economics from the Outside In*, 20.

21 *Midlander*, 1940, see Sigma Club, AGRC. *Midlander* yearbooks are located in the AGRC; online at http://library.mtsu.edu/digitalprojects/mtsumemory.php; and Special Collections, Walker Library.

22 Katherine Butler Holden, transcript QMS.1995.110, Smith Collection, AGRC.

23 Mary Lurlene Dill Rushing, transcript QMS.1995.125, Smith Collection, AGRC.

24 Geraldine Eaton Garner, transcript QMS.1995.32, Smith Collection, AGRC.

25 Thelma Jennings, transcript QMS.1995.1, Smith Collection, AGRC.

26 Holden interview.

27 James Lokey, transcript QMS.1995.113, Smith Collection, AGRC.

CHAPTER SIX

Victories and Defeats

Intercollegiate Sports History

FRED P. COLVIN

THE EARLY YEARS: 1911–1919

Middle Tennessee State Normal School opened for classes on September 11, 1911, as a combined two-year college and a four-year high school. Given the many tasks facing the administration, little attention was devoted to creating extracurricular student organizations and athletic teams in the fall quarter, but during the winter quarter two developments occurred that had a significant impact on the school's future athletic program. President Robert L. Jones appointed a committee of faculty members, Jeannette Moore King and Tommie Reynolds, and student Q. M. Smith to consider and recommend school colors to promote school spirit and affiliation. The committee selected blue and white, and the administration approved the choice. Blue and white have remained the color scheme of the school and its athletic teams throughout the school's existence. The second development was that a group of male students asked the administration to permit the formation of a baseball team to represent the school in interscholastic competition. President Jones was not opposed to a baseball team, but he told the young men that there was no coach among the school's original faculty. Max Souby, a history professor and sports fan, volunteered to supervise the players and Jones agreed to the arrangement. Baseball thus became the school's first sport and Souby the first "coach." During the spring quarter 1912, the baseball team played several nearby schools.

During the 1912–13 academic year limited progress occurred in the school's athletic program. A football team was formed during the fall and was coached by student and team member Lee "Mutt" Miller. Jeannette King, the physical education instructor, assisted Miller in securing uniforms for the young men. Only one score has survived from what was probably a short season. Middle Tennessee State Normal defeated Fitzgerald and Clark Academy of Tullahoma by a score of 6–0. There appears to have been little support for the school's first football team from either the faculty or the majority of the student body. The *Signal*, the school's first student publication, was very critical of the lack of support given to the team. Efforts by some students to form a men's basketball team in the winter failed, but the school did field a second baseball squad under Souby in the spring.

The real birth of interscholastic athletics at Middle Tennessee came in the fall of 1913, when President Jones hired Alfred B. Miles to teach biology and coach all athletic teams. Miles was a native of Rutherford County and had been a local star high school athlete in Murfreesboro. He had recently completed his studies in physical education at a normal school located in Michigan before joining the faculty. Miles's duties as an academic instructor first and coach second remained the norm for Middle Tennessee for decades to come. He had to deal with a variety of circumstances and deficiencies that shaped the character and scope of the school's sports program for years. Due to a small number of males at Middle Tennessee Normal, it was necessary to use both high school and college students on the teams. The only type of practical scheduling for athletic contests was to play nearby public high schools, private preparatory academies, and colleges. This type of mixed competition remained in effect until Middle Tennessee Normal was elevated to full college status in 1925.

Another problem early athletics faced was the lack of adequate equipment and playing facilities. Both the football and baseball teams practiced and played their home games on a large field in the general area of where Todd Hall and the science buildings are now located. There were no permanent stands; portable bleachers were positioned to accommodate the type of game being played. There was, however, a permanent baseball backstop in the area constructed of wood and chicken wire. The most serious facility problem was the lack of a gymnasium on the school's original campus.

When Miles arrived on campus, he had the nucleus of a football program inherited from Mutt Miller. The 1913 team did well, playing against largely high school teams. The team went 5-1-1, tying Vanderbilt's B team and losing only to Morgan School of Petersburg. During the winter of 1913–14, Miles organized the school's first official men's basketball squad. Only three games were scheduled that year, since they had to use the gym of a local high school. The team was beaten 53–5 by Vanderbilt in the first basketball game in the school's history. The club's only victory came in the final game of the season played in Murfreesboro; Middle Tennessee Normal defeated Dixie College, a high school which later evolved into Tennessee Tech, by the score of 27–13. The *Signal*, in its February issue, described the school's first basketball win in this fashion: "The lot fell to Dixie College and here they came—a good big bunch of freckled-faced—corn fed boys from the region of Cookeville." This less than flattering description of the "boys from Cookeville" may represent the beginning of a very intense and sometimes bitter rivalry between Middle Tennessee State and Tennessee Tech that lasted for many decades. During the spring of 1914, Miles's first baseball squad did reasonably well against local high schools, Vanderbilt, Western Kentucky, and Sewanee. It should be noted that it is hard to reconstruct the history of the early decades of Middle Tennessee baseball because of the lack of official records until the 1950s.

In 1914 Miles led the football team to a 5-0-1 record, producing the first undefeated but tied team in the school's history. Basketball was again a major disappointment. While the team went 2-2, the difficulties associated with the absence of a gymnasium led Miles and the school's administration to agree to drop the sport for the immediate future. Football and baseball became the only sports at the school for the next several years.

With the entrance of the United States into World War I in the spring of 1917, Coach Miles and many of Normal's male students left the school to join the nation's war effort. Miles joined the YMCA's program to assist American servicemen. Many colleges and universities suspended their athletic programs in 1917, but Middle Tennessee did not; however, there was no coach for the 1917 football season. Johnny "Red" Floyd, who had played for Miles in 1914 before going to Vanderbilt's program, which was now inactive, returned to Murfreesboro and convinced President Jones to allow him to coach the team. Floyd brought a spirit of determination to a squad of 17 players selected from a greatly reduced male student population. Led by Captain V. P. "Putty" Overall, Jess Neely, Cas Miles, and Rupert Smith, Floyd's squad forged the school's first undefeated, untied season, outscoring its seven opponents 201–0. Yet in 1918 Middle Tennessee suspended its athletic program for the duration of the war.

THE INTERWAR YEARS: 1919–1942

During the interwar period, 1919–1942, Middle Tennessee experienced many changes and major developments in the school and athletic program. Miles returned as coach in 1919 and remained until 1924. His 1919 football team went 6-0-0, but in his last four seasons he compiled only a 12-10-1 record. Miles produced a number of outstanding football players who went on to star at Vanderbilt. Among those were V. P. Overall, Johnny "Red" Floyd, and Jess Neely. Of these three, Neely went on to national fame as a college football coach. He served as head coach of two major universities, Clemson and Rice. He won over two hundred games in his career with a 4-3 record in bowl games. Neely was selected to the National College Football Hall of Fame in 1971.

The most significant development in Miles's last years at Middle Tennessee was the construction of a gymnasium and the resumption of basketball. The new gym was just north of Kirksey Old Main, the administration building. Miles led the men's basketball team to a record of 24-2 in his last two seasons at the school. The existence of a modern gym, plus the popularity of women's high school basketball in Tennessee as well as the strong women's intramural program at Middle Tennessee Normal, led the school to start its first interscholastic sport for women. Miss Tommie Reynolds organized the first women's team; however, she was replaced as coach by Guy Stephenson. Stephenson later replaced Miles as the primary coach in the fall of 1924.

Guy Stephenson's tenure as head coach lasted only two seasons. A major development during his era was the elevation of the school to a four-year college, and this meant that the school had to drop all games with high school teams. Stephenson had relatively little success with men's football and basketball. The women's basketball teams, however, proved to be very successful. In 1925–26, the women went undefeated. They defeated the powerful Peabody College squad, which had been the state and southern champion for the past three seasons. At the conclusion of the 1925–26 season, Stephenson's squad claimed the southern championship with a victory over the Women's College of Alabama.

In the fall of 1926 Frank Albert Faulkinberry was hired as Middle Tennessee State Teachers College head coach. During his tenure, 1926–1933, he became a very popular and influential figure among the school's faculty, student body, and the Murfreesboro community. Faulkinberry was a native of Lincoln County, and he had been a three-sport athlete at the University of the South at Sewanee. He had also been selected as an All-Southern football player, had considerable coaching experience at the high school level in Tennessee and Alabama schools, and he had served as an army officer in World War I. Faulkinberry was also a classroom instructor, teaching several sections of Latin each term. The Faulkinberry era at Middle Tennessee was one of changes, accomplishments, and ultimately great tragedy.

As football coach, Faulkinberry posted a 33-26-4 record, with only two losing seasons. He was the first coach in the school's history to schedule ten football games in a season. His 1927 football team defeated North Alabama 76–7, still the school record for the largest number of points scored in a game. The more unusual games he scheduled were a home game and an away series with the University of Miami in 1931 and 1932. Faulkinberry's teams won both games by shutouts, and the team's trip to Miami was the longest distance yet traveled by a Middle Tennessee team. Another major development was Middle Tennessee's admission to an athletic conference. In 1931 the school joined the Southern Intercollegiate Athletic Association, a large conference of small colleges spread across the Old Confederacy. Admission to a conference meant conforming to higher standards and rules. The rule that most impacted Middle Tennessee was that freshmen were ineligible for varsity teams. As a football coach, Faulkinberry produced a number of outstanding players, and among these players were John "Pink" Dixon, Winstead Moore, Henry Hackman, Smartt Parris, Robert Kerr, and Jack Delay.

In basketball Faulkinberry amassed a 48-42 record against college, club, and AAU teams. His best squad was the 1929–30 team that the *Midlander* asserted was the best in school history. The team went 16-6 with victories over Vanderbilt, Western Kentucky, and Tennessee Tech. While records are fragmentary, his baseball squad was certainly competitive as well.

Faulkinberry's greatest success, however, came with women's basketball. Inheriting an already powerful squad from Stephenson, his teams compiled an outstanding record during the late 1920s and early 1930s against colleges, YWCAs, AAUs, and industrial league teams. During this period, women's basketball may very well have been the most popular and prestigious campus sport. The 1928 *Midlander* reported that the team was held in awe by the student body, and it was "truly an honor to be coveted to be a member of the team." Faulkinberry's teams captured both the so-called state and southern championships as well as participated in several postseason tournaments with good success. The best-known female basketball star of this era was Mary Beasley, a member of the Blue Raider Hall of Fame. Other outstanding players were Wilma Towry, Bess Palmer, and Emma Dillon.

During his years as coach, Faulkinberry forged a strong relationship with players, students, alumni, and faculty. This is clear from recurring comments in the student yearbook. In 1929, the *Midlander* said that he was "held in the highest esteem by the men under him, and by the students, coach is loved and respected by all. . . ." Again in 1930 the yearbook praised him: "Mr. Faulkinberry is not only a coach, but he is a molder of character. His firm, though friendly manner of approach, has won him a place in the hearts of every student. . . ."

Yet on May 13, 1933, at approximately 10:30 a.m., Frank Faulkinberry died of a self-inflicted gunshot wound to the head at this home on Crestland Avenue. The abrupt suicide of the successful and respected coach stunned the students, faculty, and public alike. On Monday, May 15, Faulkinberry's funeral was held in the school's auditorium with an overflowing crowd of students, former players, alumni, faculty, and public in attendance. A huge motorcade accompanied the body for burial in his hometown of Blanche, Tennessee.

At the time of Faulkinberry's death, the 1933 *Midlander* was ready to go to press, but students hastily revised the publication in order to dedicate the yearbook to him. Neal Frazier, head of the English Department, wrote a memorial statement for inclusion in the yearbook, which probably captured the sentiments of the moment as well as anyone could have. Among his thoughts were these: "Shocked beyond measure was his host of friends by the tragedy of a death to which he seems to have been driven by brooding over the approaching calamity of broken health and failing strength." He added: "Many young men and young women are bowed down in grief . . . at this sudden departure. Many were close to him; many loved him." Frank Faulkinberry had a profound impact in his day. His contributions and place in MTSU's athletic history are still recognized today. He was among the earliest inductees into the Blue Raider Hall of Fame, and a campus street bears the name of this beloved coach. Faulkinberry Drive fittingly runs immediately south of the football stadium and the baseball field.

E. M. Waller, a former Vanderbilt athlete and high school coach in Alabama, succeeded Faulkinberry. He never seemed to be able to connect with his teams, and the school's athletic program declined in every sport. The school had decided to drop the women's basketball team before Waller was hired. In the fall of 1933 Waller's football teams suffered the worst defeat to date in school's history. Murray State defeated the team by a score of 70 to 7. However, two noteworthy developments occurred during Waller's brief tenure. A new football field with permanent grandstands on the west and east sides opened on October 14, 1933, when a scoreless tie was played between Middle Tennessee and Jacksonville State of Alabama. Secondly, a permanent nickname for the school's athletic teams was selected in 1934. Early Middle Tennessee squads had played under several names: Pedagogues, Normalites, Teachers, and Mid-State. The Murfreesboro *Daily News Journal* sponsored a contest to select a new name and offered a prize of five dollars for the winning entry. From over two hundred suggestions, the football team was allowed to select the winner. The team chose Blue Raiders. The suggestion came from Charles Sarver, a team member. A fan of the Colgate Red Raiders, Sarver explained that he had merely substituted blue for red to come up with the name. The Blue Raider's name was first used officially in the Thanksgiving Day game against archrival Tennessee Tech. The Raiders lost by a score of 12 to 0.

In the fall of 1936 Johnny "Red" Floyd replaced the unfortunate Waller. Floyd was well remembered as a former player and for having led the school to an undefeated season in 1917. He immediately turned the football team around, going 8-0 in his first season. The 1935 team was led by Homer Pittard, a captain and tackle. He was the largest man on the team and, as the *Midlander* phrased it, "always the fifth man in the opposition's backfield." Another star was halfback Charles Murphy, destined for greatness as a future coach of the team. Other key players were Joe Troop, Miles Baskins, Granville Waggoner, Woody Smitherson, Robert Bass, J. W. Jackson, and Hamp Thomas. The season opened with a 45–0 loss to Vanderbilt, but the Blue Raiders won their remaining seven games. Since the Raiders had won all of their SIAA Conference games in 1935 and 1936, they claimed the conference championship for those years. In 1937 Floyd's team went 6-1-1, but they fell to 2-6 in 1938.

Floyd's basketball teams performed poorly, going 15-34 in three years, but his baseball teams fared better. Among the more productive of his baseball and basketball players were Murphy, Kenneth Ezell, and John Bragg, all of whom would play major roles in future Murfreesboro affairs. In the spring of 1939 Floyd resigned his position as head coach due to the requirement to teach one academic course. Herc Alley, a high school coach from Mississippi, lasted only one season as replacement for Floyd. None of his teams performed very well; he resigned and accepted a position as an assistant at Vanderbilt. President Q. M. Smith promoted Alley's assistant, E. W. "Wink" Midgett, to the position of head coach.

Midgett had been hired to teach business courses, but he had a great interest in athletics as well. He led the Blue Raider teams for three years, and he did manage a winning record in football, but the basketball teams did very poorly, and there is no surviving complete record of the baseball squad. It should be recognized that Midgett coached at a difficult period; he and his players had to cope with distractions and concerns associated with the outbreak of World War II and the growing concerns of America's ultimate involvement in that conflict. After the 1942 football season ended, Middle Tennessee State Teachers College suspended intercollegiate athletics for the duration of the war. During this break the school was renamed Middle Tennessee State College to signify that it had developed a more diverse curriculum that went well beyond teacher training.

THE WAR YEARS: 1942–1945

During World War II hundreds of current and former Middle Tennessee State students volunteered or were drafted into the armed forces. These men and women served in every major theatre of operation. During the conflict, 37 former students died as a result of combat or service-related accidents or illnesses. Among these fatalities were former Middle Tennessee State athletes: William Burkett, Robert Fry, Robert McClintock, Bob Sarvis, Arthur Scates, James Schleicher, Robert E. Smith, William McCrory, and Lee Carlton Yates.

With the end of the war in the late summer of 1945, the world entered a new era. Atomic power and the Cold War brought drastic changes to every facet of life and society, and colleges and universities were no exception. Middle Tennessee State College entered a new age of increased student enrollments, and for the first time in the institution's history, male students far outnumbered female students. This development was due, in large measure, to returning veterans entering school on the GI Bill. These older men often resumed athletic careers abandoned years earlier in order to serve their country.

It was the women who first resumed intercollegiate athletic competition on the MTSC campus. In the fall of 1945 a revived women's basketball team took to the hardwood under Coach Nance Jordan. The Blue Raiderettes compiled an 11-4 record against a variety of colleges, industrial leagues, and YWCA teams. The team was invited to the AAU's southeastern tournament in Atlanta after the season was completed. The Raiderettes advanced to the semi-final game before being eliminated by the Goldblumes, a powerful industrial league club that had won the national AAU championship in 1945. Despite the success of the team, women's basketball at Middle Tennessee State was again discontinued after the 1946–47 season. Among the star players of the Blue Raideretts of 1947 were Betty Hart, Nancy Aikman, Mary Ann Zumbro, Betty Cloyd, Imogine Queen, Mary Ellen Roberts, and Marjorie Riggs.

THE BUBBER MURPHY ERA: 1946–1981

The Blue Raider football team returned to action in the fall of 1946 under Coach Midgett. The team, led by captains Bob Burkett and Gene McIntyre, was a mixture of returning prewar veterans and new, younger faces. The team went 5-3-1, but Midgett resigned as coach before the next season. Apparently the school's president,

Q. M. Smith, and Horace Jones, a major power on the athletic committee, felt that a new coach was needed for the long term. They were convinced that Charles "Bubber" Murphy was the man for the job.

Charles Murphy had been a star athlete at Nashville Central High School in the early 1930s, but he did not enter college immediately after graduation. He went to work for a local company, Castner Knott, and played on its industrial league basketball team. Murphy's outstanding play against Middle Tennessee's freshmen basketball team did not go unnoticed by Horace Jones. Jones was a member of the school's athletic committee and chief "recruiter" of future players for the school. He persuaded Murphy to enroll at Middle Tennessee by promising him a partial scholarship and an on-campus job. Murphy excelled in football, basketball, baseball, and tennis. Among the honors he received during his collegiate years was his selection as a Little All-American in football, the first such honor in the school's history. After completing his degree in 1938, he returned to the Nashville area where he taught and coached while playing professional baseball in the New York Giant's farm system during the summers. In 1941 he joined the navy and served until 1945. After his discharge from the navy, Murphy began graduate studies at Peabody College, and coached at Peabody Demonstration School until he returned to Murfreesboro. Murphy took control of Middle Tennessee's athletic program as head coach and athletic director in 1947.

When Murphy began his coaching duties at Middle Tennessee, the school had just helped organize a new athletic conference composed exclusively of Tennessee colleges. The charter members of the Volunteer State Athletic Conference were Middle Tennessee State College, Austin Peay State College, Tennessee Polytechnic Institute, Cumberland University, Lincoln Memorial University, David Lipscomb College, Union University, and Milligan College. Later Belmont College, Bethel College, Carson Newman College, East Tennessee State College, King College, Tennessee Wesleyan, and University of Tennessee at Martin joined the conference at various dates before it disbanded in 1968. The VSAC officially began competition in the fall of 1947. During its existence, the conference sanctioned men's teams in football, basketball, baseball, track, cross country, golf, and tennis. The conference experienced major problems from the beginning. Most of the small private schools did not offer football, making it difficult to schedule enough games to declare a conference champion every year. None of the schools fielded a team in every sport. Given the poor fit between the state and private schools, the former quickly began to look for a better conference affiliation. Middle Tennessee remained a member of the VSAC until 1958.

During Murphy's early years as head coach, he not only guided the football team, but did brief stints as a basketball and tennis coach, as well. His career and reputation as a coach are, however, overwhelmingly based upon his success as a football coach. In his first season Murphy led the Blue Raiders to a 9-1 record, losing only to Maryville College. In 1948 the squad fell to 5-5, probably because he implemented a new offense, the split T. In 1949 his team went undefeated but was tied 7–7 by

Murray State. Now the pattern was set for future successes. From 1947 to 1968 Murphy's Blue Raiders amassed a record of 155-63-8, giving Murphy the record for longest service and greatest number of victories to date in the history of the program. During 1947 to 1958, Murphy captured six VSAC football championships. Given the limitations of the VSAC, Middle Tennessee had also joined the Ohio Valley Conference in 1952. The OVC, founded in 1948 by Kentucky colleges, soon attracted other Tennessee schools as well. Middle Tennessee thus competed in two conferences from 1952–1958. Murphy's teams quickly became a major force in OVC football, winning the league championship in 1956, 1957, 1958, 1959, 1964, and 1965. He also had four undefeated seasons during his career.

Murphy led his teams to four postseason bowls, which is still the most by any Raider coach to date. The Blue Raiders' first bowl game was the Refrigerator Bowl in Evansville, Indiana, on December 1, 1956. The Raiders lost to Sam Houston State 27–13. In 1960 and 1961 the Blue Raiders played in back-to-back Tangerine Bowls in Orlando, Florida. In the 1960 game, played on January 1, 1960, the 10-0-1 Raiders defeated Presbyterian College 21–12, leading to a final number three ranking among small colleges by UPI. The next year the Raiders lost to Lamar Tech by a score of 21–14. In 1964 Middle Tennessee defeated Muskingum College 20–0 in the first Grantland Rice Bowl for the NCAA Mideast College Championship. The game was played at Horace Jones Field, the site of the bowl game until 1969.

Coach Murphy produced a large number of outstanding players at all positions. Those receiving Little All-American designation were Max Arnold, Charles Lyons, Maxie Runion, Terry Sweeney, Ralphy Massey, G. E. McCormack, Jackie Polk, George Dykes, Jimbo Pearson, Keith Atchley, Jerry Hurst, and Buck Rolan. He also coached over 40 players who were selected as All-OVC. He had two players, Teddy Morris and Keith Atchley, voted as OVC Players of the Year. In 1965 Murphy was selected as OVC Coach of the Year, as well, and was awarded the national Coach of the Year by the American Football Coaches Association.

In 1968 the MTSU football complex was renamed the Johnny "Red" Floyd Stadium/Horace Jones Field. Murphy endured the only losing season in his career that year, going 2-8 and 1-6 in the OVC. MTSU's new president, Mel Scarlett, felt it was time for a change, and he hired Don Fuoss to replace the legendary Murphy. The Raiders went 1-9 in 1969, and Fuoss was replaced by one of his assistant coaches, Bill Peck. Peck had three winning seasons in his five-year tenure, but overall barely established a winning record of 27-25-2. Ben Hurt, a former player under Murphy in the early 1950s, returned to his alma mater as head coach in 1975, but he did not return MTSU to its former glory as many had hoped. Hurt posted a record of 12-31-1, necessitating another change in leadership. Murphy, approaching retirement, orchestrated the return of yet another former player who he believed could ultimately restore the football program to its former winning spirit. That man was James "Boots" Donnelly.

While the Murphy era may be best remembered for its football teams, Charles Murphy was also the athletic director from 1947 to 1981. As athletic director he led the school's entire sports program, and much of his legacy centers on his actions in that capacity. Murphy's efforts to strengthen the other major programs of basketball and baseball were crucial. He nurtured the young tennis and golf programs that had been launched shortly before the war, and he expanded the coaching staff and allowed the introduction of new sports such as track. Among the significant and successful coaches he hired were E. K. Patty, Joe Black Hayes, Granville "Buck" Boldin, Dean Hayes, Ken Trickey, Jimmy Earle, John Stanford, and James "Boots" Donnelly. He supported the expansion and improvement of the playing facilities, and two important playing venues created in his tenure were Memorial Gymnasium (opened in 1950) and an all-purpose assembly hall and basketball facility in 1972—fittingly named Charles M. Murphy Athletic Center. Murphy Center remains a prominent feature on campus to this day. Murphy also began the process of establishing a modern women's athletic program during his tenure, in response to the federal mandate in Title IX of the Education Amendment Act of 1972.

MEN'S BASKETBALL

The men's basketball team also was revived after the end of World War II. From late 1945 until 1970 there were seven head basketball coaches. Leading the team during this era were O. L. Freeman, E. K. Patty, Charles Murphy, Charles N. Greer, Ed Diddle Jr., Bill Stokes, and Ken Trickey. Of these, only E. K. Patty had a winning record during his tenure at Middle Tennessee. The teams of this period forged a record of 242–331. While the overall performance of the basketball program was weak, it captured three VSAC championships in the 1950s. Charles N. Greer led the team into the National Association of Intercollegiate Athletics postseason tournament in 1955, where the Raiders lost to Southeastern Oklahoma. Among the better players of the VSAC–early-OVC-era were Ken Trickey, Frank Davis, Jim Burks, Nelson Forrester, Tom Hogshead, Phil Jones, Sam Smith, and Doug Shrader.

Things did not begin to change for men's basketball until 1965 when President Quill Cope and Murphy hired Ken Trickey as head coach. The changes that were about to occur were represented in the photograph of the freshmen basketball team in the 1966 *Midlander*. Two of the incoming freshmen players were African American. These players, Willie Brown and Arthur Polk, were the second and third African American athletes ever recruited to Middle Tennessee. Trickey later said that he realized when he took the job that Middle Tennessee could not become competitive in the OVC using only white players. The OVC was recognized across the nation as one of the first southern conferences to actively recruit black players. While Kentucky members of the conference had been playing African American recruits, the Tennessee members of the conference had lagged far behind. The signing of Brown and Polk by MTSU preceded by a year the much more publicized signing of Nashville's Perry Wallace with Vanderbilt, as the SEC's first African American athlete. Trickey added three more black players the next year, and these players raised the team's talent level substantially. Winning teams drew larger and larger crowds to

Memorial Gymnasium, showing the limitations of the facility for a more popular basketball program. This rising attendance was one of the factors promoting the decision to construct Murphy Center.

Trickey's success did not go unnoticed; he was hired away to Oral Roberts University. Jimmy Earle replaced Trickey and carried MTSU's basketball program to where it had never been before—the top of the OVC. Building upon the foundation of Trickey's tenure, Earle's teams continued to improve. In 1975 the Blue Raiders went 23-5 and captured the OVC Championship Tournament. For the first time in the team's history, it went to the NCAA Tournament. The Raiders played in the Mideast Regional in Lexington, Kentucky, but were eliminated in the first round by Oregon State 78–67. In 1977 Earle's club was co-champion of the conference and winner of the OVC tournament and again advanced to NCAA postseason play. The Raiders lost to Detroit in the Mideast Regional played in Baton Rouge, Louisiana. After the 1978–79 season Earle resigned as coach to pursue other options, but he had not departed permanently from the MTSU sports scene. Earle won OVC Coach of the Year Awards in 1974 and 1977. His career record of 164-103 gave him the largest number of victories to date in the program's history. He produced such notable OVC players as Herman Sykes, Jimmy Powell, Jimmy Martin, George Sorrell, Tim Sisneros, Greg Joiner, and Claude "Sleepy" Taylor. Sorrell and Sisneros were voted OVC Players of the Year. Earle's assistant, Stan Simpson, succeeded him as head coach in 1979.

BASEBALL

Baseball, like basketball, had something of a revolving coaching door in the years after World War II. Between 1946 and 1974 the Blue Raiders baseball team had 11 different coaches. Many of them served for only a year or two and were usually head or assistant coaches for other teams as well. Longer-serving coaches of this period were Durwood Stowe, Charles Murphy, Buck Rolman, Ken Trickey, Jimmy Earle, and A. H. "Lefty" Solomon. Although reliable official baseball records are not available before the late 1950s, it appears that the Blue Raiders baseball team did relatively well in the late 1940s and early 1950s. They won the VSAC championships in 1947, 1950, and 1951. The Raiders had a spirited conference rivalry with Lincoln Memorial University who defeated them for the 1954 title as part of their run of six consecutive baseball championships.

After entering the OVC, the Raiders' baseball team continued to deal with frequent coaching changes, yet the club generally had a winning record most years. During much of the 1960s, Trickey and Earle did double duty as baseball and basketball coaches. Earle's 1968 team went 23-9 and became the first team to advance to postseason play outside the conference. The team journeyed to Jackson, Tennessee, for the Mideastern College Regional. The Raiders defeated Illinois State in the first round, but they lost to Delta State in the second game. Now in the loser bracket, the Raiders defeated Illinois State once again and advanced to the finals against Delta State. The Raiders had to defeat Delta State twice to win the regional. They won the first game, then fell 3–2 against the Mississippi club in the final contest. Earle was selected OVC Coach of the Year in 1968. During the 1960s, a number of Raider players were awarded All -OVC honors. These players were Ray Purvis, Teddy Morris, Ray Hendrick, Bruce Skeen, Ken Victory, Don Tarter, Greg Cunningham, and Bill Martin.

A. H. Solomon was hired in 1971 to coach baseball exclusively and to teach in the health and recreation area. He began to schedule more games and posted three consecutive winning seasons. However, new graduate programs in his department put increasing academic demands upon him, and he decided to resign his coaching position after the 1973 season.

After Solmon's departure MTSU turned to John Stanford, a former star player for the Raiders in the early OVC era. Stanford had considerable coaching experience and success at Shelbyville High School and Motlow State Community College. Stanford quickly developed one of the most successful baseball programs in the OVC. He consistently posted winning seasons and by 1981 had won two conference championships and made two appearances in NCAA postseason play. His 1976 club played in the South Regional held in Tallahassee, Florida, where the Raiders were eliminated with consecutive losses to Auburn and Jacksonville State. In 1981 his club went 34-15 during the regular season and advanced to the South Regional in Coral Gable, Florida. There the Raiders defeated the Missouri Tigers for their first ever NCAA tournament victory. The Raiders were then eliminated for regional play with consecutive losses to the University of Miami and the Florida Gators. Coach Murphy clearly left his post as athletic director in 1981 with a good feeling about the future of baseball at MTSU.

TENNIS

While the big three sports of football, basketball, and baseball had attracted the lion's share of attention from students, alumni, and fans during the Murphy era, there was substantial progress and remarkable achievement in the smaller programs of golf, tennis, and track. Middle Tennessee's tennis program began in the late 1930s. B. B. Gracy Jr. had coached the team in its earliest seasons before the sport was suspended during World War II. The program returned to play in 1947 with Murphy as coach of the squad. Tennis, like golf and track during this era, faced the problems of few funds, no scholarships, and frequent change of coaches. After some years of disappointing results, the program took a huge step forward in 1964 when the school hired Granville "Buck" Bouldin to coach the team.

Buck Bouldin had moved to Murfreesboro in the early 1950s to practice law. As a former collegiate player and tennis fan, he followed Middle Tennessee's tennis closely, but was disappointed with the program's lack of growth and success. Knowing Bouldin's interest in the sport, Murphy urged him to accept a part-time position as tennis coach. After some negotiation Bouldin agreed to coach, but only if he received a modest number of scholarships to recruit better quality players.

From 1964 to 1971, Bouldin brought commitment, passion, and coaching skill to what had largely been a "club" type sport at Middle Tennessee. During his tenure the team competed in both the Tennessee Intercollegiate Athletic Conference and the OVC. Bouldin's teams captured five TIAC championships and performed well in the OVC competition. He was selected OVC Coach of the Year in tennis in 1965 and 1968. He also produced two OVC Players of the Year, Jean Prevost and Mike Albano. Bouldin laid the foundation for a tennis program that went on to dominate OVC competition by the 1990s. His role in the history of MTSU tennis is reflected in the naming of the school's tennis complex in his honor in 2000, as well as his induction into the Rose and Emmett Kennon Sports Hall of Fame in 2009.

GOLF

E. W. Midgett introduced golf as an intercollegiate sport at Middle Tennessee in 1939. After the 1940 season, it was suspended because of the outbreak of the war. The sport resumed play under E. K. Patty in 1946. Like other coaches of this era, Patty also helped coach other teams, although his significance to MTSU athletics rests upon his great success in golf. His early squads dominated the VSAC, winning the conference title in 1949, 1950, 1952, 1954–1957. In TIAC play the Blue Raiders captured 12 championships. Patty's clubs were also the premier programs in the OVC for years, winning the league championship 11 times from 1956 through 1978. The 1965 golf squad lifted Patty to national acclaim by capturing the NCAA College Division Championship, and team leader Larry Gilbert had the lowest individual score. Patty consistently produced top quality golfers at MTSU. He coached six NCAA All-Americans, including Gary Head and Larry Gilbert. He also produced four OVC Golfers of the Year, and he was selected OVC Coach of the Year six times in his career. E. K. Patty retired in 1991 as the school's most successful golf coach to date, and he was inducted into the National Golf Coaches Hall of Fame in 1986.

TRACK

Joe Black Hayes launched Middle Tennessee's track program in the spring of 1954. The team competed in TIAC and OVC meets with modest success for the next decade. In 1965, however, Dean Hayes was hired to coach the team, and this event marks the beginning of the gradual transformation of the program into one of the most successful in the nation. Hayes had been an outstanding athlete at Lake Forest College in Illinois. After graduate school, he coached several years at the high school level before returning to his alma mater as head cross country coach and assistant track coach. The hiring of Hayes was a break from the usual practice at MTSU. Hayes was the first coach hired from outside of the South with no prior connection to MTSU. In fact, MTSU coaches were overwhelmingly former MTSU athletes. Hayes quickly proved to be a tireless worker and skilled recruiter, factoring prominently into the school's earliest efforts to recruit African American athletes to compete at the varsity level for MTSU.

Hayes concentrated much of his early efforts on the recruitment and development of jumpers, sprinters, and relay teams. Among some of the outstanding early recruits and quality performers he developed were Greg Artis, Tommy Haynes, Harrison Salami, Brian Oldfield, Roscoe Kidd, Russell Holloway, and Barry McClure. Brian Oldfield finished second in the NCAA shot put competition in 1965. He later competed in this event at the 1972 Olympic games. In 1970 Barry McClure was the first MTSU athlete ever selected as an All-American at the Division I level. In 1974 Tommy Harper earned All-American honors as well. By the late 1970s Hayes's efforts began to produce OVC championships. The Raiders won their first outdoors track championship in 1976, and a second in 1979. The first indoor championship came in 1979 under the leadership of Hayes. Middle Tennessee track championships would multiply greatly in the future.

TITLE IX AND WOMEN'S SPORTS

During Coach Murphy's last years as athletic director, a revolutionary event occurred in American sport history. Congress passed the Education Amendment Act of 1972. One brief section of that law, Title IX, stated "no person in the United States shall, on the basis of sex, be excluded from participation in, denied the benefits of, or be subjected to discrimination under any education program or activity receiving Federal assistance." The short Title IX provision of the law had largely gone unnoticed during the bill's movement through the legislative process by members of Congress, the public in general, education administrators, and coaches at all academic levels. Once all of these parties realized what Title IX meant, the law created a great controversy that would last for some years. Despite Title IX's unpopularity with many people— male coaches, school administrators, and fans—it was the law of the land. Title IX was part of a bigger movement in civil and women's rights as a whole.

The implementation of Title IX would take time, and federal authorities gave educational institutions a grace period to begin its gradual implementation. Universities and colleges received three years to start or expand their program of women athletics. MTSU's administrators and coaches used this time to consider what steps they would take to launch a modern women's athletic program. After the consideration of many factors such as revenues, recruitment of coaches and players, and playing facilities, MTSU decided to begin their women's program with basketball, tennis, and volleyball. Women's basketball was introduced in 1974–75 with Pat Jones as coach. Women's tennis began in 1976 under the leadership of Pat Neal, and Sue Stanley led the first volleyball team in 1977.

During the first decade of women's competition, the basketball and tennis teams were far more successful than volleyball. Sandy Neal's tennis teams had winning records and captured two first-place finishes in the OVC. The basketball team, under a trio of head coaches—Pat Jones, Pat Sarver, and Larry Inman—won four

OVC regular season championships, three OVC tournaments, and appeared in three NCAA postseason tournaments. The volleyball team not only performed rather poorly, but it had six head coaches in its first decade of play; of these Diane Cummings served the longest. Through the efforts of these three original teams, Middle Tennessee had a viable women's program underway. The number of Lady Raiders sports would expand in the future, bringing considerable success and championships to the University.

In 1981 Charles Murphy retired as MTSU's Athletic Director, ending 34 years of service to the university. Murphy is probably the most "iconic" coach in MTSU history, especially among older fans and alumni. When Murphy left, a distinct era of MTSU sports history ended, and the modern sports era began and continues to unfold today. Jimmy Earle replaced Murphy, and the university's athletic program embarked upon a new era of considerable success in the OVC for the remainder of the century. A strong desire developed by the 1990s, however, for the university to rise even higher in the NCAA classification scheme of sports by gaining admission to the Division I-A ranks.

FOOTBALL: BOOTS DONNELLY, 1979–1998

A major part of MTSU's sports story in the late twentieth century was the return of the Blue Raiders as a quality football program. Credit for this success goes to James "Boots" Donnelly. Donnelly was a star athlete at Father Ryan High School before playing football for Murphy's Raiders in the early 1960s. After college he coached at Father Ryan High School in Nashville and served as an assistant at Vanderbilt before becoming head coach at Austin Peay. He won the OVC Championship in his first season there. After Donnelly's second season at Austin Peay, Ben Hurt resigned as Middle Tennessee's coach, and MTSU succeeded in bringing Donnelly back to his alma mater. When Donnelly took over the football program, it was simply at rock bottom with only a few quality returning players. Donnelly was determined to rebuild the once proud program regardless of what it took in terms of effort, determination, and hard work. In his first two seasons, 1979–80, his record was 3-17. He turned the corner in 1981 with his first winning season and more to come, as he restored the program to the upper tier of the OVC. In 1984 the Blue Raiders went 9-2 and made a first ever appearance in the NCAA playoffs. In the first round Donnelly's squad was matched against Roy Kidd's Eastern Kentucky Colonels, a fellow OVC member and team they had already beaten in the regular season. On November 4, 1984, the squad again had to travel to Kentucky, but they defeated the Colonels for a second time by a score of 27–10. The following week the Raiders defeated Indiana State 42–41 in a triple overtime game on the road. On December 8 the Blue Raiders clashed with the Louisiana Tech Bulldogs at Horace Jones Field, losing by a score of 21–13.

In 1985 Donnelly posted an 11-0 record in the regular season and returned to the NCAA playoffs as OVC champions. The Raiders were matched against Georgia

Southern, a team they had already defeated during the regular season. The Raiders also carried a number one ranking at the college division into the game. Southern prevailed in the rematch by a score of 28–13. For the next three seasons, Donnelly's Raiders posted winning records, but did not return to the playoffs until he captured the OVC in 1989 with a 9-4 record. In the first round MTSU defeated Appalachian State but lost to Georgia Southern in the second round by a wide margin. In 1990 the Raiders were co-champions of the OVC and again participated in the NCAA 1-AA playoffs. The Raiders beat Jackson State and then traveled to Boise, Idaho, to take on a strong Boise State team. The Broncos prevailed over the Raiders by a score of 20–13. In 1991 the Raiders went 9-3 in the regular season and qualified for the playoffs. The Raiders defeated Sam Houston State 20–9 before falling in the second round to their old nemesis the Eastern Kentucky Colonels. In 1992 Donnelly won the last of his four OVC championships at MTSU and returned to the NCAA I-AA playoffs for the last time. The Raiders defeated Appalachian State, but lost to Marshall University in the second round.

In his last six seasons of coaching at MTSU, Donnelly went 35-29 and was 140-87-1 for his career as head of the Raider program. Donnelly ranks second only to Murphy in most career football victories to date. Donnelly not only rebuilt a proud program over the years, but he carried the Raiders to what would be their greatest era during their history in the Ohio Valley Conference. Donnelly also produced a large number of All-OVC Players, OVC Players of the Year, and All-Americans. Among those players receiving such awards were Don Griffin, Kelly Porter, Roger Carroll, Steve McAdoo, Joe Campbell, Don Thomas, Dennis Mix, Vince Hall, Marvin Collier, Jo Nathan Quinn, Kippy Bayless, and Walter Dunston. Some of these aforementioned players were also drafted by professional teams.

MEN'S BASKETBALL: 1979–2001

The same year that Boots Donnelly became head football coach at MTSU, Stan Simpson succeeded Jimmy Earle as the head coach of the men's basketball program. In 1981–82 Simpson's Raiders went 22-8 and also won the OVC tournament by defeating Western Kentucky in the championship game. The Raiders were placed in the NCAA Mideast Regional to be played in Nashville. The Raiders were paired against the Kentucky Wildcats in the first round. On March 11, 1982, the Blue Raiders led by Jerry Beck and Rick Campbell shocked the collegiate basketball world by defeating the Wildcats 50–44 in a hard-fought defensive contest. Many Raider fans consider this victory the greatest ever in MTSU basketball. Two days later the Raiders met the Louisville Cardinals in the second round–the Cardinals won by a comfortable margin of 81–56. Over the next two seasons Simpson's clubs went 18-36 and a coaching change was made.

Bruce Stewart replaced Simpson for the 1984–85 season, and he immediately returned the Raiders to winning ways. While only going 7-7 in the OVC, Stewart's club won the conference tournament in his first year and advanced to the NCAA playoffs. The Raiders journeyed to South Bend, Indiana, to play North Carolina in the first round of the Southeast Regional. While the Raiders kept the game close in the first half, the Tarheels pulled away to win 76–57. The Raiders went 23-11 in 1985–86, but lost in the first round of the OVC tournament. The squad received the school's first ever invitation to participate in the National Invitation Tournament (NIT) postseason tournament, and suffered a defeat by Clemson in the first round. The Raiders posted a 22-7 record in 1986–87, but again lost in the OVC tournament to Austin Peay. The team received the first ever at-large bid by an OVC team to the NCAA tournament. The Raiders lost in the first round to Notre Dame 84–71. The following year the team had over 20 wins but lost in the conference tournament. MTSU received its second bid to play in the NIT, in which Stewart's club defeated Tennessee and Georgia before falling to Boston College by a score of 78–69. In 1988–89 the Blue Raiders dominated the OVC regular season and won the conference tournament. The Blue Raiders traveled to Nashville to meet the Florida State Seminoles in the NCAA Southeast Regional. Trailing well into the second half, the Raiders mounted one of the most famous comebacks in their history behind the hot shooting of Mike Buck. Going on an amazing run of 47–16, the Raiders overcame a 17-point deficit to beat the Seminoles 97–83. Two days later, the Virginia Cavaliers eliminated the Raiders by a large margin. In his final two seasons at MTSU, Stewart's teams compiled a 33-25 record with no postseason appearances. Stewart was selected OVC Coach of the Year in 1989 and his 141-76 record ranked him second to Jimmy Earle until 2011. He produced several All-OVC performers such as Duane Washington, Chris Rainey, Randy Henry, Dwayne Rainey, Warren Kidd, Kevin Wallace, and Kerry Hammond.

With Stewart's departure in 1991, MTSU basketball entered a period of decline. David Farrar led the Raider program until 1996, posting only two winning seasons. Randy Wiel followed Farrar and got off to a promising start with winning seasons in his first two years. However, the program again declined, and MTSU exited the OVC with a program in need of repair.

BASEBALL

John Stanford's baseball program excelled in the 1980s; his club again won the OVC and advanced to the NCAA Mideast Regional in Stillwater, Oklahoma. The Raiders defeated Oral Roberts, but fell to Oklahoma State in the second game. Facing elimination the Raiders rallied to defeat Minnesota, champions of the Big Ten Conference, and were one victory away from a trip to the College World Series. It was a trip they would not take; the Oklahoma State Cowboys beat them for a second time to take the regional title.

Coach Stanford continued to put winning teams on the field, but failed to capture the OVC tournament championship again until 1987. A victory over Akron in the conference finals sent the team to its fourth NCAA appearance under Stanford. The Raiders met with hard luck in the South Regional in Huntsville, Alabama. Bad weather and time delays forced the Raiders to play two games in less than twenty-four hours, and they lost to both Arkansas and Auburn.

In 1987 Stanford succeeded Jimmy Earle as the university's athletic director, ending his baseball-coaching career at Middle Tennessee. He left a considerable legacy of victories, NCAA appearances, and outstanding players. He had coached numerous All-OVC Players. Among these athletes were Danny Moore, Mike Moore, Tom Blankenship, Kenny Gerhart, Marty Smith, Steve Sonneberger, Chris Whitehead, and Tim Goff. Stanford was selected OVC Coach of the Year on five occasions in his coaching career at MTSU.

Steve Peterson followed Stanford as head coach in 1988. He was already an integral part of the baseball program, having served as Stanford's assistant on two occasions, 1976–1978 and 1985–1987. He also had a very successful program at Roane State Community College between his stints at MTSU. Steve Peterson inherited a very strong baseball program and made it even better. The Blue Raiders dominated the OVC during the team's last 12 years in the OVC. From 1988 through the 2000 season, Peterson's teams forged an overall record of 405-330 with a 166-79 mark in OVC play. The Raiders captured the regular season championship in 1988, 1990–1993, 1995–1997, and the OVC tournament title in 1988, 1990–1992, 1994–1995, and 2000. During these years, teams played in five NCAA Regionals. In 1988, in Peterson's first year as head coach, the Raiders played in the South Regional in Starksville, Mississippi, where they defeated Texas A&M before being eliminated by consecutive losses to Missouri and Mississippi State. In 1990 the team journeyed to Palo Alto, California, to play in the West I Regional. The club fell to San Diego State and Stanford. Again in 1991 the Peterson Raiders went west to California, but were quickly eliminated with losses to USC and Hawaii. Middle Tennessee fared better in their third California regional visit. The Raiders lost their first game to USC but rallied to win the second against Southwest Missouri. They were eliminated in their third game, losing to Pepperdine. The Raiders' last appearance in the NCAA Regional as a member of the OVC came in 2000, the club's last year in the conference. Playing at the Clemson Regional in South Carolina, the Raiders lost their first game to Clemson. The club scored a victory over Old Dominion in the second game and continued their rally with a victory over Illinois. In the fourth game the Raiders faced Clemson again for the regional championship, and the Tigers easily defeated them.

During Peterson's tenure in the OVC, he was selected Coach of the Year in 1990 and 1995. He also produced a large number of All-OVC Players. Among them were Eddie Pye, Chris Whitehead, Jayhawk Owens, Gary Myers, Buford "Mudcat" Brewer, Josh Pride, and Jamie Walker. Peterson's success and development of outstanding players would continue into the Sun Belt Conference era.

MEN'S GOLF, TENNIS, AND TRACK

During MTSU's last two decades in the OVC, the men's golf, tennis, and track programs continued to experience considerable success. When long-serving golf Coach E. K. Patty retired in 1981, control of the program passed successively to Jimmy Earle, 1982–1986, Walt Rogers, 1987–1989, and Johnny Moore, 1989–2000. While neither Earle nor Rogers produced an OVC championship, both did develop some outstanding golfers. Earning All-OVC honors during the 80s were Eddie Jackson, Tres Scheiber, Bud Taylor, Eric Lee, Ron Graham, and Steve Graham. The club, however, improved dramatically after John Moore became head coach in 1989. Under Moore's guidance MTSU's golf teams rose to the top of the OVC, during the 1990s, winning the OVC championship 1994–1996, 1998, and 2000, and Moore was selected OVC Coach of the Year on five occasions. He produced several All-OVC golfers, among them Jeff Cook, Steve Graham, David Reed, Nick Shelton, and Brett Alexander. Alexander was voted OVC Golfer of the Year from 1998–2000. Moore led a strong golf program into the Sun Belt Conference.

MTSU's tennis program grew even stronger under Buck Bouldin's successors. From 1972 until the end of the school's membership in the OVC four coaches, Larry Castle, Clyde Smithwick, Dick Lalance, and Dale Short, led the Raiders. During this period MTSU tennis teams won twelve OVC regular season championships, eleven OVC tournament championships, and made six NCAA Regional appearances.

While Smithwick coached only briefly, he won the OVC regular season and tournament title in 1976 and was selected OVC Coach of the Year. Lalance coached for a decade, and his team captured the OVC title in 1979, the same year he was selected OVC Coach of the Year. Lalance coached two of the better-known players of this era, Peter Hefferman and Dale Short; both were selected All-OVC twice as players. When Lalance stepped aside in 1988, Dale Short succeeded him.

Dale Short was a well-known figure in Murfreesboro and in OVC coaching circles when he was selected to head the MTSU program. He had been a star player for local Oakland High School and an All-OVC Player for the Blue Raiders. The skills and knowledge of the sport he had displayed on the playing court followed him into the coaching ranks. Within three years he produced a program that dominated the OVC for the remainder of the century. From 1991–2000 the Blue Raiders won ten consecutive OVC regular season championships and nine OVC tournament titles. In his OVC coaching career, Short's clubs were 87-6 in matches within the conference. During this run Short was voted OVC Coach of the Year eight times. He also coached in four NCAA Regional Tournaments during this period. In order to build and sustain his tennis program, Short recruited quality players at both the national and international levels. During the 1990s he produced dozens of players who received All-OVC designation, six of whom, Nick Sheumack, Keith Harrietha, Shane Scrutton, Fred Niemeyer, Anthony DeLuise, and David McNamara, were selected Players of the Year. Others who were selected All-OVC multiple times were Paul Goebel, Patrick Zackrisson, Julius Roberts, R. Gustaffson, Oliver Forean, and

Daniel Klemetz. Given his record and quality of his players, Short's program was well positioned to begin play in the Sun Belt Conference in 2001.

MTSU's men's track program dominated the OVC in the last two decades of the twentieth century. Despite the program being discontinued for three years (1987–1990) out of budgetary concerns, Hayes's squads won thirteen outdoor championships, eight indoor titles, and one cross country championship. Also, during much of this period Hayes served as the coach of the newly created women's track program.

As MTSU's track programs continued to enjoy outstanding success, they brought national and even international exposure for MTSU and coaching opportunities for Hayes. He coached athletes in meets conducted by the United States Olympic Committee and US Track and Field. Among these coaching opportunities were the Olympic Track Festival in Colorado Springs, World University Games in Kobe, Japan, World Cup in London, and World Championships in Athens, Greece. He also coached at the Seoul Olympics in 1988 and served as a referee at the Atlanta Olympics in 1996. These assignments not only enhanced Hayes's standing and reputation in the international community, but also strengthened his efforts at recruiting foreign athletes for MTSU teams. During the last decades of OVC competition, Hayes produced a large number of All-American athletes. Among them were such standouts as Roland McGhee, Dwight Johnson, Micah Otis, Andre Kirnes, Herb Newton, Tim Johnson, and Gary Mitchell. When MTSU entered the Sun Belt Conference Hayes's program was well positioned to continue its winning ways.

WOMEN'S GOLF, TENNIS, SOFTBALL

During the late OVC era MTSU fulfilled its Title IX commitment by expanding its women's athletic program. From the late 1980s until 2000 the university added outdoor and indoor track, cross country, softball, soccer, and golf to the three existing programs of basketball, tennis, and volleyball. From 1980 to 2000 MTSU's women's teams collectively won 39 OVC championships. The women's basketball squads dominated the OVC, winning 18 championships. The women's tennis teams collected eleven titles; women's indoor track captured five titles; the women's outdoor track collected three titles. The softball and volleyball teams won one each.

During the 1980s MTSU women's basketball became the most visible women's sport on campus, attracting by far the greatest number of spectators. Larry Inman led the Lady Raiders from 1978–1987 and posted a record of 161-73, winning six OVC championships. His 1982–83 squad was the first Lady Raider club to appear in the NCAA tournament, defeating Jackson State before falling to top-seeded Louisiana Tech on the road. In 1984 the Lady Raiders won the OVC again and traveled to Knoxville to play the Lady Volunteers in the first round of the NCAA tournament. Pat Summitt's Lady Vols won by a score of 70–52. The next year the Lady Raiders repeated as OVC tournament champions and faced Western Kentucky in the Mideast Regional. Again, the Lady Raiders failed to advance. In 1986 Inman's club made it to its fourth consecutive NCAA appearance. The Lady Raiders defeated South Carolina in Columbia and moved on to Baton Rouge where they were beaten by LSU. Larry Inman was selected OVC Coach of the Year four times before he resigned in 1987.

Lewis Bevins coached the Lady Raiders from 1988–1997, posting a record of 182-103. He won the OVC championship in his first year, carrying the team to its fifth NCAA appearance. The Lady Raiders were defeated by Kansas in the first round. He did not carry another team to an NCAA appearance again until 1996. The Lady Raiders again were paired against Kansas, and lost by a score of 72–57. Bevins resigned in 1997 and was succeeded by Stephany Smith.

Smith coached the club during its last years in the OVC, leading the first Lady Raiders club to a championship season in 1998. The Lady Raiders faced Duke in the first round game played at Durham, North Carolina, losing to Duke by a large margin. In Smith's second year her club won the regular season championship, but lost in the first round of the OVC tournament. This disappointing loss was offset by the club's first ever invitation to play in the NIT. The Lady Raiders traveled to Memphis were they were defeated by Memphis State in the first round. Smith led the Lady Raiders out of the OVC and into Sun Belt competition where the club would have even greater success.

The late OVC era produced some of the most talented Lady Raider basketball players whose names will long be remembered in the history of the program. At the top of the list are Jennifer McFall and Kim Webb. McFall was a four-time All-OVC Player and the 1985 OVC Player of the Year, all-time rebound leader, member of the MTSU Hall of Fame, and had many other accomplishments. Kim Webb was the first player to score 2,000 points, three time All-OVC Player, 1986 OVC Player of the Year, and a member of the MTSU Hall of Fame. Other great players of this era were Twanya Mucker, Priscella Roberson, Ester Coleman, Holly Hoover, and Sharon McClanahan.

Sandy Neal led the women's tennis teams from 1978 to 1990, establishing a strong foundation for a very strong program in the 1990s. During her 12 years as head coach, she captured three OVC titles and posted a career record of 160-113. Neal was selected OVC Coach of the Year on five occasions. She also coached numerous All-OVC Players—three of whom, Elina Durchman, Laura Martin, and Michelle Girle, were selected as OVC Players of the Year.

Dale Short succeeded Neal in 1991 while continuing to coach the men's team as well. He served in this dual capacity until 1995. Short's women's teams won three consecutive OVC championships in 1991–1993, while posting an overall record of 63-28 in his four years as coach. He was selected OVC Coach of the Year in 1993, and he produced several all-conference players, including Yael Soresman, the 1993 OVC Player of the Year.

David Thornton followed Short as coach of the women's program in 1995 and led the team during its last few years in the conference. Thorton's clubs won four OVC Championships, while posting a 96-63 record in his tenure. Thornton produced numerous all-conference players, among them Malinda Ryan, Jennifer Bryans, Clare Sevier, Amy King, Michelle North, Mechaela Gridling, Niger Kaur, Tina Hojnik, and Tanya Buchheim. Sevier was twice selected as OVC Player of the Year. Thornton won OVC Coach of the Year three times, and MTSU's women's tennis program exited the OVC having won ten championships in the past 20 years.

The women's track program under Dean Hayes quickly rose to prominence both within the OVC and across the country as a whole. From the beginning he brought to the women's program a proven record of success and numerous recruiting contacts. These, plus his work habits, very quickly produced a winning tradition in the program. Between 1988 and 2000, the women's indoor track squads won five OVC championships. The 1994 squad finished eighth in the NCAA, and the outdoor track teams won three OVC titles.

Among the outstanding performers for Hayes's program were Dione Rose, Nadia Graham, Shelly Johnson, Andreja Ribac, Jacqui Brown, Veronica Tipton, Dianne DeOliveira, Lea White, Natalie Douglas, and Sharon Smith. Dionne Rose was the 1994 OVC Track Woman of the Year and also received All-American honors—the first MTSU female athlete to do so in any sport. Rose also competed in the 1995 Atlanta Olympics. Jacqui Brown received All-American distinction, and Nadia Graham was named the OVC Female Athlete of the Year in 1996. The Lady Raiders track team continued to excel after MTSU entered the Sun Belt conference.

While the women's basketball, tennis, and track teams were far more successful than volleyball, softball, and soccer in the late OVC period, both volleyball and softball won an OVC championship. In 2000 coach Karen Green led the Lady Raiders softball team to an overall record of 39-21 and defeated Southeast Missouri for the OVC tournament champions. The Lady Raiders advanced to the NCAA Regional at Tuscon, Arizona, where they were eliminated by consecutive losses to Arizona and Illinois State. Among the star players of the 1990s were Jennifer Martinez, Shay Haskell, Allison Cheatham, Courtney Wallace, Jill Booth, and Laura Brockman. Martinez was selected OVC Pitcher of the Year in 1999 and 2000.

The women's volleyball teams had been associated since 1977 with frequent coaching changes and generally disappointing records. However, in 1995 Coach Lisa Kissee led the squad to an OVC tournament title and the team's first ever NCAA postseason play. The Lady Raiders defeated Princeton in the first round before falling to George Washington in the second contest. Some of the All-OVC selections from the early volleyball teams were Mary Rickman, Yanira Santiago, Lisa White, Judy Sain, Nidya Castillo, Angie Raffo, and Asaji Komatsu.

SUN BELT CONFERENCE ERA: 2001–PRESENT

By the early 1990s school officials were convinced that MTSU must make a move to the Division I-A level in football in order for the school to achieve its fullest athletic potential. In March 1993 the university issued a report, "Moving to the Highest

Level," outlining a plan to accomplish this objective. During the next two years, President James Walker, Athletic Director Lee Fowler, Coach James Donnelly, and others worked tirelessly to make this a reality. Two major developments occurred in August 1995, when MTSU announced plans for a $25 million renovation and expansion of Floyd Stadium and that football would move to Division I-A play. In May 1996 OVC members voted to allow MTSU's football program to leave the conference and compete as an independent, while the other teams remained in the conference. MTSU officially became a Division I-A school on September 1, 1998. On November 4, 1999, MTSU joined the Sun Belt Conference, agreeing to transfer all of its athletic teams to that conference on July 1, 2000. MTSU's admittance to the Sun Belt Conference ended almost a half-century of play in the OVC.

The Sun Belt Conference was organized in 1976. The original conference members consisted of southern schools largely located in states along the southern Atlantic and Gulf coasts. The conference was characterized by frequent membership changes in its early years. The Sun Belt Conference did not offer football as a conference sport until 2001; therefore, MTSU participated in the inaugural football season with the move to the conference.

In the first decade of Sun Belt Conference play MTSU's athletic teams have performed well. The men's football, baseball, indoor track, outdoor track, cross country, golf, and tennis teams have all won conference championships. The women's basketball, volleyball, indoor track, outdoor track, tennis, and soccer teams have won titles as well. MTSU has won the SBC's Vic Bubas All-Sports Trophy six times; this is a strong indicator of the overall success of the school's athletic teams. Another indication beyond the SBC of the growing success of the MTSU athletic program was the school's ranking in the National Learsfield Sports Directors Cup Standings for 2008–09. MTSU ranked 77 out of 271 athletic programs.

SUN BELT CONFERENCE FOOTBALL

For two years prior to its beginning play in the inaugural Sun Belt Conference football season, MTSU had competed as a Division I-A Independent team under Coach Andy McCollum. During these two years the Raiders compiled a record of 9-13, while generally playing much stronger teams than those of the OVC. MTSU played such major conference teams as Mississippi State, Arizona, Arkansas, Illinois, Florida, and Maryland, losing all of these games. These losses gave the team much needed experience with a higher level of play.

In 2001 McCollum's Raiders opened against Vanderbilt in Nashville, the tenth meeting between the two schools since 1925. Led by Wes Counts, Dwone Hicks, and a stout defense, MTSU defeated the Commodores 37–28. This victory was a major milestone in Raider football history, representing its first victory over an SEC opponent as well Vanderbilt. During the remainder of the season, the Raiders lost only three games, one to conference member North Texas by three points and others to SEC teams LSU and Mississippi. With a conference record of 5-1 the

Raiders were co-champions of the SBC with North Texas State. Because North Texas had won the head-to-head meeting with MTSU, the Mean Green represented the conference in the first New Orleans Bowl game.

From 2002–2005, McCollum's teams suffered four consecutive losing seasons. During the 2002 season the Raiders played four SEC schools, losing to Alabama, Tennessee, and Kentucky, but defeating Vanderbilt 21–20 for their second consecutive victory over the Commodores. In September of 2003 McCollum's club played games against major football powers, Georgia, Clemson, and Missouri. The Raiders lost all three, but carried Missouri into overtime before losing 41–40. McCollum's losing ways continued over the next two years. The Raiders did defeat Vanderbilt for the third time in five years on October 1, 2005, in another close game 17–15. In November 2005 McCollum was told that he would be relieved of his duties at the end of the season. The new athletic director, Chris Massaro, who had replaced James Donnelly earlier in the year, moved quickly to hire a replacement. On December 12, 2005, Rick Stockstill became the new head coach.

Rick Stockstill, a star quarterback at Florida State in the early 1980s, had extensive experience as an assistant coach and recruiter at Central Florida, East Carolina, Clemson, and South Carolina. Stockstill inherited a team that had had little success in recent years on the football field or in meeting graduation requirements. Stockstill and his assistant coaches had an immediate impact upon the football program, by placing emphasis on discipline, hard work, and academics. Stockstill revitalized the Raiders in his first season. In 2006 the Raiders went 7-5, losing to Maryland, Oklahoma, Louisville, South Carolina, and Troy. Both MTSU and Troy had only one conference loss and were co-champions of the SBC. Since Troy had won the game against Middle Tennessee, the Trojans represented the conference in the New Orleans Bowl, while MTSU received a bid to play in the Motor City Bowl in Detroit. The Motor City Bowl against Central Michigan of the Mid American Conference was the Blue Raiders' first bowl game in the Division I-A era. The Central Michigan Chippewas led by their great quarterback, Dan LeFevour, got off to a fast start, and the Raiders could never catch up—Central Michigan won 31–17. Stockstill was voted SBC Coach of the Year in 2006 in recognition of his first year's success. Equally important, Stockstill's emphasis on academics had begun a dramatic improvement in the team's academic progress rate.

In 2007 the Blue Raiders suffered a disappointing season, going 5-7. The club began the season with four consecutive losses, two to conference opponents and the others to Louisville and LSU. The remainder of season was better, but suffered a heart-breaking televised loss to Virginia on Horace Jones Field on October 6. In 2008 the Raiders again went 5-7, and this season will long be remembered for two Raider victories on Jones Field. The first came on September 6, when MTSU defeated Maryland 24–14, the school's first ever victory over an ACC team. The second was a dramatic last second victory over Florida Atlantic in a "black out" game (the Raider crowd all wore black) on national television on September 30. The Raiders had trailed the entire game, but scored two touchdowns in the last 5.2 minutes of the fourth quarter. The winning touchdown came as time was about to expire when Malcolm Beyah leaped high in the end zone to snare Joe Craddock's pass over several defenders.

The 2009 season began with an away loss to Clemson on September 5. The Raiders then reeled off three consecutive victories, including a dramatic second consecutive victory over Maryland by a score of 32–31. Stockstill's club then dropped consecutive games to Troy and Mississippi State by sizeable margins. On October 24, the Raiders defeated Western Kentucky decisively, beginning a run of six consecutive victories over conference opponents. The Raiders closed the regular season 9-3 and 7-1 in conference play. Troy had won the conference championship, going 8-0, but decided not to accept the bid to the New Orleans Bowl, instead agreeing to play Central Michigan in the GMAC Bowl in Mobile. Middle Tennessee was now selected to play Southern Mississippi from Conference USA in the New Orleans Bowl on December 20. In the first ever game with Southern Mississippi, the Raiders quickly fell behind the Golden Eagles at 14–0 at the end of the first quarter. The Raiders, however, behind the inspired play of quarterback Dwight Dasher, scored 14 points in each of the remaining three quarters to win the game 42–32. Dasher threw for two touchdowns and ran for two others. He also rushed for 201 yards in the game to set a new NCAA record for a quarterback in a bowl game, breaking Vince Young's record of 200 yards set against USC in the 2006 Rose Bowl. Dasher was also selected as the MVP of the game. The New Orleans Bowl victory gave MTSU a 10-3 record, best ever to date, and gave Stockstill a bowl record of 1-1. For his team's 2009 efforts, Stockstill was selected co-coach of the year along with Larry Blakeney of Troy.

The Blue Raider players and coaches approached the 2010 season with great expectations. However, things began to unravel before the season started; both the offensive and defensive coordinators had left to accept other coaching positions, and this produced adjustments on the part of players and coaches alike. Most serious was Dwight Dasher's suspension for four games by the NCAA for rules infractions. The Raiders opened at home against Minnesota, the Raiders first ever Big Ten opponent. The Raiders played well enough under the circumstances before eventually losing to the much larger Golden Gophers. In the next three games the Raiders went 2-1, defeating Austin Peay and the University of Louisiana–Lafayette, while losing to the Memphis Tigers. After an open date Troy came to Jones Field and manhandled the Raiders 42–13, in a televised game featuring Dasher's first start after his suspension. In the next game the Raiders lost to Georgia Tech, but did defeat the University of Louisiana–Monroe the following week. The victory over the War Hawks was followed by consecutive defeats at the hands of conference foes Arkansas State and North Texas. MTSU's football season seemed to be slipping away at this point. However, over the next three games, Stockstill's Raiders mounted a dramatic turnaround, beginning with an exciting last minute win over Western Kentucky by a score of 27–26. The Raiders closed out the season with two victories over Florida Atlantic and Florida International to become bowl eligible with a record of 6-6.

Florida International, Troy, and Middle Tennessee all received bowl bids, the first time the conference placed three teams in bowl games in a single season. Troy was selected for the New Orleans Bowl, Florida International for the Little Caesars Pizza Bowl in Detroit, and MTSU for the GoDaddy.com Bowl in Mobile. On January 6, 2011, the Blue Raiders squared off against the Miami (Ohio) Red Hawks before over 38,000 fans. The Raiders hoped to become the third SBC team to defeat a MAC opponent in 2010–11 bowl season. The two clubs played to a 14–14 tie in the first half, with the Blue Raiders scores coming from a Phillip Tanner run of 18 yards and Dwight Dasher's sprint of 49 yards. MTSU received the opening kickoff to start the second half. On the Raiders' first set of downs, Dasher threw an interception returned for a Red Hawk touchdown. In the Raiders' next offensive possession, Tanner scored his second touchdown of the game on a run of 54 yards that tied the game 21–21. From that point forward the game became one of mistakes, miscues, and missed opportunities for Raiders as Dasher threw an additional three interceptions. Raider mistakes and poor execution combined with a solid Miami defense produced a 35–21 Miami victory. The defeat produced a 6-7 record for the season and a bowl record of 1-2 for Coach Stockstill.

In the Sun Belt decade MTSU has produced numerous all-conference players. Wes Counts, Devon Hicks, Kendall Newsom, Brandon Westbrook, Kerry Wright, Jeff Littlejohn, Desmon Gee, Ranklin Dunbar, Tyrone Calico, ReShard Lee, Brian Kelly, Germanyle Franklin, Chris McCoy, Mark Thompson, Jeremy Kellum, Alex Suber, Marcus Udell, Jamari Lattimore, Danny Carmichael, Cam Robinson, Rod Issac, Phillip Tanner, Allan Gendreau, Dwight Dasher, and Quinton Stanton were all selected as All-SBC players. Wes Counts, Dwone Hicks, Jeff Littlejohn, Chris McCoy, and Jamari Lattimore were also honored as SBC Players of the Year. Brandon Westbrook and Jeff Littlejohn were recently selected as members of the Sun Belt Conference All-Decade team.

SUN BELT CONFERENCE BASKETBALL

Randy Wiel led the Blue Raiders men's basketball program into SBC play, but back-to-back poor seasons and a lack of conference wins led to his resignation in 2002. Kermit Davis replaced Wiel as the nineteenth coach in the team's history. Davis had extensive coaching experience at both the junior college and university levels. Among his coaching stops were Idaho, Texas A&M, Utah State, and LSU. He also had led teams into the NCAA tournament in his career. Davis had multiple tasks as the Raiders' head coach. He had to turn around a program with only five winning seasons since 1991–92; he had to recruit well, instill a winning spirit in his players, and reverse the poor fan attendance that had come to characterize the program in recent years.

In his first season of 2002–03, Davis led the club to a winning season going 16-14 overall with 9-5 marks in conference play. The Raiders played well in the 2003 SBC tournament, defeating South Alabama and Denver to reach the championship game against Western Kentucky. The Hilltoppers, however, defeated the Raiders and advanced to the NCAA Tournament. Davis was voted SBC Coach of the Year in recognition of his first year's efforts. From 2003 to 2007 Davis's teams consistently posted winning seasons with one exception. In all of these years his teams made it to the second round of the postseason tournament before losing in the semi-final game. In the 2007–08 campaign Davis posted a 17-15 record with a conference mark of 11-7. In the SBC tournament the team defeated Troy and South Alabama to force a championship game with Western Kentucky for the conference title and automatic bid to a NCAA Regional appearance. The Hilltoppers again defeated the Raiders 67–57. Over the next two seasons, the Blue Raiders posted winning seasons, but failed to capture a conference tournament title.

Kermit Davis is one of Middle Tennessee's most successful men's basketball coaches. The victory over Tennessee State on December 29, 2010, gave Davis 142 MTSU career wins and moved him past Bruce Stewart to second place behind Jimmy Earle's 164 victories. Davis recruited better quality players, improved average game attendance, and stressed academic progress for his players. However, the standard that Davis must meet to be considered a great MTSU basketball coach is a conference championship and appearance in the NCAA postseason tournament. The 2010–11 season is underway, and in early January the club is currently 6-9 and 1-1 in the conference.

MTSU has produced outstanding players in the SBC era, one of the best was Tommy Gunn who scored 1,528 points in his career and was an All-SBC selection from 2003–04. Lee Nosse scored 1,056 points and made the all-conference team in 2002. Also capturing All-SBC designation were Desmond Yates, Mike Dean, Kevin Kanaskie, William Pippen, and Michael Cuffee.

SUN BELT CONFERENCE BASEBALL

Steve Peterson's baseball program had enjoyed great success in the OVC, and that winning tradition has extended into the Sun Belt Conference. In 2001 the Raiders went 41-17 and 17-10 in conference play. Peterson's 41 victories were to date a career high at MTSU. In the club's first SBC tournament the Raiders won three straight over Arkansas State, Western Kentucky, and New Orleans before losing the championship to South Alabama. The Raiders, however, were an at-large selection to the NCAA tournament, traveling to play in the Knoxville Regional. In the first tournament contest Peterson started his ace pitcher, Dewon Brazelton, and Tennessee countered with Wyatt Allen. The game was a classic pitchers' duel with both hurlers going the distance. UT's All-American, Chris Burke, executed a squeeze bunt that scored the winning run in a 2–1 Volunteer victory. Without the services of two key players, Josh Renick and Justin Sims, who were injured against UT, the Raiders were eliminated in the second round by Wake Forest. For their efforts in the 2001 season, Dewon Brazelton, Josh Renick, Brandon Johnson, Justin Sims, and Jeremy Armstrong were all named All-SBC players. Renick and Brazelton were selected as All-Americans. Brazelton was also voted SBC Pitcher of the Year and the SBC

Student-Athlete of the Year.

Peterson's squad faced a rebuilding year in 2002 and suffered a losing season. The following campaign in 2003 brought better results. The club went 26-30 but only 8-16 in conference play. Still, the Raiders rose to the challenge and captured the conference tournament title and automatic berth in NCAA postseason play. The Raiders were placed in the Starkville Regional and faced a powerful Mississippi State team in the first game. The top seeded Bulldogs won 10–4 and the Missouri Tigers eliminated the Raiders in the second round. The 2002–03 club did produce outstanding players. Receiving All-SBC player honors were Justin Sims, Josh Archer, Marshall Nisbet, Chad Cooper, and Brett Carroll.

In 2004 Peterson's club again reached the 40 victories level, going 40-22 and 16-8 in SBC games. In the double-elimination postseason conference tournament the Raiders played five games before losing the championship to Western Kentucky. The Raiders, however, did receive an at-large bid to the NCAA tournament and placed in the Athens, Georgia Regional. The club was eliminated from the playoffs with two consecutive losses to Georgia and Birmingham Southern. Eric McNamee, Chris Mobley, Jeff Beachum, John Williams, and Derek Phillips received All SBC distinction. Peterson was selected as the Sun Belt Conference Coach of the Year for his success in 2004.

From 2005 to 2008 Peterson's teams won 30 or more victories three times with only one losing season, in 2008. During this time the teams usually played deep into the postseason tournament falling just short of another championship. These years saw the emergence of new stars winning all-conference recognition. Winning All-SBC distinction were Michael McHenry, Matt Scott, Jeff Beachum, Rawley Bishop, Bruce Bentz, Nate Jaggers, and Wayne Kendrick.

Before the start of the 2009 season, Steve Peterson suffered a heart attack and underwent surgery in late November 2008. This medical emergency placed Peterson's coaching career in jeopardy. He did return to coaching, but said that he intended to better balance his responsibilities of family and baseball while remaining committed to his players and a winning tradition. It was, perhaps, appropriate that the 2009 season was a record one for MTSU's most successful baseball coach.

Peterson led a strong and determined squad into the 2009 campaign. The club won a record number of victories, 44-18 and 21-8 in conference. The Raiders won both the regular season and the post-conference tournament. The tournament championship and automatic NCAA berth was the second for Peterson in the SBC era. The victory over UL–Monroe in the championship game was the 43rd of the season, establishing a new record for the Raider program. The berth in the NCAA tournament was the tenth in Peterson's career. The Raiders were placed in the Louisville Regional along with Louisville, Vanderbilt and Indiana. In the first regional game the Raiders faced the Vanderbilt Commodores who had finished second to LSU in the SEC championship tournament. The second-seeded Raiders defeated the Commodores. In the second game the club faced a powerful Louisville squad. Bryce Brentz, both an All-American outfielder and capable pitcher, pitched

7 2/3 innings before allowing a home run, which tied the score at 2–2. Coty Woods relieved Brentz and got the final out of the inning. Louisville scored another run in the top of the ninth, and closed the Raiders out in their last at bat to win. The Raiders now faced Vanderbilt again in an elimination game for both clubs. The Commodore pitching staff threw a shutout and the Raiders fell by the wayside. The win over Vanderbilt in the first round, however, was the first for MTSU in NCCA play since the 2000 Clemson Regional.

The Raiders' 2009 "Season of Seasons" was recognized when it came time to award All-Sun Belt honors. Bryce Brentz who had led the nation in batting average (.465), home runs (28), and three other statistical categories was named Sun Belt Player of the Year. He was also selected as an All-American player for the second time in his career. Others selected as All-SBC Players were Kenneth Roberts, Rawley Bishop, Coty Woods, Nathan Hines, and Drew Robertson.

The Raiders' 2010 season was a good one, but fell short of the achievements of the previous year. The Raiders went 34-23 overall and 20-13 in conference games. The club was seeded third in the postseason tournament played at Reese Smith Field. The Raiders failed to capture a title on their home field. Florida International won the championship. The club, however, was well represented in All-SBC Player selections with Byrce Brentz, Justin Miller, Justin Guidry, and Tyler Burnett receiving the distinction.

Steve Peterson is not only a great coach, but also a great recruiter of players and successful fundraiser for the Blue Raider baseball program. His coaching accomplishments have led to his inclusion in several halls of fame, and he has been selected as coach of the year in the OVC and SBC, as well as the Tennessee Junior College Athletic Association for his efforts while coaching at Roane State Community College. However, Peterson is a fundraiser with few peers. Assisted ably by John Stanford, Peterson has raised many thousands of dollars through such activities as his annual Groundhog Luncheon, Grand Slam Fish Fries, Chuck Taylor Golf Tournament, and various capital funds campaigns. These funds have been used to create a baseball stadium and complex among the best in the Southeast.

SUN BELT CONFERENCE GOLF, TENNIS, TRACK

The men's golf, tennis, and track programs have all enjoyed success in Sun Belt competition. Johnny Moore led the golf team until the summer of 2007. In his last season as head coach, his squad suffered a heart-breaking loss in the 2007 SBC championship tournament. Trailing by 13 strokes, the team rallied to tie UL–Lafayette only to lose the title in a sudden-death playoff. Moore's last team finished 47th in the national rankings, and Chas Narramore was selected to compete in the NCAA National Tournament. Whit Turnbow succeeded Moore as the sixth coach in the program.

Whit Turnbow had played his collegiate golf at MTSU and returned as Moore's assistant in 2003. He led his squad to its first SBC championship in the 2008–09 season. Among the star golfers that Moore and Turnbow produced in the SBC era were J. R. Wade, Josh Nelms, Patrick Williams, Chas Narramore, Rich Cochran, and Craig Smith.

Dale Short's tennis teams dominated the OVC in the 1990s, but the SBC featured stronger competition. Short did carry players into NCAA Regional play in 2001–02 before winning the conference championship in the 2005–06 season. Short was selected as SBC Coach of the Year on one occasion before he resigned in 2007. During his Sun Belt career, Short produced such notable players as Daniel Klemetz, Andreas Silijestrom, Marco Born, Brandon Allen, and Kai Schledorn.

David McNamara succeeded Short as head coach in 2007. He had been an All-American player at MTSU in the late 1990s. He joined Short's staff as an assistant coach in early 2006. In 2009 McNamara led his team to a victory over FAU in the conference tournament and a NCAA Regional appearance. In 2010 the Blue Raider team suffered a disappointing season, going 7-20 overall. McNamara resigned his position in May 2010. Athletic Director Chris Massaro hired Jimmy Borendame to lead the program into the 2010–11 season. Borendame had played his collegiate tennis at Butler University and served most recently as head coach at Drake University before joining MTSU.

Dean Hayes's track program had dominated late OVC competition and this trend continued into early Sun Belt competition. Hayes has won SBC championships in men's indoor and outdoor track, women's indoor and outdoor track, and men's outdoor cross country. From 2001 to 2004 both the men's and women's indoor track teams captured four consecutive championships. From 2001 to 2007, the combined outdoor squads have won five championships. Since the mid-decade, however, MTSU's control of SBC track has been challenged across the board by the rise of a powerful program at Western Kentucky. Coach Erik Jenkins's squads have captured the bulk of the titles in both the men's and women's programs. Hayes's success in SBC track has produced over a dozen Coach of the Year awards for him in the past decade.

Hayes continued to produce numerous All-American and All-SBC athletes over the last ten years. The best-known competitor of this period was Mardy Scales, a seven-time All-American and national champion in the 100 meters dash in 2003. He was also selected SBC Most Outstanding Track Performer in 2003 and 2004. Scales, along with five-time All-American Godfrey Herring, was selected to the All-Time Sun Belt Track Team in 2006. Other great performers for Hayes during these years were Juan Walker, Jasper Demps, Zamzan Sangua, Sara Lunning, Kishara George, Orlando Reid, and Rosemary Okafor.

Dean Hayes has been selected coach of the year in both the OVC and SBC numerous times in his career. He was selected NCAA Outdoor Coach of the Year in 1981. He has been inducted into many halls of fame, including the Emmett and Rose Sports Hall of Fame at MTSU. Hayes is among the few MTSU coaches to lend their names to the campus landscape. On May 8, 2009, the school's track and soccer facility was named the Dean Hayes Track and Soccer Complex.

SUN BELT WOMEN'S SPORTS

Women's golf is the most recently established athletic program at MTSU. Begun in 2001, the golf team has had three coaches in its short history. Kim St. John, Rachael Short, and Chris Adams have all led the team. St. John lasted only a semester, while Short led the club until 2007 when Adams replaced her.

The women's golf team has never won an SBC championship. The University of Denver, winning the last seven tournaments, has dominated women's golf in the Sun Belt Conference. Middle Tennessee has never placed higher than third in SBC competition. Short, however, was voted SBC Coach of the Year in 2005. While the team has never won a title, it has produced outstanding players. Tamara Munsch and Taryn Durham have been selected All-SBC golfer three times in their playing careers. Kristin Lynch and Maggie McGill have also been selected to the All-SBC squad.

The women's tennis team had four head coaches over the past decade. The team had not won a championship since it left the OVC in 2000. The club's highest finish in the championship tournament was third under Randy Holden in 2001.The club's tournament play bottomed out at ninth in the 2006 tournament. Allison Ojeda replaced Neal Stapp later that year. Ojeda inherited a weak program with only two returning players. She worked hard to recruit quality athletes and improve the team's record over the next several years. On June 30, 2010, Ojeda resigned her position at MTSU in order to accept an assistant coaching position at Baylor University. Melissa Schaub, an assistant to Ojeda, was promoted to head coach in August of 2010.

While MTSU has yet to win an SBC women's tennis title, it has produced some outstanding players. Among those who have earned All-SBC honors are Manon Kruse, Carien Venter, Stacy Varnell, Laura McNamara, Jennifer Klaschka, and Hala Sufi. Three Raider players have had success in NCAA tournament play. Mano Kruse played in three NCAA Singles Championships competition from 2002 to 2004 compiling a record of 1-3. Kruse and Stacy Varnell competed in three NCAA Doubles Championship competitions during those same years going 2-3. Kruse and Varnell earned All-American honors and were ranked tenth in the nation in 2004.

The MTSU softball team has had four coaches, Karen Green, Cindy Connelley, Leigh Podlesny, and Sue Nevar, over the last ten years. While the Raiders won the OVC championship in 2000 and participated in the NCAA tournament, the club has yet to capture a Sun Belt title. Since MTSU's admission to the Sun Belt Conference, UL–Lafayette has owned the conference, winning nine of the last ten championships. While the Raiders have yet to finish better than third in the conference tournament, the teams have produced All-Sun Belt players during this period. Cortney Mitchell, Muriel Ledbetter, Jennifer Martinez, and Stayc Preator have been two-time selections. Cortney Mitchell was voted Sun Belt Player of the Year in 2004, and she and Jennifer Martizez were selected for the All-SBC 30th Anniversary Team.

SUN BELT CONFERENCE SOCCER

The MTSU soccer teams have been very competitive in the Sun Belt Conference. Coach Scott Ginn led the program for the first two years before giving way to Aston Rhoden. Prior to coming to Middle Tennessee, Rhoden had founded and coached a very successful program at North Alabama. He installed a style of play that stressed a quick, aggressive offensive, coupled with a strong defense. After an initial losing season, Rhoden's teams have enjoyed eight consecutive winning seasons. The Raiders were co-champions of the regular season with North Texas in 2004, but the Mean Green won the tournament championship. Rhoden's 2006 squad set a program record of 17 victories in a season. The team continued to succeed, producing quality players and attracting larger crowds to its home matches. In 2010 MTSU's soccer team broke through to capture the league's tournament title and automatic bid to NCAA regional play. The 2010 club played Florida State in the Tallahassee Regional. The Raiders were defeated by a much stronger Seminole club by a score of 3–0.

Rhoden has created a winning soccer tradition at MTSU while producing honors for himself and his players. He was selected SBC Coach of the Year in 2003 and 2004. He has coached a substantial number of ALL-SBC players. Among those selected were Laura Miguez, Debs Brerton, Holly Grogan, Rebecaa Rodriquez, Claire Ward, Ingrid Christensen, Fran Howell, Regina Thomas, Vanessa Mueggler, and Whitney Jorgenson. Brerton and Miguez were selected to the All-Time SBC Women's Soccer team in 2005 to mark the 30th anniversary of the conference.

SUN BELT CONFERENCE WOMEN'S VOLLEYBALL

Lisa Kissee led MTSU's volleyball program into the Sun Belt Conference. Unfortunately, the team did not perform very well in the first four years of conference play and Matt Peck replaced her in 2004. Peck brought an impressive coaching record at Wayne State and North Alabama to MTSU, along with considerable experience in NCAA post-tournament play.

During the 2004 and 2005 seasons Peck's teams went 45-18, but NCAA sanctions vacated these two seasons results. Free of sanctions the 2006 team had a great year, posting an overall record of 27-8 and 14-3 in conference play. The Raiders won the SBC tournament championship and advanced to NCAA regional competition for the first time in the SBC era. In the NCAA Tournament the Raiders defeated Louisville before falling to Ohio State in the second round. Peck's 2007 team posted the best overall record in the program's history going 35-3 overall and 16-1 in conference matches. The club defeated Western Kentucky in the conference tournament championship match and proceeded to NCAA postseason play for the second year in a row. Peck's team defeated Louisville and Hawaii in the first two rounds played at Louisville. The Raiders made it to the "Sweet Sixteen" and headed to semifinals at Penn State. There the Raiders' dream season came crashing down at the hands of BYU. Peck's 2007 club ended the season ranked 15th in the nation in the final American Volleyball Coaches Association poll.

The 2008 squad did not match the record of the previous year but still had an excellent record of 27-8. It also lost in the second round of the conference championship tournament. They did receive an at-large bid to the NCAA Tournament. The Raiders faced Miami (Ohio) in the first round and won 3–2. Playing on their home court, the Purdue team eliminated the Raiders in the second round. Peck's teams continued to succeed in 2009 and 2010. The 2009 team did not win the conference tournament but received another at-large bid to the NCAA Tournament where it lost to Colorado State in the first round. Peck's 2010 team won both the regular season and tournament titles and made it to the NCAA Tournament for the fifth time in five years. They were eliminated in the first round by Louisville. Yet Matt Peck has carried the Raider volleyball program to the upper tier of the Sun Belt Conference. He has also produced outstanding players in doing so. Ashley Adams and Ashley Asberry have won All-American honors. Those earning All-SBC designation were Leslie Clark, Quanshell Scott, KeKe Deckard, Dara McLean, Izabela Kozon, and Stacy Oladinni.

SUN BELT CONFERENCE WOMEN'S BASKETBALL

MTSU has a tradition of winning women's basketball teams. Begun in the OVC era, this tradition has grown even larger in the Sun Belt Conference. Stephany Smith's club had a winning record in the team's first season in the SBC and received a bid to the NIT Tournament in the 2001. The Raiders lost to Indiana in the first round. While posting winning records over the next two years, the team did not win an SBC title until the 2003–04 season when it went 24-8. The Raiders got off to a good start in the 2004 NCAA Tournament defeating North Carolina 67–62 in one of the greatest victories to date in the program. The Raiders, however, fell to Notre Dame in the second round. Smith's 2004–05 team delivered 24 victories, but entered the conference tournament without a first round bye. The Raiders won four conference tournament games to advance to the NCAA playoffs. The team traveled to Dallas where it defeated North Carolina State in an exciting game 60–58. In the second round Smith's club fell behind early and Texas Tech cruised to an easy victory. Stephany Smith's two consecutive tournament titles and appearances in the NCAA playoffs did not go unnoticed. The University of Alabama hired her to head the Crimson Tide's program. Smith finished her career at MTSU with a record of 153-88.

Athletic Director Chris Massaro had just taken his position at MTSU when the women's head basketball coaching position became vacant. There was no shortage of coaches interested in the position because of the program's record of success. To the surprise of many fans, Massaro hired Rick Insell, the head coach of nearby Shelbyville High School. Some MTSU supporters believed that Massaro had made a major mistake in placing a high school coach over a Division I-A program. Insell, however, was not just another successful high school coach. He had won ten state championships and his club had finished second in five state tournaments. Insell's Golden Eaglettes set a Tennessee record for consecutive wins during one stretch in his career. At the national level, Insell was selected USA National High School Coach of the Year twice and was named as Converse National High School Coach of the Year in 1990 and 1992. Insell also had 775 wins in his high school coaching career, making him one of the most successful coaches ever in Tennessee and the nation, and he had extensive AAU coaching experience as well.

Insell's first season sent a clear message that the MTSU's women's basketball program was in capable hands. His club went 20-11 and captured the SBC tournament title. Insell's first club was led by the brilliant play of Chrissy Givens. For her play, Givens was selected as Sun Belt Player of the Year, Defensive Player of the Year, and MVP of the Sun Belt Tournament. In Insell's first trip to NCAA play, his club led Utah by one point, 68–67, with less than four minutes to play. The Raiders faltered in the final minutes losing 76–71.

Insell's 2006–07 season was a historic one. The team went 30-4 overall and 18-0 in conference play. He also captured his consecutive tournament title and made his second trip to the NCAA Tournament. The Raiders were seeded fifth in regional play at Stanford. Chrissy Givens, Amber Holt, and Krystle Horton led the Raiders to a crushing victory over Gonzaga by a score of 85–46. In the second round Marist College repeatedly broke the MTSU press and defeated the Raiders by 14 points. The defeat at the hands of the Marist Red Foxes ended MTSU's winning streak of 27 consecutive games.

The 2007–08 team could not match the performance of the previous year. While the graduation of Chrissy Given and Krystle Horton hurt the team, the play of Amber Holt and newcomer Alysha Clark carried the club to a record of 22-12 and a postseason appearance in the NIT Tournament. The Raiders began play in the NIT at Murphy Center where they won a lopsided victory over Western Carolina with a final score of 104–69. The Raiders next traveled to Lexington to play Kentucky. The Raiders came from behind to tie the Wildcats in the final seconds of regulation play. In a hard-fought overtime the Wildcats outscored the Raiders 7–5, winning the game by a score of 68–66. A major highlight of the season was the play of Amber Holt who led the nation in scoring.

Insell's 2008–09 team was another strong squad featuring the remarkable play of Alysha Clark, a transfer from Belmont. The team posted a 28-6 overall record with a conference mark of 17-1. The Raiders captured the conference tournament crown with a victory over UALR in the championship game. The team was sent to East Lansing, Michigan, for NCAA play. The Raiders were paired against Michigan State in the first round and suffered a heart-breaking one-point loss on their opponent's home court. During the season Alysha Clark led the nation in scoring. For two consecutive years MTSU had produced the nation's leading scorer. This marked the first time in NCAA history that two different players from the same team had done so in consecutive years.

Insell's 2009–10 squad again repeated as SBC conference champions, going

25-6 and capturing the conference tournament title. The Raiders were headed for another NCAA appearance for the fourth time in Insell's first five years at MTSU. The Raiders traveled to Pittsburg for the first round of NCAA play. The club lost a close game to a powerful Mississippi State club by the score of 68–64.

Rick Insell's team was off to a good start in the 2010–11 season. The club had a strong record early in the season and was 3-0 in early conference games. As of January 11, 2011 Insell's career record at MTSU was 137-43, putting him fourth on the list of career wins for the women's basketball program.

SUN BELT CONFERENCE SUPPORT

MTSU has produced many gifted players during their time in the Sun Belt Conference. The program has produced such All-SBC performers as Jamie Thomatis, Patrice Holmes, Krystle Horton, Chrissy Givens, Tia Stovall, Amber Holt, and Alysha Clark. Givens, Holt, and Clark also received All-American honors. The Sun Belt decade has produced some of the program's most outstanding players. Jamie Thomatis, Chrissy Givens, Patrice Holmes, Alysha Clark, Krystle Horton, and Amber Holt all rank in the top ten scorers to date in Raider history. The decade has produced SBC Player of the Year honors as well for the Raider program. Insell was selected SBC Women's Basketball Coach of the Year in 2007 and 2009.

While coaches and players are the very core of athletic competition, a school must have other components in place to sustain a winning program in the modern era. Among these necessary components are: capable administrators and supportive presidents; excellent playing facilities; fundraising organizations; academic support programs for student-athletes; and modern conditioning programs. MTSU has all of these in place today.

Over the past decade three athletic directors, Lee Fowler, James Donnelly, and Chris Massaro, have led the MTSU sports program during its transition to the highest level of NCAA competition and membership in a new athletic conference. These men and Diane Turnham, associate athletic director and senior women's administrator, have promoted capital campaigns for new facilities; raised the level of competition with more innovative scheduling; worked to improve the graduation rates of athletes; and made key personnel decisions. Among the hires made by these people and President Sidney McPhee are such coaches as Rick Stockstill, Rick Insell, Ashton Rhoden, Matt Peck, and others.

President McPhee has been a powerful advocate for a strong athletic program at MTSU. In addition to his role in the athletic decisions of MTSU, he has served in key positions in the Sun Belt Conference and at the national NCAA level as well. He has served two terms as president of the Sun Belt Conference and chaired the SBC's Executive Committee. He has also been very active in NCAA matters. He has served on the NCAA Division I Board of Directors and NCAA Executive Committee. He was also appointed to the President's Committee on the Future of Intercollegiate Athletics. No MTSU president has ever exercised as much influence on athletic policy at either the conference or national levels as Dr. Sidney McPhee.

The final components to a successful athletic program are the facilities and support centers. Whether it's the Monte Hale Arena in Murphy Center, Horace Jones Field, Reese Smith Field, Dean Hayes Track and Soccer Complex, or other sites, MTSU has excellent playing facilities. Too, the Academic Enhancement Center, located in the middle of the athletic facilities, is in place to assist student-athletes to meet their academic goals and maintain progress toward graduation. The university has a strong promotional and financial partner in the Blue Raider Athletic Association. Another support and education facility for MTSU athletics is the Emmett and Rose Kennon Sports Hall of Fame. And, a final and special note should also be made of the role of athletic administrative officials. As MTSU celebrates its centennial, alumni, students, and fans can take great pride in the school's athletic traditions and accomplishments. From very humble beginnings, Middle Tennessee State University has risen to the highest level of NCAA competition. What will the next century bring?

SOURCES

I. Middle Tennessee State Normal School Publications
Normalite. Spring, 1922.
Signal. December, 1912; March, 1913; May, 1913; February, 1914; May,
    1915; Fall, 1917.

II. Middle Tennessee State Teachers College Publications
Midlander. 1926, 1928, 1929, 1930, 1931, 1933.

III. Middle Tennessee State College Publications
Midlander. 1946, 1949, 1950, 1960.

IV. Middle Tennessee State University Publications
Midlander. 1966.
2009 Middle Tennessee Baseball Media Guide
2008–09 Men's Basketball Media Guide
2008–09 Middle Tennessee State Women's Basketball Media Guide
2008 Middle Tennessee Football Media Guide
2008 Middle Tennessee Golf Media Guide
2008 Middle Tennessee Soccer Media Guide
2008 Middle Tennessee Softball Media Guide
2005–06 Middle Tennessee Men's Tennis Media Guide
2008 Middle Tennessee Women's Tennis Media Guide
2008 Middle Tennessee Blue Raider Track and Field Media Guide
2008 Middle Tennessee Volleyball Media Guide

V. Emmett and Rose Kennon Sports Hall of Fame Exhibits
"Bubber" Murphy Exhibit
A Coach's Coach Exhibit
Hey Coach Exhibit
1911–1939 Exhibit
1940–1959 Exhibit

VI. Books
Newby, Bobby. *They Bled Raider Blue.* Privately published, 1996.
Nunley, Joe E. *The Raider Forties.* New York: Vantage Press, 1977.
Pittard, Homer. *The First Fifty Years: Middle Tennessee State College, 1911–
    1961.* Murfreesboro: Middle Tennessee State College, 1961.
Ware, Susan. *Title IX; A Brief History with Documents.* Boston: Bedford/
    St. Martin's, 2007.

VII. Newspapers

Murfreesboro *Daily News Journal.* 13 May 1933, 18 December 2008,
    27 April 2009, 25 May 2009, 31 May 2009, 1 June 2009, 3 June 2009,
    8 June 2009, 2 August 2009, 30 August 2009, 1 November 2009,
    6 December 2010, 19 December 2010, 21 December 2010,
    22 December 2010, 1 January 2011, 3 January 2011, 6 January 2011,
    7 January 2011.
Nashville *Banner.* 13 May 1933.
Nashville *Tennessean.* 14 May 1933, 25 May 1977.

VIII. Unpublished Study

Kirby, James T. "The History and Development of the Volunteer State
    Athletic Conference." MA thesis, Tennessee Technological University, 1969.

IX.   Web Sites

www.goblueraiders.com
www.ovcsports.com
www.sunbeltsports.org

CHAPTER SEVEN

1968 on Campus

JORDAN KIRKMAN

The year, 1968, was truly unique in the United States. American casualties mounted as a result of the war in Vietnam. Martin Luther King Jr. fell to an assassin's bullet in April, followed shortly afterward by presidential candidate Robert Kennedy, who was assassinated in June. Americans looked on in shock at the turbulent scenes coming from their television sets. Some college students, unified by their contempt for the war in Vietnam and their feelings of loss, took action. They felt empowered by their numbers and took to the streets to demonstrate against the war, the draft, and racial inequality. Many students believed that they had the power to change the world, and they refused to let the opportunity slip away. The feeling was infectious as an increasing number of students struggled to have their issues addressed. Students made their voices heard at schools across the country, including Columbia, Princeton, Berkeley, and many others.

The effects of that cataclysmic year impacted many American universities, including Middle Tennessee State University. MTSU did not experience turbulent demonstrations and appeared on the surface to be unaffected by the events in the larger United States society and abroad. Nonetheless, the shockwaves of that year hit MTSU just as they did other schools. "Nineteen sixty-eight was a knife blade that severed past from future, Then from Now," wrote Lance Marrow of *Time* magazine, and the knife undoubtedly came down at Middle Tennessee State University.[1]

The violent events of 1968 are familiar to most observers of mid-twentieth century American history. Undoubtedly, the war in Vietnam was a central issue. At the end of January, a limited peace had been declared in Vietnam to honor Tet, the Vietnamese lunar New Year. The streets of Vietnam were quiet when the North Vietnamese launched a surprise attack on American and South Vietnamese soldiers in five major cities across South Vietnam. The North Vietnamese forces failed to gain any territory from the Tet Offensive, but the incident showed the world the vulnerability of American forces in Vietnam.[2]

Leadership in America was in crisis in 1968 as well. President Lyndon Johnson, for example, faced significant disapproval from Americans due to his failing policies in Vietnam. Several members of his own Democratic Party challenged his nomination for reelection. The nation was shocked in March when President Johnson announced that he would not run for another term, making him a lame-duck president during a time when America needed a strong leader. Less than a week later, one of America's strongest leaders fell to an assassin's bullet.

Martin Luther King Jr., the leading figure in the African American struggle for equality in the United States, went to Memphis, Tennessee, in March to lead a demonstration of sanitation workers protesting unfair wages. The demonstration, in contrast to King's usual approach, ended violently. A disheartened King delivered a sermon at the Masonic Temple that proved eerily prophetic. "He [God] has allowed me to go up to the mountain, and I've looked over. And I've seen the Promised Land," ministered Dr. King. "I may not get there with you, but I want you to know tonight that we as a people will get to the Promised Land." The next day, April 4, 1968, King was struck in the jaw by an assassin's bullet outside of his hotel room and died.[3]

In response to his death, a memorial service was held in honor of Dr. King at Columbia University. Yet even this activity proved divisive and fueled social unrest. Under the leadership of university president Grayson Kirk, Columbia had acquired more than two acres of Harlem's recreational space known as Morningside Park to build a university gymnasium. Many students felt that building a new gymnasium for the students on land appropriated from a predominantly black neighborhood proved that the university had no interest in Dr. King or his ideals. In response to this hypocrisy, students gathered on April 23 to protest this racial injustice. The protest quickly escalated, and the protestors took control of five school buildings. The university was forced to close down, and Grayson Kirk decided that the student movement had to be stopped. On April 30, New York City police moved into the occupied buildings and beat any students who stood in their path, effectively ending their protest.[4]

The racial division in America was an important factor that contributed to the turbulence of the year. According to the government's Kerner Report, released in March 1968, America was splitting into two different societies: one white and one black.[5] Senator Robert Kennedy provided America with hope of joining the races together when he sought the Democratic presidential nomination in 1968. He was a symbol of compassion, hope, and inspiration for his supporters, many of whom were members of the college generation. People rallied to him and his hope of ending "the divisions within America . . . the violence."[6] On the night that King was assassinated, for instance, Kennedy, campaigning in a black neighborhood in Indianapolis, had to inform a black crowd that King was dead. As cries swept through the crowd, violence seemed imminent. Yet Kennedy calmed the crowd, telling them that he understood how they felt, having lost his brother, John Kennedy, to an assassin's bullet five years earlier. He told them to go home and pray for the King family and America. As a result, in part, of his actions, rioting did not occur in Indianapolis.[7] Kennedy was a leader who exemplified how disaster could be avoided by simply listening to, and sympathizing with, those in need. His own life soon ended when he was assassinated on June 5, 1968, at the Ambassador Hotel in downtown Los Angeles.[8] Two of America's strongest leaders had been killed within nine weeks of each other; the stability of the United States seemed questionable.

With the leading Democratic presidential candidate deceased, the Democratic National Convention, which was held in Chicago in August of that year, became a breeding ground for demonstrations. The city was under the control of Mayor Richard Daley, whose very commanding demeanor led to his being commonly referred to as the boss of Chicago. Daley had a history of enforcing law and order through brute force. When King was assassinated in April, riots ensued in Chicago. Daley dealt with the situation by giving the order, "Shoot to kill."[9] He reacted very similarly when demonstrators attempted to march to the convention in August. At Daley's command, Chicago police intervened, pressing demonstrators against the window of the Hilton Hotel, the site of the convention. The force caused the window to break, and students filled the lobby, where police continued to assault them. The entire ordeal ended with the arrests of 650 demonstrators and hundreds more injured. The demonstration had been quelled by the strong authoritarian hand of Richard Daley. The events depicted in the news, however, served to unify some college students in their struggle against authoritarianism.

For a large part of the year, MTSU remained unaffected by these events that gripped America, but that changed before the year was over. In 1968, the school's administrators focused their efforts on campus expansion rather than social change. MTSU's student enrollment was growing, and officials needed to accommodate the new influx of students. While the Student Union Building had served students since 1951, it was, undeniably, no longer big enough to accommodate the student population.[10] On March 10, 1968, the new University Center (now known as Keathley University Center) opened its doors to students. The building boasted 81,000 square feet and contained a new bookstore, a theatre, a reading library, a TV lounge, the Associated Student Body offices, and a grill with a seating capacity for 560.

While the new University Center was meant to be a sign of progress, many saw it as a symbol of the Old South, due to the plaque that was mounted over one of the entrances. The image of the Raider depicted on the plaque was a soldier in a Confederate uniform, seated proudly astride his horse. It was generally accepted that this Raider was a representation of the Confederate general Nathan Bedford Forrest, who had fought at the Battle of Stones River almost a century prior. This plaque was not the only vestige of the Confederate South on campus.[11]

Symbols of the Old South were a significant source of school spirit and were used at sporting events to rally support for the Blue Raiders. The fall 1968 football season was no exception. On September 26, in a game against Kentucky's Morehead State University, quarterback Dickie Thomas passed to freshman slot back Herbert Patterson. Patterson leaped into the air and reached out to make an amazing catch. He then dove into the end zone to bring the Raiders up over Morehead 21–6.[12] The crowd jumped to their feet and cheered as the MTSU Band of Blue began to play "Dixie," MTSU's fight song. MTSU's mascot, a representation of General Nathan Bedford Forrest, rode his horse down the sidelines in his gray and yellow Confederate uniform, and fans waved Confederate flags throughout the stands. This was a typical fall football game at MTSU, and most students were not bothered by these Confederate symbols. For them, the symbols represented southern heritage and history.

Yet for others, these vestiges of southern pride were symbols of racism that prevailed at MTSU in the 1960s. Sylvester Brooks was one of the few black students who attended MTSU in 1968. Many white students, unaccustomed to African American classmates, approached him curiously, as Brooks recalled:

> It was kind of odd, you know. Kids would walk up to you after they kind of got to know you a little bit and they'd want to like can I feel your hair or can I touch your skin. . . . How can we talk about issues that I want to talk about and deal when somebody is asking how does your hair feel? It really kind of blew my mind.[13]

Brooks felt like an outsider among his peers, unrecognized for anything other than the color of his skin.

Coupled with race issues, the threat of Vietnam was ever present in Brooks's mind, as it was with many MTSU students. The college newspaper, *Sidelines*, ran several articles about the highly feared draft. One, in particular, stated that college graduates would make up 75 percent of all soldiers drafted by July 1968.[14] College attendance was no longer a way to avoid the draft. Later that year, the draft lottery was implemented, making the draft an entirely random process. Each day of the year had a corresponding number, and low numbers were drafted first. Many students gathered outside of the MTSU radio station to see the results of the lottery. Men in the back of the crowd would call up their birth dates, and the men up in front would reply with the corresponding number. If, for example, "331" were called out in response, it meant that someone had avoided the draft, and the crowd would cheer. Conversely, the men would "boo" if the number "six" were called out because it meant that someone was on his way to Vietnam.

Sylvester Brooks was one of the students present when the results of the draft lottery were released. He felt strange about the possibility of being drafted to fight for a country where he was not readily accepted. As a staff member for *Sidelines*, he wrote of this conflict in an editorial entitled "American Negro." Brooks asked, "If Americans can fight and die together then, by God, when they come home, why can't they live together?"[15] This was a potent question directed at an overwhelmingly white student population.

A few weeks after writing this, Brooks was in a friend's room listening to music when he heard that Dr. King had been shot. The young man who told him, a white student, appeared very concerned. The two of them rushed to the new University Center where students had gathered in the TV lounge. Everyone there appeared quite anxious as they waited for news from Memphis. While they waited, a student entered the room and deliberately changed the channel with the intent of causing a problem. Many students became upset and physically removed the young man from the building. Clearly, King's assassination in Memphis had created a lot of tension at MTSU. Few students, however, were as affected as Brooks. He was from Memphis and caught a ride home the following day to be with his family. When he arrived in Memphis, he was approached by soldiers in a military jeep with a machine gun mounted on it. They informed him that there was a curfew and then gave him a pass to get around the city well enough to get home for the night. The next day Brooks participated in a memorial march to the Masonic Temple where King had delivered his last sermon. Brooks described the march:

> It was just a huge number of people. I jumped and as far as I could see ahead of me was nothing but people and as far as I could see behind me there was nothing but people. In an American city, at every intersection, or at most intersections, they had troops, they had tanks. . . . On top of the buildings, you could see . . . these policemen and soldiers with rifles looking down at this crowd. You always kind of wondered if this thing gets out of control and turns into a riot what's going to happen. Are we going to become like a shooting alley for these people? . . . It was just amazing to see that in an American city. You see it in the rest of the world, when you see people facing cannons and machine guns, but you don't really think of it in an American city. It was a strange sort of feeling to see military control of a civilian area.[16]

In his hometown, Brooks saw the impact of King's assassination firsthand as his hopes for blacks and whites living together suffered a tremendous blow.

Brooks was also a strong supporter of Robert Kennedy. Kennedy had come to Nashville in March 1968 to deliver a speech at Vanderbilt University. Brooks was in attendance and later editorialized in *Sidelines*:

> This country is on the brink of a newer world. It is up to America to determine whether or not it is to be a better world. It is essential that we have a leader of courage. Such a man is Robert Kennedy. . . . He seeks the presidential nomination in behalf of the American people who desire unity in their country and peace in the world.[17]

Brooks was so firmly behind Kennedy that he helped form a student group called "Students for Kennedy" and was appointed as a representative to the Associated Student Body, the student governing organization.[18] Brooks believed that Kennedy had the power to end the racial divisions in America. When Kennedy was assassinated in June, Brooks's hopes for a unified society were further diminished.

In the fall, Brooks attended a football game and saw the Blue Raiders as they celebrated victory with "Dixie," Nathan Bedford Forrest, and Confederate flags. "I was shocked," Brooks reflected. "I was just taken aback by this because everything in my experience relative to that flag, and even today, I associated with racism, with deprivation."[19] Brooks clearly understood these cultural symbols differently than those who adopted them. Thus, Brooks's response to these symbols was not surprising.

The song "Dixie" was written in the mid-nineteenth century by a southern musician who was performing in New York and was not pleased with the dreary northern winter. The song gained vast popularity throughout the United States but was much more treasured in the South. In 1861, "Dixie" filled the air in Montgomery, Alabama, when Jefferson Davis took the oath of office as president of the Confederate States. When the Civil War broke out, the song became synonymous with the Confederate Army. The troops sang "Dixie" to remind them of the cause for which they marched.[20] After the Civil War ended, "Dixie" continued to arouse images of the Old South. When James Meredith, the first black student to enroll at the University of Mississippi, arrived on the campus in 1962, an angry mob with violent intentions showed up in pickup trucks. The radio volume in their trucks was loud and proud as a local radio station played the old southern tune repeatedly.[21]

Brooks had reason for further concern over the image of Nathan Bedford Forrest. Forrest was a Tennessee native who sold slaves in Memphis prior to serving as "the most brilliant cavalry officer on either side" for the Confederate Army in the Civil War. In April 1864, Forrest led an attack against a large contingent of African American soldiers at Fort Pillow, Tennessee. He attacked under a black flag, which signified his intention to kill every Union soldier that he encountered. Rumors spread of black Union soldiers being lit on fire, shot upon surrendering, or even buried alive. With his past life as a slave trader, Forrest quickly became a symbol of ruthlessness and racism after the ordeal.[22] When the war ended, Forrest helped organize and lead the Ku Klux Klan, even though there is no evidence that he stayed with the organization long after it was founded.[23] Even today, the Ku Klux Klan evokes images of burning crosses, men in white hoods who preach an ideology of white supremacy, and lynchings of innocent African Americans. Whether Nathan Forrest was active with the KKK for long or not, his lasting image provides a rallying point for the Klan even today. Members of the KKK continue to meet in Forrest City, named after the Confederate general, to preach their message of hate while black residents of the city "hold their children's hands and try to explain the purpose of these men in robes."[24]

Sylvester Brooks's negative and emotional reaction to seeing these symbols is understandable. Brooks had been known to throw rocks at the image of Nathan Bedford Forrest that hung on the newly constructed University Center, and "campus officials generally accepted his symbolic posture."[25] He soon found a much more effective way, however, to fight this injustice. Having lost two of his most inspirational leaders earlier in 1968, Brooks decided that it was time he became the leader. Brooks took pen in hand and wrote an editorial that shook MTSU to its foundations.

Sidelines hit the racks with a thud on October 21. Students opened it up over breakfast in the new University Center. They focused their sleepy eyes on an article entitled "*Dixie*: What Does it Mean?" The words echoed throughout campus:

> Does it bother you that the rebel flag represents utter and unmerciful contempt of the basic human dignity of Black people? Are you proud of your school's mascot, General Nathan Bedford Forrest; the man who founded the Ku Klux Klan; the man who killed captured Black soldiers fighting for the Union; and the man who marched into Fort Pillow in West Tennessee and murdered 250 Black men, women and children? . . . Black students have just as much right to feel a part of this campus as anyone else. And if "Dixie," the Confederate flag, and General Forrest are hinderances toward that end, then they should be banned and abolished. Black Americans are not fighting and dying in Vietnam to be subjected to the symbols of bigotry and human degradation at home . . . I as a Black person am tired of the American dream being cheated by . . . those indifferent to the cares and frustrations of their fellows. To create a newer world based on understanding, we must make the effort today.[26]

The article immediately prompted responses in the October 24 edition of *Sidelines*. Student James Doyle Trigg wrote, "We must strike down all the symbols of slavery. There is not room for one," while Bobby Sands felt that "minority rights should be respected, but Mr. Brooks is using the pretense of minority rights to try and dictate to and oppress the majority." James K. Huhta, a professor in the History Department, argued that "Brooks' comments are timely, relevant, and courageous," but Beverly Barnes retorted, "I hope everyone on this campus does not take the attitude which you have taken [Mr. Brooks] . . . . That's what I call childish."[27]

The issue not only created controversy among MTSU students but among alumni as well. Tom Cannon graduated from MTSU in 1950 and saw the article while attending a Blue Raider Club meeting. "If you people can't find anything else to fill this space," Tom suggested, "why not leave it blank?"[28] Charlotte Bachler, the wife of a teacher in the Industrial Arts Department, wrote a letter of praise to Brooks. "If more people would use their intelligence and ability to inform the 'blind' in a tactful manner, as you have displayed," exclaimed Mrs. Bachler, "I'm sure more good accomplishments would be made."[29] Some MTSU students were upset that MTSU's traditions could possibly be eliminated because of complaints from one of the school's few black students. One letter written by an apparent member of the Ku Klux Klan was addressed to the "Uninformed and Ignorant." The Klansman wrote:

> The Klan is not a bunch of bigots, as you put it, but a bunch of proud Americans that is going to put a stop to this black upsurge at any minute. . . . We the Klan are more in number than you think. . . . We know how to handle people like you and your kind of filth, as we have proved in the past.[30]

Brooks found death threats taped to his door and received threatening phone calls. He was even warned that if he continued to protest he would be turned in to the FBI by a group called Project Manhattan.[31] Jim Free, president of the Associated Student Body, received similar threats via mail promising bodily harm if he attempted to have the symbols removed.[32]

Not long after the issue was brought to the forefront, a group of black students planned a protest demonstration that was to be carried out at a home football game when the Raiders scored and "Dixie" filled the air. It seemed as though MTSU was about to experience its first student demonstration. A new leader, however, had arrived at MTSU earlier that year who intended to avoid the unrest experienced on other college campuses.

Quill E. Cope had resigned as MTSU president in early 1968 to take a position at the University of Tennessee in Knoxville.[33] Dr. Mel Scarlett, the former interim chancellor of the university system in Maine, took his place at the helm of MTSU. In his inaugural address on October 1, President Scarlett, prompted by events on other campuses, said:

> You must permit students to protest. They have a right to do it. . . . I have some ideas I want to work towards, but I think you have to live in a situation for a time and become oriented to it. I want to be a learner for a while before I begin to seriously think about making changes.[34]

President Scarlett sat back with watchful eyes after Brooks's article was published in *Sidelines* and allowed the issue to evolve on its own. Dealing with the issue of race relations required strong leadership from Scarlett, who referred to the examples of other leaders of the time to help determine his course of action. There were men, like Richard Daley of Chicago and Grayson Kirk of Columbia University, who used the authority of their positions to establish their leadership. This approach, however, led to violence in both cases and actually helped to fuel disorder rather than to quell it. On the other hand, there were leaders like Robert Kennedy who had prevented violence in Indianapolis and provided lessons on how to avoid disaster with an open ear and a sympathetic heart.

When he was informed of the demonstration that a group of black students planned to carry out when the Band of Blue played "Dixie," Scarlett hesitated. It was not his policy to dictate the music staff's choices and selections, but he had to act fast. Scarlett approached the band director, Joe Smith, and requested that he not play "Dixie." Joe Smith understood the reasons for this request and instructed the band not to perform his favorite tune that night.[35] Using a non-authoritarian approach Scarlett managed to avoid a potentially volatile situation. Yet Scarlett felt that his approach set a dangerous precedent with regard to the MTSU faculty members. He quickly addressed members of the Faculty Senate and the local chapter of the American Association of University Professors on the importance of academic freedom. Newspaper coverage of his speech noted, "He pointed out that he felt any arbitrary control he attempted to exercise over organizations on campus would be a 'serious and dangerous precedent' that would threaten academic freedom in any discipline."[36] In keeping with his non-authoritarian approach, Scarlett did not force Joe Smith and the Band of Blue to remove "Dixie" from their performance catalog. The issue would have to be resolved by the students through the Associated Student Body (ASB).

The ASB was quick to act and committed itself to improving race relations on campus. ASB members appointed MTSU student Lee Webb, a representative of Creating Understanding by Effort (CUBE), as chair of a committee to investigate how these issues could best be resolved.[37] The committee delivered its report to the ASB at the beginning of December. They advocated a new "animal like" mascot and an original fight song to phase "Dixie" out over time. They also suggested that a new MTSU flag to be selected from student entries to replace the confederate "bars and stars." The ASB House of Representatives, seeing that the time for change had arrived, favored the committee's report and even amended it so the school's current mascot, "the soldier in grey," would be done away with entirely.[38] The following week, the ASB House of Representatives and Senate passed two very similar bills to get rid of Nathan Bedford Forrest as the school's symbol and mascot at athletic events.[39] Brooks never imagined that his article would generate a vote to remove Confederate vestiges from the campus.[40] Unfortunately, the failure in both chambers to pass legislation that would bring these changes to fruition meant a long delay in implementing any actual changes. Nonetheless, Brooks's article brought attention to race relations at MTSU and began a long, difficult process that continued in the following years.

Over the next several years, "Dixie" was replaced by a new school song and phased out of use at sporting events. Long after Brooks's graduation, the use of the Raider as the school mascot and symbol was abolished. In 1978, ten years after "*Dixie*: What Does It Mean?" was published in *Sidelines*, the university initials "MTSU" replaced "The Raider" as the new school symbol. So, while Brooks did not manage to do away with the Confederate vestiges on campus during the time he spent at MTSU, he did lay the groundwork for a removal process that took years to accomplish. Furthermore, he remained a symbol of the need for improved race relations on campus.

Years later, the gradual removal of Confederate vestiges continued during the Christmas break of the 1989–1990 school year when MTSU president Dr. Sam Ingram ordered that the plaque depicting the Raider be removed from the wall of the Keathley University Center. This was met with strong opposition. Angry citizens wrote their Tennessee representatives protesting the plaque's removal and urging that it be returned to the wall where it had been on display for more than 20 years. Keith Anderson Hardison, a descendant of nine Tennessee Confederate soldiers, argued that the removal was "an insult to [his] personal heritage and an affront to the men who wore the grey."[41] Despite the opposition, the plaque was sent to the Nathan Bedford Forrest State Park in Benton County, Tennessee, never to been seen at MTSU again.

In 2006, several students moved to change the name of Forrest Hall, the ROTC building that had been named for the Confederate general. As the local paper noted, "The petition to remove the Forrest name and the Student Government Association action to endorse that removal came as a surprise" because "MTSU students generally seem docile about events of the community, the nation and the world" and "seem on the periphery in regard to most social and political issues." Many students disagreed with the removal of the Forrest name, and the ROTC building still holds the name of the Confederate general. Nonetheless, it is undeniable that "the spirit of Sylvester Brooks . . . still seems to have some presence on campus."[42]

While Sylvester Brooks was the catalyst that triggered these changes in race relations on campus, an exceptional leader was required to ensure that violence did not erupt during this turbulent process. In 1970, the non-authoritarian and flexible approach that Scarlett developed two years prior was put to the test when, in December, a group of black MTSU football players noticed something glowing outside of their dormitory late one night. They soon realized that a cross had been set ablaze in the style of the Ku Klux Klan. The group, upset and angry, turned into a mob and planned to "deal" with those responsible. The ASB president, and future Tennessee congressman, Bart Gordon, arrived on the scene and discouraged a violent reaction. Rather, he encouraged them to talk with President Scarlett, and so the students marched towards his home. Scarlett awoke around midnight to a phone call from Gordon, warning him of the students who were headed his way. Scarlett went outside to talk with the students. He responded as Robert Kennedy had done a few years earlier and, along with Gordon, listened for several hours as the students aired their grievances over racial injustices that they experienced all over campus. President Scarlett thanked them for coming to talk with him and for not reacting violently. He apologized and told them that he would not be president of a university that tolerated such behavior. At about two in the morning, the students returned, peacefully, to their dorms.[43]

Soon thereafter, teachers took radios to their classes so that the entire student body could listen as President Scarlett addressed students about the situation. Scarlett stated:

> The University is a place where men and women engage in a continuing search for truth and seek to acquire knowledge, wisdom, understanding, tolerance, and compassion. . . . This University feels a strong responsibility for, and plans to protect, all its students from physical harm, and from undue harassment and humiliation.[44]

Following the speech, Scarlett, determined to improve race relations at MTSU, ordered the ASB and Faculty Senate to provide reports about whether or not the cross burning was an isolated incident. A few days later, Scarlett and his family heard a commotion outside of their home. They opened the door to find hundreds of black students singing carols of thanks in the freshly fallen snow.[45] Scarlett had managed to diffuse the situation while still moving forward to find a solution.

1968 was a year that had strong ramifications for MTSU. The shockwaves of that chaotic year hit MTSU hard, as they had other American universities. Sylvester Brooks, affected by the assassinations of two leaders whom he hoped would bring about change, and empowered by the spirit of that year, spoke out against the Confederate vestiges that had represented MTSU. As a result, the symbols of the Old South were removed, one at a time. Mel Scarlett also took over as president of MTSU in 1968, and the events of that year had a significant impact on the style of leadership that he pursued. In response to the events of that year, Scarlett chose a non-authoritarian style of leadership that he used to prevent turbulent demonstrations, such as those seen at other universities. As a result of the lessons that 1968 offered, Scarlett successfully maintained order throughout the difficult transition that began that year and lasted for two decades.

1968 ignited the fire of racial progress at MTSU and was indeed a year that severed the past from the future at Middle Tennessee State University. While the university did not experience the well-documented demonstrations of the tumultuous decade, 1968 began a fundamental cultural shift at MTSU. Undoubtedly, MTSU was a strong illustration of Bob Dylan's theme song for 1968, "The Times They Are A-Changin'."

NOTES

1   Lance Marrow, "1968: Like a Knife Blade," in "1968," ed. Kelly Knauer, *Time*, 21 July 2008, vi.

2   Jules Witcover, *The Year the Dream Died: Revisiting 1968 in America* (New York: Warner Books, 1997), 63.

3   *Martin Luther King, Jr.: A Historical Perspective*, directed by Thomas Friedman, DVD (Santa Monica, CA: Xenon Pictures, 2002).

4   Blake Slonecker, "The Columbia Coalition: African Americans, New Leftists, and Counterculture at the Columbia University Protest of 1968," *Journal of Social History* (Summer 2008): 967–96; see also Knauer, *Time*, 58–59.

5   *1968: The Year That Shaped a Generation*, directed by Stephen Talbot, DVD (Oregon Public Broadcasting, 1998).

6   Knauer, "1968," 67.

7   Jon Meacham, "1968: The Year That Made Us Who We Are," *Newsweek*, 19 November 2007, 48.

8   Evan Thomas, *Robert Kennedy: His Life* (New York: Simon & Schuster, 2000), 390–94.

9   Talbot, *1968*.

10   "SUB in Use Since 1951," *Sidelines*, 4 March 1968.

11   Horace Phillips to Representative John Bragg, 5 March 1990, Subject File: Dixie Controversy, Albert Gore Research Center (AGRC), Middle Tennessee State University, Murfreesboro, TN (hereinafter cited as Dixie Controversy File).

12   "Raiders Take Morehead," *Sidelines*, 30 September 1968.

13   Sylvester Brooks, interview by Erin Toomey, 30 September 2000, MT 0024, transcript, MT Oral History Project, AGRC, 20.

14   "Draft Facts Released," *Sidelines*, 19 February 1968.

15   Sylvester Brooks, "American Negro," *Sidelines*, 18 March 1968.

16 Brooks interview, 23.

17 Sylvester Brooks, "Kennedy 'Dissents' to 12,000 at Vanderbilt," *Sidelines*, 28 March 1968.

18 Ibid.

19 Brooks interview, 29.

20 Michael Hardy, "Look Away Dixie Land," *Civil War Times*, April 2008, 46–52.

21 Thomas, *Robert Kennedy*, 197.

22 Rodney P. Carlisle, "Forrest, Nathan Bedford," *American National Biography Online*, February 2000, http://www.anb.org/articles/04/04-00389.html.

23 Ibid.

24 "Still Riding, With a Bigger Banner," *Economist*, 8 April 2008, 29–30.

25 Jim Leonhirth, "Reliving the Past at MTSU," *Daily News Journal*, 26 November 2006, sec. B, 1.

26 Sylvester Brooks, "*Dixie*: What Does It Mean?," *Sidelines*, 21 October 1968.

27 "I'll Take My Stand in Dixieland," *Sidelines*, 24 October 1968.

28 "Student Calls for Halt to 'Dixie' Controversy," *Sidelines*, 7 November 1968.

29 Charlotte Bachler to Sylvester Brooks, October 23, 1968, Dixie Controversy File.

30 Klansman to Sylvester Brooks, Dixie Controversy File.

31 Brooks interview, 31.

32 Jim Free, interview by Lisa Pruitt, 20 July 2000, MT 0024, transcript, MT Oral History Project, AGRC, 9.

33 "Last Rites for Dr. Quill E. Cope, Former MTSU President," *Sidelines*, 26 September 1968.

34 "Scarlett Assumes MTSU Presidency, States Students Have Protest Rights," *Sidelines*, 3 October 1968.

35 Dr. Mel Scarlett and David Scarlett, "An Amazing Decade at MTSU: The Scarlett Years," unpublished manuscript, n.d., AGRC, 56.

36 "Dr. Scarlett Will Not Act to Control Music," *Daily News Journal*, 11 December 1968, sec. A, 1.

37 "Dixie, Forrest, Flag—In House Committee," *Sidelines*, 11 November 1968.

38 "House Moves on Dixie," *Sidelines*, 9 December 1968.

39 "ASB Congress Deadlocks; Forrest Decision Tuesday," *Sidelines*, 16 December 1968.

40 Brooks interview, 32.

41 Keith Anderson Hardison to Representative John T. Bragg, 7 March 1990, Dixie Controversy File.

42 Leonhirth, "Reliving the Past."

43 Scarlett, "Amazing Decade," 62--64.

44 Ibid., 66–73.

45 Ibid., 75–76.

CHAPTER EIGHT

Tyranny or Freedom?

Presidential Power and Community Relations in the Firing of Philip Mankin

JAMES HOMER WILLIAMS

"They wasn't no agitators. What they call reds. What the hell is
these reds anyways?"

—Tom Joad in
The Grapes of Wrath

Sometime in the spring of 1940, just months after the outbreak of World War
II in Europe, the specter of tyranny haunted the campus of Middle Tennessee
State Teachers College (MTSTC) in Murfreesboro. There, someone hung a hand-
penciled sign on a wall, presumably in the administration building (now known as
Kirksey Old Main). If it had stayed posted for long, everyone at the college would
have eventually seen it. The sign read, "DO WE HAVE A TYRANT ON THE
CAMPUS" (see figure 1).

While it is tempting to imagine an overwrought student displaying her or his
anxiety about German or Japanese fascism spreading into the sleepy communities of
Middle Tennessee, the actual tyrant in question was no Hitler or some other world
despot. Neither Franklin Roosevelt nor Winston Churchill would be called upon to
slay this alleged tyrant who was, in fact, someone much closer to home and familiar
to everyone on the campus and in Murfreesboro. The artist who created this sign was
referring to the third president of the college, Quintin Miller Smith, usually known as
Q. M. In asking the question, the anonymous artist spoke for many on campus and
in Murfreesboro; in the wadding up of the paper, whoever ripped down the sign and

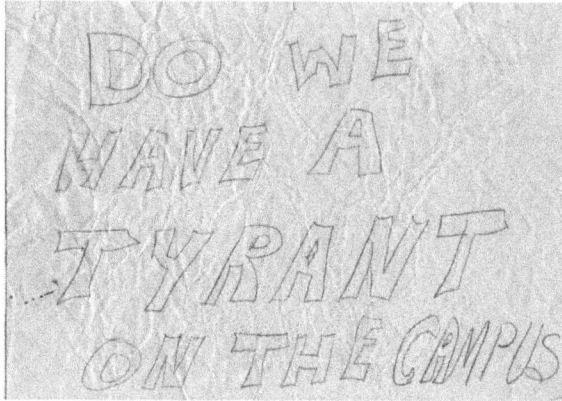

Figure 1. Hand-lettered sign. Source: Box 14, folder 6, Q. M. Smith Papers, Albert Gore Research Center, Middle Tennessee State University.

gave it to Smith signified the disgust that others felt regarding the attacks on President Smith.[1]

Not yet two years in office, Smith found himself embroiled in a controversy that stretched from campus into Murfreesboro and to the State Board of Education in Nashville. Before it was over, a veteran English professor was fired, Smith's leadership and morality were called into question, and a national academic organization found Smith guilty of serious violations of academic standards. When placed in a wider context, Smith's firing of Philip Mankin in 1940 blew the lid off a simmering pot of

Figure 2. President Q. M. Smith. Source: Smith Papers.

controversies that had plagued the campus, fractured community confidence in his leadership, and reflected national political fears and debates about academic freedom.

In selecting Smith in 1938 to take the helm of the college, board members may have pictured themselves as spreading calming oil on what were turbulent waters in Middle Tennessee toward the end of the presidency of P. A. Lyon. Smith, after all, was already a college president in the state system and had been connected to MTSTC since joining the first class of students when the normal school opened in Murfreesboro in fall 1911. No one doubted his seriousness and drive: first president of the senior class, editor of the school publication the *Signal*, and member of the football and debate teams. In 1914 he became the first president of the fledgling alumni association for Middle Tennessee Normal School (changed to Middle Tennessee State Teachers College in 1925). His meteoric rise in higher education administration took him, in 1920, to the presidency of Tennessee Polytechnic Institute (TPI, now Tennessee Technological University), where he was in 1937 when Lyon announced his desire to retire.[2]

"My appearance here is in the nature of a home coming," Smith admitted to the faculty on September 19, 1938, in his first address to his colleagues, whom he thanked for their "warm personal letters of invitation and assurances of cooperation during the period when I was considerably and even prayerfully endeavoring to make the correct decision about joining you." He assured the faculty that "we shall look to the future together . . . . We will add personnel. We have no designs on any personnel changes involving any one now here."[3]

Figure 3. Philip Mankin's last yearbook photo at MTSTC. Source: Midlander (1940).

Yet Smith's own notes from early 1939 reveal that someone on the faculty was already in his sights: Philip Mankin, shown in figure 3. What had changed from September 1938, when Smith pledged to be "a cautious observor [sic], a student, an investigator, a research worker, and an imaginative and practical designer," to March 1940, when he had announced that Mankin would be fired, setting off a firestorm that attracted national attention?

There was no hint in September 1938 that Smith would soon be accused of tyranny by members of his faculty, students, alumni, and community residents. Rather, Smith told the assembled faculty that he enjoyed "the personal and professional relationship of faculty members and their families. As we live and work together on a lifetime basis," he noted, "we know and appreciate one another in free and even confidential relationships." He described "this co-worker and neighborly combination" as "a professional relationship which I hold to be essential to good administration and to good teaching, and that should be observed as sacred and inviolate. I should like very much," he said, "for us to work toward such a mutual understanding."[4]

In looking for clues in that same speech to explain how Smith could have decided in fewer than two years that Mankin, who had taught at the college since 1927, had to go, one might settle on this remark: "We are challenged to equal in our own personal appearance and appeal the sophistication of those whose family traditions and ideals of education demand the best association for their sons and daughters seeking college opportunities here, which these families have traditionally sought in colleges much older and more beautifully decked with ivy."[5] Clearly, Smith had a plan to elevate his alma mater to greatness, and it soon became clear to him that Mankin stood in the way.

Another clue is in Smith's notes for another faculty meeting shortly after his arrival in which he described a teacher—the college faculty were not commonly referred to as professors then—as a "normal well educated person."[6] For this early graduate of the normal school, much of the first four years of his presidency would turn on the definition of normal behavior, and how much abnormality could be tolerated among the teachers under his supervision. By the middle of 1940 he was not only being accused of tyranny, but also immorality, in a quest to cleanse the college of the well educated, but decidedly not "normal," Philip Mankin.

The front-page headline of Murfreesboro's *Daily News Journal* on March 14, 1940, as it would soon become apparent, caught Smith in a lie. "Smith to recommend dismissal of Mankin at teachers college" was true enough, but the subtitle was less than accurate: "S.T.C. president states move is 'purely economy.'" In his statement, Smith claimed that he had received orders from Governor Prentice Cooper to "economize" and that he had chosen Mankin because of low enrollments in the Latin and German classes in the language department. Smith "said he had no criticism of Mankin's ability," the article reported. Mankin's work would be assumed by other members of the department, including two with doctorates and four without. A suspicious reader may have found odd this tidbit included in the article: Mankin had been in his department longer than anyone except Neal Frazier, the chair.

That this personnel decision made front-page news may be attributed to Mankin's roots in the area, also discussed in the article. Born in Rutherford County, Mankin had graduated from Central High School, and attended the normal school before graduating from Peabody College with a bachelor's degree in 1925 and a master's degree in 1927. Before joining the MTSTC faculty, he had taught at St. Andrews school near Sewanee.

When the newspaper asked for his reaction, Mankin hinted that there might be more to the story than simple economy. Smith, he said, "assigns as his reason that the move is an economy measure. This is a little surprising to me in view of the fact that the English department is one of the most heavily loaded at the college." He pointed out that faculty not necessarily best qualified to teach English—the dean of women and teachers of Latin and French—had been called upon to meet the demand. "Besides," he continued, "I am the second oldest member of the English department in point of service. This is my fourteenth year of teaching in the English department of the college. The college has always been very dear to me and my life's work has been here," he concluded, rather sadly. Readers learned that the matter would be taken up by the state board at its May 6 meeting, with Smith's recommendation to take effect during the summer session on July 17, unless student demand warranted extending Mankin's service to September 1.

While Smith claimed no criticism of Mankin in his public statements, his private papers reveal a different story. Smith had accumulated a case against Mankin dating back to December 15, 1938, fewer than three months after he embarked on his presidency with such warm and friendly words to the faculty. A note from that date states that Mankin, according to Miss Margie Mitchell, director of dormitories, had "interfered in discipline of Juanita Webb." The next charge was that several in the college had reported Mankin "as teaching questionable things regarding religion." These reports had come from a Doris Hill and a Mr. Atkin on January 20, 1939, and Smith backed them up with "other references" from Ray Cole, a Rutherford County agent, and Allie Bennett of Walterhill. Smith's third strike against Mankin apparently came from personal observations: "Noted repeatedly: untidy, wears soiled shirt, tonsled [sic] hair." Smith concludes this full page of handwritten notes with three other notes that more clearly penetrate to the heart of the matter. In the first, Lyon, then teaching as president emeritus, is said to have described Mankin as "a socialist and an atheist" on March 13, 1939. "My opinion is he will never be different," Dean N. C. Beasley is quoted as saying two days before. Finally, Smith alleges, Mankin is "not clearly and frankly Christian in belief."[7]

In John Steinbeck's words that same year in *The Grapes of Wrath*, Smith had found in his midst an agitator and a red. An unkempt socialist and atheist on his faculty could not be tolerated. Smith needed more evidence than the tittle tattle he had relied on thus far, so he went to Mankin directly. On March 25, 1939, Mankin appeared before Smith for a discussion of four topics: graduate study, Mankin's teaching, his personal appearance, and his political views. Smith's typewritten notes extend to one-and-a-half pages.[8]

The conference would have appeared entirely normal if Smith had stopped after the first topic, which he labeled "leave of absence for graduate study or study of library science." Smith noted that he suggested to Mankin "that the long range program of the State Teachers College would probably be better promoted if the younger members of the faculty would continue their graduate study, or give place to others who might be willing to do so; that it would be disastrous to the institution for those without graduate study to approach old age from a dead level of the Masters or Bachelors degree." (It did not seem to matter to Smith that he was at that "dead level" himself, while asking faculty to go beyond that to the doctorate, which he did not have.) In reply, according to Smith's notes, Mankin expressed his interest in more graduate study, maybe even in library science, "although he dislikes the idea of transferring to another field."[9]

That this topic appeared first suggests that Smith was using it as a pretense to question Mankin on issues specific to him. Under the next category, "controversial teaching," Smith suggested to Mankin "that in past years and during the present year students and others had questioned the influence of his teaching on the religious views of the students." Smith recorded that Mankin admitted past criticism of him in this regard. When Smith asked him "specifically what religious views he holds," Mankin replied, "I do not know and I could not state clearly my religious views." Smith continued to seek clarity, as if he were prodding a student to express his thoughts in class. He asked Mankin if he believed in the creation story of Genesis, the story of Noah and the flood, the prophecies of the Old Testament, and the virgin birth of Jesus, among several other biblical elements. To every question, Smith noted that Mankin "said he did not" believe. Finally, Smith inquired of Mankin about his attendance at Sunday school or church services. Mankin admitted that it had been "several years" since he had attended church but noted, perhaps in a last-ditch effort to pull himself back into the mainstream of American religious life, "that he was in sympathy with the ethical teachings of the different denominations and the moral influence of preachers and churches."[10]

Even in 1939, a college president interrogating a faculty member at a state institution about the faculty member's detailed religious beliefs would have struck many Americans as odd, if not grossly objectionable. Mankin's spiritual autobiography suggests that many of the founders of the US (particularly Thomas Jefferson and Benjamin Franklin) would have been sympathetic to his views. But Q. M. Smith's religious beliefs in 1939 more closely resembled the norm in Tennessee than Mankin's did. This cultural milieu was reflected not only in Smith's questions and the gossip he recorded about Mankin, but also in the religious atmosphere at the college then, with weekly compulsory chapel meetings of a decidedly Protestant character. The catalogs from this era make no pretense of separating church and state and, in fact, support local churches' efforts to attract student worshippers. The normal school and subsequent teachers college was, in essence, the body of a Church of Christ college in the garb of a state institution.

Thus, Mankin did not fit in. Perhaps his unorthodox religious views by themselves were not enough to motivate Smith to find an excuse to dismiss him, but other aspects of Mankin's character grated on Smith. In the third topic covered in the interrogation of March 25, Smith "suggested to Mr. Mankin that there were those who felt that he did not spend enough time or money in maintaining his personal appearance." Mankin did not plead the effects of the Great Depression or the small salaries then paid to college faculty, but he did admit, according to Smith, "that he had been careless in his personal appearance all his life and that there was a certain amount of freedom which he enjoyed as a result of this." One can imagine how this last admission must have cut to the heart of Smith's prim demeanor and belief in personal discipline. Details of Mankin's lax hygiene followed: "soiled and disarranged collar and cuffs, soiled hands and fingernails, unpressed suit, with trousers conspicuously torn in the seat."[11]

Finally, in the last, briefest section of Smith's notes, he asked for details of Mankin's political views. Mankin "stated that he believes in real democracy with the other fellow who lives 'across the railroad tracks,' and in the common man." When asked if he was a socialist, "his reply was, 'I am a Socialist.'"[12] One need not read between the lines of this shocking admission to find more nails to drive into Mankin's coffin lid. But were Mankin alive, we might wish to ask him who he included among the fellows living "across the railroad tracks." One suspects that these not only included poorer, less educated whites, but also blacks. Given Smith's later push in the 1950s to instill in the college's students a heroic posture akin to Confederate leaders such as Nathan Bedford Forrest, it would not be surprising if he objected to any hint of racial equality promoted by his faculty.

Why it took Smith another year to zero Mankin out of his proposed annual budget is not clear. Perhaps Mankin reformed his ways in the months following his meeting with the new president enough to forestall action against him. Smith may have felt he needed more evidence against Mankin or an opportunity to get rid of him without citing the true causes. Smith's papers show nothing regarding Mankin until nearly a year later when, in late February 1940, a list of students in Mankin's English 211 class appears in the files. One student from the list, Dorothy Manning, visited Smith once, or perhaps twice, in late February. Whether Smith asked her to appear as part of a larger investigation of Mankin's teaching in the class (which would explain the class list), or whether Manning asked to see Smith to discuss objectionable material in the class is not clear. Smith's notes, though brief, are damning—at least in Smith's mind. He scribbled, "Hold loved one over flame. No educated person believes in hell. Not morally wrong to drink. Christ turned water to wine, therefore not wrong to drink it."[13] Apparently, this information pushed Smith over the brink, or served to confirm a decision he had already made, for as we have already seen, in just days his decision to terminate Mankin's employment hit the newsstands.

Perhaps spurred on by state board chairman B. O. Duggan's comment to the *Daily News Journal* that "no one has the right to dismiss a member of the college faculty but the State Board of Education,"[14] supporters of Mankin sprang into action. By the end of the month, several postcards had been received at the college, all with the same pre-printed message to Smith, all postmarked in Nashville. "We are very displeased with the action you have taken toward ejecting Philip Mankin from the S.T.C. faculty," the organizer of this campaign wrote. "As a former student of the college we wish to state that we consider Mr. Mankin invaluable to the college. The action you have adopted is a poor policy for a state institution."[15]

Not one to take opposition to his decisions cheerfully, Smith began to make notes about his opponents. Some notes appear benign, as when he noted that Robert Seay was "teaching in Davidson Co." On another he wrote that Frances Sweeney was Gayle Sweeney's sister. Both had signed cards supporting Mankin.[16]

Decades later, Frances Sweeney Brandon remembered Mankin as "an oddball" and confirmed some of the charges laid against him by Smith. "You don't want to start me on Philip Mankin," she joked. "He would come to class with gravy on his tie many times. He didn't care. . . . He was profoundly absentminded. . . . His mind was really on what he was studying that day. They tell me he was a profound mathematician at the same time, and I did not ever guess it because he was so loving of literature. . . . He is exactly what you would call a nerd, today's nerd. A very lovable one." Brandon provided other insights into Mankin's eccentricities, but also his brilliance and devotion to literature. "He would frequently show us an essay or piece of work written by [the Fugitives] and he constantly begged us to read, and he brought his books, and would share his personal books with the students." She also noted how kind he was and reflected on his version of spirituality: "He would not let us kill a wasp or a fly even though it was buzzing up around. He said that that creature was alive by some material, and we didn't know about what life was, and that unless we were really being made sick or tortured we had no right to kill another animal. . . . He did not embrace any particular church, but his religion was deep. He was very much like the American Indian. He appreciated life and the mystery of life. He liked drama, and his sister was in a play one year that I was there. I think it was an Oscar Wilde play that we put on."[17]

Other anonymous flyers appeared at the college (see figure 4) and individual letters and group petitions arrived at the board of education office in April, all apparently in support of Mankin. If the authors anticipated their opinions would have been held in confidence in Nashville, they would surely have been surprised to discover that the board sent the names and addresses of all of Mankin's supporters to

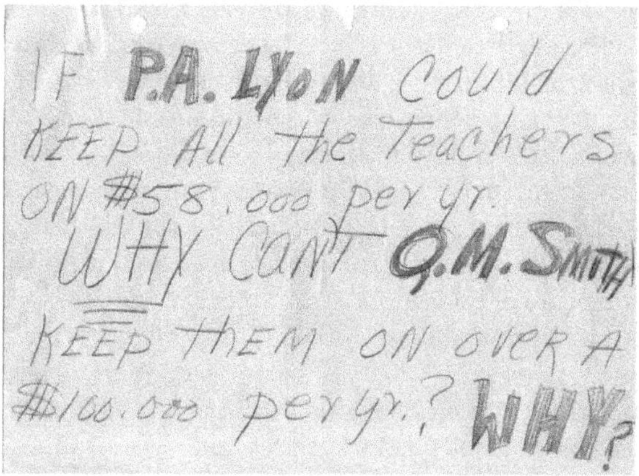

Figure 4. Anonymous Flyer from Smith-Mankin Controversy. Source: Smith Papers.

Smith. On a few of these copies, Smith revealed his pettiness, noting for instance that Miss Vivienne Petite was a "pest" and owed the college $83.50.[18]

One of the more interesting letters of support, because it offered a less parochial view of Mankin's teaching, came from Trinity College in Hartford, Connecticut, where Richard Knowles Morris was then studying. Morris wrote to Governor Cooper that he had "had the privilege of sitting in Mr. Mankin's classes in the fall and winter of 1935, and have had the opportunity since then to compare his choice of materials and methods to those of instructors at Harvard, Wesleyan and Trinity. The analogy is remarkable," he concluded, "which can be said of few on the faculty at the Teachers' College." Mankin, he continued, "by sheer force of personality and love for his subject, has given the English courses at State Teachers' College a standard for which the state can be justly proud. His quiet, kind and sincere character have enabled him to obtain a great deal from his students." And, Morris reminded the governor as the depression dragged on, "Good and intelligent citizens are economic, as well as cultural, assets to any community."[19]

In a similar letter to Commissioner Duggan, Morris noted that "Mankin's work was comparable to a high degree with the work of such a nationally important English professor as Dr. Odell Shepard," with whom he had taken several courses. He also noted that Trinity College had accepted only two of his MTSTC courses for transfer credit: Professor Davis's biology course and Mankin's English course.[20]

If Morris meant to impress the leaders of higher education in Tennessee with his comparisons to eastern faculty and colleges, one wonders if his letter had the opposite effect, since the charges against Mankin were precisely those that Smith probably would have leveled against a good number of liberal, atheistic East Coast faculty. In any event, Morris's praise of Mankin's teaching was largely beside the point, because it was Mankin's political and religious beliefs that were at issue.

A letter to Cooper from closer to home may have had a greater impact, had the governor chosen to involve himself in the controversy, which he did not even though then, as now, the governor automatically sat as a member of the higher education governing board. On April 2, 1940, Dr. James B. Jones of the Murfreesboro Bank and Trust Company wrote to Cooper expressing the view of "many of Mr. Mankin's friends," who looked "with decided disfavor" at the contemplated dismissal. "I believe that your investigation of this situation, together with your characteristic keen discernment of facts and thorough analysis of the details," Jones wrote, "will reveal that the feeling of his friends, alluded to above, reflects the sentiment of a large portion of our community and the student body and faculty of State Teachers College; which sentiment is rapidly crystalizing."[21] If community pressure would not persuade the board, perhaps alumni could.

Indeed, a petition signed by 19 alumni soon arrived in Nashville. Apparently Robert Mason, class of 1937, was the leader of this small effort. "Because of his broad scholarship, his unassailable ethics, his personal interest in the mental growth of his pupils, [and] his long period of contribution at the college," the petitioners wrote, "we, the undersigned members of the S.T.C. Alumni, do protest the dismissal of"

Mankin as "unjust and deplorable." Furthermore, they "would feel more charitable toward the administration and particularly the president of the college if Mr. Mankin is retained."[22]

As it would turn out, the most relevant letter to the board came from Mankin himself. Writing on April 22, Mankin provided a synopsis of events up to that point. He had received a letter on March 4 in which Smith had stated that "a survey of the course offerings and teaching load in the language department indicates that it is possible and advisable to reduce the teaching staff of that department by one. This is to notify you that I shall not include your name on the faculty list nor budget for 1940–41 submitted to the State Board of Education at the May meeting." Mankin replied to Smith on March 12.[23] In this letter, Mankin requested that Smith state to him—"for I feel that I have a right to know—what charges, if any, you have to make against me." Smith's reply was dated March 13 and in its entirety read, "This is to acknowledge receipt of your letter of March 12." Mankin informed the board that Smith had made his decision "without any mention of the matter to the head of the department of languages." Taking Smith at his word that the move was for economy, Mankin raised the issue of why he was chosen, given that he had worked at the college since January 1927. "Even if it were advisable to drop one member of the English department, the question would arise," he noted, "why should I be the one to go? Neither does it seem just to me to abolish foreign language classes and dismiss me, giving the basic English classes which I have been teaching to the Latin and French teachers, neither of whom has specialized in the teaching of English." Believing he could persuade the board that the economy argument was false, Mankin presented evidence that the English department's classes averaged from 26 to 33 students per class in the 1938–39 school year. "This present spring quarter," Mankin wrote, "I have in my own classes 218 students. Eighty students signed up for my short story class (an elective), and I found it necessary to divide the class. This gives me six classes, averaging 36 students per class." Further, "no criticism is offered of my scholarship or efficiency as a teacher of English. I believe I can say with complete truth that the present student body, the alumni, my colleagues, and the people of the community do not wish me to go." In fact, he continued, along the lines of the placard seen in figure 4, "during a number of the twelve years I taught in the college before Mr. Smith became its President, the school appropriation was much less that it is now, and it was not considered necessary for reasons of economy to dismiss me—even during the depression years." Mankin concluded his appeal to the board with assurances of his good feelings toward the college and Smith. "I love the school, and I have tried to do well as a teacher," he wrote. "I have always been courteous to Mr. Smith. I should like to call attention to the fact that we have had no quarrel of any sort."[24]

Another person came to Mankin's defense throughout the ordeal that was to come, and this was his sister Jane Ellen Mankin. She called Congressman Joe Henry of Tennessee's sixth district on April 20 to ask for his intervention in the matter as an ex-student of Mankin's. Unfortunately for Jane, Henry shared Smith's view of her brother, and wrote as much to his friend, attorney John R. Rucker, in Murfreesboro.

"Now, as you and I both know," Henry wrote, "this action on the part of the School, comes about ten years too late. I feel that you know better than anyone else just how I feel about this situation. Of course I can't tell Jane Ellen. However I do not feel inclined to go on record as protesting the dismissal of a teacher because of his communistic, socialistic and athiestic [sic] views and teachings. On the contrary," Henry stressed, "I feel that Mr. Smith is to be congratulated upon his action." Alas, Henry's heart was not stone cold, for he admitted that he could not "help but feel sorry for Philip. In many respects he is a very nice person." Then, as something of an afterthought, Henry added, "After rereading the above I have come to the conclusion that it is the most illogical and inconsistent line of reasoning I have ever read. But it is just the way I feel about the whole thing."[25] One wonders how much of Henry's rational skills were developed in Mankin's class.

At any rate, the stage was set. The case was left to the members of the State Board of Education to decide at their next meeting, on May 10, at which Smith presented his personnel plans for the coming year that did not include Mankin. At the request of a group of townsfolk from Murfreesboro, the board set aside time to hear their thoughts about Smith and the Mankin business, and the board also agreed to hear Mankin. The board secretary kept detailed stenographic minutes of this meeting.[26]

The board went into executive session that morning and admitted a delegation composed of Dr. W. T. Robison, Less T. Fite, and E. C. Holloway Jr. They presented a petition signed by 31 citizens of Murfreesboro and Rutherford County. The petition argued four points about MTSTC. First, it had been "for the past few years, and is at the present time, headed by ruthless and politically minded administration who have not seen fit to work for the interest of the institution along educational lines, but who have perpetuated by numerous schemes, trades, and political swaps, themselves and a selected few of their friends in office, never considering their qualifications in the interest of the student body and surrounding section of the state." Second, they described Smith as "a man of whom Middle Tennessee has little confidence in, either as an educator or as a man." They alleged that he had been "practically forced" to resign from TPI "due to his conduct unbecoming a president of a [sic] educational institution and was forced upon" MTSTC. Third, "the student body is in a state of unrest and feels insecure in obtaining the right kind of education under the present administration. . . ." And finally, the faculty "no longer feel secure in the faithful performances of their duties, but are harrassed [sic] and even threatened unless they come under the dictatoral [sic] rule of the present administration and cater to the every whims of the president, who is constantly reminding them that they are at his mercy. . . ."[27]

During the board's questioning of the delegation, Holloway referred to "a student meeting of over 500 students" held the night before, during which the students "voted to retain Mr. Mankin," with only two voting against. He opined that "that was not so much for Mr. Mankin as their expression of what they thought of Dr. Smith and what he is doing." Later, board member W. R. Landrum told Holloway that "if we elect a president we must let him select his personnel because we hold him accountable." Holloway replied, "While you hire and fire, you surely do not approve Mr. Smith's firing a teacher, who has the vote of confidence of nearly all the students. That would be a rule to follow in a foreign country." Landrum shot back, "It resolves itself into who is best to make the selection, the presidents or the students," and clearly Landrum did not think much of the students' views. Holloway retorted, "Mr. Smith said the recommendation was for economy. Everyone thinks this is not true. Last year he brought in a new teacher in the Language Department and now he is firing a man who has been there over eight years." Landrum then accused Holloway of "impuning" Smith's motives and suggested that "a committee might be appointed to go over and bring witnesses, if necessary." Holloway ended this dialogue with the ominous comment that "there are witnesses who will not speak unless they are made to do so."[28]

A few minutes later, Dr. Robison dug into the mud flying around about Smith. He referred to "the domestic cloud under which Mr. Smith came to Murfreesboro." Admitting it was hearsay, Robison continued, "He may have been perfectly justified in the steps he has taken in allowing his wife to have a divorce, and also in marrying the divorced wife of a former student. It may be on the up-and-up, I do not know. I *do* know that that is the interpretation given by the student body and the citizens. . . . 'Why is a man at the head of this institution, training young men and young women, who deserted his wife and son and married the wife of a former student,'" seemed the question on the minds of many. "I have heard some ugly things. Excuse me if I talk plainly," he said, before giving an example of the depravity that had swept over the campus. "Two boys took one of the student's [sic] who lives there in town, not to one of the regular dormitories, but to the Moffitt House which is State property, and it is said that more than a dozen boys confess to illegitimate conduct with that girl. In the course of investigation of this," Robison continued, "so I am told or informed by a reliable source, a bulletin appeared in the halls of the college to the effect, 'who are you to say what our moral conduct should be, in the light of your own past affairs?'"[29]

This went on for some time until the conversation finally came back around to Mankin. H. B. Shofner (Republican from Shelbyville) raised the subject of Mankin's religious beliefs. He had heard that Smith's dismissal was perhaps due to religion. Robison replied that he had "heard some criticism" of Mankin's views but that he "went to the head of the department [Frazier], to a man I think, if I ever saw a Christian gentleman, it is he." Frazier, Robison reported, admitted that Mankin "does bring up questions in class to try to make the students think and get up their authority for it." Robison then said that he had never discussed religion with Mankin, "but I do know his life is cleaner and higher than that lived by some of his critics."[30]

After dismissing the delegation, the board admitted Mankin who appeared, he said, in self-defense. But since Smith had laid no charges against him, other than the overall need to cut a position in languages, the board was left with little to say to Mankin, who repeatedly demurred to the board's judgment. A group of students waited in the hallway to testify on behalf of Mankin—who insisted he had had nothing to do with the meeting the night before or with the students coming that day—but Landrum argued against including them in the meeting. "I do not think the student body should be taken into consideration at all unless we want them later on, or if the committee wants to, but I think that is like dragging children into a divorce case,"[31] an apt metaphor given the accusations against Smith the divorcee.

After dismissing Mankin, the minutes noted that Dr. C. Y. Clarke (Democrat from Mt. Pleasant) "asked for a few frank expressions" from his fellow board members, whom he urged to take action that day in support of Smith's action against Mankin. "The president has a right to make a change, even if it does not save any money," he remarked. Dr. Doak S. Campbell (Democrat from Nashville) supported Clarke's "administrative policy," saying, "So far as my memory goes, this Board had sustained the recommendations of these presidents with absolute consistence even in times when we were unanimous in believing the presidents were wrong and I could cite the instances." The real debate was not to sustain Smith, but whether to sustain him after an investigating committee had done its work. Landrum had referred to this committee earlier. At its February meeting, the board had already authorized investigating committees to visit each campus and report on the situation across the state. Not sure what course to follow, the board called Smith back into the meeting and told him of its dilemma. Smith replied ominously, "I am willing for the Board to go into the whole situation and I hope it will do it. *There are forces at work at this school over which I have very little control.* [emphasis added] It is vital to the welfare of the institution and they existed prior to my administration and may continue to do so unless we can get the situation in hand." With that, the board deferred action on Mankin's case until the committee had done its work.[32]

Smith was not without his supporters. As news of the May 10 meeting became public, letters of support trickled in for Smith, mostly from friends, former student colleagues from his days at the normal school, and colleagues at other institutions. Then the investigating committee met in Murfreesboro on June 4 and 5, pursued the charges in the citizens' petition of May 10, and essentially concluded that MTSTC enjoyed a happy, growing student body and a contented faculty. Chairman Duggan reported, "Everywhere I found evidences of good order, cleanliness and correct procedure in the work of the schools." Thus the investigating committee suggested that the full board approve Smith's handling of matters at the college, including the firing of Mankin, which it did on June 17.[33]

Here the case of Philip Mankin would have ended, were it not for his persistence and an organization called the American Association of University Professors (AAUP). Mankin appealed to the AAUP for assistance, so as 1940 dragged into 1941, the AAUP sought details of Mankin's dismissal and applied its policies to his situation. As David Rowe details elsewhere in this volume, by the end of 1942, and after a meticulous review of the case—including sending an investigating team of professors from other institutions—the national office of the AAUP had determined that Mankin's academic freedom had been violated, that after 14 years of service at the college that Mankin should have enjoyed due process that was not provided to him, and therefore that the AAUP had no choice but to censure the administration of MTSTC.[34]

_____

Isolating the Mankin case from Smith's other actions as president, and from the cultural milieu in Tennessee higher education in which he matured as a college president, makes Smith appear a petty tyrant willing to destroy the career of an English professor out of dislike for his religious and political beliefs, and his personal hygiene. From our perspective 70 years later, it is difficult not to see it this way. But a better, if not more flattering, understanding of Smith's actions comes from placing the episode in a wider perspective. If the Mankin case was the main act in 1940, we should recognize that earlier episodes in the drama were staged at MTSTC and Vanderbilt in the 1930s, but without the explosive effects of national attention and censure. What had changed by 1940?

For a clue, let us turn to the sign scribbler's third creation, which asked pointedly, "WILL POLITICS REPLACE JUSTICE? WHAT DO YOU THINK ABOUT IT MR. SMITH?"[35] Justice presumably meant Mankin would be retained on his merits; politics meant his firing would stand, either because of the labeling of Mankin as a socialist or because the political appointees who constituted the board of education would collude with Smith to affirm his decision. The sign maker need not have known that the board had adopted its policy on tenure on May 6, 1927: "the State Board may dismiss a president or member of the faculty or other employee at any time for sufficient cause." (The only limitation was a requirement of 60 days' notice.)[36] This answer to the sign maker's first question clearly had come in response to the Knox Hutchinson affair of 1937–38.

The details of Hutchinson's case are not important here except to show the similarities between his dismissal and Mankin's, and the different outcomes for the presidents who did the firing. In May 1937, President P. A. Lyon recommended to the board that Hutchinson, a professor of agriculture, be left off the faculty roll for the upcoming year after charging him with negligence, too much attention to "outside enterprises," and failure to cooperate with Lyon's administration. The board deferred action until August, giving Hutchinson time to respond to Lyon's accusations.[37]

A pattern emerged that would be followed in the Mankin case, too. Hutchinson wrote to the board, asking for a hearing, which was granted. At its August meeting, the board questioned Lyon about his relationship with Hutchinson. When asked if he thought it was possible for Hutchinson to get along with him and work productively within his administration, Lyon replied, "I think it is impossible for that condition to exist for the good of the school." Further questioning revealed a deep distrust of Hutchinson's political motives toward Lyon. When asked how Hutchinson had been insubordinate, Lyon recounted, "Recently a few members of the Young Men's Democratic Committee undertook to see that I was removed from office and it is unnecessary for me to give you the reason why, but it is true that they proposed to place Mr. Hutchinson as president in my stead." Lyon further alleged that Hutchinson had told him he was an ambitious young man with a future ahead of him and "that he had 2800 farmers from the T.V.A. who would stand for him for any position he might want. The first effort was made through the Legislature. . . . The Legislature was directed to legislate the president [Lyon] out of office. The Legislature finally amended the Act." Lyon affirmed his belief that "Mr. Hutchinson joined in this and used every effort to produce that result and contacted every faculty member and got them disturbed promising them better places as well as the janitors, engineers, etc."[38]

Petitions with at least 1200 signatures poured into the governor's office and accused W. A. Bass, commissioner of education, of hostility toward Hutchinson, whose reinstatement the petitioners sought. At its November meeting, the board accepted Lyon's request to retire in January 1938 and immediately offered the job to Bass. Lyon's request spoke of his advancing age (70) but not of the recent act that, by requiring presidents of the state teachers colleges to have earned master's degrees, deprived him of office. As Lyon attempted to bow out gracefully—to the position of president emeritus at $3000 per year with teaching duties—the board then agreed to hear Hutchinson and others supporting him in Murfreesboro, another bit of anticlimax as the board had already approved his firing. Hutchinson denied the charges of neglect and "disclaimed any disloyalty to President Lyon and stated he had not approached anyone at any time with a view of obtaining the position of the presidency of the institution." Then, what really seemed to be bothering Hutchinson and his supporters came to light. Hutchinson alleged that Lyon "at one time had suggested that the negroes working on the [college] farm be taken out to vote," which Hutchinson interpreted as "a move to defeat the TVA and he did not think this was right." Governor Gordon Browning then entered the discussion, stating that "he would like to see rural electricity all over the country and as one member of this Board would hate to see any employee penalized" for supporting these efforts. Frank Hargis, a Murfreesboro attorney, returned to Lyon's alleged manipulation of the vote against TVA. He alleged that "darkies working at the State Teachers College, Murfreesboro, for over twenty years and who knew President Lyon well, said they were voting for the Tennessee Electric Power Company in order not to vote for the referendum and the light council." Browning said he had heard the power companies were going to "get" Hutchinson "if he kept on with the TVA." Several board members then seemed to fall over themselves to assure those present that they were supportive of TVA and had not prejudged Hutchinson.[39]

This discussion carried on for pages in the minutes, then shifted when Hargis asked Lyon why his highly favorable evaluations of Hutchinson had changed. Lyon replied that his opinion had changed when Hutchinson "became an active candidate for the presidency of the college." Hutchinson denied it. Lyon offered to produce eight men to affirm it. Hutchinson countered with an offer to produce four men to deny it. Having devolved into the personal squabble between sitting president and the heir apparent (perhaps behind the legislative poison that killed Lyon's active presidency), the board eventually brought the hearing to an end without reversing its August decision to support Lyon.[40]

Smith, as president of TPI and an alumnus of MTSTC, would have been aware of the Hutchinson–Lyon dispute. What lesson could he have learned? One would be that uncooperative faculty seen as damaging the "program" of the college should be dismissed. And if the president made this judgment, no matter the public or political pressure brought to bear, the State Board of Education and the governor would ultimately stand by the president.

As a Peabody College graduate and college president, Smith also would likely have followed the case of Joseph Kinmont Hart. A nationally prominent education professor hired in 1930 to create an education department at Vanderbilt University (in competition with adjacent Peabody), Hart was unceremoniously fired by Chancellor James Kirkland four years later, after Kirkland perceived he was behind student criticism of the Vanderbilt honor code in the student newspaper and had grown unpopular with a traditionalist faction of the faculty. "For those who liked the idea of a 'new [social] order,'" Deron R. Boyles points out in his study of the episode, "Kirkland referred to Hitler's Germany and invited students who wanted communism to go to Russia." Students protested Hart's dismissal, to no avail. Hart beseeched the AAUP for assistance, which helped him receive a financial settlement without further repercussions for Vanderbilt.[41]

Boyles identifies "a form of southern paternalism" at work in Kirkland's actions. Perhaps this paternalism was an unstated requirement for college leaders in the South in the 1930s, for it certainly can be seen in Q. M. Smith. Kirkland wrote to the AAUP general secretary "that college professors be advised that security of tenure could best be attained by service. He who makes himself indispensable in the college organization will never have to inquire whether he has a contract or not. I could wish that the various associations trying to protect college professors would also give this warning as to the surest means by which they would escape all need of protection."[42]

Yet Smith would also have known, as he would state later, that "there were forces at work" at Middle Tennessee State Teachers College over which the president might have little control. It is something of a wonder, then, why Smith agreed to succeed Lyon after Bass accepted the superintendency of the Nashville schools. He did not apply for the job but was recommended for it, and then chosen from among the 25 candidates in the pool.[43] We do not know for sure why he left TPI for MTSTC. We can surmise that his recent divorce and consequent scandal pushed him from Cookeville toward Murfreesboro and a return, he may have hoped, to happier times. Perhaps he also saw himself as a reformer who could whip his alma mater into shape, now that the Hutchinson–Lyon affair was ended.

Reform he did. The impression one gets from Smith's quarterly reports to the board in his first year at MTSTC was that he found most everything shabby or in disarray. He asked to sell the antiquated laundry equipment while spending more than $4000 on repairs to the library, cafeteria, dorms, and administration building. He sought to clear accounts that were past due, including a printing bill for $103.25, part of which extended back to 1929, and the bill for $300 for an imported bull that had been acquired but not paid for a few years earlier. Most significantly, he reported student accounts in arrears to the tune of at least $22,000, which he proposed to collect as best he could. And he launched a building strategy that would characterize his 20 years as president. He submitted the necessary documents to participate in the National Youth Administration college aid program and to seek $300,000 from the Public Works Administration to build a new student activities building and a gymnasium.[44] When Hutchinson, now a state senator, succeeded in passing a bill that prohibited any faculty member without a bachelor's degree from teaching at a state teachers college, Lyon and football coach Johnny "Red" Floyd were forced to leave the payroll. Hutchinson had his revenge on Lyon, and Smith seems not to have shed any tears in retiring, for good, the president emeritus who had let the college go to seed.[45]

Yet try as he might to bring the college out of the doldrums and turmoil of the late Lyon years, Smith was plagued by opponents among the student body and in town. At its meeting on February 10, 1939, just five months after Smith assumed office, the board agreed to hear a delegation from Murfreesboro, including Senator Hutchinson. Hargis once again led the group, which charged mismanagement of the college. Commissioner Duggan resorted to a familiar tactic: he suggested the board send an investigating committee. If this were done, Hargis suggested the committee ask if as much as 10 or 15 percent of the students supported their new president. Later in the questioning, Hargis stated his personal belief that "it was obnoxious to the citizens of Murfreesboro and Rutherford County, for a president to be placed there who had so recently been criticized about his domestic troubles at Cookeville, and it appeared he had been shoved off on the people at Murfreesboro." Another member of the delegation did not object to Smith's appointment but opined that "his executive ability had been very obnoxious." Later still, Pat Sutton, a student in the delegation, suggested that "the students thought Coach Floyd had been rudely treated by Mr. Smith, and on the other hand the students did not like for a 'tech' man to be on the campus." A board member asked if the students thought they should choose the faculty. "While the students were going to school there for an education and paying for it," Sutton replied, "they thought they should have some one [sic] as president who would consider them."[46] So much for Smith's happy homecoming to Middle Tennessee State Teachers College.

Under attack from nearly the start of his presidency, and with the zeal of a reformer, Smith moved forward, apparently confident in the support shown him thus far by the board. As he tidied up the campus and sought to bring to conclusion long-standing problems that Lyon had ignored, Smith inevitably turned his attention toward the atheistic, socialist English teacher in his midst. Though Mankin did not fit the profile of the "squeaky wheel" that most often attracted the attention of college presidents, he was seen as subversive of good morality and spirituality.[47] We should not be surprised that Smith sought Mankin's dismissal, but like Smith, we might be surprised that where Kirkland and Lyon had succeeded in ridding themselves of troublesome faculty members without sanction from the AAUP, Smith did not.

The main reason, it would seem, was that Smith's dismissal of Mankin in 1940 coincided with the publication of the AAUP's "1940 Statement of Principles on Academic Freedom and Tenure," which had been developing through a series of conferences since 1934. Where Hutchinson sought vengeance against Lyon in the general assembly, Mankin pursued due process through the AAUP. Where Lyon stood on firmer ground in accusing Hutchinson of negligence of his duties, Smith had initially hidden behind the facade of financial exigency, only to have it discovered that he was truly motivated by political and religious prejudices that were clear violations of AAUP principles. And perhaps, as war appeared on the horizon, Americans were more sensitive in the 1940s to charges of tyrannical leadership at home. This seemed on the mind of Frank Jones Jr. in Ann Arbor, Michigan, when he wrote to the editors of the *Nation* in late July. Jones concluded his summary of events in the Mankin case, published under the title "Dictatorship in Tennessee": "Unless this move toward fascism in the schools is stopped, we patrons of state schools must expect our children to be taught by political appointees and accidental scholars. If a fine educator can be removed at the caprice of authority without any charges, and if the powerful state board is afraid to let the people see backstage into the political involvements, then dictatorship has come to S. T. C."[48]

A year later, Philip Mankin wrote a letter to Q. M. Smith in which he informed Smith that he had finished a year of doctoral work in English and history at Vanderbilt. "Feeling that there may be a place for me in the English department of the College," Mankin wrote hopefully (and naively) "to request reinstatement in the department." Smith shared a copy of his reply with Duggan. Declaring the board's action in the case final, as far as he was concerned, Smith went on to twist the knife a bit. "The developments in the case since that recommendation was filed have strengthened my conviction that the action taken was fully justified," Smith wrote. "Your request is, therefore, denied."[49]

NOTES

1   We do not know who took down and crumpled the paper, but since Smith saved it in his papers, we know it made it into his hands somehow. It is remarkable that he felt so sure of his position that he saved, rather than destroyed, the critic's work.

2   For more details of Smith's career, see the biographical sketch at http://gorecenter. mtsu.edu/qms_bio.htm. For Lyon's retirement, see minutes of the State Board of Education, 5 November 1937, in record group 245: Tennessee State Board of Education Minutes, 1907–1983, Tennessee State Library and Archives, Nashville (hereinafter cited as RG 245).

3   Box 4, folder 9, Q. M. Smith Papers, Albert Gore Research Center (AGRC), Middle Tennessee State University, Murfreesboro, TN (hereinafter cited as Smith Papers, AGRC).

4   Ibid.

5   Ibid.

6   Ibid.

7   Handwritten notes titled "Phillip [sic] Mankin," box 14, folder 6, Smith Papers, AGRC.

8   "Interview with Philip Mankin at 9:00 o'clock, March 25, 1939," Smith Papers, AGRC.

9   Ibid. For Smith's efforts to increase the qualifications of the faculty, see David Rowe's essay in chapter nine in this volume.

10 Ibid.

11 Ibid.

12 Ibid.

13 Handwritten notes titled "P. Mankin," 28 February 1940, Smith Papers, AGRC.

14 "Smith to Recommend Dismissal of Mankin at Teachers College," *Daily News Journal,* 14 March 1940. Accompanying the story was another: "Board Considers Release of 13 Teachers from Rutherford Rolls," with "economy measures advocated by" Governor Cooper as the stated reason.

15 Postcards in Smith Papers, AGRC.

16 Ibid.

17 Howell Frances Sweeney Brandon, interview by Regina Forsythe, transcripts QMS.1995.95–96, Q. M. Smith Oral History Collection, AGRC.

18 Carbon copy, B. O. Duggan to Vivienne Petite, 22 April 1940, Smith Papers, AGRC.

19 Copy of letter from Morris to Cooper, 6 April 1940, Smith Papers, AGRC.

20 Copy of letter from Morris to Duggan, 8 April 1940, Smith Papers, AGRC.

21 Copy of letter from Jones to Cooper, 2 April 1940, Smith Papers, AGRC.

22 Undated copy of letter from alumni, Smith Papers, AGRC.

23 Curiously, only the front of the envelope survives in Smith's papers. Smith Papers, AGRC.

24 Communication from Professor Philip Mankin, 22 April 1940, Smith Papers, AGRC.

25 Copy of letter from Henry to Rucker, 20 April 1940, apparently provided Smith by Rucker, Smith Papers, AGRC.

26 Minutes of executive session, State Board of Education, 10 May 1940, Smith Papers, AGRC.

27 Copy of petition to the honorable State Board of Education, Smith Papers, AGRC.

28 Minutes, 10 May 1940.

29 Ibid. If this sign was one posted by our anonymous writer, it does not survive in the Smith papers.

30   Ibid.

31   Ibid.

32   Stenographic notes on discussion by board of interview with Professor Philip Mankin, 10 May 1940, Smith Papers, AGRC.

33   Minutes of called meeting of State Board of Education, 17 June 1940, Smith Papers, AGRC.

34   See the Committee A report in AAUP *Bulletin* 28, no. 3 (Oct. 1942): 662–77.

35   Smith Papers, AGRC.

36   Minutes, board of education, 6 May 1938, RG 245.

37   Minutes, board of education, 28 May 1937, RG 245.

38   Minutes, board of education, 20 August 20, 1937, RG 245. Nearly 50 MTSTC faculty and staff signed a petition to Commissioner Bass, dated 8 May 1937, in opposition to the legislation that seemed to target Lyon personally and that if passed, in their view, would "set a dangerous precedent, because it will tend definitely to project our institutions of higher learning into politics and thereby endanger their position with the standardizing agencies of the educational world." Interestingly, the first signatory was Philip Mankin. Record group 273: Tennessee Board of Education Records, 1874–1984, Tennessee State Library and Archives, Nashville (hereinafter cited as RG 273).

39   Minutes, board of education, 5 November 1937, RG 245.

40   Ibid.

41   Boyles, "Joseph Kinmont Hart and Vanderbilt University: Academic Freedom and the Rise and Fall of a Department of Education, 1930–1934," *History of Education Quarterly* 43, no.4 (Winter 2003): 571–609, quotation on 598.

42   Quoted in Boyles, "Joseph Kinmont Hart," 609.

43   List of names considered by the special committee for the presidency of the State Teachers College at Murfreesboro, box 150, RG 273.

44   Minutes, board of education, 28 September 1938, 9 May, 11 August, 10 November 1939, RG 245.

45 Minutes, board of education, 9 May 1939.

46 Minutes, board of education, 10 February 1939.

47 For more cases, see Ellen Schrecker, "Subversives, Squeaky Wheels, and 'Special Obligations': Threats to Academic Freedom, 1890–1960," *Social Research* 76, no. 2 (Summer 2009): 513–40.

48 *Nation*, 10 August 1940, 120.

49 Mankin to Smith, 17 September, Smith to Duggan, 22 September, Smith to Mankin, 22 September 1940, box 150, RG 273. Mankin finished his career at Eastern Kentucky University, where a scholarship in the English department is named in his memory.

CHAPTER NINE

From Teachers to Professors

Q. M. Smith, the AAUP, and Modernizing the Faculty

DAVID L. ROWE

On January 1, 1915, less than four years after Tennesseans met in Murfreesboro to celebrate the opening of Middle Tennessee State Normal School,[1] academics from leading universities around the country met in New York City. Despite the holiday, their mood was gloomy. Indeed, what had happened previously in Murfreesboro was the kind of event that had produced in them a sense of unease, even dread. A chasm separated their ideal of the professoriate's life and work from the reality for teachers in schools, like this, dedicated to teaching future teachers. To protect their craft from further decline, they gathered on this morning for the first annual meeting of the American Association of University Professors (AAUP), adopting as their raison d'être the charge its founders had promulgated the previous year:

> To promote a more general and methodical discussion of problems relating to education in higher institutions of learning; to create means for authoritative expression; to make collective action possible; and in general to maintain and advance the ideals and standards of the profession.[2]

It would have pleased them to know that the gulf between their ideal and the normal school's reality was, indeed, bridgeable and even more that the drive to build that bridge would come from the very institution that seemed so threatening. Truly astounding would be the fact that the man who epitomized for them the worst tendencies in higher education, President Q. M. Smith, would also be the man most responsible for inculcating professional faculty standards.

The problems these professors identified in 1915 sound eerily familiar to us in the twenty-first century: too few resources, low pay for teachers, attacks on their freedom in the classroom, diminished respect for learned opinion, increasingly arbitrary systems of accountability. And all this was happening in the context of rapid, even explosive, growth of higher education—in the number of institutions, professors, students, and new disciplines.[3]

Unfortunately, the professors, as they saw the situation, had become the victims of change rather than its beneficiaries. As Walter P. Metzger has put it, growth led to attenuation, "debasing academic standards" by bringing into the profession teachers who were less than adequately prepared; to usurpation of faculty authority, giving "undue power to administrations" by increasing the size of departments and colleges; and to "covert aggression" from these administrators who wished to popularize what was being taught in order to increase capital investments and budgetary appropriations, thus sacrificing both truth and academic freedom. To the AAUP the solution was for the faculty to work toward self-improvement by raising standards of preparation, self-government by assuming the authority to make decisions on curriculum and collegiate structure, and self-protection to guarantee their freedom of speech and presentation in the classroom.[4] With only slight changes in nuance over the years (for instance a shift from the call for "faculty governance" to "shared governance"), these have been the association's goals ever since.

The impetus for the AAUP seems to have received its energy from two otherwise antagonistic forces in the academy. One was the old academic establishment of East Coast, eighteenth- and nineteenth-century, some would say hoary, colleges and universities that had long served as the arbiters of American mores and culture. They approached the new academic realities as displaced elites, yearning to preserve their status and calling as a guild, Jefferson's "academic village of scholars." The second was the far more energetic, forward-looking, progressive, professional faculty from ivy league universities but also from the newer research institutions like Johns Hopkins and Stanford. Committed to applied research and being utilitarian, they developed new disciplines and academic units that, ironically, contributed to the very problems the AAUP identified. It is significant, in this regard, that the first president of the AAUP was John Dewey, professor of education and psychology at Columbia University, and the first secretary was A. O. Lovejoy, professor of philosophy at Johns Hopkins.[5]

All would have agreed, though, that Middle Tennessee State Normal School (a teachers college after 1925) illustrated the forces in higher education that most threatened the professoriate. Religious schools, state universities, and normal schools proliferated throughout the nation. While the South lagged behind the rest of the country in creating state normal schools, it caught up rapidly from 1900 to 1920, adding "more normal schools for white students than any other region"[6] including Tennessee's three regional "normals" and Tennessee A & I for African Americans.

Like others, Tennessee's schools exhibited centralized, authoritarian administrations, narrow missions and, consequently, curricula, and what appeared to be ad hoc faculties recruited locally on a non-competitive basis.[7] To members of the AAUP, such trends represented the worst tendencies of America's academic heritage and provided a major obstacle to inculcating craft/professional standards. To a great extent, they were correct.

Hard as it is to imagine today, at its inception Middle Tennessee State University was little more than a high school in a state in which few students progressed beyond the eighth grade. For example, according to Jeannette Keith, in 1900 over 8,100 students were enrolled in the first grade in the ten-county Cumberland plateau region; in the eighth grade there were only 424.[8] It was to improve this situation that the legislature passed the General Education Act of 1909 and mandated that the three regional normal schools provide teachers for the expanding number of schools and students they hoped for. A two-path curriculum at these normal schools provided a high school education, for prospective elementary school teachers who had not yet graduated, and a teacher training course of study that provided graduates with a permanent license to teach at all levels in any of the public schools in Tennessee.[9] The latter attracted some who were already teaching and who sought improved credentials, but otherwise the students were younger than today's students with weak academic preparation.

The same could be said of the faculty. Of Middle Tennessee State Normal's 19 original faculty members, only one held the doctorate and five the master's degree while six, or 37.5 percent, had not earned a bachelor's degree. Designation in 1925 as a teachers college helped raise the standards for the faculty. The percentage holding the master's degree increased dramatically in 1931 to 63.3 percent and, among the 30 teachers, nine had earned PhD's while the percentage of those earning solely a bachelor's degree or less fell dramatically. The first president, Robert Lee Jones, had worked long in school administration, but he held no academic degrees; his successor, Pritchett Alfred Lyon, held only an honorary doctorate.[10] What preparation faculty and administrators enjoyed came frequently from church-related academies and seminaries whose curricula were focused and, according to academic standards, narrow. So was the network from which they came. Jones recruited at least three men and women whom he knew personally, and he appointed his own son, Horace Grady Jones, to be the first bursar. The first librarian, Bettie Murfree, was a member of Murfreesboro's founding family. The university's historian, Homer Pittard, claimed that "without question, this first faculty was by far the best qualified of the three faculties at the state normals," but even he could describe its credentials as only "fairly adequate."[11]

If the quality of the faculty would have raised academics' eyebrows, the centralized, authoritarian administration would have created serious concerns. Since the normal school was essentially a high school, then the president was its principal. Technically accountable to the State Board of Education that hired (elected) him, in reality the presidents made all the local decisions—on hiring and firing, curriculum, budget, allocation of resources, and development. Tenure did not exist; all appointments were annual. When state board member and early school supporter Andrew L. Todd engineered Eugene Tavenner's appointment as dean of faculty without discussing it with President Jones, it caused a serious rift in their once-strong friendship.[12] Of course, presidents could only spend what the state allocated, so they devoted much of their time to lobbying legislators and state officials. But locally, their word was law.

Most problematic, though, was the normal school's strong religious culture. Church, state, and academy were not only united—they were intertwined. Morality was required of all students. As the perennial college catalog put it: "The state is under no obligation for the professional training of any persons that are not qualified to exert a wholesome spiritual influence upon the lives of children." Furthermore, the school "will not accept for entrance any person who does not show evidence of such qualification." Attendance at "chapel experience" three times a week that would include "devotional exercises" was expected of all students and faculty. The Young Men's and Young Women's Christian Associations were strong presences on campus, and the Student Christian Union sponsored vesper services every Sunday. The catalog touted Murfreesboro's "religious advantages" to recruit the interest of parents, and local ministers preached in the dormitories during the week.[13] William J. McConnell, a student and lay leader in the Episcopal Church (his nickname was the Little Parson), provided the first school song with words set to a tune from the church's hymnal (it was also the tune of the Czarist Russian national anthem).[14]

If the faculty was restive under these conditions, there is scant evidence of it. Indeed, this was the academic culture that had fostered the teachers, and they continued to nurture it. E. May Saunders, for instance, who taught music at Middle Tennessee from 1911 until 1955, assured that gospel songs and hymns were standard fare at assemblies; all half-hour sing-a-longs at assembly began with "Come Thy [sic] Almighty King." It was she who had encouraged McConnell to prepare the school song, and her successors, Neil and Margaret Wright, created the Sacred Harp Singers in 1947.[15] The school long had a reputation, despite its diversely evangelical personnel, as a Church of Christ campus, with some justification. A comparison of the faculty and staff appearing in the 1946 *Midlander* with a 1946 directory of then President Q. M. Smith's East Main Church of Christ in downtown Murfreesboro reveals that 3 of 28 faculty members, 4 of 12 staff (including Smith), and one teacher in the Training School belonged to this one congregation alone. The following year, in 1947, a large number of these members organized the North Boulevard Church of Christ to strengthen ties with the campus.[16] Long-time faculty members often recall the three questions President Quill E. Cope, Smith's successor, asked at their hiring interview as late as the 1960s: what church do you belong to; are you married; what's the lowest salary you will accept?

In light of these shared values of centralized authority and evangelical protestantism, it is no surprise to find few faculty members here joining the AAUP. From 1931 until 1936 only W. M. Mebane and A. Lloyd Taylor, both chemistry instructors at State Teachers College, Murfreesboro (STC), belonged to the AAUP, and both memberships had ended or lapsed by 1936. Early in his tenure as president, Smith precipitated a controversy that brought him head-to-head with the national organization. In 1939, he removed Professor Philip Mankin's line from the faculty budget, claiming financial exigency. When Mankin appealed the decision, first to the State Board of Education and then to the AAUP, investigations raised serious doubts about Smith's justification and pointed to several other circumstances that seemed to have been more precipitant: Mankin's refusal to attend assembly, his sloppy appearance, the long delay in completing his doctoral graduate degree, concerns about his radical politics, and whispered conjectures about his sexual identity. The case resulted, in 1942, in the AAUP's Committee on Tenure and Academic Freedom recommending censure of the administration, and the following year the AAUP complied.[17]

The effect of censure by AAUP on the campus is unclear. On the one hand, despite protests from sympathizers in the community and among students and alumni, there was support for President Smith's action, including from some teachers. In his history of MTSC's first half century, for example, Homer Pittard wrote disparagingly of Mankin's student supporters and described censure as AAUP's entering "the name of its institution in its black ledger."[18]

On the other hand, 1943 witnessed the beginning of an explosive growth in AAUP membership on the campus. How do we account for this? The Mankin firing seems to have had some immediate impact. The year began with three active members and ended with two more–long-time faculty members Eva M. Burkett (English) and Hester Rogers (Art). Four more joined the following year: Brainard B. Gracy (Agriculture) and Elizabeth Schardt (Foreign Languages) who both had arrived on campus in 1918, and relative newcomers Clayton James (Social Science) and J. C. Waller (Education).[19] But longer-term institutional change accounts for the growth as well. Upgrading the institution from a teacher's college to a four-year liberal arts college in 1943 and changing the name to Middle Tennessee State College improved its position in the academic market place. And investment in higher education through the GI Bill and government investment in research and development in the immediate post-war years certainly contributed to the school's progress.[20] Accordingly, the number of faculty members nearly quadrupled in less than 20 years, from 33 in 1941 to 70 ten years later, and 127 in 1961. The newer instructors were much more likely to be strongly credentialed as well; the proportion of the faculty holding the doctorate grew from 21 percent in 1941 to 34.6 percent in 1961.[21] AAUP membership on the campus grew apace, to 18 members in 1949 and 42 members in 1955, making it the second largest AAUP chapter in the state, exceeded only by the University of Tennessee's organization.[22]

When we scratch beneath the surface of all these circumstances of growth in the size of the school and professionalism of the faculty—increasing numbers, strengthening credentials, upgrading the nature and the mission of the college, and federal government investment—one finds the same dynamo generating all of them. Ironically, the man most responsible for the rise and development of AAUP on campus and the transformation of teachers into professors was the same man whose actions had led the AAUP to censure it: Quintin Miller Smith.

The conflict between Smith and the AAUP obscured a shared progressive vision. Both believed that education was the vehicle for social and personal improvement, but the make and model of those vehicles differed dramatically. The AAUP was the product of northern and western progressivism that tended to pit itself against the prevailing culture; it was pragmatic, secular, democratic, and meritorious. In the South, progressivism became popular, like evangelicalism in the early nineteenth century,[23] only when it adapted itself to local culture and values, among which were paternalism, patriarchy, and piety. As historian William Link puts it, southern progressives "embraced uplift and progress, yet believed in a hierarchy of race and culture," and they "endorsed measures of coercion and control" to accomplish their essentially "Protestant humanitarianism."[24]

AAUP leaders found it difficult to appreciate the mix of traditional, particularly religious, values in southern progressivism. At the turn of the twentieth century, an odd pairing of school modernizers and fundamentalists in Tennessee had produced both the free, public, central school system and the Butler anti-evolution act that led to the Scopes trial in 1925. The AAUP had participated in John T. Scopes's defense[25] and undoubtedly gained from the experience a certain disdain for both the patriarchal and pietistic qualities of contemporary southern education. When it censured the administration of State Teachers College, Murfreesboro, in 1943, the AAUP added it to a list that already included the University of Tennessee and that would include Memphis State College, the following year. Of the 12 administrations on the censure list, four came from states of the former Confederacy, and another two were in Missouri. Indeed, 1942 was the AAUP's most active year for investigating faculty complaints since its founding in 1915.[26]

Q. M. Smith was a southern progressive; he came to his presidency as a patriarch, an evangelical pietist, and a crusader for modernization. In the valedictory address to the faculty on September 19, 1938, he stated clearly what everyone in the audience already knew: "Responsibility begins and ends with the president." Shared governance, let alone faculty governance, played no role in his concept of the academic community. All faculty members served on committees, of course, but the job of a committee was to accomplish tasks, not to set policy or make decisions. Smith once described a committee as "a group of the unqualified appointed by the unwilling to do the unnecessary." Democracy consisted of each person's having a job to do and accomplishing it, thus contributing to the well-being of the whole.[27] Singularity of mind produced unity of purpose.

Nothing was more important to achieving that unity in Smith's view than personal and collective devotion to morality and religion. "Get the assembly habit," Smith said, and he repeated that call consistently throughout his presidency. Assemblies are important, he said, because there we meet "to have our devotion. To sing—people who sing together will work together." (To encourage better singing he had an organ installed in the auditorium.) As we know, Philip Mankin's absence from assembly and questions about his commitment not only to orthodoxy but to Christianity were at least contributing reasons for Smith's firing him.[28] Listing vital student activities in his opening address, Smith cited "Religious Life" second; athletics came sixth. An important job of the Public Program Committee was "to prepare chapel and other group meetings" and to "induct new students into the religious life of the campus and town." Trying to be popular, he told teachers, was "the sin of the 'holy ghost' of education." How should one act? he asked in 1949. "Go to Sunday School and Church and make friends with the preachers and teachers and leaders."[29]

With such a dominating presence of evangelicals and fundamentalists in town and on campus, Smith's secular preaching made practical sense. The fact that he arrived in Murfreesboro under a cloud of scandal, notwithstanding his strong personal religious values, could only have accentuated a need for an uncompromising public advocacy. Smith served as President of Tennessee Polytechnic Institute (Tennessee Technological University) from 1920 until shifting his presidency to STC in 1938.[30] His local welcome was not uniformly cordial. That he was divorced and remarried to a divorcee raised many evangelical eyebrows. Rumors added lurid details to the situation that lingered. On May 10, 1940, during testimony before the State Board of Education in support of Philip Mankin's reinstatement and against President Smith's "dictatorial" leadership, Dr. W. T. Robison of Murfreesboro cited as one reason for lack of confidence in Smith the "morality of a man who abandoned his wife and married the divorced wife of a former student." A petition submitted to the board at that same meeting stated that Smith "was practically forced to withdraw from the presidency [of TPI] due to his conduct unbecoming a president of a [sic] educational institution" that seriously undermined the "high moral standards that have been prevelent [sic] at the said institution for the past few years." That 81 people, mostly businessmen and attorneys, signed the petition suggests the breadth and depth of hostility toward Smith in the town, connected perhaps to bitterness which still lingered over the forced resignation of his predecessor, nearly two years after Smith's arrival.[31]

The conservative religious climate in Murfreesboro and on the campus made it easy for AAUP investigators examining Philip Mankin's firing to focus on the obvious theological differences between Smith and Mankin as the "most significant of the 'charges'" lodged against him.[32] Whereas Smith had once been the target of an evangelical campaign, now it seemed that the liberal Mankin was the victim. One wonders if the case roused memories of John Scopes in the minds of the academics on AAUP's Committee on Academic Freedom and Tenure as they voted to censure the college's administration. Whether or not Mankin's religious liberalism was the principal reason for his firing, the process that led to it clearly violated two of the AAUP's foundational values—self-governance (academic freedom) and self-protection (due process).

Lost in the controversy was the strong agreement between the AAUP and President Smith on the third of AAUP's core values, self-improvement. Controversy over a previous firing at the college that prefigured Mankin's dismissal reveals the drive for professionalization and modernization that lay at the heart of Smith's appointment and his agenda as president of Middle Tennessee State College (MTSC). Ultimately, this shared objective led Smith and the campus to a rapprochement with the AAUP and the creation of a lasting cooperative relationship between faculty and administration at Middle Tennessee.

It was the forced retirement of Smith's predecessor, the beloved Pritchett A. Lyon, that created the opportunity for his appointment. Orthodox in religion and administrative policy, Lyon's twenty-year tenure spanned both the economic boom of the 1920s and its collapse in the 1930s. Lyon had overseen the school's upgrading to state teachers college in 1925 and helped the institution weather the challenges of austerity during the Great Depression.[33] Nevertheless, toward the end of that decade he faced a direct assault from within his faculty. Knox T. Hutchinson was head of the Agriculture Department, a Democrat, and a strong supporter of the New Deal. He had come to the school in the wake of its upgrading to teachers college status and by the mid-1930s was apparently restive to see further modernization on the campus. The occasion for his assault on Lyon seems to have been popular debates beginning in 1933 over the Tennessee Valley Authority and its regional impact. TVA's promise of lower electric rates pleased everyone—except local power providers like the Tennessee Power Company. It was against their high rates that the TVA was set to compete.[34] It appears that Lyon supported the local interests; Hutchinson, on the other hand, not only supported TVA but spent much of his time in the field helping to develop the program.[35]

The disagreement became a dispute in the spring of 1937. The legislature considered a bill requiring presidents of white, state teachers colleges (this would exclude Tennessee State A & I and the Technological Polytechnic Institute) to have an earned graduate degree. Only one president did not—P. A. Lyon. Rumor had it that Hutchinson wanted the job and that he was campaigning among the faculty, promising higher salaries and promotions if he were to become president. The battle divided the community as well as the campus. The Young Democratic Club of Rutherford County lobbied the board of education on Hutchinson's behalf while one newspaper, the *Rutherford Courier*, supported Lyon and condemned the backdoor politics the bill represented. The scheme, it said, was "concocted and conceived in the brains of certain local people who have been opposed politically to P. A. Lyon (or who have been unable to get Mr. Lyon to follow their dictates as they would like)." Its whole object "is absolutely nothing more or less than an effort to get one man out of office and some other man in." It called the idea of a college president's having to hold an earned college degree "just bosh."[36] The *Daily News Journal*, on the other hand, reported about the bill and its passage but took no editorial stance in the matter, by their silence seeming to support the bill and the progressive change it represented.

Simultaneously, President Lyon submitted his report to the State Board of Education and included the recommendation that "the services of Mr. K. T. Hutchinson be discontinued." What followed was a set of hearings like the ones that soon would take place over Smith's firing of Phil Mankin. Hutchinson, said Lyon, had been in effect undermining his authority with the students and the faculty, and he did not deny his interest in becoming the new president. The board accepted Lyon's report, including the firing of Hutchinson who then appealed the decision. By November when the board heard Hutchinson's defense, the legislature had adopted the law requiring state college presidents to have an earned degree, and President Lyon had accordingly tendered his resignation, at the same time offering himself for "further service in any capacity which . . . may be advisable." He apparently wanted to continue at the college as an instructor. Hutchinson's appeal became anti-climactic, and the board sustained his firing. As a parting shot, Hutchinson ran for and won a state Senate seat the following year and submitted a bill, which passed, requiring an earned bachelor's degree for anyone teaching courses in the state colleges. This effectively put an end to Lyon's hope to be of "further service."[37]

Hutchinson's subsequent career, culminating in his appointment as assistant secretary of agriculture in President Harry Truman's administration, suggests that his ambitions truly were political and not academic.[38] But the affair had a powerful impact on Q. M. Smith's appointment and debut as president in two important ways. First, the divisions the dispute created in the town and on campus called for healing if there was to be progress. This helps to explain Smith's early emphasis on the need for unity and commonality of purpose. Several faculty members at the college, congratulating Smith on his appointment, took care to assure him of their personal loyalty and cooperation. B. B. Gracy (an AAUP member in 1943) added: "I really believe that your selection as president was a very happy solution of the whole problem and I trust that you will find Murfreesboro to be just as receptive and cooperative as we have always found it to be." The entire faculty would assuredly be "ready and willing to cooperate with you in every way."[39] All the more reason to get beyond the damage to his personal reputation that criticisms of his marriage created. Undoubtedly, controversy later over Mankin's firing aroused unpleasant memories of the bitterness surrounding Hutchinson's dismissal.

Second, the controversy focused on the weakness, or lack, of academic qualification for teaching at the state teachers colleges, and that provoked impatience with the slow pace of professionalization of faculty and administrators. Smith's appointment responded to that need. He was in Middle Tennessee State Normal School's first graduating class and held bachelor's and master's degrees from George Peabody College for Teachers.[40] It appears that modernization was in the minds of the state board.

And it was in Smith's mind, too. While he sought to exercise effective administrative leadership and to nurture morality on campus, his agenda was to turn the teachers college into a modern, professional academic institution. In his first year's addresses to the faculty he listed "Steps in Modernization of a College." Equipment needed modernizing (thus the call for the Hammond organ). So, too, did student relations. Early in his tenure Smith encouraged students to create the Associated Student Body, like the one at TPI, complete with constitution and faculty advisors so people on campus could "watch one another" and apply the "Golden Rule."[41] Most important of all, instruction required modernization. Faculty must participate more fully in the life of the profession—"spend more time in the library," attend conferences, publish papers, talk about their publications with students, and post them prominently. He encouraged faculty to join the National Education Association and the Tennessee Education Association (he had served as president of the TEA), and to enable that he established a faculty fund that provided one month's dues for anyone who joined the TEA or the NEA.[42]

Accordingly, faculty credentials needed strengthening. The Depression had weakened faculty standards by limiting instructors' opportunity to advance their education and the college's ability to hire new teachers. From 1931 to 1941 the college added only three positions, and overall faculty qualifications diminished. While 30 percent of the faculty held doctorates at the beginning of the Depression, only slightly over 21 percent held terminal degrees in 1941. Even at the end of Smith's first decade as president, while the number of faculty members holding doctorates doubled, from 7 to 14, it still represented only 20 percent of the faculty. The percentage of those holding the master's degree remained unchanged, but those holding only a bachelor's degree increased from 3 percent to 8.6 percent.[43] High on Smith's complaints about Philip Mankin was the fact that he had not shown sufficient progress toward his doctoral studies at Vanderbilt University.[44] If Mankin had been the only faculty member of whom that was true one could give more credit to Smith's charges. But one can not ignore the contribution of Smith's progressive desire to strengthen faculty credentials to his decision about Mankin.

The combined effects of economic depression and World War II created an extremely volatile job market. Early in the war it appeared the college might have to shut its doors because of the state's financial situation and the absence of male students, who were joining the armed services, and female students, who were joining the work force. But Smith saw opportunities, not just for survival but for growth, and he took them, turning challenges into rewards. His first, and some would say most important, act was to shepherd the elevation of State Teachers College, Murfreesboro, to Middle Tennessee State College. Homer Pittard credits a union of community and student desire to rename the institution Tennessee State College for initiating the drive. Competition with State Teachers College, Johnson City, for the title helped spur all these forces into action in 1941. Two years later, with little controversy, Middle Tennessee began its life as a four-year, liberal arts college.[45] Actually, promoting both campuses was almost certainly already in the minds of the board of education when it supported requiring earned degrees for state college presidents and when it hired Smith.

More than anything else, it was the growth in higher education following World War II that gave Smith the opportunity to modernize the college and to do it rapidly. Federal investment in research and development brought new teaching fields to the college, especially in engineering and technology. In 1950 the state legislature and board of education authorized MTSC to develop graduate programs, and the campus responded immediately with a new master's degree in education.[46]   Both developments required increasing numbers of highly qualified professionals to teach them. More often than before, these men and women came with doctorates from prestigious regional graduate programs and a modern professorial identity and ethic, including commitment to academic freedom and faculty governance.

Soon the AAUP rolls began to swell. Eight new members joined in 1947 alone, eight more in 1951, and six in 1952. They came from all the disciplines—science, fine arts, liberal arts and social sciences, business, industrial arts. At the time, AAUP members nominated others for membership, so it is not surprising to see AAUP concentrating in already active departments like English and history. The new members included seasoned veterans and brand new professors; many were women, including E. May Saunders, Emily Calcott, Helen Trivett, Henrietta Wade, and Mary Hall. Today many of these members' names are memorialized on campus, in the (E. May) Saunders Fine Arts Building, (Carlton C.) Sims Hall, the (Edwin W.) Midgett Building, (Howard G.) Kirksey Old Main, (Lane L.) Boutwell Dramatic Arts Building, the (Roscoe E.) Strickland Lecture Series, Miss Mary Hall, the (Neil H. and Margaret) Wright Music Building, and (Robert L.) Corlew Hall.[47]

What President Smith thought about this growth is not clear. On the one hand, given his initial negative experience with the AAUP one might speculate that he was less than thrilled to see it expand so quickly. On the other hand, by encouraging faculty to join other professional organizations he may have set the stage for AAUP's development as well. Whether he liked the organization or not, Smith was able to see the benefit its presence offered a professionalizing professoriate and to use it to the college's advantage by reversing any damage censure had caused. By 1956, George A. Shannon, chair of the AAUP's Committee A on Academic Freedom and Tenure, could report to the organization that "the President's attitude toward this administration and its principles has completely changed."[48]

What brought about the change? When the AAUP investigated the case of Phil Mankin's firing, it applied standards from its 1940 foundational policy, "Statement of Principles on Academic Freedom and Tenure."[49] At the time, the administration could afford to treat the matter lightly, but not for long. In 1941, the American Association of Colleges of Teacher Education adopted the AAUP statement as its own policy for reviewing, among other things, the status of academic freedom and tenure when accrediting institutions. In 1951, it initiated a process of institutional self-study that included an on-site visit, and on October 25, 1952, an accreditation team examined Middle Tennessee State College for the first time.[50] There is no record of Smith's conversation with them about faculty policies, though he could have pointed to the Board of Regents' "Guiding Principles in Connection with the Qualifications, Employment, Retention, and Salary Scale" of faculty members from 1946 as the governing statement about hiring and retention on this campus.[51] But with AAUP censure continuing year after year, the situation was, at best, awkward.

More was needed, nothing less than removal of censure. And that required a definitive process of hiring, retention, and dismissal that protected academic freedom and faculty governance. The presence on campus of so many AAUP members and, after 1948, a campus-wide chapter,[52] proved more a blessing than a curse; they comprised a team that could work with Smith to engineer MTSC's reinstatement.

In 1954, President Smith took the first step toward rapprochement by appointing AAUP member Gene Sloan from the Department of Journalism to write the first faculty handbook, "to replace many miscellaneous sheets that have been passed out over the years."[53] One of those sheets undoubtedly was the board's "Guiding Principles." Then, in January 1955, Howard Kirksey, dean of instruction and AAUP member, wrote to Ralph Himstead, AAUP general secretary, to pay dues as an associate member (administrators could not be full members) and to launch a trial balloon. The local chapter president had asked the AAUP "a few years ago," wrote Kirksey, to find out what the campus had to do "to remove M. T. S. C. from the association's 'black list.'" That man had not received "any definitive information," but Kirksey renewed the inquiry. "I feel that whatever is necessary to be done will be done to accomplish this objective" for the welfare of "our local chapter and the A. A. U. P. as well as this institution."[54] Himstead responded by telegram. President Smith himself should request removal of censure, forward copies of the current tenure review policy, and provide "definite assurance that principles [of] academic freedom and tenure endorsed by [this] Association, [the] Association of American Colleges, American Association of Colleges for Teacher Education, have for some time been preserved and are now being observed by Administration of institution." Kirksey responded affirmatively, but the administration wanted the local chapter to concur with the arrangement before proceeding.

On February 24, Smith provided the requisite letter and assurance that his administration was adhering to AAUP principles of tenure "in accordance with long-standing policies officially sanctioned by the governing board." The following day, the MTSC chapter sent a petition with signatures of 37 members expressing unanimously their "earnest desire to see the censure of the M. T. S. C. administration removed" since the administration was, indeed, adhering to sound principles of tenure "so far as this chapter is aware."[55] With the AAUP set to hold its annual meeting in Gatlinburg and two MTSC members, Roscoe Strickland and Richard C. Peck, in attendance to shepherd the process of reconciliation, the time seemed propitious.[56] All hoped for a resolution of the case.

It was not yet a done deal. While the AAUP believed Smith's change of heart was genuine, and although the chapter's unanimous support was very persuasive, the caveats in both Smith's letter and the chapter's resolution raised eyebrows. Was Smith using the board's statement as a cover to justify continuing inequitable processes, and were there serious infractions since 1942 of which the local chapter was unaware? To satisfy the first nagging doubt, the AAUP wanted to see no less than a definitive revision of the faculty handbook's policy on faculty hiring, retention, and tenure. A review of the document discovered six areas of concern, and George Shannon made very specific recommendations on how to revise the statement to make it accord with AAUP principles.

Second, the local chapter needed to undertake an investigation to discover "if there have been any dismissals of teachers with tenure status since 1942, or other situations involving questions of academic freedom and tenure." It's not clear whether the chapter undertook that work, and there is no surviving response from the chapter if it did. They were undoubtedly aware of Smith's firing of Durward L. Stowe, instructor in the Department of Health and Physical Education, in 1950 before the end of his probationary period, and someone in the chapter must have known of Stowe's appeal to the AAUP. That Committee A turned down the appeal because the administration had faithfully followed established policy in the matter could only have bolstered Smith's record.[57]

By now, President Smith was acceding to every request and requirement from the AAUP, even incorporating their exact recommended wording in public statements and policies. For the next edition of the faculty handbook he agreed to include this statement: "As a member of the American Association of Colleges of Teacher Education, Middle Tennessee State College accepts and abides by the principles of academic freedom and tenure of that Association, which are those set forth in the 1940 AAUP statement of freedom and tenure." At the fall convocation in 1955, Smith announced that the administration had adopted the AAUP Statement of Principles as "its official statement of policy . . . relative to tenure and academic freedom." This was, wrote chapter president Norman Parks, "a most gratifying incident to the members of the local chapter."[58]

Now it was time, wrote Parks, for removal of censure. Including the AAUP principles in the faculty handbook will "bind the present administration firmly to sound principles of tenure," and because it would be very difficult to remove it from the handbook it would "bind succeeding administrations" as well. Most important, "it would be the first step toward winning a commitment from the State Board of Education and all sister state colleges to these same principles."[59] Vanderbilt Professor and AAUP Council member Denna F. Fleming added his assurance to Shannon that the MTSC chapter members "have done just about all they can." Refusal to reinstate the administration now would create "consequences for the chapter [that] would be very serious indeed." Russell A. Nelson, member of Committee A and of the council, added a further consideration. Attacks from the House Committee on Un-American Activities and Senator Joseph McCarthy on academics across the country, and requirements of loyalty oaths after 1947, had resulted in many complaints of violations of academic freedom. The year 1956 would produce a new surge of censure resolutions. "It seems to me," wrote Nelson, "when we shall be recommending for censure so many schools, it is of utmost importance that we remove from censure those schools which have demonstrated by their actions compliance with the principles of the Association."[60]

Accordingly, at its 1956 annual meeting in St. Louis, the AAUP Council voted unanimously to reinstate Middle Tennessee State College 13 years after having censured it, one of the longest periods of censure in the association's history.[61] Perhaps it took so long to accomplish rapprochement because both parties had to decide what price it was willing to pay to get what it wanted. At the end, the AAUP won from Smith a progressive approach to faculty rights and governance and academic freedom—even if they had to swallow the uncomfortable reality that Smith would interpret all that in traditionally southern ways. Religion continued to play an important role in his leadership, as it would for his successors almost to the end of the century. But other challenges successively captured the AAUP's attention. Protecting academic freedom from the assault of national security watchdogs in the 1950s shifted toward seeking equal access to enrollment and faculty positions for African Americans during the civil rights era and then to equity for women in the 1980s. In the light of these national campaigns, the regional, cultural particularities of a small southern college (university after 1963) must have seemed insignificant.

At the same time, Smith won from the AAUP validation for his crusade to professionalize the institution, even if he had to give up the kind of centralized administrative power that had defined the school's presidency from its inception. And the partnership with local AAUP members that brought this about was a lasting legacy of his administration. Two years after Middle Tennessee State College's reinstatement, Q. M. Smith retired. Perhaps, after all, it was his desire to leave to his successor a clean slate that led him so earnestly to fix this problem. Fix it he did. Never again would an aggrieved faculty member lodge an appeal with the AAUP's Committee A that could have led once again to censure. The local chapter and its leaders from now on would negotiate on behalf of the professoriate and create solutions to vexing problems that redounded to everyone's benefit. At the end of his tenure Smith had created what he envisioned at the beginning of it, a unified, relatively cohesive team of faculty and administrators, each playing its part, not always agreeing but knowing well how to disagree.

NOTES

1   The changing status and accompanying changes in names for the university make referring to it challenging. In this essay, I will refer to the name of the normal school as indicated or as "Normal." I will refer to it after its designation as a teachers college as "State Teachers College, Murfreesboro" (STC) although I am aware that its official name was changed, in 1925, to "Middle Tennessee State Teachers College.

2   "Origins," in "A Retrospective on the Occasion of the Seventy-fifth Annual Meeting," special issue, *Academe: Bulletin of the American Association of University Professors* 75, no. 3 (May–June 1989): 4,5 (hereinafter cited as AAUP, *Bulletin*).

3   For an excellent discussion of higher education's rapid growth and its impact on faculty, see Frederick Rudolph, *The American College & University: A History* (Athens: University of Georgia Press, 1990), particularly chapter 19, "Academic Man," 394-416.

4   Walter P. Metzger, "Origins of the Association: An Anniversary Address," AAUP, *Bulletin* 51, no. 3 (Summer 1965): 231.

5   "Origins," 4. One can sense this division in the critical comments from some professors, who opposed creating such an organization, appearing in this issue, 4–6.

6   Christine A. Ogren, *The American State Normal School : "An Instrument of Great Good"* (New York: Palgrave Macmillan, 2005), 60.

7   Metzger, "Origins of the Association," 232. Metzger did not mention normal schools in his article, perhaps because academics in general would not have considered them to be legitimate institutions of higher education.

8.   Jeanette Keith, *Country People in the New South: Tennessee's Upper Cumberland* (Chapel Hill: University of North Carolina Press, 1995), 127.

9   Homer Pittard, *The First Fifty Years: Middle Tennessee State College, 1911–1961* (Murfreesboro: Middle Tennessee State College, 1961), 60–61.

10   Ibid., 217, 32, 152.

11   Ibid., 40–41, 49, 50–51.

12   Ibid., 41.

13   *Bulletin of the State Teachers College, Murfreesboro* 10, no. 2 (May 1936): 21, 25, 31, 40.

14   Pittard, *First Fifty Years*, 78.

15   Ibid., 238, 38–39, 79.

16   Box 8, folder 10, Q. M. Smith Papers, Albert Gore Research Center (AGRC), Middle Tennessee State University, Murfreesboro, TN (hereinafter cited as Smith Papers, AGRC). Smith was deeply involved in designing what became their new worship space in 1952, sketches of which appear in the same folder as the church directory. For a brief history of the North Boulevard Church of Christ, see their website, http://www.northboulevardfamiy.com/about/history.shtml.

17   For a full discussion of the Mankin case, see James Homer Williams's chapter, "Tyranny or Freedom? Presidential Power and Community Relations in the Firing of Philip Mankin," in this volume.

18   Pittard, *First Fifty Years*, 169–70.

19   *Bulletin of the State Teachers College, Murfreesboro* 29, nos. 3 and 4 (1939): 453, 603; and 30, no. 3 (1940): 476.

20   Pittard, *First Fifty Years*, 170–73. President Smith had been particularly successful in attracting federal defense funds for educating aviators and engineers during the war. See Ellen Garrison, "'Getting on the Gravy Train'—MTSU and World War II," in this volume.

21   These figures are based on Homer Pittard's statistics, 217.

22   AAUP, *Bulletin* 35, no. 1 (Spring 1949); 41, no. 1 (Spring 1955).

23   Christine Leigh Heyrman, *Southern Cross: The Beginnings of the Bible Belt* (Chapel Hill: University of North Carolina Press, 1998).

24   William A. Link, *The Paradox of Southern Progressivism* (Chapel Hill: University of North Carolina Press, 1992), xii.

25   See Charles A. Israel, *Before Scopes: Evangelicalism, Education, and Evolution in Tennessee* (Athens: University of Georgia Press, 2004). On the AAUP's role in the trial see, Edward J. Larson, *Summer for the Gods: The Scopes Trial and America's Continuing Debate over Science and Religion* (New York: Basic Books, 1997).

26 AAUP, *Bulletin* 29, no. 3 (June 1943): 446; 32, no. 1 (January 1946): 8.

27 Address to the Faculty, 19 September 1938; Notes for Faculty Meetings, Notes on Faculty Committees, 10 September 1938, box 5, folder 2, Smith Papers, AGRC.

28 Williams, "Tyranny or Freedom."

29 Meeting Notes, 5 October 1938; Address; Notes, 10 September 1938; 17 March 1941; 22 September 1949, box 5, folder 2, Smith Papers, AGRC.

30 Pittard, *First Fifty Years*, 162–63.

31 Box 4, folder 5, Smith Papers, AGRC. These claims are at best exaggerations. A file of letters to Smith congratulating him on his appointment recently added to the Q. M. Smith Collection includes several petitions from students at TPI and community organizations asking him to reject the appointment. That Smith waited a full month before accepting it suggests he was aware of the potential difficulties and was carefully weighing his options. See J. M. Smith, Chair, Board of Education to Smith, 9 May and Smith to Smith, 10 June 1938, unaccessioned file, Smith Papers.

32 AAUP, *Bulletin* 28, no. 3 (October 1942): 675. In March, 1941, William M. Hepburn visited the STC campus and the Board of Education in Nashville on behalf of the AAUP to examine Mankin's complaint. While waiting in an outer office to see State Board Chairman E. C. Duggan, he tried unsuccessfully to trap Duggan's Executive Secretary, Maude Holman, into stating that religious motivations were involved in Mankin's firing. E. C. Duggan to Doak S. Campbell, 31 March 1941, box 4, folder 5, Smith Papers, AGRC.

33 Pittard, *First Fifty Years*, particularly chapters 5–7. Challenges included a serious attempt to close the teachers colleges and move major programs, such as agriculture, to the University of Tennessee.

34 See Walter L. Creese, *TVA's Public Planning: The Vision, The Reality* (Knoxville: University of Tennessee, 1990).

35 Pittard, *First Fifty Years*, 155.

36 *Rutherford Courier*, 11 May 1937.

37 Pittard, *First Fifty Years*, 157–59.

38　*Century of Service: the first 100 years of the United States Department of Agriculture* (Washington, DC: United States Department of Agriculture, 1963), 354. A brief biography of Hutchinson (page 446) states that he had served "on staff at Murfreesboro Teachers College," but it did not mention the circumstances under which he left.

39　B. B. Gracy to Smith, 10 May 1938, unaccessioned file, Smith Papers.

40　Pittard, *First Fifty Years*, 162.

41　Ibid., 166–67.

42　Meeting Notes, 10 September, 5 October 1938; 15 January, 21 March 1939, Smith papers, AGRC.

43　Pittard, *First Fifty Years*, 217.

44　AAUP, *Bulletin* 28, no. 3 (October 1942): 669–70.

45　Pittard, *First Fifty Years*, 171–72.

46　Ibid., 196.

47　The AAUP *Bulletin* listed the names of those nominated for and then elected to membership until 1959.

48　Memorandum, 28 March 1956, Committee A, Middle Tennessee State College, General 55, box 83, AAUP Papers, Special Collections, the George Washington University.

49　AAUP, *Policy Documents and Reports*, 9th ed. (Washington, DC: American Association of University Professors, 2001), 3–10.

50　A working draft of MTSC's first self-study appears in box 6, folders 10, 11, of the Smith Papers, but there is no indication of a response from the accrediting agency.

51　A copy of this appears in the MTSC case file of the AAUP, obviously sent to the AAUP as part of the discussion that led ultimately to the school's removal from censure.

52　AAUP, *Bulletin* 35, no. 1 (Spring 1949): 171.

53 Copy from the Faculty Handbook contained in the MTSC report file, Committee A, AAUP Papers.

54 Howard Kirksey to Ralph Himstead, 27 January 1955, typed copy, AAUP Papers.

55 Ralph W. Himstead to Howard Kirksey, 4 February 1955, telegram; Kirksey to Himstead, 18 February 1955, typed copy; Q. M. Smith to AAUP, 24 February 1955; Norman L. Parks, President, MTSC AAUP Chapter, to Ralph Himstead, 25 February 1955, AAUP Papers.

56 Roscoe Strickland and Richard C. Peck to Ralph Himstead, 2 March 1955, telegram, AAUP Papers.

57 George Pope Shannon to Richard C. Peck, 26 April 1955; George Pope Shannon to D. L. Stowe, draft letter, 13 April 1950, AAUP Papers.

58 Q. M. Smith to George Pope Shannon, 30 May 1955; Norman Parks to Shannon, 7 October 1955, AAUP Papers.

59 Norman L. Parks to George Pope Shannon, 2 June 1955, AAUP Papers.

60 Russell N. Sullivan to George Pope Shannon, 6 February 1956, AAUP Papers.

61 AAUP, *Bulletin* 42, no. 2 (Summer 1956): 340.

CHAPTER TEN

Beyond the Metrics of Race

Geier and Integration

KENNETH A. SCHERZER

On September 11, 2006, Tennessee Governor Phil Bredesen assembled the parties involved in 38 years of litigation at a public ceremony in Nashville to celebrate an historic settlement. "Today, I'm proud to announce that Tennessee has met the challenge set by the Geier lawsuit—to build a unitary public higher education system that truly offers equal access to all citizens," noted the governor. Then he added, "[I]n Tennessee, the door really is open to all."[1] In the long and circuitous history of desegregation of higher education, a history which usually focuses on the dual system that maintained Tennessee State University as a primarily black institution and sought to establish a new University of Tennessee campus in Nashville largely to attract whites, Middle Tennessee State University has been little more than a footnote. Only in 1984, 16 years after Rita Sanders Geier filed her initial motion, did the expanding roster of plaintiffs enlarge the case to include all public institutions of higher education in Tennessee, both the University of Tennessee and the Tennessee Board of Regents schools. Nevertheless, *Geier* has had a profound and lasting impact on Middle Tennessee State. For African American students, it pushed the university to move beyond the tokenism of earlier integration and to create a genuine presence that embraced diversity on the Murfreesboro campus. For faculty, staff, and administrators, *Geier* brought the tools of affirmative action to bear in changing the racial composition of the university. And for the campus as a whole, the *Geier* case brought profound changes that permanently altered the funding, mission, and programs of MTSU at the same time that the university was undergoing its fastest growth. These changes continue to shape the direction of MTSU well after Bredesen made his announcement.

In May 1954, in the wake of *Brown v. Topeka Board of Education*, two recent black graduates of Murfreesboro's Holloway High School, James Scott and Walter Swafford, arrived to pick up application forms and catalogues so that they could seek admission to Middle Tennessee State College (MTSC). Dean N. C. Beasley informed them that applicants were required to be "graduates of approved high schools 16 years or over, white, of good moral character and free from communicable diseases." They applied nonetheless. The Tennessee State Board of Education, which governed state higher education, voted unanimously to deny admission to these two students along with five other African Americans who sought admission to Memphis State College in August 1954, citing statutes and the Tennessee State Constitution. While the Memphis students sued in federal court with the support of the NAACP Legal Defense Fund to win admission, the MTSC applicants declined to file an appeal.[2] The barrier of *de jure* segregation was not formally breached until 1959 when the State of Tennessee capitulated in federal district court, after losing its appeal, and agreed to allow black students to register. Desegregation finally came to MTSC in 1962, when the first black student to graduate from the university, Olivia Woods, enrolled.[3]

Nevertheless, minority students remained little more than a token presence through much of the 1960s. A telling insight into what college life was like for this small cohort of black students can be gleaned from a series of interviews conducted by MTSU graduate student Kenneth Baird Hadley. In 1969, when the 133 minority students accounted for fewer than 2 percent of the entire headcount, Hadley distributed questionnaires to all 58 male African American students on campus. Many of the 31 who agreed to be interviewed were from exceptional backgrounds; their parents had inculcated their sons with high educational aspirations. All but two were from Tennessee and most of these students came from families with strong histories of higher education: 13 had BA's in their families; ten had master's degrees; five families had members with PhD's. In terms of religion, the nine freshmen, seven sophomores, ten juniors, and five seniors represented a range of Protestant denominations: ten were Baptists, ten were Methodists, three were members of the Church of Christ, two were Presbyterians, and there were six with no religious preference. Hadley sought to show that these black students were little different from their white counterparts.

Drawing heavily upon the theoretical writing of functionalist sociologist Robert K. Merton, Hadley argued that "black male students at Middle Tennessee State University, by and large, accept the goals of our culture and the institutionalized means for obtaining them. The doors of conformity have previously been closed to the black man. Now it seems that they are partially open."[4] The ambitions expressed by the black students seemed to bear this out. Twenty planned on pursuing a master's degree after graduation, while eleven hoped to earn doctorate degrees ultimately. All but one expected to earn incomes over $10,000 a year after graduating from college (nearly $60,000 in 2010 dollars). When asked about their plans ten-years hence, 30 hoped to live in houses worth $20,000–50,000 ($120,000–$300,000 in 2010 dollars) and to build a world that would "be a better place for their children where they would not be judged by the color of their skin."[5]

Beneath these optimistic expectations for the future lurked a more troubling and less cheerful present. To be sure, earlier reminiscences of Olivia Woods and Robert Corlew, who was then chair of the History Department, asserted that Middle Tennessee State College (later to become Middle Tennessee State University) was integrated without the turmoil found on other southern campuses. Woods noted, "I guess people got used to seeing me on campus. . . . And then Margaret and Linda" and "they thought, well, they're not going to be bad." Yet Hadley uncovered a deep dissatisfaction among male students in 1969.[6] Some of this might have been due to symbols of the Old South found at MTSU, such as the plaque of Nathan Bedford Forrest on the University Center, the football team's adoption of the name "Blue Raiders," and the playing of "Dixie" at games. Indeed, in 1968, black student Sylvester Brooks sparked a campus-wide debate by attacking these symbols as representing an "utter and unmerciful contempt of the basic dignity of Black people."[7] Civil rights historian Bobby Lovett has credited these symbols with leading many black students to shy away from the university altogether.

Those who did attend expressed a broad sense of unease with the university and the town in which it was located.[8] "Most of the responses to the questions," Hadley reported, "indicated dissatisfaction with the school as a whole. They tended to view it as backward." Twenty-six respondents expressed disappointment with the school. As one student noted, "MTSU is dead. Only an atomic bomb can wake it up." Widespread complacency led to a pervasive sense of "I can't wait to get out."[9] Much the same could also be said of Murfreesboro. As one student observed, "Murfreesboro is as the South is, a slowly changing remnant of the Old South—that is the [white] people and the black people continue to exist in a somewhat discriminatory atmosphere and their attitudes are not such that there will be any radical change that will bring about better relations and understanding between the races."[10] Not surprising, since Hadley surveyed the students within a year of the assassination of Dr. Martin Luther King, twenty-two expressed admiration for the militant black power group, the Black Panthers, while only four felt that traditional organizations like the NAACP were doing the most for civil rights. When asked to name the most influential people in their lives, only four listed King, compared with the others who tended to list family members or sports figures.[11]

What accounted for the widespread alienation among this pioneering generation of black students at MTSU? The apparent cause was *not* overt racism. Although seven students felt they had received lower grades on the basis of their race, the rest did not. When it came to how white students treated them, most felt that only "a minority of the whites were hostile to them." They mainly found "white students were indifferent to them," with many white students "unsure of themselves in their relationships of blacks."[12] Such a sense of indifference was not unfounded. When the Tennessee Higher Education Commission asked President Quill E. Cope to seek input from various deans and departments on the future role of the university, only the Political Science Department mentioned a need for greater diversity, citing "a most needed increase in the percent of negro students." This was in the midst of other goals identified such as higher admissions requirements and "improved programs to assist subpar students."[13]

If the discrimination that still existed in Murfreesboro in 1969 promoted alienation, perhaps the greatest impediment for African American students was their small enrollment, which made them an "elite group" and placed them under a constant microscope. Complained one student who refused to respond to Hadley's questionnaire, "every time I turn around, somebody in the psychology department or educational department is saying 'Let's get some Negroes and find out what they think' since there are only fifty-eight Negro males on this campus." Another student, grumbling about being "over-tested," shot back at Hadley: "I wish like HELL that you oversensitive white people would leave us Negroes alone. The only way that racism is going to die is that people will stop being oversensitive. We do not need a white ghost to haunt us every day of our lives. Why don't you leave us alone!"[14]

Race relations at Tennessee colleges were on the minds of many people in the late 1960s. Just a year earlier, on May 21, 1968, a history instructor at Tennessee A&I University, Rita Sanders—who later married and became known as Rita Sanders Geier—had filed suit in Federal District Court in Nashville introducing a case that redefined race relations in higher education in Tennessee for the next four decades. Yet this was not the first time that the issues of racial equality had been challenged in Tennessee higher education. The opening of Tennessee A&I State Normal School for Negroes in Nashville, in 1912, initiated an era of dual public higher education in Tennessee that survived the 1954 federally mandated integration of public schools. Perpetually underfunded relative to white-only public colleges, Tennessee A&I State Teachers College was denied the right to offer graduate degrees in 1935. As a result, the NAACP filed suit to open graduate courses at the University of Tennessee (UT) to black students in *State of Tennessee Ex. Rel. William B. Redmond, II v. O. W. Hyman, et al.* The Tennessee General Assembly ultimately relented and allowed Tennessee A&I to offer a few graduate degrees but chose to fund out-of-state Negro scholarships for graduate degrees that it did not offer rather than allow black students to attend UT. Not until 1951 did Tennessee elevate A&I to university status—the same year that a federal court required desegregation of UT graduate programs. Otherwise, Jim Crow still governed public undergraduate admissions.[15] Consequently, Rita Sanders Geier had reason to bring suit in 1968.

Groundwork for the suit had been laid in 1947 when UT opened a branch campus in Nashville as a night school intended to service the needs of industry, business, and state employees. When, in 1968, the Tennessee General Assembly sought to convert the campus into a full-fledged, degree-granting branch of UT and university officials announced plans to construct a $5 million facility in Nashville, the Field Foundation in New York sponsored a suit by students and faculty of both UT–Nashville and TSU to prevent the expansion. In *Rita Sanders v. Governor Buford Ellington*, the plaintiff contended that expanded UT programs would "perpetuate the dual system of higher education" and that the expansion would come at the expense of A&I (which became Tennessee State University the following year). The plaintiffs, now joined by an additional group led by Ray Richardson Jr. of the NAACP Legal Defense Fund and State Senator Avon Williams, demanded greater recruitment of minority faculty and students at white institutions and the forced merger of TSU and UT–Nashville. The State of Tennessee—the defendant in the case—countered by offering limited remedial efforts to coordinate programs, recruit minorities, and boost the quality of TSU.[16]

For much of the next decade, the legal wrangling continued between the Geier plaintiffs and the state, punctuated by the protests of TSU students opposed to the expansion of UT–Nashville. On January 21, 1977, US District Judge Frank Gray Jr. finally issued his ruling that required UT–Nashville to be merged with TSU. The decision gave only passing reference to MTSU, rejecting as inadequate proposals to coordinate programs such as a Specialist in Education degree with MTSU, UT–Nashville, and TSU. Judge Gray expressed the hope that the Tennessee Board of Regents, which would manage the consolidated institution after three years, could "provide additional advantages with respect to the goal of desegregation since the other three state institutions of higher education in Middle Tennessee are under this board. Any problems of competition or duplicative programs can obviously best be handled by one governing board."[17] Regardless of Judge Gray's hopes, the University of Tennessee continued its legal appeals for another three years until the merger was completed.

A new group of plaintiffs-interveners led by Coleman McGinnis, a former professor at UT–Nashville, however, turned the case in an entirely new direction. Claiming that TSU had failed to honor its own commitment to desegregation under Judge Gray's ruling in *Geier* and was in the process of "resegregating" itself, McGinnis sought to consolidate the three boards governing higher education into one. TSU fought back, arguing that the solution proposed by his group of interveners threatened to alter "all that Tennessee State has to offer" as an historically black university.

Then in 1984, after 15 years of legal wrangling, all parties finally sat down together and were able to reach a legal understanding for the first time. The subsequent ruling, the *Stipulation of Settlement*, brought the full weight of federally mandated desegregation to all public higher education in Tennessee including MTSU. The *Stipulation*, as ratified by the court, called for the formation of a Desegregation Monitoring Committee to monitor progress for the court of TSU and all other institutions aimed at "dismantling of the dual system . . . in such a way as to increase access for black students and increase [t]he presence of black faculty and administrators overall and at the historically white institutions." The agreement directed TSU to increase white enrollment to 50 percent while maintaining admission standards that required GPA and ACT scores for admission be no lower than at MTSU. However, the *Stipulation* also contained provisions specifically directed at MTSU. It required the Board of Regents to "establish a common university calendar, publish and disseminate a joint listing of all courses" allowing students at TSU and MTSU to take up to 30 credit hours at the other institution. More important, the plan sought to establish TSU as "the regional urban university for Middle Tennessee." Not only did this involve a plan to adjust funding and improve facilities, but also to remove any "barrier to the implementation of the state's commitment to enhance TSU." To this end, TSU would be given priority for all new graduate programs while MTSU, together with Austin Peay State University, would be barred from receiving any new masters or doctoral programs for the next five years. Clearly, the continued academic growth of MTSU and Austin Peay was at a disadvantage under this plan.

The agreement mandated that all Tennessee institutions "enroll a percentage of new entering classes under alternative admissions standards" until each met desegregation goals. Newly established biracial boards would oversee an "other-race recruiting program" and help "create in each institution the image of an institution that serves the citizens of Tennessee on a non-racial basis." The TBR was specifically required to "match any existing or future scholarship program designed to increase white enrollment at TSU with an identical scholarship program designed to increase black enrollment at Middle Tennessee State University." Finally, the *Stipulation* sought to redefine hiring practices in every public institution of higher learning in Tennessee. All were required to implement a rigorous program of affirmative action to increase the number of black hires among staff and faculty, to develop a black faculty development program, and to require prior board approval for any administrative hires from the level of department chair upwards to ensure that goals of racial diversity were met.[18] As McGinnis later explained, "Though there was much disagreement (at that time) about what needed to be done at TSU, there was complete agreement on what needed to be done at the other institutions—both requirements that they do a better job of recruiting and educating minority students and that, in Middle Tennessee, MTSU (and increasingly APSU as well as, of course, UT) be prevented from encroaching on TSU's 'space' in Davidson County." The particular fear was that "MTSU coveted some specific TSU programs, especially Nursing, which happened to be one of TSU's most successful programs."[19] Under this requirement of the *Stipulation*, TSU would be protected.

The *Geier Stipulation* had its most immediate and dramatic impact upon MTSU through its freeze on new graduate programs and mandated coordination of existing programs in Middle Tennessee. In 1985 MTSU terminated its Master's degree in Public Administration and transferred its Bachelors of Science degree in Urban Planning to TSU.[20] As a result of meetings between the presidents of APSU, TSU, and MTSU to discuss consolidating duplicate programs, MTSU terminated or combined five master's level programs into a Master of Science in Wellness and Fitness and a Master of Arts in Teaching in Foreign Languages while abolishing seven additional master's level programs between 1984 and 1994. During that same period, the university added only one new graduate degree, a Master of Science in Human Sciences. By contrast, APSU offered eight fewer master's degrees in 1994 than it had in 1984 and TSU consolidated its offerings from 37 to 23. And while TSU added four new doctorate degrees, MTSU's doctorate of arts offerings were frozen at their

1984 level of five. When MTSU later sought to add two new master's level programs in education, these merely replaced existing degrees. The moratorium did not end until 1995, when the university was allowed to add a new Master of Science program in Aviation.[21]

Under terms of the *Stipulation*, MTSU committed itself to providing greater support for African American student life on campus and to establishing a closer working relationship with TSU. The two founded a consortium in the fall of 1985 to help set a common calendar with no more than two days difference between the beginning and ending of classes at each institution. The schools organized a journalism workshop together. Joint publication and dissemination of course listings allowed students to take up to 30 hours at the other institution. In the first decade after the *Stipulation*, 1,044 white students and 251 black students cross registered, although the numbers dwindled over time.[22] The Desegregation Monitoring Committee, which monitored the implementation of the *Stipulation*, boasted in its report of the election at MTSU of seven African American Homecoming Queens and one African American Student Government President between 1984 and 1994. In 1995 alone, the Murfreesboro campus sponsored 16 black-oriented events including lectures by Cornell West from Harvard and the noted political leader, Percy Sutton.[23] Finally "the University developed and established relationships that consisted of planning, programming, financial/personnel support" for "other-race" student organizations. These consisted of the African American Student Association, the MTSU Black Alumni Council, the MTSU Collegiate and Rutherford County Chapters of the NAACP, and historically African American fraternities and sororities on campus: Alpha Kappa Alpha, Alpha Phi Alpha, Delta Sigma Theta, Zeta Phi Beta, Kappa Alpha Psi, Sigma Gamma Rho, Phi Beta Sigma, and Omega Psi Phi.[24] These events and organizations clearly reflected the efforts of MTSU officials to provide for the school's African American students.

Hiring a diverse staff, faculty, and set of administrators also became a key objective of *Geier*. The Desegregation Monitoring Commission could take particular satisfaction when it proclaimed in 1991:

> Two historical achievements took place this past year in Tennessee higher education through the appointment of two executives to highly visible positions. Dr. Otis Floyd was appointed as the Chancellor of the Tennessee Board of Regents. Dr. Floyd is the first Black to hold the top position at any of Tennessee's three higher education boards and is one of the first to hold such a position in the Southeast. Dr. James Walker became the President of Middle Tennessee State University in Murfreesboro. Dr. Walker became the first Black to be selected to head an historically white university in the state of Tennessee.[25]

Otis Floyd, formerly the assistant to Commissioner of Education Sam Ingram before following him to MTSU as vice president for administration, was named president of TSU before being elevated to chancellor. The 50-year-old James E. Walker had been vice president of academic affairs and provost at the University of Northern Colorado, Greeley. This progress in hiring was followed by other successes. For example, "A Black male," referring to Dr. Thaddeus Smith, "became the permanent chair of the Department of History" in 1996 following a national search. The following year a "Black male" became associate dean of student life, then in 1999 "Dr. Gloria Bonner, an African American female," became dean of the College of Education and Behavioral Sciences.[26] By the end of the 1900s, then, MTSU was moving toward meeting the hiring objective of the *Stipulation*.

In addition, the *Stipulation* called for every institution to set five-year benchmarking goals by which to measure progress. Each institution in the TBR, from community college to university, and all branches of the University of Tennessee submitted a detailed tally of every hire, including statistics on the size and racial composition of each applicant pool. In MTSU between 1976 and 1990, the proportion of black administrative personnel increased by 800 percent, appreciably higher than at other midstate institutions. In professional staff hiring, MTSU surpassed its interim goals by 65 percent.[27] Thus, in the first five years of the *Stipulation*, MTSU witnessed its first real surge in hiring of black administrators and professionals, more than quadrupling the numbers of each (See Figure 1).

Black Hiring, 1982–1999

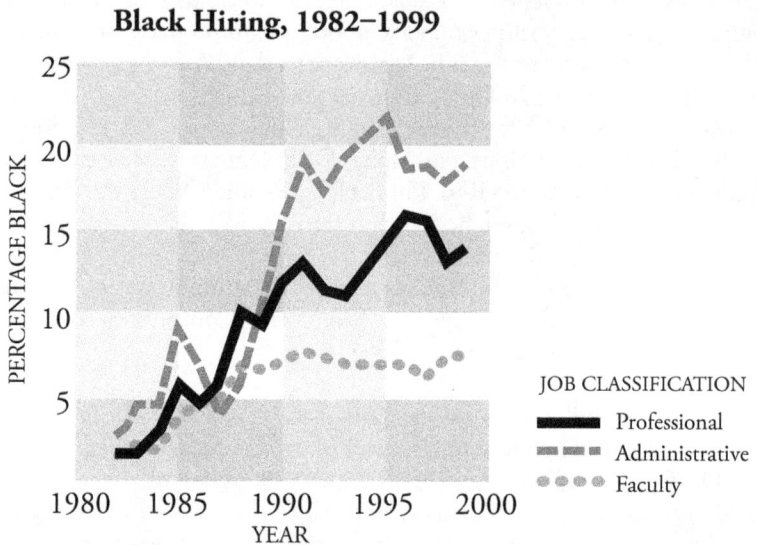

Figure 1. Source: Tennessee Higher Education Commission, Tennessee Board of Regents, and University of Tennessee, "Annual Report of the Desegregation Monitoring Committee," (1984–2000).

Beneath such high-profile successes in affirmative action lay a somewhat more mixed record. High-level administrative and lower-level staff positions, all of which were appointed by administrators, proved easier to diversify than did the ranks of the faculty, whose hiring was largely controlled by a peer group of professors. The number of minority faculty doubled from 8 in 1984 to 17 in 1985 and, once again, to 34 in 1988. In 1992, newly installed President Walker announced an ambitious goal "to increase the number of minorities on faculty and staff by 30, and the number of women by 87."[28] In 1997, MTSU fell short of the modest goals set by the Desegregation Monitoring Committee, and just prior to Walker's departure in 2000, his own goals remained unmet.

Indeed, the lack of progress in the hiring of black faculty during most of the 1990s led to considerable soul searching by administrators in 2000. MTSU reported to desegregation monitors that when "the institution fell below its goal for faculty, the provost's office began requiring the inclusion of an African-American on every faculty search committee." Furthermore, newly hired African American faculty joined with other black faculty to meet the president to "discuss strategies for future recruitment activities and retention efforts." And where "qualified African-Americans emerged through the search pools, many were invited to campus for an interview even if their credentials were not the best for the advertised position." They were either hired for "another position within the department" or groomed for future openings. [29]

As the *Geier* case entered its final phase in 2001, with the agreement of all parties to a *Consent Decree* in what was now known as *Geier v. Sundquist*, the State of Tennessee agreed to the establishment of two committees, one for each system of higher education, to examine practices in hiring and retention of minority faculty and administrators. The committees were to report to Carlos González, the court-appointed monitor overseeing the decree. Each committee was charged with hiring an outside consultant to compare compliance to national "best practices."[30] In the case of MTSU, outside consultants called on the university to "study why its retention is so poor in light of the fact that its recruitment is apparently so innovative and successful." In addition, the university was urged to utilize the "Grow Your Own" program that encouraged graduates to pursue doctorate degrees with the goal of being hired back at MTSU, and to study Miami University in Ohio and Northern Illinois State University as models for recruiting black faculty. Finally, the consultants called upon the administration to "ascertain the basis of the resentment of *Geier* and take steps to overcome the negative perception."[31] Over the remaining years in which *Geier* was in effect, the university devoted funds to supplement salaries to make them competitive and to fund minority development programs for faculty and staff. In the final year alone, MTSU funded five pre- and post-doctoral participants who ultimately received job offers while 18 other minority faculty members received $95,000 in awards for professional development.[32]

The enrollment of minority students (black students at formerly white institutions and white students at historically black TSU) was, of course, the ultimate measure of success for desegregation efforts. Starting in 1960, prior to *Geier*, open admissions served as the principle means for recruiting black students.[33] Kenneth Baird Hadley's black male MTSU undergraduate interviewees in 1969 revealed that open admission hardly meant admitting students who were unprepared for college—indeed this group may have been exceptionally well prepared.[34] Nevertheless, African American students were different from their white counterparts and showed differences, if not in high school grade point averages, then in college test scores and in performance while at MTSU.

A brief window in which to study these differences opened in 1968, when administrators began collecting information on student admissions performance by race and ethnicity. In 1968, when MTSU had only 148 blacks compared with 6540 whites, the average high school GPA was 2.656 for black students versus 2.686 for whites, not a significant difference. By 1975, GPA scores had improved to 2.823 for whites while staying at 2.661 for African American students. A more significant difference between the two groups could be found in the well-documented but controversial racial disparity in ACT test scores. Where black ACT scores had risen from 12.9 in 1968 to 13.9 by 1970, for the rest of the 1970s these scores actually declined to a low of 11.6 but regained most of their 1970 levels by 1989. White scores, which stood at 19.3 in 1968, had also declined through most of the 1974 to 1989 period, but they ended the decade at 17.5—3.8 points higher than blacks.[35]

Yet GPA and ACT scores proved to be only an imperfect measure of performance for minority students at MTSU. To be sure, the racial gap in cumulative GPA difference was shockingly wide in 1968: 1.736 for African American students compared to 2.414 for whites. This undoubtedly gave some credence to the sentiment expressed by some of Hadley's respondents that grading may have been tarnished by racism.

Cumulative GPA by Race, 1968–1989

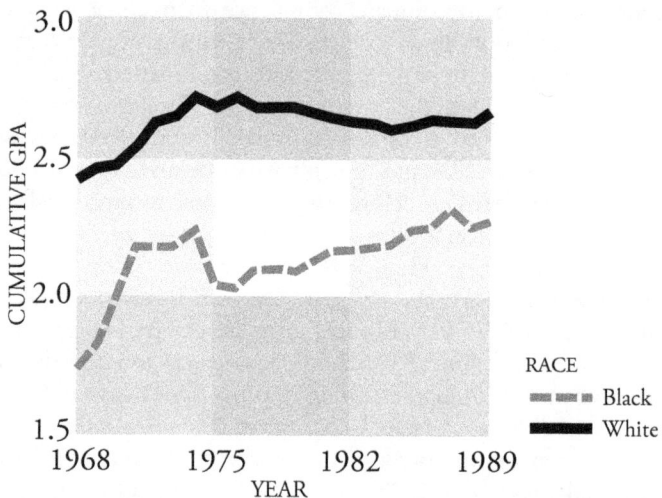

Figure 2. Source: Office of Admissions and Records, Middle Tennessee State University, Statistical Studies (For Administrative Use), Fall 1968–Fall 1989 (Murfreesboro, 1968–1990), Office of Institutional Effectiveness, Planning, and Research, Middle Tennessee State University, Murfreesboro, TN.

But, by 1971, these gaps had shrunk considerably and stood at 2.172 for black students compared to 2.545 for whites. And while white GPAs also slid during the late 1970s and early 1980s, black averages actually recovered from their initial decline in the mid-1970s and rose through most of the 1980s (See Figure 2).

By 1971, the number of African American students on campus had reached 286 or 3.3 percent of the total student population. No longer under constant scrutiny, in part because of their increasing numbers, black students expressed a new sense of confidence by constructing a permanent foundation for a university community. This was evinced by the formation of an African American student association and campus chapters of historically black Greek letter sororities and fraternities. The Eta Gamma Chapter of Kappa Alpha Psi was the first fraternity established on campus, followed in 1973 by the Iota Tau Chapter of sorority Delta Sigma Theta, the Zeta Chapter of fraternity Omega Psi Phi, and the Eta Psi Chapter of sorority Alpha Kappa Alpha. In 1975, Alpha Phi Alpha founded a Kappa Xi Chapter, followed in 1977 by the Mu Theta Chapter of sorority Zeta Phi Beta and, in 1978, these were joined by the Iota Mu Chapter of fraternity Phi Beta Sigma.[36] Black students were making their growing presence felt on the MTSU campus.

The merger of UT–Nashville and TSU mandated by *Geier* in 1977 coincided with a slowdown, even a reversal, in the growth of minority enrollment at MTSU. Where 1970s enrollment had peaked at a black enrollment of 1039 in the fall of 1979—some 9.5 percent of the total student population—the number actually dropped to 840 in 1985, or 7.4 percent of enrollment, a decline of nearly 20 percent.

Percent Black by Student, 1976–2010

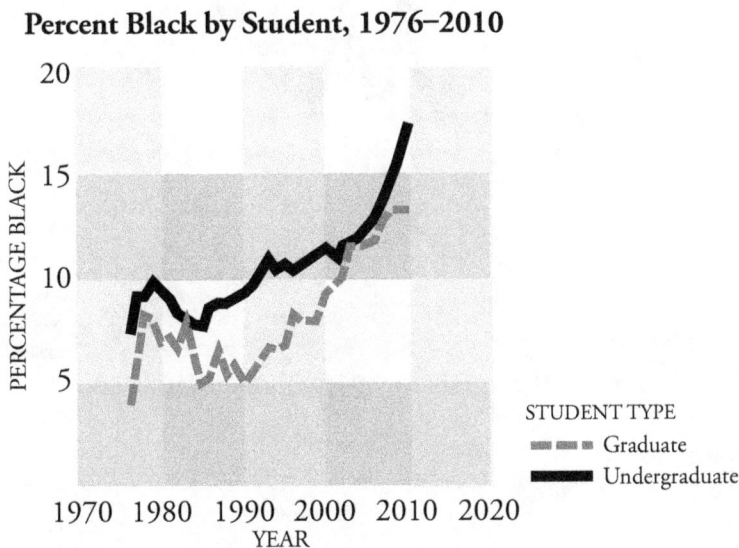

Figure 3. Source: For data through 1981 and from 2000–2010, MTSU, Statistical Studies (For Administrative Use), Fall 1968–Fall 2010. For data through 1983 and 1999 inclusive, "Annual Report of the Desegregation Monitoring Committee," (1984–2000).

The consolidation of graduate programs may have played a role in this. While the general student population stagnated in the early 1980s, and actually declined in 1981 and 1982, the greatest decline was in the number of graduate students— perhaps from the consolidation of programs and direction of resources to TSU. The number of graduate students fell from 1736 in 1979 to a low of 1125 in 1986, a net decline of 43 percent (See Figures 3 and 5).[37]

In addition, the composition of black undergraduates became more highly skewed toward women than it had been for white students. Although this gap was apparent for all classes, it became most visible for freshmen. Before 1983, white male seniors outnumbered white women, although the pattern later reversed itself, and white seniors became more strongly female, rendering a gender gap of over 20 percent female.[38] Among white freshmen, the sex ratio favored women until 2003, when men outnumbered women by a slight margin. For minority students, however, the sex ratio leaned decidedly in the direction of women and the gap has widened over time. In 2000, there were only 5.8 men for every ten black senior women and by 2010 the ratio was fewer than seven for every ten. For black freshmen, women have outnumbered men for every year for which data is available and the trend points, as of late, for the gap to widen compared to whites (See Figure 4).

Sex Ratio for Freshman by Race, 1976–2010

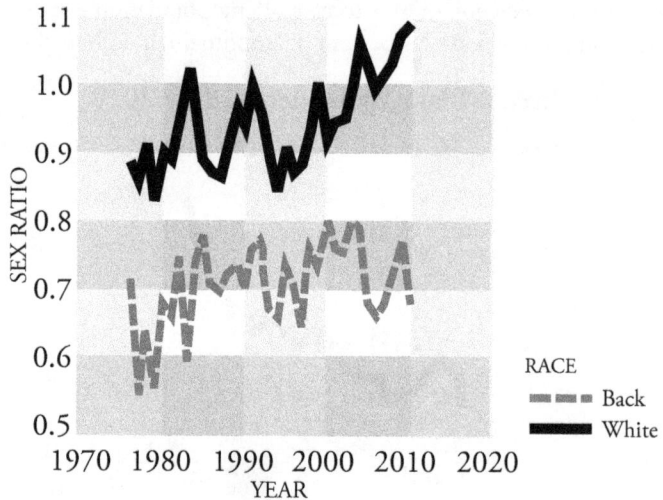

Figure 4. Source: The Office of Admissions and Records, MTSU, Statistical Studies (For Administrative Use), Fall 1976–Fall 2010 (Murfreesboro, 1968–2010).

The 1984 *Stipulation of Settlement*, which set a 50-50 target for TSU, required every other four-year Tennessee institution to undertake a "desegregation impact analysis," to adopt necessary "alternative admissions standards" to meet goals established by the analysis, and to implement "developmental education programs available to students throughout the state to promote retention of those students entering under alternative admissions standards."[39] While the landmark Supreme Court decision of *University of California v. Bakke* in 1978 precluded the federal courts from imposing specific racial quotas[40]—the *Stipulation* took pains to disavow the use of quotas—the goals it mandated involved elaborate calculations to set admissions targets not only for hiring, but also for enrollment at both the graduate and undergraduate level.

This racial metrics employed an elaborate formula that first identified which secondary school supplied students to a given university and then singled out those that provided at least two-thirds of the college student enrollment. The staff for the Desegregation Monitoring Committee then calculated a racial goal for admission by using census data to determine the county-wide black percentage for the areas in which these schools were located and then multiplied university enrollment by this number.[41] For MTSU in 1981, for example, this meant that the proportion of black undergraduates should have been 9.8 percent instead of the actual number of 9 percent, and for graduate students, 8.1 percent instead of 6.6 percent. Since the pool of potential black undergraduates rose more rapidly than that for graduate students, the targets for minority undergraduate enrollment rose to 11.5 percent in the late 1980s, 12.12 percent in the early 1990s, and 12.87 percent by the late 1990s. For graduate students the number actually fell to 6.6 percent in the 1990s. The eventual downward revision of racial goals and gradual recovery of graduate enrollment from its lows in the 1980s, however, allowed MTSU to reach its graduate targets from 1993 onward. [42]

Black Enrollment vs White/Other, 1968–2010

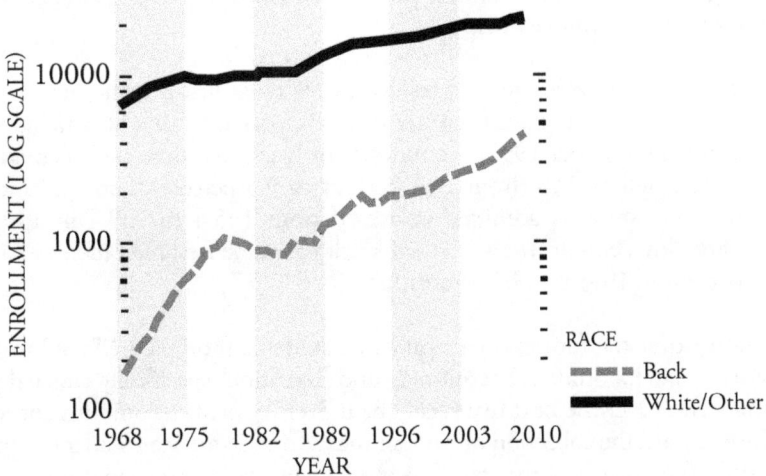

Figure 5. Source: Statistical Studies (For Administrative Use), Fall 1968–Fall 2010 (Murfreesboro, 1968–2010).

Reaching the goals for undergraduate enrollment of African American students proved far more elusive. In order to attract black undergraduates, MTSU awarded $3.4 million in matching scholarships between 1984 and 1994, compared to $6 million awarded to white and other race minority students at TSU.[43] A university publication showed one grateful black graduate of Bolivar Central High School noting, "Because of the scholarships I wouldn't have to worry about finances and I could concentrate on my studies."[44] And like other TBR institutions, MTSU instituted a developmental studies program for incoming freshmen. Using ACT and other placement test scores, the program enrolled 400 students of all races in study-skill courses, 650 in writing, and 1,300 in math courses during its initial year alone. Obviously, the program was aimed at "increasing their chances for success in college," and "avoiding the social tragedy of 'Johnny' who can't read," write, or do math.[45]

In 1993, President James Walker launched an audacious new program designed "to address MTSU's rapidly growing undergraduate population and to curtail its attrition rate" by raising the minimum ACT score required for admissions from 19 to 20 and the minimum GPA from 2.0 to 2.80. Unlike the presidential scholarships program established two years earlier to bring in students who were in the top 10 percent of their high school classes or with ACT scores of 28 or higher to MTSU, the higher admissions requirements threatened to have a devastating impact on minority enrollment. A "desegregation impact analysis" conducted by the TBR suggested that the new standards "would have little or no effect on minority applicants." Yet a new MTSU policy provided for "Admission by Committee Review" as "an alternative avenue to regular admission for anyone who fell below the minimum standards" and an "'Alternative Admission' category for applicants who could not be admitted either through regular or 'Standard Admission' or 'Admission by Committee Review.'" From a desegregation point of view, the precautions failed mightily. As the Desegregation Monitoring Committee noted:

> TBR's post-implementation review revealed that first-time freshman enrollment in Fall 1994 may have been negatively impacted by MTSU's raised standards. Compared to Fall 1992, the number of black first-time freshmen admitted to MTSU fell by 146 (from 15.1 percent to 9.3 percent), and the ratio of black to white students admitted decreased from 1::5.4 to 1::9.4 in 1994. At the same time, enrollment at TSU of black first-time freshmen increased from 86.3 percent in 1993 to 89.3 percent in 1994.[46]

Concern over the future impact on black students prompted MTSU to develop a "Master Plan for Student Recruitment and Retention" specifically targeted at African Americans. Over the next five years, the university made a commitment to increase efforts toward the collection of data on the "African American student population in Middle Tennessee and the state," to implement "earlier and more frequent contact with potential students," to work toward "improved communication, involvement, and public relations with the regional African American community," and to increase minority scholarships. All these initiatives were expected to require the expenditure of an additional $200,000 in university funds.[47]

In keeping with these efforts, in 1995, MTSU awarded 232 matching scholarships under the Otis L. Floyd Academic Scholarship program to freshmen with 3.2 GPA and minimum ACT scores of 25, and an additional 101 MTSU scholastic achievement scholarships. Floyd scholarships totaled $4,000 per annum while achievement scholarships ranged from $2,000 to $2,400 per year and renewable for four years for "African American students presenting a minimum of a 21 composite ACT and at least a 3.0 high school GPA." By 1999, MTSU was awarding 498 scholarships and awards of one form or another designed to recruit and retain black students.

As part of increased recruitment, MTSU expanded its outreach program, "Destination: MTSU," sponsoring university-funded campus visits for 150–200 prospective students and parents from Memphis, Jackson, and Chattanooga. Recruiting brochures "depicting the campus as it exists" through the use of "candid photographs" touted the university and campus organizations like the historical African American Greek letter organizations, the MTSU Black Alumni Council, the MTSU collegiate and Rutherford NAACP, and the African American Student Association. Telemarketing campaigns reached out to potential students identified in the admissions office databases.[48] Yet despite all these efforts, which mainly succeeded in reversing declines in black enrollment, MTSU was still farther away from its desegregation target in 1999 than it had been in 1993.

By the late 1990s, two trends were becoming increasingly clear. One was that TSU was moving further and further away from meeting its goal of becoming half white. The other emerging trend was that MTSU was becoming the fastest-growing institution of higher education in Tennessee. Where white undergraduates had made up 27.7 percent of TSU's enrollment in 1994, the number had dropped precipitously to 18.8 percent by 1997. Total enrollment had grown by fewer than 200 since the initial merger with UT–Nashville in 1977. By contrast, MTSU's enrollment had skyrocketed from 10,880 to 18,366 during the same period. As a commuter school, MTSU had nearly as many students from Davidson County as did TSU (3,418 vs. 3,618). This disparity in results under *Geier* increasingly became the subject of controversy. David Broad, the white chair of the TSU Faculty Senate remarked, "I look at [MTSU's] growth with envy."[49] TSU booster, State Senator Avon Williams, had once characterized MTSU as "part of a contingency plan" by Tennessee authorities "to strengthen MTSU while building up UT Nashville, but once efforts involving UT ran into trouble, state authorities increasingly saw MTSU as a residential haven for white students."[50]

Now TSU faculty and administration struggled to explain the explosive growth of the campus to the southeast. John Cade, the TSU dean of admissions and records, blamed perceptions that TSU had lower admissions standards, noting that potential applicants "make comparisons, and, often, they don't understand." Others chalked it up to general ignorance about the $100 million dollars in capital improvements made to the TSU campus as a result of *Geier*. Deborah Moore, a TSU graduate student complained, "When I see an ad for MTSU or Vol State, I wish people could see the new things we have on our campus, because they're not driving over here to see them." White professor and *Geier* intervener, Coleman McGinnis, cited "hostility to white students coming." TSU President James Hefner remarked:

> When people select MTSU over TSU, I'm sure they do it for a number of reasons. . . . I don't bemoan the students going to MTSU. I would like to get as many of those students as we can get, but I have to believe that these students obviously are aware of who we are and that we are not that far from them. I have to assume that they feel they are making a rational decision in going to MTSU.[51]

No matter the explanations, numbers were difficult to dispute.

After years of disputes, questionable results in some cases, and the desire of the state of Tennessee (and even of some alumni supporters of TSU) to have the court order finally lifted, in 2000, all parties finally entered into mediation that produced the consent degree under *Geier v. Sundquist* that the court at last accepted on January 5, 2001. The court appointed Carlos González as monitor to oversee the disposition of the case prior to final settlement and, in return, the agreement freed state colleges from the strict goals that had governed admissions and hiring since 1984.

To a great extent, the court was merely reflecting the changed legal climate following the 1997 Supreme Court case, *United States v. Fordice*, but in a more targeted manner. If *Fordice* upheld the right of the federal government to compel affirmative action to correct the remnants of *de jure* segregation, the 2003 decision of *Grutter v. Bollinger* moved the standard beyond one race being injured, to the question of the broader good that would flow from diversity, provided remedies were "narrowly tailored." In the decree, the court released TSU from the strict target of 50-50 other-race students, while leaving admission directors at the other TBR four-year universities and community colleges with the obligation only to undertake studies "for the recruitment of other-race high school other-race community college students." MTSU had the added satisfaction of not being singled out, as had Austin Peay State University, East Tennessee State University, the University of Tennessee in Memphis, and the University of Tennessee in Knoxville, for not closing "the 'persistence gap' between black and white students."[52]

In sum, the Consent Degree offered MTSU the freedom to pursue its policy of continued expansion. To be sure, the institution was still required to coordinate its programs and calendar with other mid-state TBR institutions and the ruling specifically barred the university from offering "courses for credit at any physical location in Davidson County." But MTSU won the cherished right to pursue the phased conversion of its doctor of arts to PhD programs, enhancing its status as a graduate-degree-granting university.[53] To that end, in November 2002, the TBR approved the conversion of three doctor of arts programs, English, human performance, and economics, to PhD programs, as the university planned for subsequent conversions of DA degrees in history/historic preservation and chemistry. President Sidney McPhee hoped the conversion would "allow us to be more competitive for external funding, like federal funding . . . National Endowment for the Humanities, National Science Foundation funds."[54] Since the end of the case was in sight, MTSU looked to a future where institutional and system-wide concerns would dictate its direction rather than a battle with TSU for programs and resources. On September 21, 2006, Judge Thomas A. Wiseman Jr. ruled that Tennessee had, at long last, removed "any vestiges of segregation" and now operated "a unitary system of public higher education."[55] Yet the MTSU student newspaper, *Sidelines*, greeted the dismissal of 38 years of *Geier* with a derisive editorial, questioning the whole premise of the case. As the editorial noted, "It seems that whether or not the state, the governor and the Tennessee Board of Regents chose to keep the Geier Degree programs or not, students will still be subjected to a form of racial grouping. . . . Selecting students to hold up, to support or to favor over another based on race is nothing but another form of racism."[56]

What had the case accomplished at MTSU? At the peak of black enrollment prior to the court-mandated merger in 1979, 9.8 percent of MTSU undergrads and 8.1 percent of graduate students were black. In the fall of 2006, with dismissal of the case, the numbers stood at 12.9 and 11.8 percent black, respectively. In the intervening years, racial composition of the student population at MTSU had plunged and did not fully recover its earlier levels until 1993, for undergraduates, and 2000, for graduate students (see Figure 3). The case had channeled $200 million to upgrade buildings at TSU and to correct a legacy of preference to white institutions.[57] Yet the physical improvements to TSU may have come at the expense of operating funds at all three mid state institutions. One fiscal study by John William (Jay) Sanders and Toto Sutarso, on the impact of *Geier* on state funding of higher education from 1983 to 2003, concluded that resources had shifted to the two flagship institutions in each state system, the University of Tennessee in Knoxville and the University of Memphis, along with Tennessee Technical University. By contrast, all three Middle Tennessee schools—APSU, TSU, and particularly MTSU—"lost ground since the Geier Settlement in 1984" as measured by FTE (headcount of students converted to the equivalent in full-time students).[58] This study shows that these institutions paid a high price as a result of *Geier*.

Nevertheless, the status of black students at MTSU has changed not only since Olivia Woods first registered at the school, but also since the 1984 *Stipulation of Settlement* first brought the full impact of desegregation to MTSU. Even if significant academic differences still remain between white and black students, *Geier* sought to address retention levels and increase the number of scholarships available to minority students. This reversed the earlier pattern that had made black freshmen less likely than whites to return for a second year. By 1986 retention for black freshmen was higher than for whites; while 71.6 percent of white freshman returned to campus the following year in 1987, the figure for black freshman stood at 81.2.[59]

If the effect of 38 years of *Geier* on MTSU was mixed, the aftermath of its settlement has had a remarkable impact on campus diversity. In 2007, the percentage of undergraduates who were black began a steep ascent, rising to levels unheard of during the duration of the case, reaching 14.9 percent in 2008, 16.3 percent in 2009, and more than 17.4 in 2011. TSU, like many historically black colleges and universities, has been beset by flat enrollment and difficulties attracting a diverse student body. Yet at the eve of the second decade of the twenty-first century, African American students at MTSU have finally achieved what many had long sought: minority enrollment has finally reached (if not surpassed) the percentage of black residents in Tennessee, which according to the 2009 census surveys stood at 16.8 percent. Four years after Governor Bredesen's announcement, at least at MTSU, the promise of *Geier* has been achieved—albeit without *Geier*.[60]

NOTES

1   "Governor Announces End of Geier Lawsuit," http://www.tennesseeanytime. org/governor/viewArticleContent.do?id=862.

2   George N. Redd, "Educational Desegregation in Tennessee—One Year Afterward," *Journal of Negro Education* 24, no. 3, The Desegregation Decision— One Year Afterward (Summer, 1955): 340; *Daily News Journal*, 23 May 1954, 1; Bobby K. Lovett, *The Civil Rights Movement in Tennessee: A Narrative History* (Knoxville: University of Tennessee Press, 2005), 344–45.

3   Stenia Olivia Murray Woods, interview by Betty Rowland, 19 June 2001, Middle Tennessee Oral History Project, audio clips, http://content.mtsu.edu/cdm4/ audiofiles/wood/woods4.mp3 (hereinafter cited as MT Oral History Project.) Transcripts of interviews in MT Oral History Project are housed in the Albert Gore Research Center (AGRC), Middle Tennessee State University, Murfreesboro, TN; Leah Massey, "First black graduate to be recognized at ceremony tomorrow: Woods studied elementary education; earned Master's," *Sidelines*, 29 February 2004, http:// www.mtsusidelines.com/2.3115/first-black-graduate-to-be-recognized-at-ceremony-tomorrow-1.317011.

4   Kenneth Baird Hadley, "A Functional Analysis of the American Ideological System and the Part Therein Played By the Negro Male Student at Middle Tennessee State University" (MA thesis, Middle Tennessee State University, May 1969), 40–41, 45. CPI calculation to 2010 dollars using Federal Reserve Bank of Minneapolis, "What is a dollar worth?" http://www.minneapolisfed.org/.

5   By comparison, 2010 black students were disproportionately represented in the following majors: chemistry, social work, human performance, psychology, and marketing and management while less likely to choose majors in recording industry, agriculture, history, English, and art. White students, by contrast, showed no strong patterns save for an affinity for recording industry and a lower level of selecting chemistry. MTSU Office of Institutional Effectiveness, Planning and Research, *Student Profiles Fall 2010*, 35–43, http://www.mtsu.edu/iepr/student_profiles/profiles10f/Profiles_F10.pdf.

6   Woods interview; Robert Corlew, interview by Regina Forsyth, 5 September 1995, Q. M. Smith Oral History Collection, audio clips, http://library.mtsu.edu/ digitalprojects/mtsumemory.php. Transcripts of interviews in Q. M. Smith Oral History Collection are housed at AGRC.

7   Sylvester Brooks, "*Dixie*: What Does it Mean?," *Sidelines*, 21 October 1968; Holly Barnett, Nancy Morgan, and Lisa Pruitt, *Middle Tennessee State University*

(Charleston: Arcadia Publishing, 2001), 114; *Middle Tennessee State University Diamond Anniversary,* 7 September 1986, Special Collections, JamesWalker Library, Middle Tennessee State University, 10; and Sylvester Brooks, interview by Erin Toomey, 30 September 2000, MT Oral History Project, audio clips, http://content.mtsu.edu/cdm4/item_viewer.php.

8   Lovett, *The Civil Rights Movement,* 354. Lovett wrongly attributes integration to the Civil Rights Act of 1964, two years after the enrollment of the first black student.

9   Hadley, "A Functional Analysis," 48.

10 Ibid., 46.

11 Ibid., 47.

12 Ibid., 43, 47.

13 Memo to President Cope from the Political Science Department, 29 April 1968, page 2 in "Statement of future institutional role and scope," (MTSU, 1968). Typescript in Special Collections, Walker Library.

14 Hadley, "A Functional Analysis," 55–56.

15 Lovett, *The Civil Rights Movement,* 24, 338–341, 344. The establishment of four normal schools by 1912 called for funding to be divided into seven shares, two each for the three white institutions—including Middle Tennessee State Normal School and remaining share for Tennessee A&I State Normal School. H. Coleman McGinnis, "Geier Case History," http://www.tnstate.edu/interior.asp?mid=940. See also Testimony of Christine Modisher, United States Commission on Civil Rights, Tennessee State Advisory Committee, *Desegregation of Public Higher Education in Tennessee: A Summary Report* (Washington, DC: The Commission, 1989), 1–2; John Egerton, *Black Public Colleges: Integration and Disintegration* (Nashville: Race Relations Information Center, 1971), 9–14; David D. Owensby, "Affirmative Action and Desegregating Tennessee's Higher-Education System: The Geier Case in Perspective," *Tennessee Law Review* 69, no. 3 (Spring, 2002): 703; and Alfreda A. Sellers Diamond, "The Gordian Knot: Higher Education Desegregation in Tennessee," *National Black Law Journal* 21, no 2 (July 13, 2009): 81–121.

16 Egerton, *Black Public Colleges,* 9–10; Lovett, *The Civil Rights Movement,* 350–53.

17 Lovett, *The Civil Rights Movement,* 355–70; and *Geier v. Blanton,* http://

tn.findacase.com/research/wfrmDocViewer.aspx/xq/fac.%2FFDCT%2FMTN%2 F1977%2F19770131_0000001.MTN.htm/qx .

18 "The Stipulation of Settlement," http://www.tnstate.edu/interior.asp?mid=4186.

19 H. Coleman McGinnis, e-mail message to the author, 20 October 2010.

20 Tennessee Higher Education Commission, Tennessee Board of Regents, and University of Tennessee, "Annual Report of the Desegregation Monitoring Committee," (1995) 32. Reports (1984–2000) on file at Tennessee Higher Education Commission, Nashville, TN. The 2000 report is also available at http://www.tn.gov/thec/Index/News/desgmeet.pdf.

21 "Annual Report of the Desegregation Monitoring Committee" (1995), 32; (1996), 30; (2000), 31.

22 "Annual Report of the Desegregation Monitoring Committee" (1996), 36.

23 "Annual Report of the Desegregation Monitoring Committee" (1995), 35; (1996), 16.

24 "Annual Report of the Desegregation Monitoring Committee" (2000), 14.

25 "Annual Report of the Desegregation Monitoring Committee" (1990), 1.

26 "Floyd Named Interim Prexy at Tenn. State University," *Jet*, 21 July 1986, 27; Lovett, *The Civil Rights Movement*, 387; "Dr. James Walker 1st Black Prexy Of Middle Tenn. State," *Jet*, 27 July 1991, 38; "Annual Report of the Desegregation Monitoring Committee" (1996), 1, 20; (1997), 1; (2000), 24.

27 Ellen Brett Davis, "Twenty Years After Sanders v. Ellington: Desegregation of Public Higher Education in Middle Tennessee" (EdD dissertation, Memphis State University, 1992), 61, 69, 79. See also Jewell Winn, "The *Geier* Consent Decree Years: Fulfilled or Unfulfilled Promises?," (EdD dissertation, Tennessee State University, 2008), 65. Figure 1 shows a decline in white administrators of 10 percent compared to a black increase of 7 percent.

28 James E. Walker, *The President's Report: Middle Tennessee State University*, 1991–92 (Murfreesboro: 1992), 2.

29 "Annual Report of the Desegregation Monitoring Committee" (2000), 23–24.

30 *Rita Sanders Geier, et al. v. Don Sundquist, et al.*, Consent Decree 128 F.Supp.2d 519 (2001), http://www.justice.gov/crt/edo/documents/geiersettle.php.

31 Citied in Winn, "The *Geier* Consent Decree," 70–71.

32 Ibid., 81, 83.

33 Davis, "Twenty Years After," 6; McGinnis, "Geier Case History."

34 Hadley, "A Functional Analysis," 41.

35 MTSU Office of Admissions and Records, and subsequently, MTSU Office of Institutional Research and Planning, Statistical studies (for Administrative use), Fall, 1966–Spring 1990 (Murfreesboro, 1966-1990), AGRC. A complete set from Fall 1966 to Fall 2010 is located at the MTSU Office of Institutional Effectiveness, Planning, and Research. Reports from fall 2003 through fall 2010 under the title "Student Profiles" can be found online at http://www.mtsu.edu/iepr/profiles.shtml.

36 http://frank.mtsu.edu/~aasa/. For fraternities and sororities, see *Middle Tennessee State University Diamond Anniversary*, 39. MTSU later added the Kappa Tau Chapter of Sigma Gamma Rho and a chapter of Iota Phi Theta, http://www.mtsu.edu/greeks/nphc/index.shtml.

37 The figures for fall 2010 include a new definition of "Black or African American."

38 "The Stipulation of Settlement."

39 Ibid.

40 *University of California Regents v. Bakke*, 438 U.S. 265 (1978), http://caselaw.lp.findlaw.com/scripts/getcase.pl?navby=CASE&court=US&vol=438&page=265 .

41 Davis, "Twenty Years After," 16.

42 Calculated from "Annual Report of the Desegregation Monitoring Committee" (1984–2000).

43 "Annual Report of the Desegregation Monitoring Committee" (1995), 35.

44 Walker, *The President's Report*, 9.

45 Michael R. Turner, "New Program Helps Remedial Students," *Midlander*, 1986, 110–11, AGRC. Midlander yearbooks are located in the AGRC; online at http://library.mtsu.edu/digitalprojects/mtsumemory.php; and Special Collections, Walker Library.

46 "Annual Report of the Desegregation Monitoring Committee" (1995), 8.

47 Ibid.

48 "Annual Report of the Desegregation Monitoring Committee" (1996), 7–8, 16; (1998) 13, 18; (2000) 8, 14, 18.

49 Liz Murray Garrigan, "Lightening Up: If TSU is courting white students, where are the white faces?," *Nashville Scene,* 6 November 1997, http://www.nashvillescene.com/nashville/lightening-up/Content?oid=1181722.

50 Lovett, *The Civil Rights Movement*, 354.

51 Garrigan, "Lightening Up."

52 See Diamond, "The Gordian Knot: Higher Education Desegregation in Tennessee"; *United States v. Fordice*, 505 US 717 (1992), http://caselaw.lp.findlaw.com/scripts/getcase.pl?navby=CASE&court=US&vol=505&page=717 and *Grutter v. Bollinger* (02–241) 539 US 306 (2003), http://www.law.cornell.edu/supct/html/02-241.ZS.html

53 *Geier v. Sundquist*, Civil Action: 5077. For national news coverage, see "National News Briefs; Tennessee Reaches Deal To End Racial Quotas," *New York Times*, 22 December 2000, http://www.nytimes.com/2000/12/22/us/national-news-briefs-tennessee-reaches-deal-to-end-racial-quotas.html.

54 Patrick Chinnery and Stephanie Hill, "First-ever Ph.D. programs approved: English, economics two of the accepted proposals," *Sidelines*, 18 November 2003, http://www.mtsusidelines.com/2.3115/first-ever-ph-d-programs-approved-1.320616.

55 Final order of Dismissal, *Rita Geier v. Phil Bredesen*, 21 September 2006, http://fp.tbr.edu/general_counsel/Geier%20Dismissal/Final%20Order%20of%20Dismissal.pdf.

56 Editorial Board, "Categorizing students by their race," *Sidelines*, 13 September 2006, http://www.mtsusidelines.com/2.3113/categorizing-students-by-their-race-1.312301.

236MIDDLE TENNESSEE STATE UNIVERSITY: *A Centennial Legacy*

57 Brad Schrade, "Settlement of desegregation lawsuit brings $200 million, mixed opinions," (Nashville) *Tennessean,* 11 July 2010, http://www.tennessean.com/article/20100711/NEWS04/7110342.

58 John William (Jay) Sanders and Toto Sutarso, paper "A 32-Year Study of the Equitability of Funding in Tennessee's 4-Year Universities Pre-*Geier* Settlement (1971–1983) vs. Post-*Geier* Settlement (1984–2003)" (Murfreesboro: Middle Tennessee State University, 2005), 17, available at http://www.johnwmsanders.com/HE%20funding%2071-04-2-11-05.doc.

59 "Annual Report of the Desegregation Monitoring Committee" (1984–2000), computed from statistical tables measuring the percentage of first time freshman enrolled at any level the following year.

60 The percentage of first-time black freshmen stood at 18.5 percent. Office of Institutional Effectiveness, Planning and Research, *Student Profiles: Fall 2010,* 41, and *2010 Fact Book* (Murfreesboro: Middle Tennessee State University, 2010), 16, http://www.mtsu.edu/iepr/factbook/factbook10/factbook_10.pdf; US Census Bureau, *QuickFacts from the US Census Bureau: Tennessee,* 16 August 2010, http://quickfacts.census.gov/qfd/states/47000.html. For TSU, see Jaime Sarrio and Brad Schrade, "Enrollment booms bypass TSU: School shifts focus to boosting its graduation and retention rates," *Tennessean,* 11 July 2010, http://www.tennessean.com/article/20100711/NEWS04/7110343/Enrollment-booms-bypass-TSU. See also Marybeth Gasman, "Coffee Table to Classroom: A Review of Recent Scholarship on Historically Black Colleges and Universities," *Educational Researcher* 34 (October 2005): 32–39; Jack Stripling, "HBCUs Drawing Scrutiny," *Inside Higher Education,* 20 January 2009, http://www.insidehighered.com/news/2009/01/30/hbcu; "The Persisting Myth That the Black Colleges Are Becoming Whiter," *Journal of Blacks in Higher Education* (2005), http://www.jbhe.com/news_views/47_myth_blackcolleges.html.

CHAPTER ELEVEN

Gettin' on the Gravy Train

MTSC and World War II

ELLEN GARRISON

"How many of you can teach mathematics or physics?" President Quintin Miller Smith asked the Middle Tennessee State Teachers College (STC) faculty at its first meeting in January 1943.[1] Characteristically, he did not explain why he needed that information and no one asked. Most faculty probably understood that whatever his plans, he would, as his colleague Homer Pittard later wrote, be "adamant in his course of action" without any intention of compromise.[2] Some may also have realized that something had to be done to ensure the survival of the school during what had become tumultuous political as well as economic times. And most knew that Smith had already displayed considerable talent for devising and implementing such survival schemes.

Since his controversial appointment as president of his alma mater in August 1938, Smith had enjoyed the full authority and support of the state board, in spite of "ill-wishers in his official family and in the area beyond the campus."[3] He had also continued to nurture his network of state and national political connections, especially his close working relationship with Governor Prentice Cooper.[4] Smith also shared Cooper's belief in the importance of the new aviation industry to the future of the state and the college. Less than a year after his appointment, he had taken advantage of funding from the New Deal's National Youth Administration (NYA) and Civilian Conservation Corps (CCC) programs to construct an airstrip and a flight hanger on campus. The next summer, the college, again with government financial support, had launched a Civilian Pilot Training Club; by the fall of 1941 31 students had received their flight certificates after completing the 35-hour course offered by the club.[5]

Building on these earlier successes, Smith proved equally adept at securing funding for the college when the national government's priorities shifted from economic recovery to military preparedness. Completion of the NYA-funded Voorhies Industrial Arts building in the early 1940s, for example, enabled him to snag a federal subsidy in 1942 to conduct defense training classes in sheet metal work, draftsmanship, and woodworking for civilians. Not long after, the college announced the availability of a public course in first aid and training in the new defense nutrition program, also funded by the NYA.[6]

When Japan bombed Pearl Harbor on December 7, 1941, sophomore Jane Maxwell and others on campus felt "as if a shade was pulled." "Teachers' expectations dropped," she remembered, and the campus became more serious, quieter, with less laughter. Students, Maxwell added, would go to class just to see who would be next, as her male classmates "simply disappeared"[7] into the armed services. For Smith, however, Japan's attack merely accelerated the search for new federal funding that would enable the school to survive. After the loss of 23 football players to the armed services in the fall of 1942, for example, Smith secured funding from the War Production Board to pay football coach Wink Midgett to teach non-credit courses in industrial accounting.[8] The next month the college urged the women who remained on campus to enroll in the new credit courses in engineering drawing, architecture, sheet metal working, and drafting in order to be ready to replace men in war industries. These new courses, the notice added, could be taken at no cost because the government was paying the salaries of the instructors.[9]

When he announced, in late July 1942, that the college would open a week early because of the war, Smith added that the curriculum "would lay heavy emphasis on defense courses."[10] The week before classes began he even outlined a detailed plan for courses that would accommodate wartime needs, including a new emphasis on Spanish "as a gesture to Pan-American solidarity."[11] In spite of Smith's efforts to align college programs with war needs, only 120 freshmen, preponderantly women, arrived on campus that fall, and upperclass enrollment continued to drop during the semester.[12]

Loss of income, in large part due to this dropping student enrollment, soon topped the list of challenges facing the college, and Smith "began to negotiate for some of the military training programs which could be housed on campus," calling on his vast network of political allies, especially Governor Prentice Cooper, for help.[13] Smith and his allies focused their attention on the opportunities and possibilities in military aviation, a discipline for which the community, as well as the college, had already developed an extensive support network. By 1942 the city of Murfreesboro had already begun lobbying the Tennessee Bureau of Aeronautics for funds to construct a municipal airport, and that summer the Army Air Forces had launched courses for combat crews and for ferry pilots at Stewart Air Force Base in nearby Smyrna.[14] Clearly, the college's best prospects for attracting new federal income lay in training aviators.

Thanks to "an intense publicity campaign" by the Army Air Forces itself, the public already viewed the air corps as the elite branch of military service.[15] When the War Department, in an effort to create a backlog of qualified applicants ready for advanced aviation training, set up the Air Corps Enlisted Reserve (ACER) in April 1942 the program quickly enrolled 93,000 potential pilots, navigators, and bombardiers nationwide. By the fall of 1942 many of these men had been waiting impatiently to be called to active service for as long as six months, and this large pool of highly qualified but idle men had attracted the attention of both the Selective Service System and the War Manpower Commission.[16] To forestall the possibility of losing these applicants to other branches, H. H. "Hap" Arnold, commanding general of the Army Air Forces, proposed activating ACER members and assigning them to colleges prepared to provide training to make up their "educational deficiencies."[17]

Smith and his allies sprang into action before Secretary of War Henry Stimson even agreed to Arnold's proposal. When the War Manpower Commission contacted the Tennessee Bureau of Aeronautics about potential sites for flight training in the state, its director, Colonel Herbert Fox, immediately notified Smith, enabling him to submit a report to the commission on staff and facilities available at the college before the War Department launched the program on January 23, 1943.[18] On the next day, Smith announced that all STC application materials for an ACER unit had been sent to the army. That same day Colonel Fox left for Washington to confer with army officials on behalf of the college.[19]

A week later, officials from the Army Air Forces inspected the campus and met with Smith and other college administrators in Washington to resolve the details of the government contract. On February 6, Congressman Jim McCord telegraphed Smith that the joint committee had approved STC's application for a training detachment, and the next day the War Manpower Commission announced that STC and 280 other colleges had been selected to provide "specialized military training" for cadets who had completed a 13-week basic training course and been accepted for aviation. The colleges could expect their first cadets to arrive on March 1.[20]

On February 11, 1943, Smith wrote Governor Cooper that in order to fulfill the proposed contract by that date it would "be necessary to make improvements at the college . . . amounting to approximately $30,000."[21] Fortunately, state Representative Shelton Edwards had already introduced a bill that was passed by the legislature on February 11, 1943, providing funds to STC and three other state schools "for military purposes," enabling Cooper to provide STC with $10,000 for a new physics laboratory and $20,000 for repairs and new equipment for two dormitories and the cafeteria, within two days of Smith's request.[22]

Following this news, events moved quickly at STC. At 11:00 a.m. on February 20, STC girls living in Lyon Hall received instructions to move all their personal belongings to Rutledge Hall by 4:00 p.m.[23] On the following day, Lieutenant [Len] Everett Blaylock, who had joined the Army Air Corps in 1939, arrived on campus to take command of what had been designated the 11th College Training Detachment (CTD).[24] Blaylock later observed that in addition to acting as commandant he had to function as "Training Officer, Mess Officer, Finance Officer and Recreation

Officer" and was also "heavily involved in the sale of war bonds."[25] Then on March 1, the initial group of cadets, whose last names all began with the letter P, arrived on campus. That morning, Murfreesboro's local paper, the *Daily News Journal,* carried an appeal from President Smith to residents to bring wood, metal or paper coat hangers for the cadets to Room 50 of the STC administration building.[26] The next morning the girls in Rutledge awoke to "the tramp, tramp, tramp of boots" as the cadets marched to breakfast. With that "the 11th College Training Detachment was underway."[27]

Marching to meals, class, and other activities constituted part of the military training provided to cadets by the Army Air Forces cadre, which the War Department charged with overall management of the entire program. The Department's Flight Training Command (FTC) developed the entire five-month curriculum, both academic and military, supplied all textbooks, and constructed all tests. Blaylock employed his own staff of 20 officers and NCOs to provide instruction in military drill (84 hours, including marching to class and meals), ceremonies and inspections (40 hours), first aid (20 hours), customs and courtesies (10 hours), hygiene and sanitation (10 hours), and guard duty (6 hours).[28] Fifteen STC faculty members, broadly advised by Blaylock, provided almost 500 hours of academic instruction to each class of cadets including 80 hours of math, 180 hours of physics, 60 hours of current history, 60 hours of geography, 60 hours of English, and 24 hours of civil air regulations.[29]

English professor Eva Burkett, assigned by Smith to teach math to cadets, found the experience unsettling. She told one of her STC students that when all of the "boys" stood up and came to attention when she walked into the classroom the first day "it scared me to death."[30] She probably also felt worked to death, since the FTC required that, in addition to teaching, faculty members submit weekly letter grades for each cadet in each subject, which Dean Nathanial Craig Beasley then compiled and sent to Lt. Blaylock.[31]

By the end of 1943, Blaylock had contracted with civilian instructors to provide optional flight training for the cadets on the field just east of the campus. He later described these instructors as "really trying to make the kids time in the air productive."[32] Best known of these instructors was "Miss Piggy," Mary E. Pigg, a native of Maury County, Tennessee, who had begun her flying career in 1941 and had graduated as a full-fledged flight instructor two years later.[33]

Cadets and coeds remained completely separate not only in their classes, which were held on different floors of the administrative building, but elsewhere on campus. Although the cafeteria had been tripled in size, the two groups ate at different times, and the cadets had exclusive use of the library on Saturdays and of the tennis courts on Sunday.[34] Lt. Blaylock recognized, however, that the female students "needed to spend some time with some young men."[35] So his wife Lynn sponsored weekly dances organized by a committee made up of cadet and student body representatives. "A wonderful orchestra sent down from Stewart called the 'Stewart Bombardiers'" provided the music, a coed later recalled.[36] And the committee, Blaylock remembered, "always had a cake and drinks and stuff like that . . . and it was a lot of fun."[37] A few couples who met at the dances did get married, although one coed later "wondered how all that came about," considering that each class of cadets remained on campus such a short time.[38]

Over the next 15 months, 12 classes graduated from the program, and at various times three different groups of cadets were at different stages in the program. Regular classes also continued, and the female students who remained on campus filled the student government offices and edited the yearbook, the *Midlander*. The second coed to serve as student body president did not think of herself as "fulfilling a leadership position," however. She and her classmates, she later said, were "just finding our own niche in the war effort . . . while the capable people were doing more important things."[39]

The Army Air Forces "received what they needed from the money they spent" at the college, according to Lt. Blaylock,[40] and most of the cadets who served in the 11th Cadet Training Detachment went on to serve as pilots, bombardiers, and navigators with the Army Air Forces in Europe. In March 1944, however, President Smith received notice that the AAF had "reached the point where they had enough" flight officers so the school's (now Middle Tennessee State College) training contract would not be renewed. A few weeks later Smith invited the faculty to a final celebration for the CTD permanent party, which departed from campus on June 30, 1944.[41]

By the time of the party, Smith had already turned his attention to preparing for the future. On the same day in 1943 that he had received word that the campus had been selected for a military training program, Smith also announced that the state legislature had changed the institution's name from Middle Tennessee State Teachers College to Middle Tennessee State College. This new name, he said, connoted "the future scope and function of the college more appropriately" than its label as a teacher's college.[42]

Time would demonstrate Smith's shrewdness and perspicacity. He had kept the campus alive during the war years, thanks to what Homer Pittard called "a financial windfall from the federal government,"[43] and in September 1944 he appointed Dean Beasley as chair of a new committee on Veteran's Education.[44] In November 1944, he could write a former student that the college had enrolled six ex-service members under the GI Bill of Rights "which promises to be a fruitful source of students in the future as well as the occasion for a considerable revision in the college curricula structure."[45] President Q. M. Smith had clearly proved himself and his school to be survivors.

NOTES

1   Faculty Meeting Agenda, 18 January 1943, Q. M. Smith Papers, Albert Gore Research Center (AGRC), Middle Tennessee State University, Murfreesboro, TN (hereinafter cited as Smith Papers, AGRC). Although the official name of the school was Middle Tennessee State Teachers College, it was widely known as State Teachers College, Murfreesboro. Until 1943, students often referred to the school as "Teachers College."

2   Homer Pittard, *The First Fifty Years: Middle Tennessee State College, 1911–1961* (Murfreesboro: Middle Tennessee State College, 1961), 161.

3   Ibid., 166.

4   See scattered letters between Smith and Cooper, 1938–1943, especially a note from Cooper, 27 June 1942, thanking Smith for signing a petition to qualify Cooper as a candidate in the August Democratic primary. Smith Papers, AGRC.

5   "Bring Us Your Coat Hangers: The 11th College Training Detachment at Middle Tennessee State University," n.d. unpublished paper, vertical file: CTD Cadets, WWII, AGRC, 7. Federal funding of aviation facilities at STC paralleled the War Department's growing emphasis on the role of the airplane in combat. As early as 1939, the Army Air Corps, led by General H. H. "Hap" Arnold, had established an accelerated training program for military pilots that qualified candidates in less than nine months. Wesley Frank Craven and James Lea Cate, *The Army Air Forces in World War II,* Volume 6: *Men and Planes* (Office of Air Force History, 1983), 454.

6   Faculty Meeting Agenda, 2 January, 29 April, 6 October, and 12 October 1941. That fall STC also opened a recreational program for soldiers on campus. Pittard, *First Fifty Years,* 177.

7   Jane Maxwell Tucker, interview by Betty Rowland, 29 February 2002, MT 074, transcript, Middle Tennessee Oral History Project, Albert Gore Research Center (AGRC), Middle Tennessee State University, Murfreesboro, TN (hereinafter cited as MT Oral History Project, AGRC).

8   *Daily News Journal,* 25 August 1942. The Raiders none the less completed a "creditable season" with four wins, one tie, and two losses. *Daily News Journal,* 29 November 1942. This would be the last football season during the war. Pittard, *First Fifty Years,* 178.

9   *Daily News Journal*, 6 September 1942.

10   *Daily News Journal*, 21 July 1942. See also editorial, 22 July 1942.

11   *Daily News Journal*, 8 September 1942. See also the outline of Smith's presentation at the first college assembly on 18 September 1942. Smith Papers, AGRC.

12   Jane Maxwell Tucker remembered that by graduation there were only two men in her class. One had a disability and the other was one of three preachers on campus. Tucker interview, 25.

13   Joe Nunley, *The Raider Forties* (New York: Vantage Press, 1977), 38. Smith also applied directly to both the army and the navy as soon as each service announced plans to utilize college facilities to train military specialists. Faculty Meeting Agenda, 7 December 1942. STC later received what Smith described as a "routine query" about the school's interest in participating in one or both programs. *Daily News Journal*, 17 and 18 December 1942.

14   *Daily News Journal*, 12 June and 16 July 1942, 7 February 1943. Smith himself had also been appointed to the national Naval Aviation Committee. *Daily News Journal*, 29 July 1942.

15   "Coat Hangers," AGRC, 8. This campaign included publication of a nonfiction account of his experiences with US Army Air Force bomber crews by John Steinbeck. John Steinbeck, *Bombs Away* (Viking Press, 1942).

16   "Coat Hangers," AGRC, 10. Established in 1926, the Army Air Corps served as the aviation branch of the United States Army until the creation of the Army Air Forces on 20 June 1941. The Air Corps continued to serve as the training arm of the Air Forces until 1947.

17   Craven and Cate, *Men and Planes*, 562–63. After January 1942 the Army no longer required applicants for flight training to have a college degree.

18   *Sidelines*, 8 January 1943. The next evening Colonel Fox spoke to the annual dinner meeting of the Rutherford County Chamber of Commerce about the program. *Daily News Journal*, 10 January 1943.

19   *Daily News Journal*, 24 January 1943. Fox also met with officials of the Civil Aviation Administration, which had just approved the funding for construction of a $10,000 hanger at the new municipal airport.

20 *Sidelines*, 6 February 1943; *Daily News Journal*, 7 February 1943. On February 17 the Murfreesboro Girls Cotillion Club announced plans to hold a dance for cadets scheduled to arrive on March 1. *Daily News Journal*, 17 February 1943.

21 Q. M. Smith to Prentice Cooper, 11 February 1943, Smith Papers, AGRC.

22 *Daily News Journal*, 10 and 11 February 1943. The contract also required the college to replace students who worked in the cafeteria, all of whom were football players, with civilian employees. Nunley, *The Raider Forties*, 49.

23 "Coat Hangers," AGRC, 22. Girls who were away from campus found the dorm locked and all their possessions moved to Rutledge when they came back from the weekend. One student later recalled that for the next three years they all "became very close" living five or six to a room in the only women's dormitory on campus. Blanche Cook McClure, interview by Betty Rowland, 22 February 2006, MT 0281, transcript, MT Oral History Project, AGRC, 17.

24 *Daily News Journal*, 21 February 1943. The newspaper incorrectly listed the officer as Lt. Eugene Blasdel.

25 Biographical Data Form, Len Everett Blaylock Interview File, AGRC. When the program at STC ended in June 1944 Blaylock would be assigned to the program at Tuskegee Institute. He was later sent with the 8th Air Force to England, where he often ran into former students from the 11th. Len Everett Blaylock, interview by Betty Rowland, 18 June 2002, MT 0124, transcript, MT Oral History Project, AGRC, 20.

26 Craven and Cate, *Men and Planes*, 477; McClure interview, 22. *Daily News Journal*, 1 March 1943.

27 Tucker interview, 13; "Coat Hangers," AGRC, 17.

28 *Daily News Journal*, 25 February 1943; *Sidelines*, 20 February 1943. The cadre also provided at least one hour daily of physical training, including calisthenics, running, and competitive sports. Blaylock later wryly noted that the latter included only "touch" football. Blaylock interview, 19.

29 Faculty Meeting Agenda, 15 February 1943; *Sidelines* 20 February 1943; *Daily News Journal*, 1 March 1943.

30 McClure interview, 13.

31 Memo to College Faculty from Dean-Registrar N.C. Beasley, 4 June 1943, Smith Papers, AGRC.

32 Blaylock interview, 17.

33 Article in *Skylines* magazine, 7 August 1943, in the Smith Papers. Pigg had also earned ground instructor ratings in meteorology, navigation, and aircraft engines.

34 McClure interview, 21; Tucker interview, 23–24; "Coat Hangers," AGRC, 21–22.

35 Blaylock interview, 16. The college also encouraged coeds to mingle with cadets as a "patriotic duty," although one student considered it "a kind of a sad duty." Tucker interview, 19.

36 Tucker interview, 21.

37 Blaylock interview, 18.

38 McClure interview, 23.

39 Tucker interview, 25; see also McClure interview, 18.

40 Blaylock interview, 27.

41 Faculty Meeting Agenda, 20 March and 5 June 1944, Smith Papers, AGRC.

42 *Daily News Journal,* 7 February 1943.

43 Pittard, *First Fifty Years,* 178; Nunley, *The Raider Forties,* 665.

44 Faculty Meeting Agenda, 4 September 1944, Smith Papers, AGRC.

45 Smith to Lieutenant Colonel Ferris U. Foster, 22 November 1944, Smith Papers, AGRC.

CHAPTER TWELVE

Honors Education:

A Story of Grand Dreams and Noble Work

PHILIP M. MATHIS

If we work on marble, it will perish; if we work on brass, time will efface it; if we rear temples, they will crumble to dust. But, if we work on immortal minds, and impress upon them high principles . . . we engrave on those tablets something which no time can efface.
— Daniel Webster, 1852

THE COLLEGIATE HONORS MOVEMENT IN AMERICA

When the honors program was first established at Middle Tennessee State University in 1973, the National Collegiate Honors Council had only been in existence for seven years, but the movement that it represented was much older. Indeed, suggestions of an impending honors movement were seen as early as 1873 at Harvard[1] and continued through the late 1800s and early 1900s at such places as Oregon's Reed College, the University of Michigan, Princeton University, and Columbia University.[2] In 1903, Harvard President Abbot Lawrence Lowell went so far as to advocate the founding of an honors *college*,[3] but recognizable honors programs did not exist until after World War I, and the first honors college—Clark Honors College at the University of Oregon—was not established until 1960.

Organized, programmatic honors education in America dates from 1922, when Frank Aydelotte established the pass/honors system at Pennsylvania's Swarthmore College. As the new president of Swarthmore, Aydelotte seized the chance to adapt what he saw as the best practices of European higher education to the American scene. Within months, not years, the Socratic dialogue, the Oxford tutorial, and the German seminar became a part of honors education at Swarthmore.[4] As a Rhodes Scholar at Oxford, Aydelotte discovered the effectiveness of the tutorial system of instruction and became a strong proponent of the system and of the idea that true education is ultimately self-education.[5]

The launching of Sputnik in 1957 called attention to the need to foster intellectual talent, and thereby catalyzed the development of honors programs throughout the 1960s and 1970s. During this time, J. W. Cohen, director of the Honors Program at the University of Colorado and an advocate for the needs of high-achieving students, founded the Interdisciplinary Committee on the Superior Student (ICSS). The ICSS and its journal, the *Superior Student*, were funded through grants provided by the Carnegie Corporation of New York. When funds ran out in the mid-1960s, the ICSS ceased to function, but much of its role was ultimately assumed by the newly formed National Collegiate Honors Council (NCHC), an organization that continues to serve collegiate honors programs and member institutions.[6]

During its existence between 1957 and 1965, the ICSS had a profound effect on the spread of honors education in America; in those few years, the number of honors programs more than tripled,[7] spreading from a group of mostly small, private, eastern colleges to large public universities, four-year colleges, and community colleges throughout the nation. Today, the number of honors colleges grows every year,[8] and Cohen's role in the rise of a robust honors movement cannot be overstated.

Honors education was catapulted upward by the influence of Sputnik on the development of America's best minds. Pre-Sputnik notions of educational equality emphasized opportunity through standardization. Post-Sputnik, equality of educational opportunity came to mean education appropriate to each individual's gifts or talents. President John F. Kennedy declared, "All of us do not have equal talent, but all of us should have an equal opportunity to develop our talent."[9] Clearly, such a statement opens the door to the idea that varied talents should be a consideration in planning for equal educational opportunity.

Frank Aydelotte railed against the inappropriate and inequitable instruction of America's most talented college students. In his book, *Breaking the Academic Lockstep*, Adeylotte observes that ". . . instruction of the average American student has been standardized beyond the point where uniformity has value" and that the American system fails to ". . . pay him [the individual student] the compliment of assuming that his ability is very great or that he has any consuming interest in his studies." He concluded that docility was the most rewarded virtue in American higher education and acknowledged that it had its use, but maintained that independence and initiative were virtues of a higher order. Thus, the collegiate educational imperative of the 1920s was, in his mind, to provide instructional programs that would appropriately challenge and reward the most gifted and voracious minds.[10]

The success in establishing honors programs to challenge gifted minds understandably resulted in accusations of elitism. After all, honors programs are, by design, elite. Even critics, who accepted the notion that education for the gifted should be different, sometimes attacked honors programs on grounds of elitism. One argument against honors held that the establishment of programs that challenge the best students competes with the need to establish programs that appropriately challenge non-honors students.[11] Perhaps the most insidious form of the elitism charge calls attention to the high cost of honors programs. Critics allege that although honors programs may be desirable from a strictly educational perspective, they are expensive and deny other students their proportionate share of resources.[12] These and many other issues surfaced during the early history of honors education at MTSU.[13]

The spread of honors in American higher education led to varied programs as individual colleges and universities minted new models and adapted existing ones to their own desires and needs. In terms of functional organization, most programs today bear only faint resemblance to the first program at Swarthmore. Variation is the order of the day. There are programs in departmental honors; programs in general honors; two-year programs at two-year colleges; two-year programs at four-year colleges; four-year programs at four-year colleges; programs that require independent study, research, and a scholarly thesis; programs that utilize external examiners and programs that do not; programs that emphasize seminars, colloquia, and Socratic-style instruction; programs based on the English tutorial method; programs that emphasize curricular acceleration; programs that emphasize curricular enrichment; programs administered through semiautonomous honors colleges; and programs administered through honors colleges where faculty and students are shared with other academic units within the same institution.

Widespread program variation clearly suggests that standardization is not a sought-after goal within the honors community; nevertheless, common threads *do* run through the fabric of American honors education. Most programs have high admissions standards, limit class size, seek to prepare graduates for advanced study, and strive to establish a sense of community among students and faculty. They value global perspectives, interdisciplinary courses, and opportunities for teacher-student and student-student interaction. Moreover, the National Collegiate Honors Council's programmatic benchmarks for "fully developed" honors programs or colleges represent additional factors that honors programs and colleges generally embrace.[14] Examples include distinctive diplomas for graduates, academic autonomy, high-level administrative recognition, provision for an external advisory board, and provision for a rich, residential college experience.

FOUNDING OF THE HONORS PROGRAM

In less than a decade after gaining university status, Middle Tennessee State University established an honors program for the benefit of a limited number of high-achieving students. In so doing, the university positioned itself to found the first honors college at a public university in Tennessee and to become a regional leader in honors education. The honors *program*, which in 1998 transitioned into the honors *college*, was founded by President M. G. Scarlett, following a three-year study by a faculty

President M.G. Scarlett

committee chaired by Dr. William Holland of the English Department. President Scarlett was not greatly influenced by the nation-wide surge in honors programs or by prior education and work experience. He simply believed that an honors program could provide curricular enrichment without undue elitism, add to faculty and student prestige, and possibly increase the university's attractiveness to potential students and faculty.[15]

President Scarlett appointed Dr. June Hall McCash (then Martin) to lead the new program, thereby making her the founding director of the MTSU Honors Program. McCash's qualifications included degrees from Agnes Scott College and Emory University, institutions that honors guru Frank Aydelotte[16] recognized as having well-crafted, department-based plans for honors. Her education in the liberal arts, along with relevant experience and a strong work ethic, positioned her for success in her new role.

Dr. June Hall McCash

Early in 1973, the new director began to make plans for a program that would welcome its first students during the fall semester of 1973. Key support for the program came from a newly appointed Honors Council, which served as the director's sounding board in all matters pertaining to honors. Included on the first council were representatives from each of the four undergraduate schools: Dr. Barbara Haskew (Business), Dr. James Huhta (Liberal Arts), Dr. Robert Prytula (Education), and Dr. Alvin E. Woods (Basic and Applied Sciences). The council also included two at-large faculty appointees, Drs. William Holland and William Windham, and two students, David Dodd and Laura Smith. Dr. Howard Kirksey, vice president for academic affairs, served in an ad hoc capacity.[17]

The council held its first meeting on January 22, 1973. The initial task was to draft and approve a set of honors goals, guidelines for admission, and programmatic requirements. These guidelines established the program's admission standards for entering freshmen as either a composite score of 25 on the American College Test (ACT) or a rank in the upper 10 percent of the student's high school class. The guidelines required upperclassmen to have a "B" average (3.0 grade point average on a 4.0 scale) in order to enroll in honors courses. The council sought to establish a program that would mimic the educational experience provided by small liberal arts colleges of high quality, but with the added advantages made possible by the greater resources of a large university. At the outset, honors courses were established in general studies as well as in major programs.

Completion of the honors course of study required that a student accumulate a minimum of 24 semester hours of credit in honors, including at least 12 hours of lower-division work and 12 hours of upper-division work. It was further stipulated that the upper-division work would include at least six semester hours of coursework in an academic department and six semester hours in specially designed University Honors courses. The initial list of course offerings in University Honors included UH 360 (Medieval Experience), UH 361 (Seminar in Popular Culture Studies), UH 362 (Physical Science and Philosophy), UH 363 (The City), UH 460 (Senior Interdisciplinary Seminar), and UH 495 (Honors Independent Research).[18] In the early days of the Honors Program, all interdisciplinary minors were administered through the Honors Program.[19] Moreover, the Honors Program itself emphasized interdisciplinary perspectives as a counterbalance to the more narrowly focused work in an academic major.[20] Although the MTSU *Bulletin* did not initially specify the requirement of a thesis (UH 495), it soon became an expectation, and by 1976 the requirement of a thesis was included.[21]

The first great challenge of the honors director was to convince department chairs to develop and provide honors courses in their respective departments. On philosophical grounds, some departments were unconvinced of the desirability of actually having an honors program. Athough philosophically unopposed to honors education, others were reluctant to assign professors to teach small classes because such a practice usually required other faculty members to teach greater numbers of students. To her lasting credit, however, McCash ultimately succeeded, and 12 departments initially agreed to offer honors courses. Several more soon followed suit, and by the late 1970s the number of departments offering honors courses in a major field of study had grown to 18.[22] Honors enrollment in the fall of 1973 was 129 students. By the spring semester, 207 students were registered for classes.[23]

Under McCash's leadership, the Honors Program's fundamental structure was established. During its first year of operation, Faculty Firesides were instituted. In time, these gatherings to discuss important issues became a valued tradition. At the outset, McCash realized the importance of bringing to campus recognized leaders who might inspire or serve as role models for students. Because of travel costs, students sometimes gained access to influential scholars via a speaker phone arrangement; however, provision was also sometimes made for in-person visits. Examples include B. F. Skinner's telephonic exchange with students and Margaret Mead's in-person visit and lecture on November 1, 1974.[24]

The first honors thesis was written by Mary Wilgus in 1973; but her contemporary, Paul W. Martin Jr. became the first person to actually graduate with University Honors. Wilgus went on to earn a PhD degree in history at Vanderbilt University. Martin went on to law school and to a successful business career. Student leaders of the 1970s included Debra (Hopkins) Hollingsworth and Mark Hall, members of the first Honors Student Advisory Council, established in 1976, and later members of the first Honors College Board of Visitors. Others who served on the first Student Advisory Council included Mike Dagley, Mark Mathis, Karen Nelson, Pam White, Ramona Pope, Beth McClary, and Hugh Sharber.[25]

An honors newsletter, *Honors in Perspective*, was begun during the program's first year of operation. An interesting account in the initial issue traced the trek of Honors Council members to the National Collegiate Honors Council's October 1973 convention in Williamsburg, Virginia.[26] Afterwards, the Honors Program asserted its leadership within the growing honors movement by hosting the second annual meeting of the Southern Regional Honors Council (SRHC) and by hosting meetings of the Tennessee Collegiate Honors Council (TCHC) in both 1978 and 1979.[27]

The Honors Program functioned as designed until 1978 when program requirements were revised to provide for three tracks, or options, for graduation with University Honors. The first option, Option A, reasserted the program's original requirements. It allowed the student to take 12 hours of lower-division work, followed by 6 hours of upper-division departmental honors work in the major or minor, and 6 hours of University Honors work including the thesis. Option B specified 18 hours of general honors work plus 9 hours of upper-division University Honors courses including the thesis. Option C required 18 hours of general honors work, 3 hours of departmental work, and 6 hours in University Honors, again including the thesis.

Near the end of McCash's tenure as director, the Honors Lecture Series was established as a weekly forum where important topics and issues could be explored by students, interested faculty, and the community at large. In the years since its establishment, the lecture series has grown in stature and impact due to several factors, including the selection of timely topics, success in attracting off-campus speakers, and unwavering support from the faculty. During the spring semester of 1975, McCash received a grant from the National Endowment for the Humanities that allowed her to conduct research in France. In her absence, Dr. William (Bill) Windham of the History Department served as the program's acting director. Otherwise, McCash served continuously from 1973 until 1980, when she relinquished the director's post to become chair of the Department of Foreign Languages. Her decisions have now been time tested, and the strength of her leadership is more evident today than in 1980. Despite her ultimate effectiveness, she was not a likely choice for the director's job in 1973. As she suggested, during a recorded interview at the Albert Gore Research Center, President Scarlett took a bold step in authorizing a new Honors Program, but perhaps even bolder was his decision to name a *female* as its leader.[28]

BUILDING AN HONORS COMMUNITY

At the outset, the Honors Program office was located in room 11 of the Drawing Building (now the Tom H. Jackson Building) but, within three years, the director had succeeded in obtaining a two-room space in Keathley University Center. Rooms 304 and 306 in Keathley became known as the Honors Center and provided the first semblance of space where honors students and faculty could gather to meet, socialize, and give or receive advice. Rinn and others cite a number of positive outcomes that may accrue when honors students are provided with dedicated space for study, living, and social discourse, and note that the importance of building space, as a means of fostering a sense of community, cannot be overemphasized.[29]

In 1980, Dr. Ron Messier, a history professor, succeeded McCash as director of the Honors Program. He had distinguished himself among honors educators by inaugurating a popular and innovative course, Honors Seminar on Historical Characters (UH 460), and by developing a special program on Napoleon for

Dr. Ronald A. Messier

presentation in the Environmental Simulation Lab of the Learning Resources Center, a facility dedicated to instructional innovation and support. Like his predecessor, Messier possessed outstanding educational qualifications, enormous energy, and an unsurpassed determination to succeed. During almost 11 years as director, the unspoken but actively communicated theme of his leadership was community building. Friendly and with wide-ranging knowledge and interests, Messier was a magnet who energized students and brought new attention to the Honors Program. In retrospect, the acquisition of a larger and more strategically placed Honors Center may be seen as a particularly significant accomplishment of his early administration.

The new Honors Center was located in Peck Hall. Still small, the center consisted of a director's office large enough to double as a conference room, an adjacent classroom, and a small space that served as a student lounge. Over time, a group of students known as Lounge Lizards claimed the small space for their own. Writing in the *Honor Guard*, Serenity Sutton described the group that inhabited the space:

> The lounge is at times a haven. You can go there and commune with your own personal karma or discuss the horrors of retail. Some of the greatest comedic minds in the nation convene in the lounge daily, minds loaded with useless trivia and enviable rhyming skills. There is also great diversity in the geographic regions represented. At least one of every Southern accent in the middle Tennessee area is represented. Beyond all this, there is real life. The kinds of people in the lounge are those who face problems and pressures, whether it be school, marriage, or mismatched socks. And the odds are good that someone has change for a dollar.[30]

Messier recognized that space for the Honors Program could foster the growth of a vibrant honors community and quickly agreed to cooperate with the Housing Office in the creation of an honors living-learning center in the Monohan-Schardt-Reynolds Hall complex, colloquially dubbed MonSchaRey. A page one newsletter article noted that 30 women and 15 men were expected to reside in different wings of the complex during the 1985 fall semester.[31] Plans were laid to furnish study rooms with reference materials and to use the commons area for recreational activities, social events, and Honors Student Association (HSA) meetings. Despite some initial excitement, the honors living-learning experiment was short lived, but it did succeed in planting the idea for the center that would open at Wood and Felder Halls in 1997.

Although space was important, Messier understood that creating a sense of community entailed more than the need for space. Despite a minimal budget, arrangements were made for community-building opportunities to serve more than 400 students. There were film fests, camping trips, Faculty Firesides, Halloween parties, Christmas parties, Valentine's Day parties, fund-raising activities, meetings of the Honors Student Association (founded in 1981), Honors Day activities, awards banquets, student travel to the SRHC and NCHC meetings, guest speakers, opportunities to serve on the Honors Student Advisory Council, small-group interactions with people of note including a Nobel Prize winner, a nationally known environmentalist, and a presidential candidate.[32]

Honors faculty members who collaborated with the director and provided significant leadership during the 1980s included Bob Corcoran (economics), Bill Connelly (English), Jill Hague (English), and David Rowe (history). Among the many student leaders and award winners of the period were Linda Pence, Linda Sarsfield, Becky Ingram, David Lee Gregor, Susan Henry, Hugh Shelton, Kathy Brady, David Tirpak, Alicia Adkerson, Ross Meyer, Tanya Jackson, Jean Howe, Kory Green, Amy Wilson, Patti Cavitt, Jill McWorter, Mark Morris, Mark Hahnert, Melissa Hahnert, Jenny McMillion, Victor Vale, John Damon, Kirk Hooten, Barbara Rockenbach, Terry Robertson, Karen DeBarry, Pongracz Sennyey, Kathy Kirkman, Dahli White, and George Wood.[33]

Throughout the early 1980s, a sense of shared excitement permeated the honors community, and by 1985 enrollment had reached 500.[34] Toward the end of the decade, however, progress slowed, spirits fell, and student enrollment declined, mostly in response to frustrations associated with inadequate funding. A cruel irony was that the scarcity of resources may have actually enhanced the growing sense of community.

In 1986, students came up with the fund-raising idea of an HSA-sponsored "Playathon." With announcements like "Faster than a speeding High Rise cockroach, stronger than a Blue Raider's gym socks, able to leap over calculus texts in a single bound . . ." otherwise uninterested individuals were drawn into the advertisement's vortex of intrigue. The Playathon itself involved an around-the-clock, 24-hour extravaganza of games and competitions, played concurrently at various stations in Murphy Center. Board games, poker, volleyball, and other games and sports were included. Pledges and high fees for participation combined with relatively small cash prizes for winners ensured a desired outcome! The grand total for the first Playathon amounted to $2,300, most of which was profit.[35]

CHALLENGES: OLD AND NEW

Despite evidence of student interest in honors courses, the number of students who actually graduated with University Honors remained low. This fact was attributed to two primary factors: the thesis requirement and the lack of available upper-division honors courses in many majors. The first problem was addressed through an overhaul of the thesis approval and development process.[36] The new process required a three-member thesis advisory committee appointed by the director, set timelines for progress, and required that a progress report be given to the Honors Council by the middle of the semester during which the student was registered for UH495 (thesis). The second problem was addressed through creation of what came to be called the H-option.[37] The H-option allowed qualified students to take *non-honors* courses for honors credit. It required the student to work with the course instructor to develop an individualized plan of study appropriate for an honors student and to gain advance approval of the plan through the Honors Council and honors director.

Insufficient financial resources were cited in the 1983 Self-Study as a noteworthy problem. The following quote makes the point in unambiguous terms: ". . . the effectiveness and efficiency of the program would be greatly enhanced if additional monies could be allocated to the program." The study went on to cite specific needs for a capital outlay budget, an increased budget to pay travel expenses for guest speakers, and an increased budget for clerical support.[38] In a recorded interview, the director corroborated the Self-Study's conclusion, recalling that insufficient funding had been a chronic and frustrating problem, one that finally forced him to seek private support from Rusty Burns, a local builder, and others. Burns's help, combined with the fund-raising success of the student-run Playathon and the generosity of Paul W. Martin Jr. helped to alleviate budgetary shortfalls and to provide for modest student scholarships.[39]

The summer of 1988 culminated in Messier's discovery of the remains of Sijilmasa, a once-thriving medieval trading center in the Sahara Desert. This drew his attention in a new direction, as he shared the excitement of his findings at meetings of the American Archeological Association and through invited lectures at such universities as Harvard, Northwestern, and Transylvania.[40] In a Faculty Fireside only months after the Sijilmasa discovery, he suggested the need for a review of the Honors Program to assess past practices and to project future needs.[41] He attempted to meld his research interests with the needs of honors students by arranging for a Moroccan Honors Semester Abroad; however, the outbreak of Desert Storm prevented it from becoming a reality. Despite a decade of community building and many successes, the die was cast. In the fall of 1990, he announced that he would be leaving as honors director to return to full-time teaching and research.[42]

During his tenure as director, Messier emphasized student recruitment, moved toward the establishment of an honors living-learning center, developed a computer-augmented study center for students, established the Honors Student Association (HSA), increased the flexibility of the honors curriculum by introducing the H-option, and improved guidelines pertaining to the capstone thesis project. Through Faculty Firesides, the innovative HSA-sponsored fund-raising Playathon, and by the frequent hosting of student groups in his home, Messier energized the honors community. Despite limited travel funds, he managed to attend meetings of the National Collegiate Honors Council, the Southern Regional Honors Council, and the Tennessee Collegiate Honors Council and to involve students as well. His successor, John Paul Montgomery, said of Messier, "I have not known a man in my life who pursues a goal more doggedly or determinedly than Ron Messier. He is absolutely miraculous."[43]

GROWTH, CHANGE, AND TRANSITION

Dr. John Paul Montgomery, professor of English, became the third director of the Honors Program in January 1990. He embraced his new role with firm ambition and with the same sort of determination that he had attributed to his predecessor.

Dr. John Paul Montgomery

It is doubtful, though, that even he could have envisioned the growth and progress that would come about before his retirement in June 2004.

One of the first changes made during the 1990s involved strengthening the admission policy to require an ACT score of 26 or higher or a high school GPA of at least 3.7 or a rank in the upper 10 percent of the student's high school class. The three options for meeting requirements for graduation with University Honors that had been in place for more than a decade were abandoned in favor a universal requirement that included a total of 24 semester hours, 12 at the lower-division level and 12 at the upper-division level. Of course the new requirements were not really new; instead, they represented a return to the requirements of the early years of the McCash administration.

Many of the community-building activities of the 1970s and 80s were continued as new programs were added. During the fall of 1991, the Honors Lyceum was introduced.[44] In a newsletter column, titled "Greeting the New World Autumn," Montgomery announced that future Lyceum events could be expected to involve poetry readings, music concerts, film festivals, and other forms of entertainment and cultural enrichment.[45] The first Lyceum event featured Celtic folk music.[46]

By 1992, the name of the honors newsletter, the *Honor Guard*, had been changed to the *Honors Alternative*. As might be expected, the name change was accompanied by a change in graphic imagery. The *Guard's* masthead that had included an armored knight, a Freemason-like seal, and the slogan, *E tenebrius lux* (out of darkness, light), was replaced with a new masthead that depicted three stylized Greco-Roman columns, a flaming torch, and a bolt of lightening that appeared to strike a globe of the earth at the exact location of Middle Tennessee State University. Elements of the *Honors Alternative's* early masthead were soon modified to form a seal, one that has since become emblematic of the Honors College. Since 1993, honors graduates have received the Honors Medallion, a three-dimensional replica of the Honors Seal.[47] Made of die-cast brass, the medallion depicts a lighted torch, symbolically, the search for truth; three ionic columns, representing unwavering commitment to the pursuit of knowledge; and a lightening bolt, suggesting a flash of creative energy.

During the early 1990s, attention was given to enhancing student interest in the Honors Program and to providing the amenities of a small, liberal arts college. A study in the mid-1990s noted that the Honors Program combined the best features of a small, private college with the greater resources of a large university, a goal set during the program's formative years.[48] It went on to report the viability of the program in terms of student interest (333 courses offered between the fall semester of 1985 and the spring semester of 1993) and student satisfaction. Ninety-four percent of honors students surveyed indicated honors courses contributed necessary professional skills, and a full 100 percent indicated that honors courses were more conducive to learning than courses in the regular curriculum. By 1994, annual enrollment was approaching 600; 22 departments offered honors courses; and progress was being made toward the objective of making more upper-division honors courses available to interested students. Still, problems related to curricular offerings remained, with the paucity of available courses in the sciences being a particularly acute problem.[49]

Montgomery's leadership style was characterized by careful attention to needs and attitudes of students, frequent one-on-one meetings with members of the honors faculty, and a focus on making key administrators aware of the growing success of the program. Much of the success of the 1990s hinged on good relations with department heads and faculty members, publicizing individual and programmatic successes, and direct contact with students. Montgomery's approachability, interest in motorcycles, and flare for the dramatic made him popular with students. On one occasion, his flare for the dramatic was illustrated when he personally engaged a stretch limo to transport a group of students to catch a plane departing from Nashville for the NCHC convention in San Antonio, Texas.[50] His vision for Honors meshed well with university-wide trends toward growth in terms of student numbers and student quality. As a result, Honors benefited from the university's steady growth and, especially, from the Presidential Scholarship program founded by President James E. Walker in 1993. Between 1990 and 1997, the number of honors classes offered per semester almost doubled, from 26 to 51.[51]

During the lead-up to the Honors Program's becoming an Honors *College*, a new Honors Living-Learning Center was opened at Wood and Felder Halls fulfilling the unrealized dream of the earlier living-learning center at Monohan, Schardt, and Reynolds Halls. According to one announcement, the new center included a classroom, a computer center, living accommodations for 100 women (Wood Hall) and 100 men (Felder Hall), and a spacious lobby that connected the two residence halls. Concurrent with the opening of Wood-Felder, Dr. Greg Schmidt of the Psychology Department became Honors Program liaison and student advisor.[52] When the Honors Program transitioned to the college status, Schmidt became the College's first associate dean, a position that combined teaching and administrative duties.

FOUNDING OF THE HONORS COLLEGE

The Tennessee Board of Regents approved the transformation of the Honors Program into the University Honors College on August 1, 1998. Their action made the College the first of its kind in a public university in Tennessee, and J. P. Montgomery became its first dean. The transformation was a just reward for the planning and work of many, including Montgomery in particular. It should be noted, however, that it was James E. Walker, then president of MTSU, and Barbara Haskew, then provost of the university and a member of the university's first Honors Council, who initiated the process that led to the Honors Program becoming the Honors College. According to Dr. Haskew, the epiphanous moment came outside of Miss Mary Bobo's, a well-known eating establishment in Lynchburg, where a group of MTSU administrators had held a luncheon meeting. It was on a day when Montgomery was in a particularly ebullient mood. His luncheon presentation filled the room with facts, figures, and dreams as he developed a vivid picture of the Honors Program and its eventual evolution. Haskew acknowledged that she and President Walker were quite impressed. As they made their way into the parking lot outside the restaurant, they looked at one another and exclaimed, simultaneously, "We should make the Honors Program an Honors College!"[53] Shortly thereafter, the concept was endorsed by the committee that developed the university's first Academic Master Plan (1997–98), and university officials subsequently prepared the recommendation for the board's August 1, 1998 action.[54] On May 8, 1999, Janet Patterson became the first graduate of the Honors *College.*[55]

With the advancement to college status, minimal requirements for graduation with University Honors were advanced from 24 to 36 semester hours. The enhanced requirement called for a minimum of 18 hours in lower-division honors work and 18 hours in specified upper-division work. Specified upper-division work included six hours in interdisciplinary honors seminars, eight hours in general honors work (usually to be taken in the major and minor fields of study), and three hours of thesis work. Also included was a new, one-hour thesis tutorial requirement, which had been recognized as a critical need during the Self-Study of 1994. The need was forcefully highlighted: "A most glaring weakness in the Honors curriculum is the absence of 'gateway courses' leading to the development of an Honors thesis or reading courses designed to develop and support the thesis process."[56]

Admission requirements adopted early in Montgomery's tenure as director were again modified. The requirement that freshmen students have a composite score of 26 on the ACT *or* a high school GPA of 3.7 *or* a high school class rank in the upper 10 percent was changed to allow admission by one of two routes. The new requirement became a minimal score of 26 on the ACT *and* a high school GPA of at least 3.0 *or* an ACT minimum of 22 *and* a high school GPA of at least 3.5. Whether the new standards were more stringent than the ones they replaced can be argued, and some might contend that the newly created second route for admission actually represented a relaxation in standards. The requirement of a cumulative GPA of at least 3.0 was retained as the standard for established students, as was the requirement of a 3.25 GPA for graduation with University Honors. Whether the new standards for freshman admission were more selective than the old ones may never be fully resolved; however, it is an established fact that they did not greatly impede further enrollment growth. Between the 1998 fall semester and 2004 fall semester, Honors student enrollment rose from 729 to an all-time high of 1,182.[57]

THE MARTIN HONORS BUILDING

Middle Tennessee State University's success in establishing the first honors college at a public university in Tennessee led to a cascade of further successes, beginning with the construction of a wonderfully functional and architecturally attractive facility: the Paul W. Martin Sr. Honors Building. A formal agreement dated June 26, 2000, and signed by H. Lee Martin, Paul W. Martin, MTSU President James E. Walker, and MTSU Foundation President Don Moser outlined the terms and conditions for a two-million dollar gift to the MTSU Foundation ". . . for the purpose of constructing a building on campus to house the MTSU College of University Honors." Among the conditions were that the benefactors transfer the pledged funds to the MTSU Foundation within 45 days. The agreement required that MTSU raise a matching amount of two million dollars within 18 months and that the funds provided by the Martins were to be temporarily maintained in an account invested in the Local Government Investment Pool of the State of Tennessee in order to receive earnings. The agreement further provided that the interest accrued prior to the beginning of construction "shall be used to increase the principal of the Paul Martin Honors

Lee and Paul Martin Jr.

Scholarship fund." A final provision of the agreement included an MTSU pledge to recommend to the Tennessee Board of Regents that the Honors College building be named the Paul W. Martin Sr. Honors College Building.[58]

The Martins' pledge generated great excitement, of course, but it came during a period of change in the university's presidential leadership. Within months after signing the Martin Agreement, President Walker resigned in order to accept a similar position at Southern Illinois University, and Dr. Gene Smith was named interim president.

During the critical months that followed the signing of the Martin Agreement, Dean Montgomery worked toward the goal of obtaining the required two million dollar match with notable success. Nevertheless, when Dr. Sidney A. McPhee was named the university's tenth president, more than three-fourths of the total remained to be raised and there was only about six months' time in which to complete the task.[59]

President Sidney A. McPhee

President McPhee's prior experience included work with honors programs at the University of Louisville and at Memphis State University. He was therefore convinced of the value of honors education prior to his arrival at MTSU. As he assumed his new post, he recognized the importance of raising the required funds and considered the possible impact of failure on his new administration. Accordingly, his first priority became fund-raising for the Honors College. He estimates that he spent about 80 percent of his time on fund-raising during his first six months at MTSU.[60] With momentum brought about by the transition of the Honors Program to college status and with the clout of the MTSU presidency on his side, McPhee quickly won pledges from individuals and private businesses, alike. Major pledges came from the Rust Foundation, the Sallie Mae Fund, Conwood Company, LP, and Professional Project Services, Inc. (Pro2Serve). Gifts of $100,000 or more were received from the Bridgestone America's Trust Fund, Cingular Wireless Corporation and BellSouth Corporation (now AT&T), Don C. and Carolyn G. Midgett, D. E. Simmons and the family of Kathleen Martin Simmons, the Estate of John C. Hoover, and the Estate of Esther Jetton Cunningham. During the last available month for fund-raising, alumnus Andrew W. (Woody) Miller's gift of $250,000 put MTSU "over the top" in its quest to raise the required two million dollar match.[61] The fund-raising drive came to a successful end on December 12, 2001, with President McPhee's announcement that the required match had been met. Montgomery later wrote, "The administration, faculty, alumni, community members, and industry leaders all came together to support the Honors College. We are particularly grateful for President McPhee's leadership during the final six months of our fund-raising effort."[62]

Prior mention was made with regard to the unique status of Paul W. Martin Jr. as the first graduate of the Honors Program. The development of his affinity for his alma mater and the Honors Program in particular could be a case study in alumni relations. His long history of support transcends personal involvement; he also takes a measure of credit for reinforcing Lee's interest in MTSU.[63] Both Paul and Lee acknowledge a personal love for the Murfreesboro community where they spent many boyhood days. Connections to the Martins run through a four-decades-long succession of MTSU leaders starting with President M. G. Scarlett's involvement of Paul and Lee with the MTSU Foundation and continuing through Drs. June McCash, Ron Messier, J. P. Montgomery, and others.[64]

In reflecting upon the Martin Gift, Lee Martin corroborated his brother's claim of reinforcing attitudes favorable to MTSU and also commented on the ease of working with MTSU's comparatively "thin" administrative bureaucracy. From earlier days, he recalled impressions of MTSU as a friendly and hospitable

Paul W. Martin Sr. Honors Building

place. But perhaps the greatest impetus for his ultimate decision to support the construction of an honors building was his recollection of his father's admonition: "Son, get as much education as you can. No one can take that away."[65] Apparently, the two Martin sons took their father's advice to heart. Lee earned three degrees in engineering, including a PhD from the University of Tennessee, and Paul earned two degrees, a bachelor's degree with University Honors from MTSU and a JD from the Nashville School of Law.

The building contractor for the Martin Building was 101 Construction of Brentwood, Tennessee. The Nashville architectural firm of Everton Oglesby Askew was in charge of building plans and overall design. Key features included an amphitheatre for lectures and special events, three classrooms, a science lab, a computer lab, offices for faculty and staff, a library, a conference room, and areas for study, conversation, and lounging. An architectural rendering of the building appeared on the first page of the *Honors Alternative* during the fall of 2001, and the official ground breaking took place on March 13, 2002.[66] A year later, construction was underway and excitement was building. Montgomery exuded hopeful anticipation as he spoke of the prospect of students defending their theses in "the tower" and how the new building would "allow us to continue to create the sense of community that is so vital to the Honors experience."[67] Although the final building design was rendered by a Nashville architectural firm, Montgomery's personal imprint is evident in the design of the second floor study area, the bell tower, the inclusion of fireplaces, and in other details. Honors staff members moved into the Martin Honors Building on December 17, 2003, a semester prior to the official dedication and grand opening of the building on May 3, 2004.[68]

CHANGING OF THE GUARD

Montgomery retired in June, 2004, less than two months after the dedication of the Martin Honors Building. Former directors June McCash and Ron Messier also retired in 2004, and the College felt the additional loss of its first associate dean, Greg Schmidt, who returned to full-time teaching in the Department of Psychology. Thus, the Honors College lost all of its former leaders within a single year.

President McPhee named Dr. Philip M. Mathis, professor of biology, to the post of interim dean in July, 2004. Weeks later, Dr. Lara (Womack) Daniel, associate professor of accounting, was named interim associate dean. Mathis and Daniel inherited an established program, a new building, a supportive administration and Honors Council, and a newly expanded staff that included three secretaries, an event coordinator, and an academic advisor. The expanded staff combined with momentum borne of sustained progress helped to counterbalance the loss of experienced leadership and paved the way for further progress.

Dr. Philip M. Mathis

MEETING NEW CHALLENGES

By the time Mathis assumed his duties in the summer of 2004, the 36-hour requirement for graduation, adopted in concert with the move to college status, had been reduced to 31 hours, including 15 lower-division hours and 16 upper-division hours. Upper-division requirements specified six hours in general upper-division work in the major or an allied field, six hours in interdisciplinary seminars, one hour of thesis tutorial credit, and three hours of thesis credit.

In charging Mathis to assume his position as dean, President McPhee emphasized three points: first, the importance of maintaining the momentum gained through the opening of the Martin Building; second, the need to increase the number of students who graduate with University Honors; and, third, the importance of establishing a clear vision for the future. Early initiatives that contributed to sustained momentum included revitalization of HSA and the Honors College Residential Society (HCRS), improvements to the student commons, and placement of study-abroad displays throughout the building. Frequent scheduling of entertainment events, Faculty Firesides, festivals, and colloquia reinforced the College's tradition as a place for intellectual discourse and social interaction. Successful collaborations with Dr. Claudia Barnett, professor of English (Visiting Artist Program), Dr. Nancy Goldberg, professor of foreign languages and literatures (Visiting International Scholars Program), and Dr. Shelley Thomas, professor of foreign languages and literatures (Foreign Language Institute), contributed further to the growing number of enrichment opportunities.

The thesis requirement had long been considered a key factor in the College's low graduation rate. The Self-Study of 1994 stated: "The major stumbling block to graduation appears to be the Honors thesis."[69] Even though the thesis was thought to be a "stumbling block," Mathis considered it to be the hallmark of an honors education and was unwilling to support its removal as a requirement for graduation. Instead, he focused on the disparity between the College's specified requirements for graduation and its actual course offerings. Between 1985 and 1993, 333 honors courses were offered: 57 sponsored by University Honors (*all* upper-division level) and 276 by departments (45 percent upper-division level). Lower-division and upper-division offerings were therefore roughly proportional to graduation requirements that specified 12 lower-division hours and 12 upper-division hours.[70]

By 2004, however, upper-division requirements had risen to slightly more than 50 percent of the specified curriculum (16 out of 31 semester hours) while the proportion of upper-division courses actually offered had fallen to less than one in five (*Honors Alternative* 2004). Given that honors course offerings were largely determined by individual departments, and not by the honors administration, the problem was addressed by adjusting the ratio of lower-division to upper-division requirements. With the disparity between curricular requirements and curricular offerings in mind, the 31-hour requirement for graduation with University Honors was modified to require a minimum of 20 lower-division hours and 11 upper-division hours following a review by the Honors Council and approval by the University Curriculum Committee in May, 2005. The modification apparently had its intended effect. During the academic year of 2003–2004, only seven students graduated with University Honors. Four years later, the annual number of graduates reached 27.[71]

In keeping with his charge to develop a vision for the College, Mathis presented a 12-page report to President McPhee and Executive Vice President and Provost Kaylene Gebert in January 2005. The report, titled *A Focus for the Future*, outlined a range of problems, possible solutions, and new directions that the Honors College might take. It was well received and may have played a role in President McPhee's Spring 2005 decision to remove the "interim" from Mathis's title, an action that made him the Honors College's second dean. *A Focus for the Future* suggested the need to (1) simplify admission standards and raise retention standards; (2) establish a fellowship program that would require a new and exclusive interdisciplinary curriculum; (3) increase study abroad opportunities and student participation; (4) restrain enrollment but increase graduation rates; (5) emphasize leading-edge instructional technology; (6) establish a distinguished speakers program; (7) provide opportunity for student leadership development; (8) enhance student services; (9) develop a faculty excellence program; (10) adopt and develop "points of pride"; and (11) plan for the future of the Honors Living and Learning Center.[72]

The period between 2004 and 2008 was characterized by a systematic realization of the goals suggested in *A Focus for the Future*. Retention standards were raised (from an overall GPA equal to or greater than 3.00 to 3.25), and admission standards were simplified and raised (Composite ACT score equal to or greater than 25 *and* a high school GPA of 3.50). In response to higher admission and retention standards, enrollment declined; but, counter-intuitively, graduation rates rose. Displays of study abroad materials were spread throughout the Martin Building, provisions were made for study abroad scholarships, and study abroad was promoted through workshops, guest speakers and acquisitions for the College's Martinelli Library. At a cost of approximately $280,000, the Cingular Wireless Computer Lab (Room 218, Martin Honors Building) was transformed into the AT&T Advanced Classroom Technology Laboratory, a next-generation classroom.[73]

During the fall of 2004, Mathis successfully petitioned top MTSU administrators to have *Collage*, a campus-based arts and literature publication, transferred to the custody of the Honors College where he hoped Honors students would contribute to its revitalization and future success. As *Collage* was transferred to Honors, Lara Daniel (interim associate dean) and Michelle Arnold (academic advisor) forged a new partnership with the McNair Scholars Program, one that recognized common goals of the Honors College and the McNair Program, including the emphasis on research and preparation for post-graduate work.[74]

During 2004–2005, the Institute of Leadership Excellence (ILE) was founded. Dr. David Foote, associate professor of management and marketing, assumed the role of institute director with assistance from his colleague, Dr. Earl Thomas, also a professor of management and marketing. Financial support for the ILE was provided by Dr. Lee Martin, whose generosity also allowed for the establishment of the Paul W. Martin Sr. Honors Lectureship in December, 2004.

Other initiatives undertaken during 2004–2005 included transformation of the computer lab into the AT&T Advanced Classroom Technology Lab, creation of a scholarship display in the thesis defense room, cataloging the Martinelli Library's approximately 2,000 volumes, and adding special library resources and mini-scholarships for students planning post-graduate study. Special library resources included study guides, a catalog of websites, and computer-assisted learning activities. Interest in these resources was heightened by the success of honors students in being admitted to prestigious graduate schools including Harvard (Kimberly Myers), Oxford (Eric Freundt), Yale (Ranin Kazamy), and the California Institute of Technology (Taylor Arnold Barnes).

HONORS PUBLICATIONS

Like his predecessors, Mathis believed that honors publications could facilitate communication and reinforce a positive image of the Honors College. Soon after his appointment, he began working with staff members to develop new publications (brochures, booklets, etc.) and to transform the newsletter, the *Honors Alternative*, in terms of content and graphic appeal. The newsletter that emerged was a longer publication with greater visual appeal, one that served the College's need to communicate important dates and announcements as well as to highlight the many successes of students, alumni, faculty, and staff members.

The *Honors Alternative* quickly won recognition for excellence. In November 2007 it placed second in a national competition sponsored by the National Collegiate Honors Council, a feat that was repeated the following year. Dr. Scott Carnicom, associate dean, commented that "The newsletter is a great source of pride . . . special thanks must go to editor Karen Demonbreum and Sherry Wiser George in Publications and Graphics."[75]

Collage represented a means of showcasing the creativity of honors students and non-honors students alike. During the fall of 2004, an ad hoc committee was appointed and charged with the development of a set of operational standards to guide *Collage* staff members toward professional practices that would ensure contributors of a fair-minded, knowledge-based review of their work. Committee members were: chair, Dr. Martha Hixon (English); Dr. Gaylord Brewer (English); Ms. Suma Clark (publications and graphics); Ms. Jenny Crouch (former *Collage* staff advisor); Dr. Virginia Donnell (speech and theatre); Ms. Amy Foster (student representative); Mr. Seth Johnson (art); Dr. John Minichello (English); Ms. Teresa Pickering (student representative); Ms. Marsha Powers (Honors College); Dr. Tom Strawman (English); and Dr. Lara Daniel (Honors College).

The group recommended that the journal's name become, *Collage: A Journal of Creative Expression*; that it be entirely student-run with anonymous review of all submitted work; and that a faculty oversight board, chaired by the vice chair of the Honors Council, be created and charged with appointing the editor in chief and with subsequent confirmation of the editor's recommendations for staff appointments. In conjunction with the Honors College's takeover of *Collage*, approval was obtained for the conversion of a secretarial staff position into a coordinator's position for publications and special projects. Day-to-day oversight of *Collage* operations was among the enumerated duties of the new coordinator, Marsha Powers.

Collage flourished as a publication of the Honors College. Since 2005, eight issues have been judged by the Columbia Scholastic Press Association (CSPA), an arm of Columbia University's School of Journalism. Four issues have received Gold Medalist Certificates and two have received the even more prestigious Silver Crown Awards. Each year, CSPA reviews nearly 2,000 student publications from across the nation; less than 2 percent receive the Silver Crown Award.[76]

After the 2004–2005 academic year, Lara Daniel returned to full-time teaching in the Jones College of Business. During her year in the Honors College, she contributed greatly to the oversight of the College's Institutional Effectiveness Plan, the transition of *Collage* to the Honors College, event coordination, partnership establishment, administration of the Honors Lecture Series, College recruitment efforts, and coordination of class offerings and schedules.

The following year, Dr. Angela (Jill) Hague, professor of English, assumed the position of interim associate dean. During 2005–2006, she worked in concert with the newly appointed dean and other members of the honors staff to publicize the Honors College, review and revise program policies, and oversee course offerings. The Buchanan Fellows program, the elite scholarship program envisioned in *A Focus for the Future* was approved, and she helped to develop and shape the program. Hague effectively implemented many good ideas, but her interests and professional identity were tied closely to teaching. When the associate dean's position was converted to a full-time administrative position in the fall of 2006, she elected to return to full-time teaching rather than to seek a full-time administrative appointment, setting the stage for the appointment of Dr. Scott Carnicom as the College's first full-time associate dean.

DR. JAMES M. BUCHANAN AND THE BUCHANAN FELLOWS

The Buchanan family tree is deeply rooted in the rocky soil of Middle Tennessee. Ancestors of Dr. James M. Buchanan, Jr. were among the first Europeans to settle in the area. During the 1780s, they established Buchanan's Station, near Nashville, and successfully defended it against a large scale Indian attack in 1792. John Price Buchanan, a later ancestor, was the 28th governor (1891–1893) of the state of Tennessee.

Dr. Buchanan's connections to Tennessee's past include growing up in the Buchanan Community, south of Murfreesboro, and connections to Middle Tennessee State University. In 1940, he graduated from State Teachers College, Murfreesboro, a forerunner to Middle Tennessee State University. After earning a master's degree from the University of Tennessee and a PhD from the University of Chicago, he embarked on a noteworthy and fecund academic career that led to his winning the 1986 Nobel Prize in economics.

Dr. James M. Buchanan

Buchanan's interest in his alma mater and in high-achieving, first-generation college students was evident prior to the inauguration of the Buchanan Fellows Program in October 2007. During the 1990s, he periodically provided funds to support cultural enrichment opportunities for a select group of students identified through the provost's office. Students who benefited from these gifts were informally referred to as the "Buchanan Scholars." By the new millennium, however, funds were largely depleted, and the Buchanan Scholars were no longer an identifiable group.[77] The stage was set for renewed support from Buchanan and for full implementation of the Buchanan *Fellows* Program.

As formulated, the Buchanan Fellows Program consisted of two components: a financial aid package, or scholarship, and a special curriculum that required members of each class to complete a sequence of six courses as an intact group. The Program called for a pool of applicants to compete for an annual allotment of 20 awards and for successful applicants to enroll in the Buchanan Seminars. Key elements of the financial aid package included full payment of tuition and fees for four years, an annual book allowance of $1,000, and special consideration for receipt of financial support to study abroad. Seminars reserved for Buchanan Fellows included: A Historical and Philosophical Journey through the Universe (science course taught by Dr. Eric Klumpe); Chemistry and Crime (science course taught by Dr. Tammy Melton); Greek Origins of Western Culture (humanities course taught by Dr. Angela Hague); Questing Toward the Modern (humanities course taught by Dr. Tom Strawman); Bigger than America, Brazen as Politics, Better than Plowing (economics course taught by Dr. Richard Hannah); and Who Gets What, When, and How (government course taught by Dr. Karen Petersen).

During the 2009 fall semester nearly 60 Buchanan Fellows were enrolled, with an expectation of as many as 80 by the fall of 2010. Since continuous enrollment in the Honors College is a stipulated requirement for Buchanan Fellows, the total number of Honors College graduates is projected to reach more than 40 per year by 2011.

OTHER INITIATIVES AND SUCCESSES

In August 2006, Dr. Scott Carnicom joined the Honors College as associate dean after having founded and directed a fledgling honors program at Marymount University (Arlington, Virginia). He was lured to MTSU by several factors including evidence of administrative support for honors, the Martin Honors Building, and the opportunity to help build a nationally acclaimed honors college. Like his predecessor, Jill Hague, he brought new ideas along with support for established goals and on-going initiatives. Between 2006 and 2008, he worked in concert with the dean and other members of the honors staff to effect change and operational efficiency. Noteworthy were his contributions to the AT&T Advanced Classroom Lab, the thesis advising process, priority registration for honors students, selection of Buchanan Fellows, coordination of the Honors Lecture Series, and execution of programmed events, including the College's hosting of the 2008 meeting of the Tennessee Collegiate Honors Council.

The period between 2006 and 2008 witnessed staff and student involvement in honors-related professional organizations, sponsorship of the Institute for Leadership Excellence, and the founding of the Buchanan Fellows Program. The establishment of the Undergraduate Fellowship Office (UFO) as a campus-wide service led to winners of highly competitive national scholarships. Taylor Arnold Barnes (Goldwater), Brandon Armstrong (Fulbright), Matthew Bullington (Phi Kappa Phi), and Gretchen Jenkins (Phi Kappa Phi) were among the honors students who won awards.

During this period, the Honors College became home to MTSU's chapter of Phi Kappa Phi and welcomed other campus honor societies (Tau Sigma, Golden Key International, and the National Society of Collegiate Scholars) as affiliates of the Honors College. Staff members and students became involved in the annual MTSU Homecoming event and in hosting distinguished lecturers, visiting scholars, visiting artists, and prospective students, including high school valedictorians and finalists for National Merit Scholarships. Other highlights of the 2006–2008 time period included relocation of the Honors Living-Learning Center from the Wood-Felder complex to Lyon Hall, placement of a future honors living-learning center on the Campus Master Plan, and the signing of partnership agreements with honors directors and key administrators at area community colleges and with the Discovery School at Reeves-Rogers, a Murfreesboro elementary school for high achievers.[78]

The period also witnessed progress in terms of gifts received and the establishment of new scholarship programs including the previously mentioned Buchanan Fellowships, the James M. Buchanan Study Abroad Scholarships, and the Hannah/Harris Honors Study Abroad Endowed Scholarships that honor Drs. Richard L. Hannah and K. Watson Harris. Major gifts were received from H. Lee Martin that provided for two new programs: the Martin Lectureship and the Institute of Leadership. Also providing significant gifts in support of scholarships or other Honors College needs were Paul W. Martin Jr.; Dr. Jan Hayes and her husband, Dean; Elaine G. Royal; Mark A. Hall; and Michael D. Martinelli Sr. and his wife, Gloria Kharibian. Recognition of a continuing need for broad-based private support for the College was a key consideration in actions that led to the creation of the Board of Visitors.[79]

THE BOARD OF VISITORS

The Board of Visitors was established to: (1) help the Honors College realize a distinctive niche within the domain of higher education; (2) consult with the dean concerning societal and student needs in a changing world; (3) promote public awareness of the academic programs of the College; and (4) enhance academic quality through gifts and by identifiying external funding sources.[80] The board's *Mission and By-Laws* were developed concurrently with the recruitment and appointment of members of the first board. They were officially adopted on July 1, 2007, and ratified by the board at its inaugural meeting, on December 7, 2007.[81] A detailed account of the board's founding and possible role for the future appears elsewhere.[82] Named to the board were:

John F. (Jeff) Whorley Jr. (Chair), Executive Vice President–Debt Management (retired), SLM Corporation
James H. Bailey III (Vice Chair), Johnson + Bailey Architects, PC
Don R. Ash, Circuit Court Judge, 16th District of Tennessee
Albert Cauz, Headmaster, The Webb School
Emily P. Ellis, Vice President for STAR Culture, Gaylord Entertainment
Mark A. Hall, Turnage Professor of Law, Wake Forest University
Emil Hassan, Senior Vice President (retired), Nissan North America
Debra H. Hopkins, Southeast Regional Director, National Geographic

H. Lee Martin, Chairman, Abunga.com, LLC
Paul W. Martin Jr., Chief Managing Member, Clarity Resources, LLC
Chasity Wilson Nicoll, Partner, Law Office of Nicoll & Nicoll
Utpal P. Patel, Physician, Murfreesboro Medical Clinic and SurgiCenter
Byron Smith, Chief Marketing Officer (retired), Asurion Corporation
Holly Thompson, WSMV Co-anchor
James A. Thorpe, Vice President and General Manager, AT&T
Jim Tracy, Tennessee State Senator, 16th Congressional District
Vincent Windrow, Vice President, Zycron Computers–Nashville.

In addition, Drs. James M. Buchanan and June Hall McCash were named to the board as Distinguished Members. Ex officio members included President Sidney A. McPhee, Provost Kaylene Gebert, Senior Vice President John W. Cothern, Vice President for Development Joseph Bales, and Dean Phil Mathis.

During its first two years of operation, the board proved to be a valuable resource. In addition to providing useful ideas on new methods of publicizing the College, numerous board members made direct gifts or guided staff members toward funding sources that totaled more than $65,000. Key support and leadership was provided by John F. (Jeff) Whorley, James H. Bailey III, James M. Buchanan, Greg F. Morton, Emil Hassan, June H. McCash, John R. Vile, Don Ash, Philip M. Mathis, and others. Gifts and grants received were applied mainly to scholarships, outreach programs, and books for the Martinelli Memorial Library.

According to schedule, several members rotated off the board in 2010 thereby allowing new members to be seated. New members included Don Midgett (elected board chair), Keta Barnes, Mary Lee Barnes, Gordon Bell, Eddith Dashiel, Elliot Dawson, Raiko Henderson, Shane Reeves, and Don Witherspoon. Several members of the group have already made significant contributions through gift-giving and useful ideas. Based on pledges already made, board gifts will certainly rise to new heights during 2011, the Centennial Year.

THE HONORS CREED, BELL TOLLING, AND THE *BOOK OF TOWN AND GOWN*

The Honors Student Advisory Council, established during McCash's tenure as director, was revived by Mathis and proved to be a source of many useful ideas. It supported the proposal that allowed honors students to gain priority status during registration as well as a proposal to create a different and distinctive diploma for students graduating with University Honors.[83]   Other Advisory Council contributions included involvement in the establishment of an official Honors Creed, endorsement of the idea of a *Book of Town and Gown,* and support for the "tolling of the bells" following the successful defense of each thesis.

The Honors Creed was adopted on February 3, 2006.[84] Its recitation at the inauguration of each class of Buchanan Fellows and on other ceremonial occasions is now a developing tradition. The Creed takes as its outline the virtues engraved on the north facade of the Martin Honors Building. The entire Creed follows.

THE HONORS CREED
University Honors College at Middle Tennessee State University

It is evident that a set of guiding principles is useful in charting a course
for the future; therefore we, the students and faculty of the University
Honors College, embrace THE HONORS CREED and acknowledge
before others our deeply held beliefs that:

CHARACTER,
more than anything else, defines the worth of a man or a woman,

COMMITMENT
is a virtue that sustains us, guides us, and inspires others during uncertain times,

CREATIVITY
is the essential factor that promotes invention, adaptation to our environment,
and personal fulfillment,

CURIOSITY,
more than anything else, compels human beings to explore and learn,

DISCIPLINE
is essential to a culture of order, whether on a personal level or
within a political system,

FAITH
and its cousin hope are foundational to human knowledge,
whether applied to religion or to science,

HONOR
is a virtue not to be equated with glory, but with respect and purity, and finally that

INTEGRITY
is the cornerstone of every creed, every code, every profession,

every civilization, and every enterprise.
Without integrity, truth—the virtual goal of the academic
enterprise—can never be found.

Adopted February 3, 2006

The *Book of Town and Gown* is a book of nineteenth-century origin, purchased for $120 at the Murfreesboro Antique Dealers Association's 2006 Summer Show and Sale. The book is fully leather bound, embossed, and adorned with gold leaf. At the time of its purchase on behalf of the Honors College, it consisted of 300 *blank* pages. Marsha Powers, publications coordinator for the College, retained a calligrapher to inscribe headings that divide the book into sections and added a bookplate that describes its history and intended use. According to the bookplate, "The purpose of the *Book of Town and Gown* is to record the signatures of key individuals who helped shape the University Honors College in the year 2006 and beyond."

The book's name acknowledges the important and long-standing relationship between the academic realm, or "gown," and the broader societal realm, or "town." At present, gown signatories include the MTSU president and senior academic officers, multiple student winners of Goldwater and Fulbright awards, multiple *Collage* editors, HSA presidents, several chairs of the Honors Council, award-winning honors faculty, and four classes of Buchanan Fellows. Signatories under the heading of "town" include a Nobel Prize winner, a former chairman of the US Military's Joint Chiefs-of-Staff, an eminent Tennessee jurist, several visiting artists, scholars and visiting dignitaries from Europe and Asia, special patrons and friends, members of the Board of Visitors, and numerous government officials, including retired US Congressman Bart Gordon and former Governor Phil Bredesen.

The bell tower of the Martin Honors Building is situated immediately above Room 203B, the room in which every completed thesis is finally defended before a committee of three or more faculty members. The four cast bronze bells of the bell tower carillon are automatically programmed to chime on the quarter hour and strike on the hour; however, a hand-held remote control device allows a person sitting in Room 203B to activate a minutes-long peal of the bells by simply pushing the "peal" button on the remote control device. On November 8, 2005, at the thesis defense of Brandon Armstrong, the new thesis-defense-ending practice was begun.[85] Dr. Sonja Hedgepeth, professor of German and Armstrong's thesis co-advisor, was the first to execute the ritual now referred to as "the tolling of the bells."

Dr. John R. Vile

QUESTING FOR NATIONAL RECOGNITION

Dr. John R. Vile, former chair of the MTSU Department of Political Science, became the fifth principal officer and third dean of the Honors College in July 2008. Like his predecessor, Phil Mathis, Vile embraced his new role by drafting a plan for the future. Vile's plan, titled, *A Vision for the Future: Master Plan for the Honors College, 2009–2019*, was presented to President McPhee in March 2009.[86] The 22-page report reviewed the College's past, current goals, curriculum, enrollment and graduation trends, and gauged the University Honors College against 11 recognized characteristics, or standards, set forth by the National Collegiate Honors Council as indicators of a "mature honors college."[87] His conclusion, with regard to the latter, was that the Honors College was in full compliance with NCHC standards. Despite the past successes implied by broad compliance with national standards, the report outlined several new goals and emphasized the academic master plan's lofty objective: "to promote the Honors College as a national model program." [88]

Envisioned as immediate or near-term goals were the needs to hire a fund raiser, establish a leadership society, increase publicity about the Honors College, systematically monitor the successes of honors graduates, streamline procedures for thesis supervision, increase transfers from community colleges, facilitate publication of honors-related books, initiate an additional scholarship program as a complement to the Buchanan Fellows Program, and raise monies for existing scholarships. Longer term, the desirability of expanding *Collage*, supplementing the pay of faculty housed in the Martin Honors Building, constructing a new living-learning center, establishing a sister institution for foreign exchange, and establishing exchanges with other honors colleges were recognized.

INTERNATIONAL BACCALAUREATE SCHOLARSHIPS
AND OTHER SCHOLARSHIPS

The approval of a new scholarship program designed to benefit the Honors College and the entire university was a key development of Vile's early administration. Beginning in 2010, Middle Tennessee State University became the first public university in Tennessee to offer special scholarships to incoming freshmen who have earned an international baccalaureate diploma while maintaining a GPA of 3.5 or greater. Currently, the IB diploma is awarded by a limited number of high schools for completion of a rigorous academic curriculum that includes creativity, action, and service components. Winners of IB scholarships will receive an award of $1,000 per year for four years and be allowed to combine their IB award dollars with any other MTSU academic scholarship except the Buchanan Fellowship. Other scholarships added during Vile's tenure as dean include new Buchanan Study Abroad Awards, the June McCash Founder's Award, a scholarship that supports study abroad, and the permanently endowed Marilyn M. and Philip M. Mathis Honors Research Award.

SCIENTIA ET HUMANITAS

The Honors College continues to build a culture of research and publication through sponsorship of special journals and publication opportunities for students. In 2009, a special website, listing appropriate journals and contact information, was created as a means of guiding students toward publication of their research. The success of *Collage* as a publication for the creative arts provided inspiration for a new honors publication. With cooperation of Dean Tom Cheatham (College of Basic and Applied Sciences), the on-line journal *Scientia*, a Middle Tennessee student-run publication since 1997, is being expanded and revitalized as an Honors College publication. The new journal, *Scientia et Humanitas*, will feature research reports and scholarly essays in the sciences and humanities. Its journal office was recently relocated to the Martin Building, adjacent to the *Collage* office. Marsha Powers, staff publications coordinator, will oversee operations for both *Collage* and *Scientia et Humanitas*.

PROGRESS IN CHALLENGING TIMES

In less than three years as dean, Vile has successfully maintained the momentum of prior years in the face of new budgetary constraints brought about by a national economic downturn. Despite the less than ideal economic situation, progress continues. During 2008, the semiannual newsletter was expanded and renamed, the *Honors Edition,* concurrent with the naming of a new editor, Marsha Powers. Recently, the Honors College worked with the Department of Political Science to establish a campus chapter of Rotaract, an affiliate of Rotary International. Following an October 21, 2009, site visit by officials of Omicron Delta Kappa (an honors leadership society), approval was given for the establishment of a new ODK chapter in the Honors College, and a charter chapter was created on April 30, 2010.

Efforts to support students in applying for prestigious scholarships have been redoubled. Record numbers of applicants are now seeking and receiving nationally competitive scholarships. Patrick Pratt, Kimberly Yarborough, Kaitlen Howell, and Eric Little recently won nationally competitive Fulbright awards to study in Tanzania, Spain, Germany, and Portugal, respectively. Evan Craig and Robert Ehemann were 2011 winners of the nation's most coveted undergraduate award in science—the Goldwater Scholarship. Merranda Holmes received a $5,000 cash award and national recognition from the honor society Phi Kappa Phi, and Anna Yacovone won the Benjamin Gilman International Scholarship. In a singular success, 2010 graduate and MTSU Presidential Award winner Jasmine Gray became the university's first-ever member of *USA Today*'s Academic First Team.

Dr. Kaylene Gebert, former provost, moved to the Martin Honors Building and the Honors College in 2009, a move that permitted the College to offer two new speech classes for honors students. A year later, Dr. Diane Miller, mathematics professor and former interim provost, added further to the College's prestige by joining Gebert and other distinguished colleagues in the Martin Building. The AT&T Advanced Classroom Technology Lab was retrofitted with emerging digital technologies for instruction during the spring semester of 2010. Record numbers of applicants are also now being received for Buchanan Fellowships. Record numbers of thesis writers and prospective honors graduates are also in the pipeline. Prospects for the future are, indeed, promising. Given time and the assumption of economic recovery, there is little doubt that the bold objectives set forth in Vile's visionary plan can be realized, and when they are, increased national recognition will follow.

SUMMARY AND CONCLUSION

The Honors Program was founded in 1973, about 50 years after Frank Aydelotte launched the collegiate honors movement in America. Despite the time lag, MTSU was not a latecomer to the honors movement; rather, it was a contributor to the post-Sputnik surge in the founding of honors programs throughout the country. Within Tennessee, the university was an early leader in honors education. In fact, only the Helen Hardin Honors Program at the University of Memphis, founded in 1972, predates the MTSU Honors Program. Moreover, the Program's conversion to college status in 1998 established the University Honors College as the *first* such college at a public university in Tennessee.

Since the earliest days of the Honors Program, university officials have sought to attract top students by adding new scholarships for honors students. One study noted the positive impact of Presidential Scholarships and Freshman Honors Scholarships on student participation in Honors.[89] Although IB scholarships represent the latest success, other scholarships established over time add immeasurably to the College's growing number of available scholarships and awards; included are the Paul W. Martin Sr. Scholarships, the Michael Martinelli Memorial Scholarship, the Bart McCash Scholarship, the Honors Achievement Scholarship, the Ingram-Montgomery Honors College Thesis Research Scholarship, the Hannah/Harris Honors Study Abroad Endowed Scholarships, the James M. Buchanan Study Abroad Scholarships, and the Marilyn M. and Philip M. Mathis Honors Research Award. Other long-established non-monetary recognitions include the Outstanding Freshman, Sophmore, Junior, and Senior Awards. Going forward, the College must manage its existing resources well and seek to add new awards and scholarships in order to continue to attract capable and motivated students.

Strong and sustained support at the presidential level, especially including M. G. Scarlett, James E. Walker, and Sidney A. McPhee, has allowed a succession of directors and deans to build an Honors College that attracts academically talented students from near and far. Their support is reflected in many ways, including growth in budget lines for Honors staff members. At the outset, there was a half-time director and a part-time secretary; today, there are seven full-time staff members including a dean and an associate dean. In recent years, National Merit and National Achievement Scholars have joined the student population in ever increasing numbers. Graduates and former students of the Honors College have entered and succeeded in some of the world's most prestigious graduate programs including Oxford (UK), Harvard, Yale, and the California Institute of Technology. In 2010, *Collage*, the College's award-winning publication won the Columbia Scholastic Press Association's elite Silver Crown Award, a recognition given to less than 2 percent of publications reviewed. Since the early days of its founding, the College has sought uncompromised excellence, a tribute to founding director, June H. McCash, and many others.

There is little doubt that the College's reputation for excellence is growing as it has attracted visitors from colleges and universities throughout the region and the world. It is a settled fact that much of the success of the past decade has come about due to the decision to convert from program level to college level and from the generosity of many, including the Martin and Buchanan families. Without Lee and Paul Martin and the individual patrons and corporate sponsors who matched their $2 million gift, the beautiful and functional Paul W. Martin

Sr. Honors Building could not have been built. Without Dr. Buchanan's willingness to lend his name to a new program, the Buchanan Fellows Program, and to contribute to its support, it would have been impossible to attract the gifted student population now resident in the College. Without the leadership of Don Midgett (chair, Board of Visitors) and his wife, Carolyn, the 2011 Centennial Scholarship honoring Ralph and Elizabeth Gwaltney would have been impossible. Generous gifts and leadership from several members of the Board of Visitors, including Jeff Whorley (former chair), Elliot Dawson, Don Witherspoon, and Raiko Henderson, have placed the College's most cherished goals within arm's reach. Others who further the board's work or who contribute to the College's progress in other ways are periodically recognized in the *Honors Edition*.

Indicators of excellence include outstanding students, faculty, and facilities. But other factors contribute to excellence. Over time, the Honors curriculum has retained its defining elements: interdisciplinary seminars and a capstone thesis project. Small classes, the thesis tutorial, and independent research have survived as reminders of the Oxfordian origins of honors education. Civic engagement and involvement in service, cultural, and leadership activities have added to the well-roundedness of an honors education. Since the 1980s, the College has maintained a commitment to community building through programmed events and an on-campus living and learning center. Broad compliance with each of the National Collegiate Honors Council's "Characteristics of a Mature Honors College" represents a further indication of excellence.

Looking back, the rapid development of the Honors College is clearly evident. Looking forward, the College rests upon a firm foundation of past accomplishment, and there is reason to hope that the best is yet to come. Strong leadership and continued support from the university administration, the Board of Visitors, and corporate friends and patrons will help propel the College into a future where generations of students will realize personal dreams and where the College itself will gain deserved recognition as a national model in honors education.

NOTES

1   Joseph W. Cohen, *The Superior Student in American Higher Education* (New York: McGraw-Hill, 1966), 13.

2   Frederick Rudolph, *The American College and University* (New York: Alfred A. Knopf, 1962); Anne N. Rinn, "Rhodes Scholarships, Frank Aydelotte, and Collegiate Honors Edcuation," *Journal of the National Collegiate Honors Council* 4, no. 1 (2003).

3   Cohen, *The Superior Student*, 14.

4   Grey C. Austin, "Orientation to Honors Education," in *Fostering Academic Excellence Through Honors Programs*, ed. Paul G. Friedman and Reva C. Jenkins-Friedman (San Francisco, CA: Jossey-Bass, 1986), 6.

5   Rinn, "Rhodes Scholarships."

6   Austin, "Orientation to Honors," 6.

7   Cohen, *The Superior Student*, xii.

8   Peter C. Sederburg, ed. "Characteristics of the Contemporary Honors College," in *NCHC Monogram Series, The Honors College Phenomenon* (Lincoln, NE: National Collegiate Honors Council, 2008), 25.

9   John F. Kennedy, President of the United States of America, Civil Rights Speech, 11 June 1963, Washington, DC, *American Rhetoric: Top 100 Speeches* <http://www.american rhetoric.com/speeches/jfkcivilrights.htm>.

10   Frank Adeylotte, *Breaking the Academic Lockstep* (New York: Harper & Brothers, 1944), 12–13.

11   Richard J. Cummings, "Exploring Values, Issues, and Controversies," in Friedman and Jenkins-Friedman, *Fostering Academic Excellence*, 19.

12   Ted Humphrey, "The Genesis of and Idea," in Sederburg, *The Honors College Phenomenon*, 15.

13   June McCash, "Why Honors? Precedents, Perceptions, and Perspectives," lecture, Middle Tennessee State University Honors Lecture Series, 2 February 2009.

14   Rosalie Otero and Robert Spurrier, *Assessing and Evaluating Honors Programs and Honors Colleges: A Practical Handbook* in *NCHC Monograph Series*, ed. Jeffrey A. Portney (Lincoln, NE: National Collegiate Honors Council, 2005), 25–27.

15   Melvin G. Scarlett, interview by Philip Mathis and James Williams, 17 April 2009, MT 402, tape recording, Middle Tennessee Oral History Project, Albert Gore Research Center (AGRC), Middle Tennessee State University, TN (hereinafter cited as MT Oral History Project, AGRC).

16   Adeylotte, *Breaking,* 55.

17   June H. McCash, "The History of the Honors Program at MTSU, 1973–2004," *Honors Alternative* (Spring 2007).

18   *Bulletin of the Middle Tennessee State University* 47 (1974): 258–59.

19   *Bulletin, MTSU* 49 (1976): 291–92.

20   *Bulletin, MTSU* 48 (1975): 292.

21   *Bulletin, MTSU* 50 (1977): 348.

22   Ibid.

23   *Honors in Perspective* 1, no. 1 (Spring 1974).

24   *Honors in Perspective* 1, no. 2 (Fall 1974).

25   *Focus on Honors* (March 1977).

26   *Honors in Perspective* 1, no. 1 (Spring 1974).

27   *Focus on Honors* (March 1978); *Honors News & Views* (February 1979).

28   McCash, "Why Honors?"

29   Anne N. Rinn, "Academic and Social Effects of Living in Honors Residence Halls," *Journal of the National Collegiate Honors Council* 5 no. 2 (2004): 67–79; Eric Daffron and Christopher J. Holland, "Honors Living-Learning Communities: A Model of Success and Collaboration," *Honors in Practice* 5 (2009): 197–210.

30   Serenity Sutton, "Lounge Lizards," *Honor Guard* (March 1989): 4.

31 *Honors Syndrome* (February 1985).

32 Self-Study, *Report of the Honors Program*, Middle Tennessee State University Self-Study, Administrative Reports, 1982–83 (year of record). Prepared for the Commission on Colleges, Southern Association of Colleges and Schools (1983).

33 *Honors Syndrome* (March 1985); *Honor Guard* (May 1988).

34 *Honors Syndrome* (May 1985).

35 *Honor Guard* (April 1986).

36 *Honors Syndrome* (February 1985).

37 Ronald Messier, interview by Philip Mathis and James Williams, 24 February 2009, MT 399, recording, MT Oral History Project, AGRC.

38 Self-Study, (1983): 23.

39 Messier interview.

40 *Honor Guard* (November 1990).

41 *Honor Guard* (November 1989).

42 *Honor Guard* (November 1990).

43 Ibid.

44 *Honor Guard* (October 1991).

45 *Honors Alternative* (Autumn 1992).

46 *Honor Guard* (March 1992).

47 *Honors Alternative* (Fall 2006).

48 Self-Study, *Traditions Realities Opportunities*, Middle Tennessee State University Self-Study Report, 1, part B. Prepared for the Commission on Colleges, Southern Association of Colleges and Schools (1994): 199.

49 Ibid., 202.

50   *Honors Alternative* (1995).

51   *Honor Guard* (November 1989); *Honors Alternative* (Spring 1997).

52   *Honors Alternative* (1997).

53   Barbara Haskew, interview by Philip Mathis and James Williams, 17 February 2009, MT 398, recording, MT Oral History Project, AGRC.

54   McCash, *Honors Alternative* (Spring 2007).

55   *Honors Alternative* (1999).

56   Self-Study, (1994): 217.

57   Honors College Data Base: Enrollment and Graduation Statistics.   Karen Demonbreum, Manager.

58   *Agreement between Carla L. and H. Lee Martin, Phyllis B. Martin and Paul W. Martin, Jr., Middle Tennessee State University,* (and the) *Middle Tennessee State University Foundation,* 26 June 2000.

59   Sidney A. McPhee, interview by Philip Mathis and James Williams, 10 February 2009, MT 397, recording, MT Oral History Project, AGRC.

60   Ibid.

61   Ibid.

62   *Honors Alternative* (Spring 2002).

63   Paul W. Martin Jr., interview by Philip Mathis and James Williams, 7 February 2009, MT 394, recording, MT Oral History Project, AGRC.

64   Scarlett interview.

65   Lee Martin, interview by Philip Mathis and James Williams, 9 February 2009, MT 396, recording, MT Oral History Project, AGRC.

66   Randy Weiler, *Record: A Bi-weekly Publication for the Middle Tennessee State University Community* 10, no. 17 (2002): 1.

67   *Honors Alternative* (Fall 2002).

68   *Honors Alternative* (Spring 2004).

69   Self-Study, (1994): 204.

70   Ibid., 199–200.

71   Honors College Data Base.

72   Philip M. Mathis, *The University Honors College at Middle Tennessee: A Focus for the Future,* report to President Sidney McPhee, Executive Vice President and Provost Kaylene Gebert, and Vice President for Academic Affairs Jack Thomas, January 2005.

73   Scott Carnicom, K. Watson Harris, Barbara Draude, Scott McDaniel, and Philip M. Mathis, "The Advanced Classroom Technology Laboratory: Cultivating Innovative Pedagogy," *Honors in Practice* 3 (2007): 121–27.

74   *Honors Alternative* (Fall 2005).

75   *Honors Alternative* (Spring 2008).

76   Ibid.

77   Faye Johnson, personal communication with author, 29 September 2009.

78   *Honors Alternative* (Spring 2006; Spring 2007; Fall 2007; Spring 2008).

79   *Honors Alternative* (Spring 2008).

80   *Board of Visitors Mission and By-Laws* (Murfreesboro: Middle Tennessee State University Publications and Graphics, 2007).

81   *Board of Visitors Mission and By-Laws*; *Honors Alternative* (Spring 2008).

82   Scott Carnicom and Philip M. Mathis, "Building an Honors Development Board," *Honors in Practice* 5 (2009): 41–46.

83   *Honors Alternative* (Spring 2006).

84   *Board of Visitors Mission and By-Laws.*

85   *Honors Alternative* (Spring 2006).

86   John R. Vile, *A Vision for the Future: Master Plan for the Honors College, 2009–2019*, report to President Sidney McPhee, March 2009.

87   Otero and Spurrier, *Assessing and Evaluating*.

88   *Building on the Blueprint for Excellence*.   Middle Tennessee State University Academic Master Plan for 2007–2017.

89   Self-Study, (1994): 216.

Conclusion

JANICE M. LEONE

As MTSU moves into its second century, its prospects for continued growth and development are bright. What began as a school for teachers with 125 students, five buildings on a hundred acres, and 20 faculty members, is today a university with more than 26,000 students, 930 full time faculty, a campus of 515 acres, an increasing number of PhD programs, and Division I-A sports. Clearly, it would be difficult to argue that Middle Tennessee State Normal School has had anything but a very successful first one hundred years.

David Rowe correctly noted in the introduction to this collection that researching and writing these essays was truly a labor of respect and love as well as perseverance on the part of contributors. And although this collection cannot tell the entire story of MTSU's centennial legacy, in part because we have not always been careful stewards of the school's past, we have tried to eliminate the apocryphal and to be clear and correct in recounting this history. We hope that we have provided an understanding not only of the development of this institution but also of the people and town that welcomed and guided its creation over the past century.

We quickly discovered in our efforts to recreate MTSU's history that the route to success was neither easy nor straightforward, not for those people directly involved with the school's growth and activities or for those of us trying to uncover their stories. As several of our essays show, officials who guided the school's development faced numerous obstacles and challenges. They overcame many of these hurdles successfully, although others proved more difficult to conquer, whether it was the search for a usable identity, the struggle to work with inadequate funding, or the need to respond to major societal events and changes such as world wars or social reform movements. Then, as we worked to document their efforts, it would have been very satisfying, for example, to have had records of the conversations and discussions held by those involved in choosing the site for the normal schools. In other cases, more complete presidential and administrative records would likely have helped answer questions about why officials made certain decisions that influenced the school's progress. And still, even without complete records, historical hindsight tempts us, as contributors and readers alike, to assume that we surely would have made different decisions or shaped the school in other ways had we been in charge. As we have found, however, administrators, faculty, staff, and students involved in moving the school in certain directions usually had the school's best interests at heart. So even though MTSU's centennial legacy, as we've presented it here, has gaps and warts along with proud moments and major accomplishments, our wish for the next one hundred years is the continued growth, success, and celebration of Middle Tennessee State University.

NOTES ON CONTRIBUTORS

Fred P. Colvin, Professor Emeritus, joined the Department of History at MTSU in 1969 and retired in 2010. He taught a wide variety of courses in European and American history, served on various departmental and university committees, and was Director of Graduate Studies for the History Department for a number of years. Colvin was selected as an MTSU Foundation Outstanding Teacher for 1978–1979 and served as Faculty Senate President for 1979–1980.

Derek Frisby is an associate professor of history at MTSU, specializing in military and Tennessee history, and has led several study abroad courses to Iwo Jima, Guam, Peleliu, Normandy, and Western Europe. He is an MTSU alum, a recipient of the 2008–2009 MTSU Outstanding Teaching Award, and a USMC Desert Shield/Storm veteran. He also serves on the MTSU Veterans Affairs and Memorial Committee as well as the Centennial Executive Committee.

Ellen Garrison received her MA and PhD degrees in American history from Stanford University and is a Fellow of the Society of American Archivists and the Society of Georgia Archivists. She served in academic and government archives in five states before joining the history faculty at MTSU in 2000 as an associate professor. Before her retirement from the university in 2010 she designed and launched the archival curriculum in the public history program and collaborated on the development of the doctoral program in public history.

Jordan Kirkman is a 2010 graduate of the MTSU Department of History. His interests included the history of MTSU as well as Russian Studies, and he spent a summer in Russia with the Study Abroad Program. He will begin graduate studies in American history at MTSU in fall 2011.

Reuben Kyle is Professor Emeritus of Economics. He taught for 34 years as a member of the MTSU Economics and Finance Department. Over the course of those years he served in many capacities and was privileged to teach many students.

Janice M. Leone joined the MTSU Department of History in 1989 and currently serves as Interim Associate Dean in the College of Liberal Arts as well as professor in the Department of History. Her teaching and research interests focus on American women's history, the history of education, and the preparation of history majors and pre-service history teachers.

John Lodl is an alumnus of MTSU, having received his BA in Music Industry in 1998 and his MA in History in 2004. He has worked as a senior archivist at the State Archives of Georgia, director of the Bradley Academy Museum & Cultural Center in Murfreesboro, and the Sam Davis Home & Museum in Smyrna. For the past five years he has been director of the Rutherford County Archives. He is also an adjunct professor of history at MTSU.

Philip M. Mathis served Middle Tennessee State University for four decades as professor of biology and dean of the Honors College from 2004 to 2008. He recently edited and contributed to *Time and Tradition: A Poetry Anthology* (Twin Oaks Press, 2011), a publication that celebrates the MTSU Centennial and the Honors College's long-standing embrace of creative expression.

Rebecca Cawood McIntyre is associate professor of history at MTSU. She specializes in southern history and tourism, and her book, *Souvenirs of the Old South: Northern Tourism and Southern Mythology*, was recently published by University Press of Florida. She also directs the regional History Day competition held at MTSU each year.

D. Lorne McWatters, a 1979 University of Florida graduate, taught at the University of Illinois at Urbana–Champaign before joining three colleagues in 1983 to create HMS Associates, a history consulting firm. In 1993 he returned to teaching at MTSU where, after six years as Co-Director of the Public History Program, he founded and oversees the History Department's Digital History Studio (http://mtsu.edu/digitalhistory/).

David L. Rowe came to the Department of History at MTSU in 1981, building on a career in architectural history and historic preservation in upstate New York. He worked for state and county agencies and directed a regional not-for-profit organization. His research field is American religion, and he is the author of several articles and two books on the Millerite movement including a biography of its founder, William Miller.

Nancy Ellen Rupprecht, professor of history at MTSU, chairs the Holocaust Studies Program and is a former director of the Women's Studies Program. She has published articles in the fields of German, Holocaust and European Women's History, and edited two books on the Holocaust. She is a member of the editorial board of German Studies Review and the Advisory Boards for the Annual Scholars Conference on the Holocaust and the Remember Women Foundation.

Kenneth A. Scherzer, a graduate of Columbia College and Harvard University, has taught in the Department of History at MTSU since 1988. He is the author of *The Unbounded Community: Neighborhood Life and Social Structure in New York City, 1830–1875* (Durham, NC: Duke University Press, 1992).

James Homer Williams directs the Albert Gore Research Center in the College of Liberal Arts at MTSU. As such, he oversees the ever-growing university archive. A specialist in colonial American history, he has been a member of the Department of History at MTSU since 1996, and is a member of the MTSU Centennial Planning Committee.

INDEX

www.ingramcontent.com/pod-product-compliance
Lightning Source LLC
Chambersburg PA
CBHW030939150426
42812CB00064B/3066/J